EXPECT GREAT THINGS

The Life and Search of
HENRY DAVID THOREAU

by
KEVIN DANN

A TARCHERPERIGEE BOOK

tarcherperigee

An imprint of Penguin Random House LLC
375 Hudson Street
New York, New York 10014

Most TarcherPerigee books are available at special quantity discounts
for bulk purchase for sales promotions, premiums, fund-raising, and
educational needs. Special books or book excerpts also can
be created to fit specific needs.
For details, write:
SpecialMarkets@penguinrandomhouse.com.

Page iii: "Thoreau's cove, Lake Walden, Concord, Mass.," © Detroit Publishing Co.,
c. 1908, Detroit Publishing Company Photograph Collection, accessed June 28, 2016,
https://www.loc.gov/item/det1994020348/PP/.

Names: Dann, Kevin T., 1956– author.
Title: Expect great things: the life and search of
Henry David Thoreau / by Kevin Dann.
Description: New York, New York: TarcherPerigee, [2017]
Identifiers: LCCN 2016023294 (print) | LCCN 2016040654 (ebook) |
ISBN 9780399184666 (hardback) | ISBN 9780399184680 (ebook)
Subjects: LCSH: Thoreau, Henry David, 1817–1862. | Authors, American—19th
century—Biography. | Naturalists—United States—Biography. |
Transcendentalists (New England)—Biography. | Mysticism and literature. |
Spirituality in literature. | BISAC: BIOGRAPHY & AUTOBIOGRAPHY /
Historical. | BIOGRAPHY & AUTOBIOGRAPHY / Literary. |
BIOGRAPHY & AUTOBIOGRAPHY / Religious.
Classification: LCC PS3053 .D35 2017 (print) |
LCC PS3053 (ebook) | DDC 818/.309 [B]—dc23

Printed in the United States of America
1 3 5 7 9 10 8 6 4 2

Book design by Katy Riegel

For Cathline

ACKNOWLEDGMENTS

I'm deeply grateful to Tom Slaughter for having given me the opportunity to study Thoreau's life; to Gordon Miller and Thomas LeBien for their helpful editorial counsel; and to Mitch Horowitz for his faithful adherence to and celebration of Thoreau's core credo.

CONTENTS

CHAPTER 1

Declarations of Independence

This town, too, lies out under the sky, a port of entry and departure
for souls to and from heaven.   —*Journal*, July 10 to 12, 1841

The twelfth of July 1817 saw the arrival of the first of those sultry, sweaty summer days that Concord's farmers knew as dog days. Their almanacs marked these as beginning July 3 and ending August 11—the forty-day period preceding the rising of the Dog Star, Sirius— but they knew that the first furnace blast of austral air could come a week or more on either side of the third. This was good grass-growing weather; red-top, herd's-grass, sheep's fescue, and Canadian bluegrass and the ripening rye and wheat presented a checkerboard of greens, purples, reds, and golds. Working the fields were haymakers in white shirts and straw hats, occasionally setting aside their scythes and calling out to one another.

Cynthia Dunbar Thoreau had moved to the Virginia Road house when she was eleven, after her widowed mother had remarried. From her bedroom in the northeast corner of the second floor, she could hear the haymakers out on the Bedford Levels. Their swishing scythes sent ground-nesting mother birds and their young aloft for safety. She heard bobolinks, killdeer, meadowlarks, and sparrows. Kingbirds twittered from fence posts, and a yellowthroat sang "ecstasy, ecstasy" from a nearby alder thicket. As dusk fell and a solitary singing toad or soaring nighthawk occasionally broke the quiet, she could hear the lowing of the cows, the cackling of geese, the beating of a far-off drum, their neighbor Joe Meriam whistling to his team. Years later, she would recall that she used to get up at midnight, when all in the house were asleep, and sit on the doorstep. Then she could hear nothing in the world but the ticking of the clock in the house behind her. At some unknown hour on July 12, 1817, Cynthia Thoreau's newborn son uttered his first cry, joining his voice with the chorus of dog-day sounds.[1]

His mother's memories were among the few images that David Henry Thoreau ever recorded from his boyhood. She once told him that his uncle David, for whom he was named, had died when he was six weeks old and that when Dr. Ezra Ripley submerged him, at just three months old, in the baptismal waters, he had not cried. Nor had he cried when, knocked unconscious after falling down a flight of stairs, she had tossed two pails of water on his head to wake him up. She also recalled that he had cut his toes once with a hatchet; been knocked over by a rooster; on another occasion he was kicked down by a passing ox.[2] It was not surprising that his mother should have selected these falls and missteps as the highlights of her son's youth. As his caretaker, the accidents happened on her watch, and they marked the moments when his life seemed particularly precarious, haphazard. Thoreau's own memories of his boyhood stood in sharp contrast, conveying instead a distinct sense of purposefulness. He had pointed recollections of having been sent, at the age of ten, to fetch huckleberries for a pudding for some special dinner guest and unwaveringly adhering to his self-imposed rule to never eat one until his pail was full. Going "a-graping" was another early memory; for the rest of his life he would point out the particular vine in Walden Woods where he had picked his first wild grapes as a boy. Foraging became his special talent, as did the celebration of wildness and the freedom that such early expeditions afforded him. "I would not now exchange such an expansion of all my being for all the learning in the world," he later declared.[3]

As young children, Henry and his older brother, John, slept in a trundle bed in their parents' room, and while John would go to sleep at once, Henry would often lie awake for a long time, looking up at the stars. When his mother once asked him why he didn't go to sleep, he replied, "Mother, I have been looking through the stars to see if I couldn't see God behind them." The boy had a precocious gift for expansiveness, as keen an eye for the heavens as for huckleberries.[4]

As an adult, Thoreau never failed to be amazed by July's overwhelming fecundity as he observed the season's warmth turn flowers into fruits and awaken the locust's incessant buzzing. Inclined to "make a separate season of those days when the locust is heard," Thoreau would come to discover countless signs marking separate seasons—the reddening of the river shore with the year's crop of red maple seedlings, their winged samaras still attached; morning glories and yellow pond lilies blossoming synchronously with the rising of the sun; the smell of milkweed and basswood flowers; pogonias and calopogons abundant in the meadows; luna moths abroad at nightfall, their gigantism suggesting "what productions Nature would run if all the year were a July"; the last lingering pink stars of the mountain laurel; bream on their nests at the bottom of the rivers; turtle embryos ripening in the warm sands underneath the Concord River. Thoreau's birthday, which, like Christmas, always went completely uncelebrated in his journals, fell at the apex of the growing season, when the forces of growth and ripening were strongest. During his thirty-seventh July in Concord, Thoreau would declare: "Methinks the season culminated about the middle of this month,—that the year was of indefinite promise before, but that, after the first intense heats, we postponed the fulfillment of many of our hopes for this year, and having as it were attained the ridge of the summer, commenced to descend the long slope toward winter, the afternoon and down-hill of the year."[5]

This sort of fine-grained phenology took many summers to ripen. In his eleventh or twelfth year, while a student at Concord Academy, Thoreau composed a brief essay on the seasons. It survives as the very first composition from the hand that would pen over 2 million words in a journal whose principal object became the precise chronicling of Concord's seasons. "Why do the Seasons change? / and why / Does Winter's stormy brow appear?" he asked. The young Thoreau settled for only four seasons—ice-thawing, tree-budding, grass-greening, bird-returning spring; blossoming summer; fruit-laden autumn; and winter, when sleigh bells replaced birdsong as the morning sound.[6] With such a vague description of seasonal change, it was premature to ask why—premature not just for Thoreau but for America, which still needed to fully explore the what of its prodigious, rapidly expanding self.

Concord's haymakers swung their scythes through clover and timothy—European plants that for nearly two centuries had been sending their roots into the soil of a new continent. For the few native herbs and shrubs familiar to them, the people of Concord had names their Puritan ancestors had carried across the Atlantic from England: *hawthorne, hazel, oak,* and *alder* were all Anglo-Saxon words. The New England menagerie was equally Old English in name: *hare, harrier, lark,* and *robin.* Their churches, their homes, and the layout of their farms were all modeled on English patterns. Only five years before Thoreau's birth, Concord citizens—including his father—had fought a second war for independence against Great Britain. Growing up, Concord children were tutored in the tales of the Revolution, frequently by those who had taken part in the events. Henry heard from his mother's mother, Mary Jones Dunbar, that after her Tory brothers had been arrested during the Revolution, she'd smuggled metal files to them in a meal she brought to the Concord jail. After they freed themselves from their cell, they escaped to Loyalist Canada on horses that she had provided. One elderly woman told Thoreau that her brother, having gone off after midnight with his fellow Minutemen to the battle, came back in the morning for provisions of cider and cheese.[7] And the story of the Concord Fight, the April 19 skirmish that marked the opening of the American Revolution, was Concord's creation myth, marking, at least for the locals, the birth of the national body and mind.

Fortuna

In 1817 James Monroe was inaugurated, and in that year the period of prosperity and relative political harmony following victory in the War of 1812 was christened the Era of Good Feelings in America. Fortuna would not be so good to the Thoreau family, however. Just weeks after Henry's birth, his father, John Thoreau, was forced to sign over his share of his family's home in Boston to pay off creditors of the small store he operated in Concord. Within the year, the family gave up the farm on Virginia Road, as the house was sold to settle Cynthia Thoreau's mother's estate. In the fall of 1818, John moved the family about ten miles north to Chelmsford, where he opened another grocery store and painted signs. This venture failed within two years, apparently due to his lax business practices; he extended credit to all of his customers, even the insolvent ones. John then taught in his native Boston until in 1823 an opportunity came to him through his brother-in-law, Charles Dunbar. Henry's uncle Charles was, in the family's eyes, the least likely agent of fortune. An eccentric bachelor who suffered from narcolepsy and was celebrated for his card tricks, wrestling prowess, and feats of physical strength, Charles lived a gypsy life, alternately vagabonding to odd jobs throughout New England and settling in for a few months at a time with the Thoreaus.

In his wanderings, Charles had come upon a graphite deposit in New Hampshire, bought the mineral rights, and gone into the mining business with a Concord partner, Cyrus Stow. After the graphite from their mine was certified by prominent chemists to be superior to any other American source, Dunbar and Stow hoped to compete with Concord cabinetmaker William Munroe, who, stimulated by the embargo on European goods during the War of 1812, had manufactured America's first pencils.[8] Not long after joining his brother-in-law's endeavor, John Thoreau became its sole proprietor, as Dunbar and Stow dropped out. John Thoreau & Company pencils, particularly after improvements made to their manufacturing process by his son, were by the 1840s competing successfully with Munroe.

Shortly after the Thoreaus moved into the house on the southwest corner of Walden and Everett streets, in March 1823, Henry began attending Miss Phoebe Wheeler's private school, thereafter going on to the public grammar school on Concord Common. Then, in 1828, he and his brother, John, entered the Concord Academy, which had been founded in 1822 by a number of leading Concord men as a college preparatory school. Thoreau's "Seasons" essay was composed for his academy schoolmaster Phineas Allen, a Harvard graduate who taught Hesiod, Sophocles, Euripides, Homer, and Xenophon in Greek; Virgil, Tacitus, Cicero, and Caesar in Latin; and Voltaire, Molière, and Racine in French. The geography, history, botany, and natural history he taught were similarly rooted in the Old World, and the texts for astronomy, mathematics, and natural philosophy were uniformly works by European authors. At the end of each twelve-week quarter, the young scholars "declaimed" on selected topics; among Thoreau's recitations were "The Death of Leonidas," "Lines Written in 1821 on Hearing That the Austrians Had Entered Naples," "Prince Henry and Falstaff," and "Bonaparte's Address to His Army." At meetings of Allen's Concord Academic Debating Society, students argued such questions as "Have the Crusades been a benefit to the Christian nations of Europe?"; "Has Italy produced as great a man as Greece?"; and "Was the French Revolution a benefit to Europe?" American people, places, and events were totally absent from all of this epic storytelling.[9]

Thoreau failed to impress his schoolmates, both at Concord Academy and later at Harvard, who recalled him as shy and "not given to play or to fellowship with boys." In reality, no one ever took play and fellowship as seriously as Henry Thoreau, and he was far from shy. It was just that he had his eye and hand set to an earnest purpose that remained unseen by most of his contemporaries. Early on his intensity and sureness earned him a nickname, the Judge. Whereas college classmates and Concord townspeople recall him walking with his head down, eyes scanning the ground, Thoreau, echoing his mother's memory of him staring at the night sky, recalls gazing at the clouds, intent upon finding a gap where he might "get a peep at the world beyond which they seem intended to keep from our view."[10]

During this great age of oratory in America, Thoreau never distinguished himself as a public speaker, and he showed his lack of distinction early. His very first debate was on the question "Does it require more talents to make a good writer than a good extemporaneous speaker?" Thoreau took the affirmative position and lost to his opponent Rockwood Hoar. A month later, he took the negative in a debate as to whether a scholar was better served by a good memory than by good "understanding"; though he was declared the winner of this debate, the recording secretary commented, "Such a debate, if it may be called so, ... I hope never again will be witnessed in this house." The third and final debate in which Thoreau participated paired him with two others to take the negative on the question "Ought lotteries to be granted for any use?"[11]

The lottery debate was at that moment raging in Massachusetts and would continue to generate heated discussion throughout America in the 1820s and 1830s. Since the mid-eighteenth century, Americans had gambled their hard-earned coin on everything from private real estate lotteries sponsored by land speculators to state- and city-sponsored lotteries created to raise funds for roads, bridges, schools, and other civic projects. Though providing scarce capital for the fledgling republic, it was feared that lotteries posed a perennial threat to republican virtue.[12]

Whatever the state might decide about public lotteries, Concordians ran their own wheels of fortune on a daily basis. Young men threw dice on Concord Common, while girls drew lots to cipher the names of suitors. Concord's landscape, like most towns in New England, was pockmarked with excavations made by "money-diggers," whose every move during the treasure hunt was prescribed by strict magical rules. Lucky stones were carried about in the pockets of young and old.

Fishermen, hunters, and trappers were bound by ritual protocols that ranged from spitting on baited hooks and traps to prohibitions about diet and behavior before the hunt. Horseshoes hung over many a Concord doorway to bring good luck if not still to ward off witches as in earlier times. Almanacs listed each month's lucky and unlucky days. Owls, nighthawks, and bluebirds were all singularly oracular, their calls signaling things to come. While only a few human oracles, such as Lynn's Moll Pitcher, gained regional or national fame, every American village had its resident fortune-teller. Out on the outskirts of Concord, in the scrubby woods near Walden Pond, Fenda Freeman read palms and soothsaid by reading tea leaves.

If America during Henry Thoreau's formative years was a wide-open economic and social landscape ruled chaotically by Lady Luck, it was equally a moral and religious landscape where Puritan notions of Providence, though waning among young people, still held sway among the Revolutionary generation. They had been raised on a steady diet of prodigies and providences as narrated by divines like Increase and Cotton Mather, whose catalogs of "publick calamityes" went beyond the Salem witchcraft catastrophe to dark days, earthquakes, and comets as portents sent by God. But this generation had survived the traumatic turmoil of Indian wars and a revolution against an empire, and their successes caused them to shed some of their Puritan forefathers' fatalism. When Dr. Ripley, whose theology and personality dominated Concord for over half a century, watched the weather like a sea captain and petitioned for rain or good weather or prayed that lightning might be driven off "that it may not lick up our spirits," he expected a favorable answer.[13]

Thoreau's generation inherited both attitudes—Puritan ideals of humility and Promethean hubris. At Concord Academy, George Moore— Thoreau's teammate for the lottery debate—opened his composition on Alexander Pope's optimistic dictum "Whatever is, is right" by stating that man's inhumanity to man and the catastrophes of nature seemed to argue against the maxim. Still, Moore felt that earthquakes and other natural "convulsions" were "overruled by a kind providence," the actions of a God whose governance was as yet mysterious to man. Thoreau no doubt agreed, for he felt himself the luckiest of men. "I was born in the most estimable place in the world, and in the nick of time, too," he declared.[14]

Shooting Stars

Two months after he and his fellow Concordian Charles Stearns Wheeler settled into Harvard's Hollis Hall as roommates, all America's eyes were directed at the night sky. Beginning at about ten P.M. on the evening of November 13, 1833, and continuing until the sun rose the following morning, people from the Great Lakes to the Gulf of Mexico and from the Atlantic to the Pacific Coast watched the most prodigious celestial display ever to occur in recorded history. A constant succession of fireballs from the Leonid meteor swarm, many trailing vivid phosphorescent streaks behind them, radiated in all directions from a point southeast of the zenith. The stars fell "like snowflakes"; Denison Olmsted, professor of mathematics and natural philosophy at Yale University, later estimated that 34,640 shooting stars could be seen each hour. On a dark evening when the waxing crescent moon was only two days old, the light from the exploding sky was so bright that a man in Baltimore said he could read the time on his pocket watch hanging across his bedroom on the wall above the fireplace mantel; a New Haven surveyor said that at midnight it was bright enough to see the color of a man's beard. Observers reported eccentric meteors—some of which remained visible for up to five or ten minutes—that took the shape and mimicked the motion of serpents. There were red, blue, and yellow shooting stars, shooting stars the color of "fish blood," shooting stars that snapped, crackled, sizzled, or popped, and shooting stars that smelled like rotten eggs or onions. A correspondent of the *New York American* at Acquackanonk, New Jersey, claimed that a shooting star exploded right before his face.

In Cambridge and Boston, as in every city in eastern North America, awestruck and terrified citizens gathered in the streets to watch the spectacle. There is no record as to whether Thoreau, perennial admirer of the night and the stars, was among the throng gathered on the Harvard quad. Back in Concord, Dr. Ezra Ripley's son Samuel was wakened by his little boy, who told him that all the stars were falling down. His father sent him back to sleep and did the same himself. (Emerson judged that "the boy was the better philosopher.")[15] It seems unlikely that the perennial stargazer and night owl Thoreau would have slept through such celestial and civil commotion.

The event awakened both religious and scientific fervor. Elders who could recall the Dark Day of May 19, 1780 (when clouds, fog, and forest-fire smoke produced a darkness that required candles at noon) saw the 1833 starfall as another herald of the Apocalypse and searched the Bible for some explanation. In upstate New York, where Baptist apocalypticist William Miller had been sounding the alarm of approaching doom, the falling stars lent credence to Miller's prognostications, and brought him new followers. Americans needed no particular millennial prophet to frighten them, knowing by heart the passage from Revelation (6:13) that spoke of "the stars of heaven [falling] unto the earth." For many American blacks, both slave and free, November 13, 1833, held promise of deliverance. Frederick Douglass wrote, "I witnessed this gorgeous spectacle, and was awe-struck. The air seemed filled with bright descending messengers from the sky. It was about daybreak when I saw this sublime scene. I was not without the suggestion, at the moment, that it might be the harbinger of the coming of the Son of Man; and in my then state of mind I was prepared to hail Him as my friend and deliverer." For those less given to biblical interpretation, it was still profoundly unsettling to see nature's routines upset.[16]

Uniquely favored by the display, America had few facilities to study it. Harvard University had no astronomer in 1833, and the nation had only three observatories, none of which were in Cambridge. Thousands, perhaps millions, of Americans had witnessed the event, however, and their reports reached newspapers in every region of the country. Two observers—Olmsted at Yale and Alexander Twining of West Point—collected the reports and delivered their summaries in Benjamin Silliman's *American Journal of Science*. Olmsted began by citing Wilhelm von Humboldt's observations of a meteor shower on the same date and at the same hours in 1799. Humboldt had been the first to indicate the point of common origin in meteoric showers, a fact that Olmsted and most of his correspondents also observed in 1833. With the experience of lesser showers on November 13 in 1831 and 1832, the 1833 display offered convincing evidence that it was a periodic phenomenon.

Despite the comforting commonality of coincident dates and a radiant point in the constellation Leo, a whole range of other observations made it difficult for Olmsted to explain the origin of the meteors. Of four possible causes—electricity, magnetism, hydrogen gas combustion, and cometary debris—Olmsted favored the last. Twining objected to a celestial origin due to his own and many others' observations of at least four spectacular meteors that left luminous clouds that were blown by the wind in the direction opposite to the meteor's path. Clearly these trails had to have been located within the atmosphere of Earth. The shooting stars were seemingly atmospheric too in their coincidence with a wide range of weather phenomena. In Mobile, Alabama, it had been 80° Fahrenheit on the morning of the thirteenth, then 40° that evening, and there followed two weeks of the most severe weather that the city had ever experienced. New Haven surveyor James Palmer noticed that after a strong gust of wind at four A.M., the meteors had increased "astonishingly" and had continued to increase in number whenever the gust returned at intervals. Palmer, noting that his compass needle was shaking, had pulled out a silk handkerchief, and as he drew it through his hands, it produced long, intense sparks, confirming an increase in the local electromagnetic field. Auroral displays were common, and in Fredonia, New York, a man reported that the tips of his horse's ears had become luminous for some minutes.

Twining reported that ships at sea had experienced heavy gales coincident with the shower, and, curiously, those ships in calm weather with clear skies saw no meteors at all. At Harvard, Massachusetts, there were reports of a cloudless sky that delivered a downpour. Rain was not the only thing reported to fall on November 13, whether from cloudy or cloudless skies. In Rahway, New Jersey, people found "lumps of jelly" after a "fiery rain," while in Newark, residents found a mass of a substance like "soft soap" that evaporated when burned. A woman at West Point reported to Twining that while she had been out milking a cow, something that looked like boiled starch splashed on the ground in front of her. When she returned a few hours later to show neighbors, it was gone, but a boy spotted pin-size white particles that turned into ash as he picked them up. While odd things fell from the sky to earth on November 13, the earth itself also fell in some places. In Hudson, New York, a one-and-a-half-acre woodland sank thirty feet, so that the treetops stood at ground level. In Lynchburg, Virginia, there had been a series of small earthquakes.

Olmsted showed no distrust of these observers, concluding, "The fact that the supposed deposits were so uniformly described as gelatinous substance forms a presumption in favor of the supposition that they had the origin ascribed to them." His *American Journal of Science* article found plenty of supportive evidence for all the reported meteorological and geological oddities in historical reports, from a shower of black dust at Constantinople in 472 A.D. to reports of red rains on November 13, 1755, in several European countries. Perhaps the most extraordinary mystery about the 1833 meteor shower is that throughout the duration of the shower, as the rotation of the earth effected a change in the apparent position of the constellation Leo, the meteors' radiant point moved with the constellation, rather than remaining stationary, which is the rule for such showers. Along with the radical weather phenomena, falling debris, and meteor trails blown by the wind, this observation suggested to contemporary scientists that at least some of these meteors had an atmospheric rather than an extra-atmospheric origin. All of these anomalous observations quickly disappeared from all subsequent scientific discussion of the 1833 shower.

The attempt to understand the November 13, 1833, meteor shower marked a moment in American science when all citizens still had standing as reliable observers of natural phenomena. Just a week before Boston was lit up by shooting stars, Ralph Waldo Emerson had delivered the inaugural lecture before the newly organized Boston Society of Natural History. Emerson opened his talk with a characteristically democratic declaration: "It seems to have been designed, if anything was, that men should be students of Natural History. Man is, by nature, a farmer, a hunter, a shepherd and a fisherman, who are all practical naturalists and by their observations the true founders of all societies for the pursuit of science."[17] Cow-milking farm women and curious boys could be trusted to be as empirically minded as civil engineers and professors of natural philosophy. Free of abstract and elaborate theoretical constructions, the untutored folk of America in fact sometimes saw things clearer than the professors.

The hazy boundary between the factual and the fabulous was on display in the very next issue of the *American Journal of Science*, which carried a translation of an article from the *Bulletin d'Histoire Naturelle de la Societé Linnéene de Bordeaux*, arguing emphatically for the existence of unicorns. "To say that it is impossible that there should be . . . such an animal as the land unicorn would be to go astray from acquired knowledge, to credit an absurd fable, in a word, to affect singularity." After citing the Bible, Pliny, and Leibniz as authorities, the unicorn enthusiast quoted Buffon concerning the prospect of unfolding new mysteries: "It is not by contracting the sphere of nature and confining her within a narrow circle that we shall be able to understand her . . . it is necessary to consider nothing as impossible, to look for every thing, and to suppose that whatever can exist, really does." A generous principle of plenitude respecting nature still held its own against increasing scientific skepticism.[18]

Antebellum America shared with France a fascination with the fabulous. Emerson regaled his Boston audience of natural historians with descriptions of the giraffes, elephants, hyenas, leopards, and monkeys he had recently seen at the Jardin des Plantes in Paris. Dazzled by the hummingbirds, peacocks, pheasants, toucans, and birds of paradise, even the mineral exhibits shocked Emerson with the realization of nature's extravagance. When he quoted Wordsworth and Coleridge and declared that to gain anything of nature, one "must go in the spirit of a little child. The naturalist commands nature by obeying her," even the eldest and most cultivated of the Boston naturalists wholeheartedly agreed.[19]

A Love for Story

Harvard's library afforded Thoreau great opportunities for travel and exploration; during his first year, he read Washington Irving's *Chronicle of the Conquest of Grenada*, George Waddington's *Journal of a Visit to Parts of Ethiopia*, William Bullock's *Six Months Residence and Travels in Mexico*, and Irving's *Life and Voyages of Christopher Columbus* and *Companions of Columbus*. It was not surprising then, that, asked to write an essay on "the anxieties and Delights of a Discoverer of whatever class," Thoreau would have chosen Columbus over a land-bound discoverer of new worlds, such as Herschel or Newton. What delighted young Henry Thoreau most about Columbus was his persistence in the face of overwhelming skepticism and derision; it already seemed that the seventeen-year-old Thoreau was speaking about himself.[20]

Thoreau's Harvard essays, written for Professor Edward Channing, presage themes, sentiments, and aspirations that would occupy him the rest of his life—an animus against materialism, wholehearted admiration for faithfully following one's inner calling, a deep respect for solitude, championing an energetic engagement with the physical world equally with an ascetic withdrawal from the wordly, and a love of plain speaking. Both in Channing's assigned themes and Thoreau's response to them there ran a strong current of questioning tradition. "The majority of mankind are too easily induced to follow any course which accord with the opinion of the world," Thoreau declared in a January 1835 essay. He feared that most men were too concerned with meeting others' expectations, rather than crafting their own, so that their lives were ruled by chance rather than design. Ashamed of being considered "singular or eccentric," their conformity became habit, preventing them from realizing their singular destinies.[21]

However strong the impulse toward seeing and making new worlds may have been for Thoreau, Harvard's curriculum and culture firmly rooted him in the old worlds of classical and Christian thought. He was always more likely to quote Plato, Socrates, Cicero, Virgil, and Scripture than John Locke, Adam Smith, or even Shakespeare. His Harvard essays show his intimate acquaintance with the pantheon of Greek gods and goddesses—Zeus, Demeter, Aphrodite, Apollo, Athena, and Ares. Lesser deities, such as Zephyr and Aurora, were for Thoreau living beings, for whom he would forever find places in his writing. Fate, a concept that fairly obsessed the transcendentalists and their Romantic brethren, was almost always imagined plurally, as the three thread-spinning, thread-weaving, and thread-cutting sisters Clotho, Lachesis, and Atropos. Thoreau knew Pan as the ancients did, the universal spirit of Nature, who is as often destructive as constructive of matter's forms. Also drawn to Nordic mythology, Thoreau felt its consonance with the rugged Northern wilderness. "Their conceptions were as subtle and un-approachable as their own mountain mists, every retired glen, every beetling crag, every dark unfathomable abyss, had its peculiar spirit."[22]

Thoreau found this "neglect of the material, this fondness for the dark and mysterious, this propensity to the spiritual" most pronounced in the poetry of John Milton, whose poems reanimated the gods for the modern imagination. Milton believed that, as he declared in *Paradise Lost*, "Millions of spiritual creatures walk the earth unseen, both when we wake, and when we sleep." These ranged from the di-minutive and largely benevolent spirits of *Comus*—"pert faeries," "dapper elves," "flowery-kirtled Naiades," "Yellow-skirted Fayes"—to the arch-adversaries of *Paradise Lost*, waging war in Heaven. Thoreau easily discerned in Milton's descriptions of the devils Satan, Moloch, Belial, Mammon, and Beelzebub qualities he knew well to be ever afoot upon the earth.[23]

At the heart of Homer, Virgil, Milton, Shakespeare, and all of the other authors he loved throughout his youth, Thoreau found story. "The Love of Stories and of Story-telling, cherishes a purity of heart, a frankness and candor of disposition, a respect for what is generous and elevated, a contempt for what is mean and dishonorable, a proper regard *for*, and independence *of*, the petty trials of life, & tends to multiply merry companions and never-failing friends." Holding such a power-fully redemptive view of narrative, he had the good fortune to come of age when America's first generation of indigenous storytellers with truly national audiences was writing.[24]

Thoreau's own appetite for story carried within it the seed of his vo-cation, both as writer and naturalist. He believed that all humans craved story because they forever craved the new. "The earth we tread upon is as curious as the stars we gaze upon," he declared, quoting for support one of his own—and America's—favorite storytellers, Washington Irving: "To the thinking mind, the whole world is enveloped in mystery, and everything is full of type and portent." Thoreau theorized that each child accidentally comes upon something that unveils a new truth to him, noting that if this new object of discovery has been pleasurable, the child becomes a hunter of novelty. Pursuing the "strange" or "re-markable" becomes a lifelong pastime, the "principle of our principles," so that the innocent Mother Goose rhymes of youth give way to adult curiosity about the mysteries of nature and history. Thoreau loved par-ticularly the Mother Goose tale of the three wise men of Gotham, who "went to sea in a bowl." The Gotham "wise men" were actually holy fools whose lack of wisdom got them into deep waters among their fellow men, but who always emerged unharmed and uncannily blessed.[25]

Thoreau likely knew Gotham's wise men from his mother's story-telling, but in his youth most American children in literate households would have also known the tale from the chapbooks sold door to door by itinerant peddlers. These little pamphlets held wonderful worlds within, where characters often not unlike the peddler adventured among ghosts, goblins, mermaids, and elves. Stories religious, diabolical, supernatural, superstitious, romantic, humorous, legendary, historical, biographical, and even criminal filled the flimsy tomes in which American children first met Jack Horner, Jack the Giant Killer, Robinson Crusoe, Reynard the Fox, Robin Hood, and Doctor Faustus. In the chapbook world, dream and omen loomed large, so children also met celebrated prophets like Mother Shipton and Robert Nixon of Cheshire. The heroes were usually children or young adults: Fortunatus, the young man who finds a purse that cannot be emptied and a hat that carries him anywhere he wishes to be; Guy, the Earl of Warwick, who overcomes sixteen assassins, slays boars and dragons, and then goes on his pilgrimage to the Holy Land; even Saint George the dragon slayer was a young man in the chapbook tales. Before Barnum made a household word of a stage midget by the same name, Tom Thumb was a chapbook adventurer whose history of "Marvellous Acts of Manhood Full of Wonder and Merriment" were known to all American boys and girls. Chapbook humor was raw and bawdy, and the chief beauty of the tales was that of all fairy tale and fable—everything appeared to happen by chance, and so *nothing* seemed anything less than absolutely fated.

The World of Faerie

In the first few decades of the nineteenth century, Harvard boys were never far from the dream world of the chapbooks. Thoreau's Harvard notebooks show his predilection not just for Elizabethan poetry, but also for the world of faerie, the midsummer night's dream where time and space are fluid, mobile settings for adventures in the uncanny.[26] One of the very first books he borrowed from the Institute of 1770 Library at Harvard was Washington Irving's *Abbotsford and Newstead Abbey*, from which Thoreau wrote out a long extract about Irving's visit in 1817 with Sir Walter Scott.

Scott took Irving to see the Eildon Tree, beneath which Thomas the Rhymer had, according to tradition, given forth his famous prophesies after his seven-year bondage in the netherworld of the Faerie Queen. Scott pointed out—and Thoreau copied down—every feature of the landscape that figured in the ballad. In his notes on Milton's "L'Allegro," "Il Penseroso," *Comus*, and "Lycidas," Thoreau transcribed particularly the editorial commentary on the nymphs, goblins, lubber fiends, Oreads, Nereids, Stridentii, Furies, and other members of the faerie world. This commentary gave Thoreau a fairly complete tutelage in early modern British fairy lore.[27] Magical allusions also held special interest for Thoreau, and his notebook lists favorite phrases concerning "magian & cabalistic lore" gleaned from Shakespeare, Milton, and Chaucer.

Thoreau's youthful fascination with faerie was more representative than singular. Nathaniel Hawthorne, while an undergraduate at Bowdoin, borrowed from Shakespeare's *Midsummer Night's Dream* the pen name Auberon, the French rendering of the German Alberich, or Elf King. It had come to Shakespeare through Spenser, who in turn had borrowed it from thirteenth-century troubadour tales. While at Harvard, Ralph Waldo Emerson—who belonged to a literary club called the Knights of the Square Table—dreamed of composing an Arthurian romance full of faerie. At the end of his junior year at Harvard, when Emerson bid adieu to these same spirits, his farewell address hints how Janus-faced these "tutelary soules" could be: "Abandoning your allegiance he throws you to the winds, recklessly defying your malice & fun. Pinch the red nose; lead him astray after will-o'-the-wisps over wilderness & fen; fright him with ghastly hobgoblins—wreak your vengeance as you will."[28]

For Thoreau, Emerson, Hawthorne, and other well-educated high-romantic youths, the fascination for faerie seemed a happy prolongation of youth into adulthood, and it was encouraged by the wider world. Constant staging in the early Victorian era of Shakespeare's two "fairy plays"—*A Midsummer Night's Dream* and *The Tempest*—along with the romantic fairy ballets *La Sylphide* and *Giselle* made Puck, Auberon, and hosts of flower fairies pop-cultural icons. Fairy paintings fostered the same images as the theater. In the living room of the Emerson home hung a large engraving of David Scott's 1837 painting, "Puck Fleeing from the Dawn," rendering the last scene of *A Midsummer Night's Dream*. In 1854, Louisa May Alcott published her first book, *Flower Fables*, dedicated to Emerson's daughter Ellen, for whom she had first fashioned these stories of flower fairies on outings in Concord woods and meadows.[29]

This preoccupation with the realm of faerie was not restricted to dreamy teenagers and genteel village Victorians but was shared by Boston and Concord Brahmins. In April 1834 at the Concord Lyceum, B. B. Thatcher of Boston lectured on "The Popular Belief in Witchcraft & Fairies." Fairies were no doubt discussed during the very first lyceum lecture, "Popular Superstitions," given to an audience of three hundred on January 31, 1829, by Reverend Bernard Whitman of Waltham. The second lecture of the lyceum's inaugural season was on alchemy and astrology, magical arts that utilized the elemental spirits of Nature. Subjects touching on the dark mysteries of human consciousness—witchcraft, Egyptian hieroglyphics, phrenology, sleep and dreams, animal magnetism—were nearly as numerous in the lyceum's offerings as social progress, education, vegetarianism, "national greatness," and natural history.[30]

The lyceum lecturers told what was already well known to most Concord villagers, that their rural neighbors still trafficked, albeit warily, with the fairy folk. Throughout New England circulated stories echoing all of the dangers associated with faerie. Infant children were stolen and deformed changeling children left in their stead. Wives and husbands were fair prey also; they could only be recovered by confronting the fairies on a certain night, within a day and a year after the loss. No livestock were off limits, and fairies would kill or maim chickens and cows as well as steal them. A host of prescriptive rules were known to protect against or remedy fairy enchantment. The most common was to turn one's clothes inside out. In an 1837 lecture, Emerson gave frank testimony that Concord participated in these traditions. "All the postulates of elfin annals—that the fairies do not like to be named; that their gifts are capricious and not to be trusted; that who seeks a treasure must not speak; and the like—I find true in Concord, however they might be in Cornwall or Bretagne." [31]

Thoreau's favorite character out of faerie was Robin Goodfellow, whom he had first encountered in Milton's *L'Allegro* and Shakespeare's *Midsummer Night's Dream*. His Harvard notebooks contain extracts from a variety of sources about this "greenwood spirit," whose pedigree sometimes described him as the son of Oberon. Thoreau copied out a ballad from around 1600 that refers to Robin Goodfellow's ability to shape-shift, to project an array of voices to call travelers astray, and to become a "walking fire," i.e., a luminous will-o'-the-wisp. Another ballad recorded by Thoreau had Robin stealing newborn babes and leaving elfin children in their stead, pinching the limbs of sleeping women who were poor housekeepers, receiving gifts of food and drink, and bestowing gifts of gold coins upon tidy housemaids. Though this "hob-goblin" or "mad crisp" delighted in tormenting human beings, Robin's laudatory surname was consistent with the widespread belief that one must practice extraordinary deference toward the beings of faerie. "Goodfellow" was the specific epithet that echoed the more generic "good folk," "good neighbors," "men of peace," and other polite euphemisms. Thoreau's deep affection for Robin Goodfellow reflected the fact that in Robin survived the honest, healthy, carefree joy in life that once permeated a greater share of fairy mythology. [32]

Perhaps the most popular source for understanding the danger and the dread of the faerie world drawn upon so freely by the Elizabethan poets was Sir Walter Scott's *Letters on Demonology and Witchcraft*, published in 1830. In the spring of his senior year at Harvard, just three days before he checked out Emerson's *Nature*, Thoreau borrowed Scott's demonological work from the library. Thoreau had read all of Scott's novels, which were shot through with his theories about the origin and nature of the fairies. Scott's writings about fairies were especially influential because in the 1830s, America had almost no indigenous literary tradition of faerie beyond the occasional collection of regional folktales. The first American author to take local folk material and reach a wider audience was Washington Irving, whose "Rip Van Winkle" was inspired by a Hudson Valley version of Thomas the Rhymer's experience of being abducted into the Otherworld.

Thoreau's own demonology extended beyond Elizabethan poetry and modern folkloric analysis to ancient Greek thought. For the Greeks, the daimones were not inner, subjective psychological principles but outer, objective realities, capable of very powerful interactions with all humans. All of the Greek philosophers agreed that each person from birth had a special deity—an *idios daimon*—as his own guard and companion, who determined to a great extent the destiny of the individual. The most celebrated daimon in Greek literature was Socrates's, who often intervened by whispering "No!" at critical moments in the great philosopher's life. Thoreau knew from his reading in Roman mythology of the Fatuae, a race of beautiful, immortal damsels who lived in places inaccessible to man, but sometimes made themselves visible to him. Their name preserves the long-forgotten but essential linkage between fate (*fata*) and faerie (or *fée* in medieval France, "fay" in Old English); these gossamer, ghostly beings whose very existence was forever being questioned were universally understood to have extraordinary influence over individual human lives.

Just how close Thoreau's generation was to actual belief in the existence of daimones is evident in the work of another Harvard graduate, Marshall Tufts, who in 1832 published a memoir of his college experience whose second half was a survey of "The Ancient and Popular Pneumatology." Along with presenting a rabid critique of Cartesianism, Tufts's pneumatology suggests the degree to which Harvard students of the 1830s trafficked with spirits of various sorts. Tufts preferred Scott's faith-full demonology to that of Harvard's skeptical "metaphysical" professors, and easily entertained the idea that the daimones could occasionally appear in bodily form. Tufts concluded his work by quoting Jean Le Clerc's *Pneumatologia*: "They may do many things without man's notice, and many things also when seen by him; in a form for the most part human, but more august and holy. The Greeks relate the like of their divinities, as is every where seen in their poets and historians." [33]

Along with this prescriptive knowledge of daimonic behavior, Thoreau carried with him on his outings into the Concord landscape a detailed taxonomy gleaned from classical mythology. The Dryades—nymphs of forests, glens, and groves—included Adryades and Hamadryades (spirits of oak and poplar forests), Oreiades and Orodemniades (mountain pine and oak forests), Mēliades (fruit trees), Epimelides (sheep and goats), Aigeiroi (black poplars), Ampeloi (grape vines), Balanis (food-acorn oaks), Karyai (hazel and other nut trees), Kraneiai (cherry trees), Moreai (mulberry trees), Pteleai (elms), Sykei (fig trees), Hamamēliades (witch hazels), Daphnaiai (laurels), and Kissiai (ivies), as well as less specialized dryads like the Aulōniades (mountain pastures and ravines), Alseides (groves), Napaiai (glens and dells), and Hylēōroi ("Watchers of the Wood"). The Naiades—freshwater nymphs—were classified by their particular aquatic habitat: Pegaiai (springs), Krinaiai (fountains), Potameides (rivers and streams), Limnades (lakes), and Eleionomai (marshes). Although no similar indigenous New England classification scheme existed for the subtle beings standing behind nature, Thoreau remained comfortable all of his adult life invoking nameless spirits of place.

A Theory of Animated Nature

Deep in reverie over the active spirits of nature as surveyed in Scott's *Demonology,* Thoreau came upon these sentences in the other book he was reading in April 1837:

At present, man applies to nature but half his force.... Meantime, in the thick darkness, there are not wanting gleams of a better light— occasional examples of the action of man upon nature with his entire force—with reason as well as understanding. Such examples are the miracles in the earliest antiquity of all nations; the history of Jesus Christ; . . . the miracles of enthusiasm, as those reported of Swedenborg, Hohenlohe, and the Shakers; many obscure and yet contested facts, now arranged under the name of Animal Magnetism; prayer; eloquence; self-healing; and the wisdom of children. These are examples of Reason's momentary grasp of the sceptre; the exertions of a power which exists not in time or space, but an instantaneous in-streaming causing power.[34]

Uttered by the anonymous "Orphic poet" at the conclusion of Ralph Waldo Emerson's manifesto calling for a new relationship with nature, these words were a kind of counterpoint to the trend of Thoreau's study in his final months at Harvard. Emerson's 1836 book *Nature*, while recognizing and celebrating nature as a dynamic cosmos of activity, emphasized the human being as himself a cosmos, capable of supreme magical action upon the very powers of nature—the daimones—that awed antique and early modern minds.

The Orphic poet was no doubt Emerson's own genius, or, as he frequently spoke of it, his daimon. Though his prodigious youthful intellect devoured literature, theology, and philosophy, and he had quite unsurprisingly chosen the ministry as his vocation, his guiding star kept speaking "Yes!" to him each time he turned his fiery mind in the direction of natural science. In 1832, in the wake of a dispute with church elders over his reluctance to administer communion, Emerson, then an ordained Unitarian minister, retreated to the White Mountains, where his daimon prompted him to resign his post. A year later, in the Jardin des Plantes in Paris, the apostate minister, entranced by the "bewildering series of animated forms, the hazy butterflies, the carved shells, the birds, beasts, fishes, insects, snakes, and the upheaving principle of life everywhere," felt his personal daimon speak authoritatively once again. "I feel the centipede in me—cayman, carp, eagle, and fox. I am moved by strange sympathies. I say continually, I will be a naturalist."

Leaving Liverpool for home, he knew already what the title of his first book would be, and he again attributed his instinctual homing on a true course to an invisible being: "That which I cannot yet declare has been my angel from childhood until now. It has separated me from men. It has watered my pillow; it has driven sleep from my bed. It has tortured me for my guilt. It has inspired me with hope. It cannot be defeated by my defeats. It cannot be questioned though all the martyrs apostatize. It is always the glory that shall be revealed; it is the 'open secret' of the universe." [35]

Having long outgrown his infatuation with the fairy world, still the genii loci haunt the edges of Emerson's thought: "The greatest delight which the fields and woods administer is the suggestion of an occult relation between man and the vegetable. I am not alone and unacknowledged. They nod to me and I to them." A paragraph later he alludes to the "frolic of the nymphs," and then quotes George Herbert's statement that "More servants wait on man / Than he'll take notice of." Wholly forward-looking in its radical reliance on Nature, not God, as the arbiter of truth, the essay's embrace of participatory consciousness yet allied it with more traditional cosmologies. The essay's argument is itself largely a modern restatement of the ancient esoteric doctrine of correspondences, and its prophetic conclusion, "Prospects," returns to a language of hidden mystery: "In a cabinet of natural history, we become sensible of a certain occult recognition and sympathy in regard to the most unwieldy and eccentric form of beast, fish, and insect." [36] Emerson, whose intensive reading in seventeenth-century English poetry preceded Thoreau's parallel reading program by just one year, included Herbert's "Man" as a prelude to his essay's Orphic apotheosis. Thoreau loved the poem as much as Emerson did, copying it out in full in his notebook.

Herbert's poem presented the highest expression of the doctrine of correspondences, the ancient assertion that man was microcosm, embodying the macrocosm—not just the Earth but the planets and stars as well. Herbert's poem affirmed a cosmic hospitality that both Emerson and Thoreau knew personally. Emerson acknowledged that the reciprocal hospitality between man and nature was broken, not by virtue of human degradation of wild nature, but because modern man mistook himself for a material, rather than spiritual, creation. "A man is a god in ruin.... Man is the dwarf of himself. Once he was permeated and dissolved by spirit. He filled nature with his over-flowing currents.... But ... he is shrunk to a drop." As remedy for this disenchantment, Emerson's *Nature* offered the vague outlines of a transcendental—and what was to become a transcendentalist—research program. Men could not be naturalists until they redeemed their soul and spirit natures, and birthed from themselves higher faculties. When that moment arrived, facts, not fables, would feed man.[37]

Emerson believed he was outlining his own future life's work but certainly had no idea that he was instead prophesying the vocation of a Harvard senior whom he had met the previous February. If Thoreau could only dimly discern that Emerson's manifesto pointed directly at him, he at least recognized *Nature* as a magisterial summary of his own maturing ideas and attitudes. He checked the book out again in June and purchased a copy to give as a graduation gift to his classmate William Allen. As luck—or fate—would have it, the Sunday after reading Emerson's book, Emerson's sister-in-law Lucy Jackson Brown, a boarder at the Thoreau home on Main Street in Concord, brought Thoreau to visit Emerson at his home. Over the mantel in Emerson's study hung New Bedford artist William Wall's painting of *The Three Fates*, a copy of a painting that Emerson had seen in the Pitti Palace in Florence on his life-changing pilgrimage in 1833. Within the year, the spinning sisters Clotho, Lachesis, and Atropos would weave together Emerson's and Thoreau's destinies more tightly than they could imagine.[38]

Secrets

Both before and after the April 9, 1837, meeting, the two men kept slipping past each other, seemingly eluding the Fates' designs. In

September 1835, just days before Emerson remarried and moved to Concord, he had given the main address (the printed speech was Emerson's first real publication) at Concord's two-hundredth-anniversary celebration, but Thoreau had just gone off to begin his junior year at Harvard. On July 4, 1837, Emerson was the obvious speaker of choice for Concord's Independence Day ceremonies, which were especially auspicious, as they were the occasion for the unveiling of the North Bridge Battle monument. Emerson could not attend, but the audience—which included Thoreau, who sang in the choir—heard Emerson's commemorative verse "Concord Hymn" read in absentia.

> By the rude bridge that arched the flood,
> Their flag to April's breeze unfurled,
> Here once the embattled farmers stood
> And fired the shot heard round the world.

Emerson had been a member of the committee that crafted the inscription borne on the twenty-foot-tall granite obelisk: "The first forcible resistance to British aggression." Commemorating the April 19, 1775, battle led to a second Concord Fight, which laid bare the social dynamics of antebellum Concord. This latter fight began in 1825, the fiftieth anniversary of the two- or three-minute skirmish out at North Bridge. This commemoration was itself inspired partially by the Marquis de Lafayette's 1824 American tour (the itinerary included Concord, where a lavish invitation-only reception had been held for the celebrity), which had fueled a nostalgic longing to honor Revolutionary-era heroes and landmarks. The original plan had been for a monument in the center of Concord village, which along with being the focal point of regional commercial and civic life was also the staging ground for the descendants of the Minutemen, the Concord Artillery, and the Light Infantry. Though militia units occasionally drilled and camped out by the North Bridge battlefield, it was more popular as a place for locals to fish or boat.[39]

The 1825 celebration included a parade, military exercises, the firing of cannon, Ezra Ripley's prayer, Edward Everett's oration, a twelve-piece band, and a dinner with thirteen toasts, one for each state of the original union. The climax of the day was the solemn laying of a huge granite cornerstone for the monument on the little green in front of the courthouse, close to the banks, mills, and mechanics' shops that made Concord a thriving industrial and commercial hub. Not long after, however, a twenty-foot-high pile of tar barrels and boards appeared on the cornerstone, with a note declaring that the monument was meant for another location—North Bridge. The next night the mock monument was set afire, ruining the cornerstone. Directly after this, the *Yeoman's Gazette* ran a series of essays by a certain "Middlesex," who argued for the North Bridge location by declaring that a patriotic pilgrimage needed to transport the pilgrim from the profane bustle of everyday life to a sacred space and that the North Bridge site was the proper setting for such sacred communion.

In 1827, when *Gazette* editor Herman Atwell published Dr. Ezra Ripley's *History of the Fight at Concord*, the identity of "Middlesex" was revealed—Ripley, whose letter-writing campaign was carried out pseudonymously because he had of late alienated much of his parish with his extreme Federalist preaching. At the very moment that his letters were appearing in the *Gazette*, disaffected church members were buying land and making plans to build a new church, to house the breakaway Second Congregational Society. By 1837, Concord's booming economy, which enriched a few and impoverished others (in 1835, 64 percent of Concord's adult males were landless, while the top tenth—just fifty men—controlled almost half the town's wealth), added social discord to the existing religious discord. No one represented the local aristocracy more conspicuously than Ripley, the "Pope of Concord," who, as it happened, was also the owner of the North Bridge battlefield site. From his Old Manse ivory tower, which overlooked the bridge, Ripley conceived of donating the property to the town as a philanthropic act that would unite the pope with the populists by fostering common devotion to the memory of the heroic Revolutionary battle. Ripley's philanthropy had a distinct pecuniary strain; in an address to the Concord Lyceum, he noted that real estate values were 12 to 20 percent higher in towns marked by civic peace.

The day of the dedication was a sultry, sweaty dog day. At noon the bells of the village churches brought hundreds of Concord citizens to the common, from which they walked north to the Old Manse and then followed the path to the new monument. Ripley's assistant, Reverend Barzillai Frost, led the opening prayer, and then Sam Hoar, lawyer and member of Concord's leading family, gave a patriotic speech. Ripley gave the benediction. Hoar's and Ripley's prominence in the ceremony were a reminder to some Concordians that another division lay behind this second Concord Fight, which the dedication of the monument seemingly brought to a truce. Ripley had been a member of Concord's Corinthian Lodge of Ancient and Accepted Masons since its founding in 1798. In 1826, Freemason William Morgan wrote an exposé of Free-masonry revealing its secret rituals but was kidnapped and murdered by several Masons before publication. The resulting uproar made the book a bestseller, shattered American Freemasonry, and led to the rise of the Anti-Masonic Party. At the time, Ripley was grand chaplain of the Most Worshipful Grand Lodge of Massachusetts. Freemasons had orches-trated much of the activity dedicated to commemorating the American Revolution and were particularly conspicuous in the laying of corner-stones for public monuments. Lafayette, a Mason, had participated in at least half a dozen cornerstone-laying ceremonies on his 1824 tour. The Corinthian Lodge had laid the cornerstone of the original Concord Fight monument in 1825, along with burying a leaden box filled with historical manuscripts as a message to posterity.[40]

The populist fear of Freemasonry as a conspiratorial alliance of aris-tocrats led to the demise of hundreds of lodges throughout America, but the Corinthian Lodge, though it ceased regular meetings in 1831 (leasing out its hall to the Concord Lyceum) and enrolled only three new members between 1832 and 1844, never surrendered its charter. Indeed, in the year following the Morgan affair, ten new members were initiated, including *Yeoman's Gazette* publisher and editor Herman Atwell, who was proposed for membership by town historian and local Brahmin Lemuel Shattuck. But by 1833, even the Boston region, heart of Revolutionary-era Freemasonry, was wracked by Anti-Masonic fervor, thanks largely to the revelations of Atwell, who published a series of editorials attacking Freemasonry. In March 1834, Atwell appeared before an investigative committee of the Massachusetts legislature to give testimony about the nature of his initiation into the first three Freemasonic degrees. He described being stripped naked, getting "hoodwinked"—a black hood placed over the eyes—and feeling a noose placed around his neck before he was led to the altar to take a series of oaths. The secret initiatory practices of Freemasonic lodges were widely known after the publication of Morgan's exposé; what set Atwell's revelations apart was his insight into the rationale behind the initiation rituals. He understood that the ceremonies were designed to confuse and terrify the candidate in order to put him completely in the power of those doing the initiation. Most damning was Atwell's testimony that during the summer of 1833 he had heard a prominent citizen of Concord who was a Royal Arch Mason state "in a calm, dispassionate manner" that he approved of the murder of William Morgan as just punishment for his having violated his pledge of secrecy.[41]

In the wake of Atwell's testimony, some 54 Concord voters joined a statewide campaign against Freemasonry, and in 1834, this rose to 152, or half of the town's voters. During the same 1834 town meeting at which Ripley made his offer of land, they threw his fellow Freemason Dr. Abiel Heywood out of the town clerk's office that he had held for thirty-eight straight years and replaced him with Thoreau's old Concord Academy preceptor Phineas Allen. Just nine months before his July Fourth address, Freemason Sam Hoar had been defeated for reelection to Congress by an Anti-Masonic coalition.

The Thoreau family was strictly Anti-Masonic, and Thoreau never mentioned Freemasonry in his writing, but like all young boys in

Concord, he surely was aware of the secret society in their midst. Thoreau biographer Frank Sanborn recalled: "The Masonic hall was over the school-house . . . we boys used to wonder and be very much awestruck when we looked through the keyhole and saw the carpentry, supposed to be coffins and scaffolds, and the regalia, supposed to typify all the glory of the days of Solomon and Hiram. Occasionally Elisha Tolman, the tyler [doorkeeper], was seen at the entrance with his drawn sword. In those days John Keyes was king, and William Whiting was priest, and Dr. Ripley high dignitary of the order."[42]

Jacksonian America—like young Frank Sanborn and every other boy who snuck into a Masonic lodge for a peep through the keyhole— had a passion for secrets, for their crafting, exposure, celebration, and damnation. The suspicions and scrutiny leveled at Freemasons, Catholics, and Mormons were also democratically directed toward peddlers, stage entertainers, and politicians, all of whom were seen as potentially criminal keepers of secrets. On August 11, 1834, in Charlestown, outside of Boston, a mob stormed and ransacked a Catholic convent, driven to this violence by their uncontrollable curiosity about the mysterious rites they imagined performed within. This tragic attack on cloistered, powerless religious women highlights the limits on America's distrust of secrecy; no similar mobs tore up the Masonic altars where influential men gathered to exchange secret oaths. But the rhetorical attacks upon Freemasonry show just how virulent a poison Masonic secrecy was seen to be. In a series of impassioned Anti-Masonic tracts, John Quincy Adams of Boston acknowledged the powerful seduction of secrecy:

> A more perfect agent for the devising and execution of conspiracies against church or state could scarcely have been conceived. At the outer door stands the image of secrecy, stimulating the passion of curiosity. And the world which habitually takes the unknown to be sublime, could scarcely avoid inferring that the untold mysteries which were supposed to have been transmitted undivulged to any external

ear, from generation to generation, must have in them some secret or power richly worth the knowing. Here was the temptation to enter the portal...[43]

The secret "richly worth the knowing" that drew in hopeful candidates was the same Promethean power forever sought by humanity—the knowledge of nature. In the Second Degree ceremony the Masonic candidate was asked, "What are the peculiar objects of research in this degree?" to which he was required to answer, "The hidden mysteries of nature and science." On completion of the ritual he was told, "You are now expected to make the liberal arts and sciences your future study." Few Freemasons actually gained the knowledge of nature's arcana promised, and the ones who did came by that knowledge not from fellow Freemasons but from their own study. While most Masons were content to gain the expected business or social advantages conferred upon the elect, others—like Herman Atwell—were disappointed to learn that the lodge was built not upon Solomon's wisdom but on ersatz mysteries designed principally to bind the initiated to ignorance. Charles Pinckney Sumner, sheriff of Suffolk County, Massachusetts, became a Mason in 1801 because he was told it was "a Noble Science founded on Geometry," but after reaching the third degree, he discovered that Freemasonry did not "enable its adepts to solve questions of either Science or Philology." The public face of Freemasonry happily maintained the charade of esoteric knowledge, however. Louis Surette's history of the Corinthian Lodge, like every lodge history, claimed descent from the ancient Egyptian mysteries; Surette admitted that Masonry had "experienced many changes, both exoteric and esoteric," but maintained that "in its great doctrines and principle it is the same now that it was in the dim centuries of antiquity." In this era of Champollion and the Rosetta Stone, Freemasonry's borrowing of Egyptian symbols gave it a particular fascination for the popular mind. In his address at the dedication of the Masonic Hall in Concord in 1820, Benjamin Gleason let on that there was a good deal of mystification mixed in with the Masonic mysteries, yet he still allied them with serious esoteric traditions:

> Some suppose you conjure "spirits from the vasty deep"—that you are familiar with demons—that you have miraculous gifts—that you are different from other men; but how mistaken is the world, in all these wild and bewildering conjectures!... Some foolishly suppose your associations ridiculous—that you have charms and incantations—profane mysteries—bacchanalian frolics and abusive behavior; and that others, rendered spellbound, may share the surprise and the ridicule—that you keep secret as a reserve torment, or amusement, for those, whose curiosity induced them to become candidates. What would the Athenians and Romans have thought of such opinions, in relation to their celebrated *Olympiads* and *Lustrums*? And particularly their *Eleusinian Mysteries*—which continued 1800 years, called the "most sacred and solemn of all the festivals observed by the Greeks...." [44]

In the ancient mysteries, the picture language and ritual procedures—particularly the mock "death" experience—were designed to open the candidate's spiritual sight. For the modern consciousness, the arcane symbols on the letter boards and aprons that once held the key to a language of correspondences were mere atavistic obfuscations. *Sacred* and *secret* shared the same linguistic root, but they now needed to branch apart, as the new natural sciences were daily demonstrating. Emerson's *Nature* invited the open-air exoteric exploration of nature's correspondences at the very moment when the esoteric path was exhausting itself in the decadence of Freemasonry. In his emphasis upon the individual spirit as the crucible for knowing nature—"a dream may let us deeper into the secret of nature than a hundred experiments," he declared in the concluding section of *Nature*—Emerson allied himself with the ancients, but he was preparing a wholly democratic, demonstrative, declarative—and yet still sacred—science. Its emblems and symbols could not be pyramids and trowels and compass and square, nor its oaths bound with secret handshakes. Little did he know that the new spiritual science's first emblems would be drawn from his own woodlot on the outskirts of Concord.

"The American Scholar"

Emerson issued his call for an indigenous American mythopoetic landscape the day after Thoreau's Harvard commencement ceremony. Speaking at Brattle Street Church just outside the main gate to Harvard Yard, Emerson looked out upon an audience that included U.S. Supreme Court Justice Joseph Story, Massachusetts Supreme Court Chief Justice Lemuel Shaw, Oliver Wendell Holmes, James Russell Lowell, Richard Henry Dana, Wendell Phillips, Edward Everett, and Edward Channing. Once again Emerson began by pointing heavenward and asking, "Who can doubt that poetry will revive and lead in a new age, as the star in the constellation Harp, which now flames in our zenith, astronomers announce, shall one day be the polestar for a thousand years?" And once again he stressed Nature as the polestar that any "Man Thinking"—the universal and democratic exemplar he was calling upon the graduating students to become—must dedicate himself to study. The new breed of scholar—by which he meant not the hemmed-in Harvard bookworm but any American thinking for himself—would practice a relational, sympathetic science, matching his individual soul to nature, hence discovering that "nature is the opposite of the soul, answering to it part for part." Rhythm, or "Undulation," was the great law of both, and the incipient American scholar would accommodate the new knowledge of nature as easily and naturally as the inspiring and expiring of the breath.

The hour-and-a-half address climaxed in a confident injunction to become native to the American land and spirit and to each and every individual's own sovereign continent of self. "The world is nothing, the man is all; in yourself is the law of nature, and you know not yet how a globule of sap ascends; in yourself slumbers the whole of Reason; it is for you to know all; it is for you to dare all. . . . We have listened too long to the courtly muses of Europe. . . . We will walk on our own feet; we will work with our own hands; we will speak our own minds."[45]

If Emerson was with these words prophesying the course of any particular Harvard senior, it was David Henry Thoreau, but Thoreau had already left Cambridge for Concord and did not hear the address. The day before, Thoreau had delivered his own declaration of independence with his contribution to a conference titled "The Commercial Spirit of Modern Times," in which he participated along with classmates Charles Wyatt Rice of Brookfield and Henry Vose of Dorchester. Rice wanly lamented that the economic crisis of the 1830s was perhaps caused by the desire for gain. Vose delivered a sycophantic supplication to merchants for patronage of literature and science, seeing the era's rampant commercial spirit as "unit[ing] the nations of the earth." Thoreau, however, critiqued the commercial spirit in America, saying it would inevitably become the *ruling* spirit and lead to selfishness in domestic relations, patriotism, and religion. A bit of Emerson, borrowed from *Nature*, showed up in his address; he imagines observing the Earth from an observatory among the stars and questions all the bustling activity, "hammering and chipping, baking and brewing . . . buying and selling, money-changing and speech-making," but the rest is pure Thoreau.

He declares that freedom is the salient characteristic of the age: "Man thinks faster and freer than ever before." He notes the "profuse beauty of our orb" and "its varied zones and seasons." He says getting one's living should be the *means* but not the *end* of life, and celebrates nature's inexhaustible novelty and beauty. He gives his rule of thumb that the seventh day should be man's day of toil, rather than Sabbath. Thoreau even demonstrates his characteristic contrariness and optimism by finding in the commercial enterprise that he critiques an example of the unparalleled freedom of his age and a definite indication of the progressive nature of history. He concludes with his most familiar gesture, pointing the way from Earth to Heaven: "We glory in these very excesses which are a source of anxiety to the wise and good, as an evidence that man will not always be the slave of matter, but erelong, casting off those earth-born desires which identify him with the brute, shall pass the days of his sojourn in this his nether paradise as becomes the Lord of Creation."[46]

Scholarship—in its conventional, non-Emersonian sense—was surely on the horizon as Thoreau's vocation. He had already done a few months teaching in Canton, Massachusetts, during a leave taken from Harvard in his junior year, and his hope upon graduation was to secure a position as schoolmaster. Unfortunately, 1837 was hardly an auspicious time to be job hunting. The United States had just entered a depression; banks were closing, and there was a mood of crisis. Thoreau's good fortune, however, brought him an offer from the Concord school committee of one of the two principal positions in the Concord public school system—schoolmaster at the Center Grammar School. The salary of five hundred dollars a year was only a hundred dollars less than what the First Church paid Dr. Ripley as minister. There were more than three hundred pupils in the Center School, one-third of whom would be in Thoreau's charge.

One-room schoolhouses in New England were often hardscrabble places where students were ruled by iron-fisted masters—or else the masters quickly lost what little control they had. In Thoreau's second week of teaching at the Center School, a school-board member, Nehemiah Ball, visited Thoreau's classroom to observe him. Ball called the new teacher into the hallway and reprimanded him for not using the cane more liberally to enforce discipline. Thoreau went back into the classroom, selected six students at random, and struck them with the cane. He then resigned.[47]

The impulsive twenty-year-old was not turning his back on teaching as a profession; he spent the next nine months diligently searching for a teaching job, writing to Harvard classmates, seeking out recommendations from influential friends and former professors, inquiring after jobs in Massachusetts, New York, and Virginia. He offered himself as a private tutor and proposed to his brother John, then teaching in Taunton, that they travel west in search of a school that would hire them. Their sister Helen had secured a teaching position in Roxbury, and it looked as if their younger sister, Sophia, might also be hired there. Despite the incident at the Center School, everyone enthusiastically backed him; Ezra Ripley wrote a letter saying that Thoreau's "scholarship and moral quality will bear the strictest scrutiny"; Emerson's letter of recommendation claimed that Thoreau was "an excellent scholar, a man of energy and kindness, and I shall esteem the town fortunate that secures his services."[48]

Emerson had already lent Thoreau a hundred dollars to help tide him over while he conducted his job search; in May 1838, he lent him another ten dollars to fund a voyage to Maine, where Thoreau hoped that his cousins in Bangor, the Thatchers, might assist his search. He met many strangers, as he traveled through Brunswick, Bath, Gardiner, Hallowell, Augusta, China, Bangor, Old Town, Belfast, Castine, and back to Portland via Belfast and Bath. His sails were set heroically for distant parts, his fate very much at stake: "What indeed is this earth to us of New England but a field for Yankee speculation?" But whereas the chapbook lad Fortunatus had discovered serendipitous, magical opportunity at every turn, Thoreau instead found only disappointment. He returned home without a single job offer.[49]

A week before setting out for Maine, Thoreau had written a poem about a bluebird box that his family had erected in their yard the year before, in hopes of "a transient pair to coax." A pair did arrive, "reared a happy brood," and then departed as "Boreas came blust'ring down from the north." That April, anticipating the return of the bluebirds to the nest box, as "the earth jogged steadily on," he had been caught up in an extraordinary ecstasy:

> . . . never before from the hour of my birth
> Had I wandered so thoughtfully . . .
>
> I dreamed that I was a waking thought—
> A something I hardly knew—

Not a solid piece, nor an empty nought,
But a drop of morning dew . . .[50]

Before his Maine journey, the provincial, homebound young
Thoreau had yet been "at a game of bo-peep" with the world, deep at
home existentially. When at last he heard the faint warble of the bluebird
that had come winging from the south over the Concord meadows to
nest in the box by Thoreau's door, the poet was confident that the bird
"opened wide his slender mouth, / On purpose to sing" for *him*. A few
days after he got back home, he wrote a poem that recorded another
daydream ecstasy:

How long I slept I know not, but at last
I felt my consciousness returning fast,
For Zephyr rustled past with leafy tread,
And heedlessly with one heel grazed my head.

My eyelids opened on a field of blue,
For close above a nodding violet grew,
A part of heaven it seemed, which one could scent,
Its blue commingling with the firmament.[51]

If the wider world had not opened its arms to embrace the vocation-
seeking lad, still his natal place seemed to affirm that his destiny lay
there in Concord. School boards elsewhere might deny him, but the
gods of Concord were happy to have him back.

His Own Magic Circle

Thoreau's destiny seemed to be unfolding its true course in smaller,
subtler moments. One such moment cannot be chronicled but certainly
was Thoreau's most dramatic youthful declaration of independence;

sometime between his August graduation and his first publication—an obituary notice in a November issue of the *Yeoman's Gazette*—David Henry Thoreau began to call himself Henry David Thoreau. Another moment, perhaps simultaneous with his rechristening, came on October 22, 1837, when he encountered his new friend Ralph Waldo Emerson. Emerson asked him, "What are you doing now? Do you keep a journal?"

"So I make my first entry to-day" are the first words in his journal. With this question, Emerson truly set Thoreau on the path to his life's work. The pattern of near misses in their earliest acquaintance was past; now nearly every meeting between the two men would be filled with significance.

Thoreau titled the first volume of his journal "Gleanings or What Time Has Not Reaped of My Journal," suggesting that he had edited these earliest entries, making them all the more telling of Thoreau's own conception of what was significant at that moment in his life. Whereas the later journal would be filled with countless stories, the early entries are distinguished by a conspicuous absence of narrative. After a series of entries consisting almost entirely of quotations from his reading, with two brief impressionistic natural history descriptions—about fog and a pair of ducks on a local pond—the very first story told by Thoreau is one about an "accident" that he absolutely knows is no accident at all. The "curious" incident (which Thoreau even highlights by saying he "thought it worth the while to record") had happened some four to six weeks before, only a couple of days before the caning incident at the school. Thoreau had been out searching for Indian relics with his brother John, their "heads full of the past and its remains." At the brow of a little hill near the mouth of Swamp Bridge Brook, Thoreau, gesturing dramatically toward Nashawtuc Hill, "broke forth into an extravagant eulogy": "How often they have stood on this very spot, at this very hour . . . and communed with the spirits of their fathers gone before them, to the land of the shades!" "Here," he continued, "stood Tahatawan; and there is Tahatawan's arrowhead." Reaching for an ordinary stone and picking it up, it "proved a most perfect arrowhead, as sharp as if just from the hands of the Indian fabricator."

Many who knew Thoreau would come to comment upon his seemingly uncanny ability to find what he was looking for—particularly arrowheads and rare plants—but this lucky find was more on the order of Fortunatus's habit of being aided by unseen helpers.[52]

At the time when Thoreau wrote out this account, he was reading Goethe's *Torquato Tasso*, from which he copied out a passage describing the poet as seeking "something which we know not, / And perhaps after all he knows not." Goethe's conception of the poet was one to which Thoreau clearly aspired—one who found unity in diversity, whose mind took in all sensations, and who "In his own magic circle wanders." The magician's circle circumscribed a microcosmos where he became master of the elemental beings of nature, with whose help he could make things appear and disappear. Concord would become the magic circle into which this nascent master of the elementals would soon draw his own—and America's—destiny.[53]

CHAPTER 2

Seeing the Unseen

"Sing Thou, O Muse"

It was an article of faith among Thoreau's contemporaries that the independent "Man Thinking," which Emerson's "American Scholar" address endeavored to call forth out of the American soil, would utter his thoughts in verse. Emerson had in mind a poet who might—like Chaucer, Marvell, Dryden, Shakespeare—speak to future centuries as well as their own. In his study, on the wall across from the round oak table where he did all of his writing, there was a lithograph titled "Poesis," which pictured a lovely maiden wearing a band of stars as a laurel wreath round her head. He liked to point out to his children that her two-toned garment of light and darkness represented Day and Night, and that the arm of her chair bore the likeness of Homer.

Of all the stars in Poesis's firmament, Thoreau, who was fluent in Greek, loved Homer first, last, and always. He called the *Iliad*—which was the one book he took with him to Walden Pond—"fit to be remembered in our wisest hours . . . brightest in the serenest days." Troy was never long ago and far away for Thoreau, who would look upon a Concord neighbor at town meeting as a "fire-eyed Agamemnon" or see in the woodchopper Alex Therien a "Homeric or Paphlagonian man." The Greek gods—Zeus, Aphrodite, Ares, Apollo, and Pallas Athene—

were as real to Thoreau as Homer's heroes—Achilleus, Agamemnon, Helen, and Hektor—so the Homeric epics lived in Thoreau as historical narrative rather than poetic fancy.[54]

If Thoreau held Homer in high esteem, he held Poesis herself even higher. With Emerson, Thoreau believed that all of the greatest wisdom had been and would always be communicated in rhyme: "It is the simplest relation of phenomena, and describes the commonest sensations with more truth than science does." There were two types of poetry— inspired works of genius, and all the rest, which held no interest for Thoreau. Inspired poetry was "always correct... vibrates and pulsates with life forever... sacred... to be read with reverence, as the works of nature are studied." Again, Thoreau's sensibility about the source of poetry was more akin to the ancient Greeks' than to that of his own age. He took it for granted that "inspired" literally meant that the poet heard the voice of a god. Homer's heroes were forever heeding the voice of Ares or Athena; so did Homer—who always began his epics "Sing Thou, O Muse"—and so would Thoreau.[55]

The clairaudience of the ancient bards persisted into later ages via the world of dream. Chaucer, whom Thoreau called "the Homer of the English poets," voiced his faith in the inspired nature of dreams in many of his tales, which were themselves often renderings of his dreams. In the preface to *The Romaunt of the Rose* Chaucer says, "You may call me a fool for it, but I believe some dreams are prophetic." In the "House of Fame," Chaucer gave a full oneiromantic theory: Some dreams are oracles and revelations; others are phantoms that "never come." In the "Parliament of Fowls," Chaucer falls asleep reading "Tullius of the Dream of Scipio," and dreams that Scipio guides him through the spiritual world as Virgil guided Dante. Thoreau recorded many of the prophetic poetic passages in his notebooks, and he clearly harbored his own hopes for prophecy in his poetry. In an early journal entry, Thoreau declared that the poet "must be something more than natural—even supernatural."[56]

His earliest efforts at verse were voiced in the language of dream.

The very first surviving poetic lines, from around age nineteen, sail back to his beloved chapbook tales, recalling the three men of Gotham who set sail in a bowl.

A number of these early poems record ecstatic experiences brought on by hearing some simple sound, for just as Homer's "blindness" had bequeathed him such sharp ears that he could hear the intertwining rhythms of the cosmos, Thoreau attuned his voracious ear to the world's rhythms. Emerson's call for an indigenous literature had affirmed the dignity of the vernacular as a fit medium for poetry; "I embrace the common, I explore and sit at the feet of the familiar, the low." In Thoreau's poems, there were bluebirds and veeries, Yankee woodsmen and Massachusetts streamlets, Algonquian place-names, church bells and children, even his weathered walking boots. If Thoreau always used the Greek Zephyr to denote a significant breeze, still he let the landscape below speak through him. By 1839, Emerson proclaimed Thoreau's poetry "the purest strain, and the loftiest I think, that has yet pealed from this unpoetic American forest" and wrote to his friend Thomas Carlyle that Thoreau "writes the truest verses." Fewer than half of the two hundred poems that Thoreau wrote were ever published, and they have received almost no critical attention, even though Emerson declared in his funeral address for Thoreau that "his biography is in his verses." 57

The summer and fall of 1841 was the most fertile period for Thoreau's verse, and in the poems from this season of song, one can hear most clearly the "spiritual perception" that Emerson pointed to as the source of Thoreau's poetry. In "Inspiration," Thoreau describes the "divine electuary," which "comes unsought, unseen, . . . And I, who had but sensual been / Grow sensible, and as God is, am wary."

> Such is the Muse, the heavenly maid,
>   The star that guides our mortal course,
> Which shows where life's true kernel's laid,
>   Its wheat's fine flour, and its undying force.

> She with one breath attunes the spheres,
> 　And also my poor human heart,
> With one impulse propels the years
> 　Around, and gives my throbbing pulse its start.

Written years before he would come to hone his skills as a naturalist, Thoreau was yet at this moment a committed empiricist for whom "Muse," "heavenly maid," and "Eternity" were not tropes but Truths. Gods spoke in Thoreau's ear, and he spoke in reply. Almost half of the poems written from 1841 to 1845 are prayers, addressed humbly and anonymously to the "Maker." Emerson recognized the deeply religious nature of Thoreau's verse: "His habitual thought makes all his poetry a hymn to the Cause of causes, the Spirit which vivifies and controls his own."[58]

At a meeting of the Transcendental Club at Emerson's home, Bush, in May 1840, the topic was "the Inspiration of the Prophet and Bard, the nature of Poetry, and the causes of sterility of poetic inspiration in our Age and country." In February 1843, Bronson Alcott led one of his "Conversations" at Bush, on "What is Prophecy? Who is a Prophet?" Emerson, Thoreau, and their fellow transcendentalists had a strong inner sense of their own role as prophets and an equally strong sense that any prophecy they produced would sound forth as poetry. Thoreau was writing verse as compelling as any American poet of the 1840s, though as yet there was hardly a hint of the prophetic in it.[59]

"Somewhat Military in His Nature"

The introspection to which Thoreau dedicated himself as he began his journal quickly yielded episodes of self-awareness. "I yet lack the discernment to distinguish the whole lesson of to-day; but it is not lost,—it will come to me at last. My desire is to know *what* I have lived, that I may know *how* to live henceforth." On the cusp of adulthood, he had lost none of his youthful seriousness and self-discipline. In early December

1837, Emerson was on his way to Boston to deliver the first lecture of his Human Culture series, and stopped to pick up Henry, to whom he had given a ticket to the lecture. He discovered that Thoreau had set out on foot that morning, walking the nineteen miles because he couldn't spare the stagecoach fare. Thoreau at twenty was still all boy as well. Writing to John, then teaching school at Taunton, Henry assumed the mock voice of his boyhood hero, Tahatawan, to tell John about recent election politics and other local gossip.[60]

Thoreau played with Indian identities all his life. On a walk to Nashawtuc Hill, the site of Tahatawan's village, Thoreau imagined an epitaph atop it:

> Stop, thou who has mounted!
> Here
> A son of Nature
> Tahattawan, Sachimaupan
> The last of the Indians
> Hunted, in this stream he fished.
> Over fields, meadows, and hills he held sway,
> But if report must be credited
> He possessed no distant bands
> A Man, Chief, Christian,
> Although unschooled not unlamented.
> In character austere and without levity;
> In language lofty, charming and withal sparing!!
> In integrity and resolution tried and found pre-eminent.
> This cliff shall be his cenotaph.
> O Indians, alas! Where in the world are they?

Along with believing himself possessed of the qualities he imagined embodied in Tahatawan—stoicism, eloquence but economy in language, impeccable character, and firm resolve—Thoreau envisioned himself as having in some way inherited Tahatawan's majestic title: "He that was prince here." Musing on a stone pestle that he had unearthed on a walk, Thoreau again spoke of himself as he imagined the tool's maker: "The Indian must have possessed no small share of vital energy—to have rubbed industriously stone upon stone for long months, till at length he had rubbed out an axe or pestle—As though he had said in the face of the constant flux of things—I at least will live an enduring life." [61]

At the center of Thoreau's model of himself and all selves was the absolute sovereignty of the individual human being. In his first public lecture, "Society," delivered to the Concord Lyceum in April 1838, he declared, "Man is not at once born into society, hardly into the world. The world he is hides for a time the world that he inhabits. . . . That which properly constitutes the life of every man is a profound secret. Yet this is what every one would give most to know, but is himself most backward to impart." Even though he was still trying out different identities and different voices in his writing, his genius, his daimon, was emerging. Tahatawan was prince in times of peace, but more important, in times of war, and he was for Thoreau only the most local of his heroes who were distinguished by their martial valor—the *Iliad*'s warriors, King Arthur, the princes of the *Mahabharata*, and Arjuna, the great fighter of the *Bhagavad Gita*; "I have a deep sympathy with war" he confided to his journal, and though he attributed this to the poignancy of war as a universal image of the soul's epic struggle, his affinity for Mars was more personal. Emerson discerned this: "There was somewhat military in his nature, not to be subdued, always manly and able, but rarely tender, as if he did not feel himself except in opposition." Thoreau's inner allegiance to Mars rings out from his most familiar saying: "If a man does not keep pace with his companions, perhaps it is because he hears a different drummer." [62] Although the Revolutionary soldier had become the icon of courage, Thoreau was more likely to draw upon classical warriors, and his fidelity to the martial ideal never moved him to militarism. He valued the discipline of the soldier as training to do battle with immorality and injustice in the social arena.[63]

America awaited its Homer; so it awaited its Achilles, its archetypal war hero. When Thoreau set out to anticipate the New World hero, he naturally found a warrior, one dressed in celestial armor, his mount in sidereal motion. In December 1840, he finished "The Service," which, instead of offering historical examples, put forward an unequivocal definition of bravery, using the language of astronomy to flesh out the brave man: "He rides as wide of this earth's gravity as a star, and by yielding incessantly to all the impulses of the soul, is constantly drawn upward and becomes a fixed star." Sword and shield were unnecessary prosthetics, for as with the "all pervading ether," being struck by lightning only enhanced his purity. Immeasurable as the cosmos, his eye made centripetal the rays from all suns and stars. Like the vault of heaven, the Hero was a perfect sphere; "what shame then, that our lives, which might so well be the source of planetary motion, and sanction the order of the spheres, should be full of abruptness and angulosity, so as not to roll nor move majestically."[64]

For all his martial bluster, Venus, rather than Mars, would forever be Thoreau's ruling planet. In the "Society" lecture, he lamented human insincerity, longing for true and authentic human communion. It seems altogether fitting that Thoreau's first publication was a loving celebration of a Concord crone, Anna Jones. His obituary notice praised her "amiableness and benevolence . . . she was never known to speak ill of anyone." As a member of Concord's Revolutionary generation, Miss Jones had been during Thoreau's youth a living link to the patriotic past, but more impressive was her piety. "Of her last years it may truly be said, that they were passed in the society of the apostles and prophets." The last line of Thoreau's eulogy, omitted from publication by the *Gazette*'s editor, likely due to its heterodoxy, hints that Thoreau, already at age twenty, had entertained the doctrine of transmigration of souls: "And who shall say that under much that was conventional there burned not a living and inextinguishable flame." Whatever his view of personal immortality, Thoreau's tribute to Miss Jones showed that he saw through the physical surface to value her existence as a unique spiritual being.[65]

This capacity was constant in Thoreau. An April 1838 poem suggests that his "philanthropy"—in the antebellum period commonly understood as the "brotherly love of humankind," rather than the strictly pecuniary connotation of today—was not restricted for family and bosom acquaintances, but extended to strangers, "Both great and small / That ever lived on earth."[66]

With such universal love in his heart, it is not surprising that Thoreau had a particular genius for friendship. Generations of biographers have accentuated the difficulties of his friendship with Emerson and slighted the extraordinary depth of a much wider circle of friendships, so that this gifted philanthrope has been repeatedly mistaken for a misanthrope. He wrote three different poems called "Friendship," the first one in April 1838, exactly one day before the anniversary of his first meeting with Emerson. Thoreau admitted in the poem that the love of a friend—his "greatest happiness" and the "closest connecting link / 'Tween heaven and earth"—was inexplicable. Thoreau and his friend— in this poem surely Emerson—were "two sturdy oaks" withstanding any weather. Above, the oaks barely touched, but below, at their "deepest source," their roots were "intertwined / Insep'rably." Thoreau seemed to intuit a relationship with Emerson that had begun before their meeting the year before, indeed, before this lifetime.[67]

All who knew Henry Thoreau well loved him, beginning with his mother and sisters Helen and Sophia. The fraternal bond with John was immense, and though there is little direct evidence of his relationship with his father, it too was one of mutual affection. Children universally adored Thoreau, as he did them. "I love . . ." is perhaps the most frequent phrase to appear in his journal. "I love a broad margin in my life." "I love the wild not less than the good." "I love to see the yellow knots and their lengthened stain on the dry, unpainted pitch-pine boards on barns." "I love to gaze at the low island in the pond—at any island or inaccessible land. The isle at which you look always seems fairer than the mainland on which you stand." "I love to see anything that implies a simpler mode of life and greater nearness to the earth." [68]

A halo of innocence enveloped Thoreau's gestures of love. For years Thoreau had been a happy helpmeet to Emerson's sister-in-law Lucy Brown, coming to her aid whenever she called. Though a college senior a generation younger than Mrs. Brown, his feelings for her were strong enough that he wrapped one of his poems with a garland of flowers and tossed it through her window. The poem was most likely "Sic Vita," whose lines express the ephemerality of human life by analogy with the very nosegay Thoreau had appended to the poem. His poems and journal entries are shot through with gratitude, and his perennial proclamation was thankfulness for being singularly blessed.

As Thoreau approached the advent of what the ancient Greek philosophers thought of as the Sun period of life, beginning at age twenty-one, there was an abundance of sunlight in Thoreau's life. A month before his twenty-first birthday, he composed a paean to the eternal aspirations: "Truth—Goodness—Beauty—those celestial thrins [triplets]." His sunny outlook and easy intimacy with Nature allowed him to feel a particular providentiality: "Strange that so many fickle gods, as fickle as the weather, / Throughout Dame Nature's provinces should always pull together." On July 8, after a walk with Emerson to the Fair Haven Cliffs, he wrote a poem that speaks clearly of how every walk brought communion. And on the same day he wrote to his sister Helen, who was teaching in Roxbury, answering her query about suggestions for readings in "mental philosophy" for one of her students. "I should think an abridgement of 'Miscellaneous Thoughts,'" Thoreau wrote. "Set one up to a window, to note what passes in the street . . . or let her gaze in the fire, or into a corner where there is a spider's web, and philosophize, moralize, theorize or what not. What their hands find to putter about, or their minds to think about, that let them write about. . . ." Here he was outlining his own curriculum and practice. [69]

On the day after his twenty-first birthday, he had settled into a calm confidence about his own heroic destiny, a timeless path that was lost to the ambitious, restless America of the 1830s:

> What a hero one can be without moving a finger! The world is not a field worthy of us, nor can we be satisfied with the plains of Troy. A glorious strife seems waging within us, yet so noiselessly that we but just catch the sound of the clarion ringing of victory, borne to us on the breeze. There are in each the seeds of a heroic ardor, which needs only to be stirred in with the *soil where they lie,* by an inspired voice or pen, to bear fruit of a divine flavor.

Thoreau had taken root in his native soil. A few weeks before, he had given up the search for a teaching position and opened his own school—with but four students—in his parents' house.[70]

"This Refulgent Summer"

Three days after Thoreau's birthday, Ralph Emerson was back in Cambridge, to give the graduation address to the Harvard Divinity School. "In this refulgent summer," he began, "it has been a luxury to draw the breath of life." The birdsong, pine pollen, and new-mown hay of July were markers of the Earth's perennial divinity and thus a reminder of the divinity within each of the "planters, the mechanics, the inventors, the astronomers, the builders of cities, the captains" and all others alive and upon the ripening earth at that moment. Thereafter attacking the Unitarians and all other Christian sects for driving Christ from their houses and from the hearts of their congregants, Emerson declared "The word Miracle," which Christ proclaimed throughout his life as an affirmation of the God nature of each human being, had become "Monster" in the mouths of Christian ministers.

The divinity students got exactly what they wished for in inviting Emerson, for along with his critique of contemporary Christianity, he delivered an impassioned invitation to them to revitalize religion. His advice was essentially the same he had offered Thoreau's graduating class the year before: The time for revelation is *now*, and it is your task to speak and live it. Emerson's words infuriated the clergy present, and many others who learned of the address, so that Harvard issued a public disclaimer, and Emerson was not invited back for almost thirty years.[71]

Thoreau's twenty-first summer was indeed "refulgent," radiant with his sanguine self. His feeling of being divinely favored still expressed itself by recognizing the activity of individually appointed spiritual beings: "In the vulgar daylight of our self-conceit, good genii are still overlooking and conducting us; as the stars look down on us by day as by night." Truth, as Emerson had told the divinity students, Thoreau knew to come to any who sought it earnestly enough. "Whatever of past or present wisdom has published itself to the world, is palpable falsehood till it come and utter itself by my side." Thoreau's optimism was of that rare sort that always found opportunity in the midst of disappointment, and when he looked at both society and nature, Thoreau found only good: "No faculty of man was created with a useless or sinister intent; in no respect can he be wholly bad, but the worst passions have their root in the best,—as anger, for instance, may be only a perverted sense of wrong which yet retains some trace of its origin." Here was the highest form of bravery, the expectation ever of the good. When lines like "We make our own Fortune" or "Man is the artificer of his own happiness" appeared in his journal, these were not episodic exhilarations but glimpses of his core belief.[72]

August, typically the month when summer's heat muffled birdsong and stream song, rang out instead with music for Thoreau. No discordant note nor erratic rhythm could dampen his aural ardor. While "weeping, and wailing, and gnashing of teeth" went on during a revival meeting held at the Academy Hall, he still discerned "sphere music" rising from the building. Sonic resonances between himself and nature caught his ear: "Every pulse-beat is in exact time with the cricket's chant, and the tickings of the death-watch in the wall. Alternate with these if you can." Even the earth's moan or wail was "never so loud... but it seemed to taper off into a piercing melody and note of joy." Nature's sounds unfailingly affected Thoreau as joyously as her sights: "We listen and are capable of no mean act or thought—We tread to Olympus and participate in the councils of the gods." Thoreau's gift for spiritualized hearing ran in two directions; he could hear the gods when they spoke, and his ear translated terrestrial sounds and conveyed them heavenward.[73]

Some inner instrument of Thoreau's seemed to be able to attune to a whole range of rhythms. Toward the end of this refulgent summer he declared, "For the first time it occurred to me this afternoon what a piece of wonder a river is. A huge volume of matter ceaselessly rolling through the fields and meadows of this substantial earth...." Richly riparian Concord afforded him endless opportunities for such merger of inner and outer cadences, the first of which he recorded on August 13, 1838:

> If with closed ears and eyes I consult consciousness for a moment, immediately are the walls and barriers dissipated, earth rolls from under me, and I float, by the impetus derived from the earth and the system, a subjective, heavily laden thought, in the midst of an unknown and infinite sea, or else heave and swell like a vast ocean of thought, without rock or headland, where all riddles solved, all straight lines making there their two ends to meet, eternity and space gambolling familiarly through my depths. I am from the beginning, knowing no end, no aim. No sun illumines me, for I dissolve all lesser lights in my own intenser and steadier light. I am a restful kernel in the magazine of the universe.

Thoreau was not the only transcendentalist to have an overwhelming transcendental experience at age twenty-one. Emerson's "transparent eyeball" episode while crossing a bare common occurred in his twenty-first year. Margaret Fuller was twenty-one when, while walking the fields of Groton after church on Thanksgiving Day, she went into an ecstasy that forever after she believed to have been a turning point in her life.[74]

In his twenty-first year, Thoreau was himself a refulgent summer sun, radiating his finest qualities into the world. He was exercising his Muse, producing poetry whose cadences and dialect were altogether new, more of the future than the past. Ralph Waldo Emerson, America's premier prophet, had become his best friend. His vocation seemed finally to be maturing; in September, he moved his school out of his parents' home and into the Masonic Hall, as Concord Academy. Enrollment began to climb, and he asked John to come serve as second teacher. In the fall, he was elected secretary and curator of the Concord Lyceum. Deeply immersed in the idiosyncratic forms, colors, and sounds of his beloved, neatly bounded Concord, it was easy for him to "consult consciousness" and instantaneously leap out of bounds into Eternity. For all his commonness, Thoreau wore a magisterial, royal mantle, king of a wide country. At the moment that America was most fiercely meting out lots, driving out the land's native inhabitants, and claiming sovereignty with fences and cavalries, back in Concord—the first inland settlement of the Massachusetts Bay Colony—a vagabond for truth was awarding himself a license to trespass. The highest fences and boldest Keep Out signs would become invitations to Thoreau to walk right in.[75]

Sympathy, Act I: A Gentle Boy

As fall turned to winter and Concord's ponds and streams glazed over with ice, the brilliant warmth of Thoreau's refulgent summer kept him melting into his surroundings. In mid-December he wrote "Fair Haven," a poem about the broad bay in the Sudbury River whose name for Thoreau always suggested sanctuary for soul as well as body. The "pent-house" of ice only served to prompt him to think that "the summer still is nigh, / And lurketh underneath." A week later, he wrote a poem about the return of spring, and in early January, "The Thaw" recorded his continuing ecstatic condition:

> Fain would I stretch me by the highway side,
> To thaw and trickle with the melting snow,
> That mingled soul and body with the tide,
> I too may through the pores of nature flow.

By the time spring came in earnest, he had written a half dozen more verses giving voice to his inspired condition, and on April 4, an outing on Walden Pond provoked another ecstasy: "Drifting in a sultry day on the sluggish waters of the pond, I almost cease to live—and begin to be. A boat-man stretched on the deck of his craft, and dallying with the noon, would be as apt an emblem of eternity for me, as the serpent with the tail in his mouth. I am never so prone to lose my identity. I am dissolved in the haze."[76] As with the *ouroboros*, something in Thoreau was being dissolved, and something was simultaneously being born. On the eve of his twenty-second birthday, he composed a poem entitled "Sympathy."

Shortly after turning twenty-two, Thoreau had met eleven-year-old Edmund Sewall, the grandson of one of his mother's boarders, Prudence Ward. Thoreau had an instant affection for the boy and took Edmund sailing and hiking to the Cliffs and Walden Pond. He wrote in his journal:

> I have within the last few days come into contact with a pure, uncompromising spirit, that is somewhere wandering in the atmosphere, but settles not positively anywhere. Some persons carry about them the air and conviction of virtue, though they themselves are unconscious of it, and are even backward to appreciate it in others. Such it is impossible not to love; still is their loveliness, as it were, independent of them, so that you seem not to lose it when they are absent, for when they are near it is like an invisible presence which attends you.

On the eve of his birthday, Thoreau penned the poem "Sympathy," two stanzas of which read:

> We two were one while we did sympathize
> So could we not the simplest bargain drive;
> And what avails it now that we are wise,
>
> If absence doth this doubleness contrive?
> Eternity may not the chance repeat,
> But I must tread my single way alone,
>   In sad remembrance that we once did meet,
> And know that bliss irrevocably gone.

All of Thoreau's biographers have assumed that the subject of "Sympathy" was this "pure, uncompromising spirit," who in June 1839 enrolled in the Concord Academy. But Edmund Sewall's deep and instant familiarity only served to remind Thoreau of another "gentle boy" whom he knew much more intimately—his own youthful self. The journal entry admitted that Thoreau could see in Edmund only that which he knew to be true in himself. The poem's tone of lamentation marked this aspect of Thoreau's self as having a separate, and wholly past, existence. The series of ecstasies that Thoreau experienced in his twenty-first year marked the rending of the sympathetic bond between his adult sun-self and the boy who was "Beauty's toy," but Thoreau testified that the "kernel" of his youth endured and was always available to him, "if I but love that virtue which he is."[77]

Three poems—"The Assabet," "The Breeze's Invitation," and "Stanzas"—in which the elegiac tone vanished followed close on the heels of this one, but the doubleness was preserved in each as a narrative "we." In "The Breeze's Invitation," Thoreau beckons his companion: "Come let's roam the breezy pastures, / Where the freest zephyrs blow . . . Like two careless swifts let's sail." Then he imagines the pair as a gnat and a bee making a concert of "merry minstrelsy" at a willow tree, and finally as king and queen to whose music "Time will linger." Written on the day that he met Edmund's beautiful sister, seventeen-year-old Ellen Sewall, Thoreau's fanciful reverie appears to be a love poem for her. During her two-week visit to Concord, Thoreau accompanied Ellen (with her aunt Prudence and Mrs. Thoreau) to see a giraffe; he took her and her aunt on a river outing and for a drive; he walked to the Cliffs with Ellen, Mrs. Ward, and John, and even took her alone for a sail and a number of other walks. The breeze's invitation seems to have been issued to these two new lovers, and five days after Ellen's arrival, Thoreau wrote, "There is no remedy for love but to love more," suggesting that the stoic Henry had gone all agog over a girl.[78]

The most demonstrative of lovers, Thoreau was equally the most discreet. No doubt he wrote poetry and love letters to Ellen, but "The Breeze's Invitation" is not addressed to her. In shedding his juvenile self at age twenty-one, Thoreau was fully ready to sympathize with a beautiful, cultured, gracious young woman, but a much more profound strain of sympathy linked him with a steadier and older mistress— Dame Natura. Though he could address Her more openly in his odes, still he does not give voice to half of what he has seen and heard.[79]

Rivering and Revering

Months before Ellen Sewall turned the Thoreau brothers' heads, they had prepared to give their hearts to another Siren—the Musketaquid, or "Grass Ground River" (a reference to its many adjacent marshes), known lately as the Concord River. In the spring, they had spent a week building the vessel for their intended river journey. Like a fisherman's dory in form, it was fifteen feet long by three and a half wide, painted green below, bordered in blue, to mimic "the two elements in which it was to spend its existence." Two sets of oars, some sapling poles for shallow straits, a sail, and two masts—one of which would serve as ridgepole for a cotton cloth tent—completed the rig. On the last day of

August 1839, having the day before loaded it with potatoes and melons from their kitchen garden, John and Henry rolled their boat—christened the *Musketaquid*—down to its namesake's southern shore. That morning's drizzle had ceased, and the afternoon sun drew an outward breath from the drying landscape as the Thoreau brothers pushed out from a bank of blue flag and bulrushes.[80]

A few friends gathered to see them off, but the farewell ceremonies had already taken place the night before, when Henry and John hosted one of their famous melon parties at the Thoreau home. Just before they passed beneath the famed North Bridge, Henry and John fired off a two-gun salute that echoed through the Concord woods and fields. Then they floated down through the Great Meadows, meandering round Ball's Hill to turn due north along Carlisle Reach. A mile wide in many places during the spring floods, the river was in August still some one hundred to three hundred feet wide, with a pitch of perhaps an eighth of an inch per mile. Thoreau had read the accounts of exploring the Nile and the Orinoco, the Mississippi and the Ganges, whose every reach brought exotic sights and sounds. As the sounds of Concord village faded, he contented himself with familiar vistas of bream and pickerel below, bitterns rising from the marsh reeds at their approach, and turtles dropping off logs.[81]

After stealing alongshore "like sly water-rats" in search of a campsite, they ate a dinner of bread and sugar, and cocoa made with river water. Thoreau lay awake listening to the night sounds—cowbells tinkling along the riverbank, foxes rustling dead leaves, muskrats fumbling about with the produce in their boat, fire alarm bells in Lowell, barking dogs. The next morning, they entered the Middlesex Canal at Billerica and, wishing to make good time on this humdrum stretch of their journey, took turns running along the towpath drawing the *Musketaquid* by a cord, while the other kept it away from the bank with a pole. Not only did they break the four-mile-per-hour speed limit (completing the six-mile section in an hour), but by breaking the Sabbath, they also upset the faithful coming out of church. At Middlesex,

Massachusetts, the lockkeeper dropped them twenty-seven feet through three stone locks into the Merrimack River.[82]

Thoreau's journal records only the barest details of the two-week trip—their campsites and, after leaving their boat below Hookset Falls, their itineraries on foot and by stage to Franconia Notch, where they viewed the Old Man of the Mountain. Though the alpine summit of Mount Washington was the Ultima Thule of their voyage, Thoreau's journal entry reads only, "Ascended the mountain and rode to Conway." The real adventure was Thoreau's continued excursion to much loftier heights than the White Mountains. Within weeks after their return, Thoreau was making a study and translation of Aeschylus's *Prometheus Bound*. Thoreau identified himself with Aeschylus, a "seer in his day," and the subject of the Greek poet's play was familiar terrain for Thoreau, full of gods, nymphs, and oracles. Prometheus and his brother Epimetheus (Foresight and Hindsight) were the sons of the Titan Iapetus, who was himself the son of Uranus and Gaia, Heaven and Earth. Zeus had created the human race, but they had become rebellious, and Zeus was sorely tempted to do away with them. Prometheus, as humanity's representative, devised a plan enabling humans to become independent from Zeus and thus save themselves. Zeus as retribution chained Prometheus to the Caucasus bedrock and an eagle gnawed continuously at his liver. Prometheus, however, knows some secret, which Zeus tries to discover by sending Hermes to question him. He refuses to answer, and as thunder, lightning, and earthquakes rattle about him, he declares defiantly: "O revered Mother, O Ether / Revolving common light to all, / You see me, how unjust things I endure!"[83]

"What a range of meanings and what perpetual pertinence has the story of Prometheus!" Emerson had declared, and Thoreau agreed. His journal entries suggest, however, that Thoreau was most interested in the Orphic dimension of Prometheus, his gifts of knowledge and civilization; Prometheus taught humanity astronomy, numbers ("chief of inventions"), domestication of animals, architecture, shipbuilding, medicine, divination, and metallurgy. In his journals, along with noting

Prometheus's philanthropy toward mankind, Thoreau began entering translations of key dramatic passages: Kratos's weak attempt to comfort Prometheus as he binds him to the rock, Prometheus's despairing cry "Behold me—what, a God, I suffer at the hands of Gods," his account to the chorus of his misfortunes, Io's request to know what the future holds for her, and Prometheus's revelation.[84]

The Prometheus myth as preserved by Aeschylus and translated by Thoreau is actually the story of human evolution as it would have been imparted to initiates in the Eleusinian Mysteries, showing the necessity of the ego ("fire") to overcome the tainted animal nature (the "eagle") in order to achieve true freedom. Prometheus is chained to a rock, representing the human being's mineral/physical nature, and his liver—which represents the vital principle imparting life to all inanimate matter—is attacked by the eagle's animalic passion and desire. In the second drama of the trilogy, *Prometheus Unbound*, Aeschylus tells how the initiate Hercules (his "twelve labors" signifying the stages of initiation) penetrates the physical realm—the Caucasus—to free Prometheus, but he must sacrifice the centaur Chiron, the human being's half-animal nature. The goal in all the mystery traditions was the freeing of the life body from the imprisonment of the physical body, to facilitate clairvoyance of the spiritual world. Despite the explosion of interest in ancient mythology in the early nineteenth century, the scholarship was completely "Epimethean" rather than Promethean, "thinking in advance."

While Prometheus embodied the image of the future human being, freed from the materialistic thinking that prevented him from perceiving the spiritual world, his brother, Epimetheus, thought "afterward," reflecting wholly out of that which was given by his senses. Comparative mythology at the time viewed the myths of Greece, Rome, India, Scandinavia, and other ancient cultures as pretty pictures that, for all their poetry and heroism, depicted no historical truth. Webster's *Compendious Dictionary* of 1806 defined mythology as "a system of fables," and "fables" had by then come to mean "untruths." In American letters, even the most enthusiastic champions for a new mythology, such as Emerson and Thoreau, held a wholly exoteric, mundane view of mythology. They lacked a "language of the birds"—the vocabulary of the mystery traditions—that would unlock the esoteric significance of myth. Emerson, for all his heavenly aspiration, comes off as quite pedestrian when he declares "Astor, Watt, Fulton, Arkwright, Peel, Russell, Rothschild, George Stephenson, Fourier are our mythological names." An Epimethean outlook like this assured that Emerson and Thoreau and their contemporaries could find Aeschylus's *Prometheus Bound* merely the "story of the invention of the mechanic Arts." [85]

Though Thoreau may not have understood the esoteric meaning of the Prometheus story, he was living through the Titan's suffering. The initiates in the ancient mystery centers where the myth was told knew that it pointed to a time in the future, when humans would lose their ability to see and hear the gods. By the time of the Rosicrucian mystery tradition beginning in the fifteenth century, the far-off year 1840 was prophesied as "the Abyss," the historical moment when humanity would be furthest removed from knowledge of its divine origin. This falling away from God was absolutely necessary to enable man to stand on his own two feet, but it was only a prelude to man completely fulfilling his destiny by lifting himself back into the perception of the divine world whence he came. Even Emerson, the seer most fit to warn America of its own godlessness, was sometimes apt to bind Prometheus rather than set him free. What impressed him about the Thoreau brothers' river expedition was its raw physicality, as an antidote to modern life: "Now here are my wise young neighbors who instead of getting like the workmen into a railroad car where they have not even the activity of holding the reins, have got into a boat which they have built with their own hands, with sails which they have contrived to serve as a tent by night, and gone up the Merrimack to live by their wits on the fish of the stream & berries of the wood." In his celebration of Thoreau's capacity for self-reliance, he slighted the higher purposes to which Thoreau's adventure was dedicated, purposes that would be revealed only when Thoreau published his account of the trip ten years later. [86]

On the Merrimack trip and in his daily life in Concord, Thoreau was Promethean in taming his own animal nature, much like another of his heroes, King Arthur, whose battles with dragons were an imaginative picture of the same Promethean struggle against the universal seduction of the physical world. His terse journal entries from those two weeks mask an epic encounter with and triumph over the eagle. There are hints in Thoreau's "Long Book"—the journal kept in parallel principally for the years 1842 to 1848, but which opens with scattered notes from September 1839—of the inner voyage Thoreau was making at the time of the Concord and Merrimack expedition. The very first entry shows that his bow was pointed heavenward: "The celestial phenomena answer to the poetical or ideal in man—The stars are distant and unobtrusive, but bright and enduring, answering to our aspirations." Contemplating the Harvest and Hunter's moons, Thoreau delighted in the fact that their movements should have been known to unlettered husbandmen before the learned astronomer, and that "All great laws are really known to the simple necessities of men before they become the subject of science." Perhaps too optimistically, he stated that "Science knows that the isolated mountains in the horizon are but portions of an unseen range." [87]

The unseen range, not the Presidentials looming over the sublime scene at Crawford Notch, held Thoreau's gaze each day of the river trip and every day after their return. When Thoreau thrilled to see his first shadbush along the Merrimack or took Emerson to see his first Concord grove of mountain laurel, these discoveries only pointed to higher groves. "There is a depth in Autumn which no poetry has fathomed—Behind the rustling leaves . . . I am sensible of a wholly new life—which no man has lived. . . . Who can hear the wind in October rustling the wood without believing that this earth has more mysterious and nobler inhabitants than Fauns and Satyrs Elves and Fairies—In the fading hues of sunset we see the portal to other mansions of our Father's house." This "wholly new life—which no man has lived" is Thoreau's anticipation of the future clairvoyance held within the heart—and liver—of the mythical hero Prometheus, which Thoreau felt himself approaching.[88]

Thoreau intuited the Promethean task as a solitary one, casting himself as the protagonist of "The Fisher's Son," a poem written in December 1839 and early January 1840. In it he recorded his own small Promethean saga, turning away from the land of the physical world toward the sea—heaven and God. Knowing that heaven's "feeble beat is elsewhere felt by few," and resigned to the fact that even America's most earnest seekers—"neighbors" literally, as Concord was the epicenter of antebellum spiritual aspiration—get only "weeds and ballast," Thoreau found himself with "no fellow laborer on the shore."

> My years are like a stroll upon the beach,
> As near the ocean's edge as I can go;
> My tardy steps its waves do oft o'erreach;
> Sometimes I stay to let them overflow.
>
> Infinite work my hands find there to do,
> Gathering the relics which the waves upcast;
> Each storm doth scour the deep for something new,
> And every time the strangest is the last.
>
> My sole employment 'tis and scrupulous care,
> To place my gains beyond the reach of tides,
> Each smoother pebble and each shell more rare,
> Which ocean kindly to my hand confides.
>
> I have no fellow-laborer on the shore;
> They scorn the strand who sail upon the sea;
> Sometimes I think the ocean they've sailed o'er
> Is deeper known upon the strand to me.[89]

The metronomic regularity of the iambic pentameter and the simple alternating rhymes, the inward and outward breath of Thoreau's verse, mirror the constancy of his daily, hourly, eternally alternating passage upon metaphoric land and sea. The "infinite work" of communing with the divine, each time bringing him strange new "relics," was his "sole" and "scrupulous" employment. This message in a bottle washed up on America's shore at the very moment of the prophesied Abyss—January 1840—ensuring that its contents would stay "beyond the reach of tides."

Ethereal Flesh and Blood

From the spiritualist viewpoint, it was during Thoreau's lifetime that humanity most completely lost sight of the Creator's "many mansions," just as it was mastering the technological application of two great invisible forces—electricity and magnetism. Nineteenth-century science increasingly denied the reality of any mansion but the material world, even as it was discovering new ways to make the unseen seen. In 1787, Ernst Chladni drew a violin bow across a resin-covered plate and noticed complex regular patterns form. The experiment suggested that sound could act as an invisible formative force working in the physical world. In December 1840, Thoreau, reading Coleridge's *Table Talk*, made notes about Chladni's experiment, struck by its resonance as a model for bravery. Emerson went further than Thoreau in his interpretation of the result, which became a favorite metaphor for the Romantic conception of material creation. "Chladni's experiment seems to me central. He strewed sand on glass, & then struck the glass with tuneful accords, & the sand assumed symmetrical figures. . . . It seems, then, that Orpheus is no fable: You have only to sing, and the rocks will crystallize; sing, and the plant will organize; sing, and the animal will be born." [90]

Through the spring and summer of 1840, Thoreau was working through a much more fully elaborated contemplation of the shoreline where sand met sea. Cambridge Platonist Ralph Cudworth's 1678 *The*

True Intellectual System of the Universe was a four-volume survey of ancient pneumatology, which opened with an attack on the materialism of the Stoics and on determinist tendencies within ancient astrology. Cudworth's range was extraordinary, digesting the Sybilline Oracles, Hermes Trismegistus, Athanasius Kircher, Zoroaster, Mithras, Dionysius the Pseudo-Areopagite, Plato, Proclus, Pythagoras, the Chaldean Oracles, Synesius, Iamblichus, and a host of other sources of esoteric wisdom. *The True Intellectual System of the Universe* was essentially a history of pagan consciousness, with extensive discussions comparing the ancients' ideas about soul and spirit with Christian doctrine. The running heads give some sense of Cudworth's scope: Pan, God Diffused Through All; Demons Lament the Death of Great Pan; How the Trismegistic Books Insist Upon God's Being All Things; Isis One and All Things; Osiris and Serapis the Supreme Numen; Osiris Cut in Pieces by Typhon; Homer's Gods All Generated from Jupiter and the Ocean; Pythagoras' Monad the Sole Principle of All Things; Heraclitus' God Whose Temple the Whole World; Plato and Aristotle; Polytheism; Stoics Honored the Supreme God Above All. Though Cudworth concluded that all these pagan gods were "mere fiction and fancy," the splitting up of the "one supreme Numen," his survey offered a comprehensive summary of how humanity had approached the question of its own physical and spiritual constitution. Thoreau absorbed an enormous body of philosophy from Cudworth, without settling on any particular theory of soul and spirit: "When I read Cudworth I find I can tolerate all—atomists, pneumatologists, atheists, and theists—Plato, Aristotle, Leucippus, Democritus, and Pythagoras. It is the attitude of these men, more than any communication, which charms me. . . . As it is, each takes me up into the serene heavens, and paints earth and sky." [91]

Ether and its adjectival form *ethereal* began the nineteenth century with at least enough vestige of its Western philosophical heritage that it was borrowed repeatedly by the physical sciences to name the mysterious medium in which light, electricity, and magnetism traveled, but as the century closed, "the ethereal" came to mean immaterial, intangible.

Thoreau used the term somewhat sparingly, most frequently in its original Greek sense of "heaven," but he also employed *ethereal* to describe other "intangibles" that were to him quite substantial. Contemplating the forms of elms reflected in the Concord River, he mused that every tree is the outer expression of "a graceful ethereal tree" unseen by "our groveling senses."[92]

Shortly after reading Cudworth, Thoreau made a survey of German *Naturphilosophie* in C. C. Felton's *German Literature* and copied out long extracts that grappled with a metaphysics of nature that would allow for a spiritual animating principle. From Gotthilf Heinrich von Schubert, Thoreau extracted a passage describing breathing as the imbibing of the spiritual element in which we live. Von Schubert suggested that man and animals and plants aspire upward toward the divine. "They are the breathings and the pulsations of the inner life. . . . The artificial magnet inhales an invisible magnetic stream, which flows through all earthly things, that its inner and living action may continue." Another *Naturphilosophe*, Lorenz Oken, following Schelling, conceived of ether as a dynamic, active medium animated by three "powers"—light, gravity, and warmth. Oken's conception of the working of the elements and the manifestations of life within the ether was a hybrid of classical and alchemical ideas, which appealed greatly to Thoreau for both its vitalist flavor and poetic holism.[93]

Emerson in the fall of 1840 was taking in similar notions and spoke of ether as naturally as air and water. He had a dream in which he "floated at will in the great Ether," alongside a diminutive Earth, which an angel took in hand and gave to him, saying "This must thou eat." The appetites and ambitions of both men at this moment were nothing if not "ethereal"—that is, encompassing the vault of heaven as well as all earth. While Emerson had embraced the Hermetic maxim of the identity of the microcosm (man) with the macrocosm (the cosmos) through his study of Swedenborg, Thoreau worked through to this understanding in response to almost all the texts that he met—both written books and the wide world as a hieroglyphic demanding to be read imaginatively. "Man is in very truth a child of the Universe, an inseparable part thereof, and consequently he has in him everything— manifest or unmanifest—that the Universe has, as Proclus, the Greek Neo-Platonic philosopher, says in substance: The elements which form the composition of our bodies are but a portion of those which form the Universe on the great scale."[94]

In his reading in Cudworth, Thoreau encountered many ancients who took for granted that the human microcosm literally had star stuff within, and that the stars thus measured and marked man. Struck by Origen's rule that "the stars do not make but signify; and that the heavens are a kind of divine volume, in whose characters they that are skilled may read or spell out human events," Thoreau seemed willing to grant more than just a physiological identification—"the elements which form the composition of our bodies"—with the astral realm: "Nothing can be truer, and yet astrology is possible. Men seem to be just on the point of discerning a truth when the imposition is greatest." This spring and summer his journal was full—as it would continue to be for many years—of astral allusions: "I need not make haste to explore the whole secret of a star; if it were vanished quite out of the firmament, so that no telescope could longer discover it, I should not despair of knowing it entirely one day."

Thoreau avidly kept up with his era's astronomical discoveries, so that "the stars" were more than mere metaphors for destiny or a shorthand for heaven. "To myself I am as pliant as osier, and my courses seem not so easy to be calculated as Encke's comet." In Emerson's study hung an engraving of "Philosophia" that was based on Raphael's design for the Stanza della Segnatura in the Vatican. Emerson's daughter Edith recalled that Emerson would point out the symbolic ruby on her forehead—"one that Margaret Fuller loved"—and showed her that the stars upon her upper garment symbolized astronomy, while the figures on her lower garment signified natural history, basing her upholding of moral law upon natural law. For Thoreau and his fellow transcendentalists, the study of the stars was always equally a study of terrestrial nature and the human being within.[95]

Transcendentalism and the Hermetic Method

On July 1, 1840, the day that Thoreau entered in his journal the comment about the most significant deeds engraving themselves in the constellations, a small star—a new magazine called the *Dial*, incubated primarily by Emerson—finally appeared. The Transcendental Club was also known variously by its members as the Symposium, Hedge's Club, and the Aesthetic Club. Ever since it had first met in Cambridge in 1836, Emerson and other leading members had hoped to initiate a journal to promote their rejuvenation of American life and letters. Widely perceived in their own (and even in our) day as impractical dreamers, the transcendentalists were radical activists who, while mostly avoiding their generation's most conspicuous reform enthusiasms, still engaged in personal political and social action to improve the American civitas. Beginning with the small circle who attended the second "symposium"—Emerson, Henry Hedge, George Ripley, Bronson Alcott, James Clarke, Orestes Brownson, Convers Francis, and some Harvard divinity students—the group attending meetings came to include perhaps two dozen individuals, including Thoreau. By the time the *Dial* was fledged, the gatherings had ceased, giving some sense of the fluidity and ephemerality of American transcendentalism. The transcendentalist movement is perhaps America's most dramatic proof of Thoreau's maxim about human activity, for although it failed to transform America into a nation actively achieving "atonement," it continues to inspire—individual by individual, rather than collectively, as its contemporary spiritual impulses universally sought—"at-one-ment," the reconciliation of spirit and matter called for in the *Dial*'s opening pages.

Edited by Emerson and Margaret Fuller, the first issue of the *Dial* included Thoreau's essay "Aulus Persius Flaccus" and his poem "Sympathy." The editors' introduction was unequivocal as to the mission of the journal and the movement: "Here then is the mission of the present. We are to reconcile spirit and matter; that is, we must realize this atonement. Nothing else remains for us to do. Stand still we cannot. To go back is equally impossible." Transcendentalism looked to guide the nation forward to what they and other Americans called the Newness— the revolutionary spirit of the times that saw humans "withdrawing from all old form, seeking in all that is new somewhat to meet their inappeasable longings." Both Margaret Fuller's essays on Jean Paul Richter and Washington Allston and Thoreau's essay on the Roman satirist fell short of this revolutionary rhetoric; much more striking were Bronson Alcott's "Orphic Sayings," which became a regular feature of the *Dial*. The magazine's name was echoed in an aphorism of Alcott's which combined the transcendentalist taste for celestial imagery with its emphasis on the heart forces: "Thou art, my heart, a soulflower, facing ever and following the motions of thy sun, opening thyself to her vivifying ray, and pleading thy affinity with the celestial orbs. Thou dost the livelong day Dial on time thine own eternity." Alcott's often cryptic Orphic sayings were intelligible at least to the inner circle of transcendentalists, who recognized Alcott's inspirational, oracular language as akin to the one spoken sometimes by their own daimones. The pragmatic impulse within the Concord circle stepped back whenever Alcott spoke, allowing him free rein to claim the reality of revelation, while warning against the desire for earthly messiahs.[96]

Alcott's Hermeticism today seems aberrant, but the esteem with which he was held by Thoreau, Emerson, and others suggests that behind the transcendentalist's principal initiative of working out a practical ethos for living in the modern world was a vast cosmos of esoteric thought. Emerson, in the very first paragraph of *Nature*, had asked: "Why should we not also enjoy an original relation to the universe? Why should not we have a poetry and philosophy of insight and not of tradition, and a religion by revelation to us, and not the history of theirs?"[97] Emerson was as steeped in tradition as any of his fellow transcendentalists, studying for years the sacred texts of India, Persia, Egypt, and Greece as well as Christianity, but he read in these works only to supplement his living experience of the oversoul shining through all history to the present. Plato, Plotinus, Pythagoras, Zoroaster, Böhme, Swedenborg—every manner of mystic echoed truths that existed apart from any line of historical transmission of ideas; their words, like those of Orpheus, came straight out of the ether.

The most consistent aspect of Hermetic thought had been its "hermeticism"—its inscrutability, exclusivity, and secrecy. Hermetic knowledge had for millennia been kept out of the hands of noninitiates through both its linguistic obscurity and social rules that prescribed silence. Transcendentalism—and more widely, Romanticism—represented a marked exotericization of the esoteric, an opening of the gates to the well-guarded mystery temples of antiquity. Margaret Fuller, whom Emerson and others felt an incarnation of the daimonic, pursued a hermetic path openly. She loved gemstones, ciphers, talismans, omens, and coincidences, was devoted to the planet Jupiter, and was well versed in hermetic correspondences among planets, gems, colors, and musical tones. In her letters she frequently sketched hermetic and alchemical symbols—the serpent biting its own tail, the Seal of Solomon, the Sphinx—and the original edition of her book *Woman in the Nineteenth Century* had as frontispiece illustration an ouroboros wrapped around Solomon's Seal—a pair of triangles, one white, one black. These symbols were important elements in the practice of ritual magic, and Fuller commonly used the language of magical practice in her literary work, believing in the supreme principle that the magician draws toward him that which is desired. When, after Christian theosopher James Pierrepont Greaves's death in 1843, Greaves's library of over a thousand volumes of esoteric literature was sent to his friend Bronson Alcott at Fruitlands, it included many of the major works in the Western magical corpus, such as Cornelius Agrippa's *Occult Philosophy* (1651), Roger Bacon's *Opus Magus* (1597) and *Mirror of Alchymy*, Ebenezer Sibly's *Key to Physic and Occult Science* (1821), and Paracelsus's *Archidoxus* (1663).

Emerson was always skeptical, even slightly fearful, of practical magic, but in his most Dionysiac flights toward prophecy, when his daimon—which he variously named Guy, Uriel, and Osman—spoke freely, Emerson approached the persona of millennial magician. Fuller shared Emerson's millennial expectations and expressed them in language akin to Swedenborg and other Christian theosophers. In the preface to *Woman in the Nineteenth Century*, Fuller claims that it is "the destiny of Man, in the course of the ages, to ascertain and fulfill the law of his being, so that his life shall be seen, as a whole, to that of an angel or messenger ... [whose] holy work ... is to make the earth a part of heaven." Not only do the angels await humanity's redemption of nature; humanity *becomes* angelic in this redemptive work.[98]

Thoreau never borrowed any of the occult treasures from Fruitlands, but during the 1840s he steeped himself in the hermetic worldview through his reading of Elizabethan writers. Thoreau loved to refer to the poet as the "arch chymic," an Elizabethan term for the alchemist. He knew Sir Walter Raleigh to have practiced alchemy along with his more outward exploits; Raleigh's biographer John Aubrey wrote that Raleigh made intensive alchemical studies on his sea voyages when there were no distractions, and that during his tower imprisonment, he used his alchemical knowledge to make Paracelsian medicines for other prisoners. Thoreau transcribed entire poems in his notebooks, such as George Herbert's "The Elixir," whose alchemical language portrays God as the "famous stone," His will the "tincture." Alchemy—along with natural magic the principal prescientific avenue of exploration of nature—sought nature's secrets not for the purpose of achieving dominion over it but to align with and augment its creative powers. Both alchemy and magic were like poetry in demanding enormous powers of concentration, which, when properly trained, transformed the poet into the Philosopher's Stone. From the poetry of Herbert, Sir Thomas Browne, John Donne, Ben Jonson, Thomas Lodge, John Milton, Francis Quarles, Sir Walter Raleigh, Shakespeare, Edmund Spenser, Henry Vaughn, and other English metaphysical poets, Thoreau received a thorough indoctrination into the Hermetic method.

Reading Geoffrey Chaucer's *Canterbury Tales*, Thoreau copied out long sections of "The Canon Yeoman's Prologue," which satirizes false alchemy—the materialistic attempt to fashion material, instead of spiritual, gold. In classic Hermetic fashion, Chaucer managed to expose the charlatans while at the same time smuggling in authentic alchemical allusions meant only for the initiated, who would recognize him as a fellow adept. Thoreau began his transcription with a stanza that foreshadows the theme of forbidden knowledge and continued with the section that has the canon yeoman confessing the addictive nature of materialist alchemy. The poem ends with the yeoman affirming that the true mystery of the Philosopher's Stone rests in Christ and is His to dispense individually to deserving men.[99]

In Chaucer, Herbert, and other early modern poets whose esoteric allegiances had to be couched in obscure symbols, Thoreau found fellow members of the craft of circumspection. From early Christian times, Hermeticism occulted itself in the face of repressive rule, to surface when and where it could, in new guises. The Renaissance Hermeticism that blossomed both in poetry and in the practical and philosophical treatises of Paracelsus, Giordano Bruno, Jakob Böhme, and the Rosicrucian Brotherhood had been eclipsed during the Enlightenment but was reborn in the Romantics, who took up again the task of putting Imagination into the retort.

The popular reception of Thoreau's earliest literary efforts suggests how arcane the hermetic method had become. Even Margaret Fuller consistently misread Thoreau's contributions to the *Dial*; Emerson constantly had to argue in their favor against Fuller's disfavor. Shortly before the first issue appeared, Emerson wrote to Fuller about the Persius essay: "There is too much manner in it . . . & too little method . . . yet it has always a spiritual meaning even when the literal does not hold." Emerson was correct, but neither he nor Fuller seemed to discern that the Roman satirist Persius was hardly the subject of the essay. Thoreau was instead performing as subterranean satirist, using the Roman poet's lines to his own ends while making a feint in the direction of critical review. The sly satirist Thoreau hides in plain sight as he says,

"But the divinest poem, or the life of a great man, is the severest satire; as impersonal as nature herself, and like the sighs of her winds in the woods, which convey ever a slight reproof to the hearer. The greater the genius, the keener the edge of the satire." [100]

The essay is simultaneously a reproach against false esotericism and an invitation to worship the most sacred gods in full view. Again quoting Persius, Thoreau says, "It is not easy for every one to take murmurs and low / Whispers out of the temples, and live with open vow." This modest essay then makes the most immodest—but wholly true—claim: "The life of a wise man is most of all extemporaneous, for he lives out of an eternity that includes all time." Thoreau left unsaid the corollary truism that the wise man living out of eternity is always misunderstood *by* his time, and with each of his literary efforts, he came to experience this personally. Though Thoreau eventually published thirty-one poems, essays, and translations in the *Dial*'s run of sixteen issues, his work was repeatedly rejected—and misconstrued—by Margaret Fuller and other editors. "The Service," written around the same time as "Aulus Persius Flaccus," Fuller sent back with the remark "I cannot read it through without *pain*." [101]

Housekeeping

Dauntless, Thoreau felt Fuller's rejections more as victory than defeat. The true hero enacted the highest principles in his words and deeds and accepted the consequences, even when they seemed not to favor him. But just three weeks before Fuller's rejection letter, Thoreau received a more devastating refusal: Ellen Sewall, at the insistence of her father, turned down his proposal of marriage. He was the second Thoreau to be turned down. In July 1840, just as the first issue of the *Dial* appeared with Henry's twin odes to sympathy and satire, John had proposed to Ellen while walking on a Scituate beach. After accepting John's proposal, Ellen then refused him. Henry might have undergone the same traumatic reversal of fortune save that Ellen this time asked her father's permission before responding to Henry's proposal. "I never felt so badly at sending a letter in my life," Ellen wrote to her aunt Prudence. "I could not bear to think that both those friends whom I have enjoyed so much with would now no longer be able to have the free pleasant intercourse with us as formerly. . . . I do feel so sorry H. wrote to me. It was such a pity." Ellen's remarks betray the limits of her love for both the Thoreau brothers; she is clearly more concerned that they are now unable to enjoy her company than she theirs. "I have always loved her," Henry told his sister on his deathbed, yet unlike his other great loves, this love would have almost certainly gone unreciprocated. After this, he occasionally took an interest in women, but they were always older or married. When Sophia Ford, a tutor living with the Emersons, proposed to him, he unhesitatingly refused. Ellen's rejection of Henry freed him to focus his love on the Creation and the Creator.[102]

Even as he was entering more and more directly into the physical world, Thoreau valued its gifts only to the degree that they passed intensely through the crucible of his consciousness. "It is more proper for a spiritual fact to have suggested an analogous natural one, than for the natural fact to have preceded the spiritual in our minds." Dreams, the nightly dwelling in the spiritual world experienced by everyone, always afforded Thoreau particular renewal. "Sometimes I find that I have frequented a higher society during my sleep, and my thoughts and actions proceed on a higher level in the morning." He had direct experience at night of the working of his daimon. Sublimity was ever tempered by the ridiculous, as Thoreau was always ready to drink a "deep and refreshing draught of silliness," to become Harlequin even when treading Elysian Fields. "I exult in stark inanity, leering on nature and the soul. We think the gods reveal themselves only to sedate and musing gentlemen. But not so; the buffoon in the midst of his antics catches unobserved glimpses, which he treasures for the lonely hour. When I have been playing tom-fool, I have been driven to exchange the old for a more liberal and catholic philosophy."[103]

The fool's other great pleasure during the winter of 1841 was his friend Emerson, who was at that moment reaching the pinnacle of his powers as lecturer, writer, and mentor of young talent. Speaking anonymously of Emerson, as he always did in his journal when the sentiments were intimate, Thoreau said, "The world has never learned what men can build each other up to be—when both master and pupil work in love." The two friends shared their thoughts daily, so that their reflections seemed to merge. As Emerson corrected the proofs of his "History," "Self-Reliance," "Love," and "Friendship" essays for his first published collection, Thoreau delved into these same themes, particularly the last. When Thoreau was sick in bed with bronchitis, Emerson—feeling low himself—visited, and Thoreau felt perhaps more than ever Emerson's tenderness. "Nothing will reconcile friends but love," he declared. Thoreau thought Emerson's friendship to be "an infusion of love from a great soul." [104]

Thoreau always excelled his friend in extending more than just tolerance or appreciation toward others. The word *sympathy* appears so often in Thoreau's writing because it best characterized his relationship with his fellows—a "feeling with" that Emerson almost always fell short of even in his most intimate friendships. Thoreau was always able to appreciate the nobility of the humblest gestures, a quality that made him a uniquely sensitive friend. Emerson—America's greatest democrat, always intellectually generous—was constitutionally regal, slightly aloof. [105]

These two friends, who had more to say than almost any other Americans about the rewards and responsibilities of friendship, were both sought out to become members of a wider circle of friends. In November 1840, Emerson's friend Reverend George Ripley invited him to join a new community he was initiating on a 160-acre farm in West Roxbury. All of the aims of the initiative—balancing intellectual and manual labor, promoting cooperation over competition, abolishing servitude, extending the benefits of education and the fruits of production to all, and enriching the cultural life—were dear to Emerson, but he declined Ripley's invitation. A few months later, an invitation to join what was now being called Brook Farm came to Thoreau; he declined immediately. The utopian design behind Brook Farm and the more than forty other American intentional communities begun in the 1840s disquieted both Thoreau and Emerson, who feared that collectivist activity would undermine the self-reform that must precede all social and spiritual progress. Brook Farm aimed to rejuvenate both the land—through reform of farming and landholding practices—and the people, projects to which Thoreau was surely dedicated, but he was too fiercely individualist to imagine this form of communal housekeeping.[106]

In April 1841, although the school was doing well, Concord Academy closed; John was suffering from tuberculosis and needed respite from the strain of teaching. Henry met this disappointment with characteristic resolve: "I will build my lodge on the southern slope of some hill, and take there the life the gods send me. Will it not be employment enough to accept gratefully all that is yielded me between sun and sun?" Instead of a hillside lodge, Thoreau moved into the Emerson house, intending to stay for a year (he stayed two). Emerson wrote to Thomas Carlyle telling him of his new boarder, "Henry Thoreau—a poet whom you may one day be proud of;—a noble, manly youth, full of melodies and inventions. We work together by day in my garden, and I grow well and strong." Thoreau was to do "whatever he wishes" for his room and board, and that came to include not only gardening, carpentry, woodchopping, and other chores, but serving as surrogate husband to Lidian and father to the three Emerson children while Emerson was away on lecture tours. When Thoreau would come in at the side door to fill the wood box, the children ran to hug him, and he would turn his woods walks into fables for them. He did magic tricks, popped popcorn, made panpipes from squash and pumpkin stalks, and taught them how to camp and cook.[107]

Emerson, too, learned many things from Thoreau. Just after moving in, he taught Emerson how to graft apple trees, and on walks he showed his friend his most treasured places. In June, out with Emerson for a crepuscular paddle on the Concord, Thoreau shared with his friend his especial dwelling—the night: "Then the good river-god has taken the form of my valiant Henry Thoreau here & introduced me to the riches of his shadowy, starlit, moonlit stream, a lovely new world lying as close & yet as unknown to this vulgar trite one of streets and shops as death to life, or poetry to prose. Through one field only we went to the boat and then left all time, all science, all history, behind us, and entered into Nature with one stroke of a paddle." Emerson had now lived in Concord for six years, but had yet to inhabit the place as Thoreau did, as inside a second skin. Emerson always craved the sort of *ekstasis* he had experienced as a young man crossing that "bare common" when he felt himself become transparent, and on the moonlit river with his friend, Emerson felt caught up in "A holiday, a *villegiatura*, a royal revel, the proudest, most magnificent, most heart-rejoicing festival that valor and beauty, power and poetry ever decked and enjoyed—it is here, it is this." Thoreau's journal records no similar ecstasy, but what for Emerson were episodic encounters were for Thoreau nearly quotidian. A week before their evening outing, Thoreau had been out alone in his boat on Walden Pond, charming the perch with his flute.[108]

Reposing on God's Croft

As Thoreau's home in Nature came to have more and more rooms, he grew wilder, yet simultaneously tamer. He wrote to Lucy Brown, "I grow savager and savager every day, as if I fed on raw meat, and my tameness is only the repose of untamableness. I dream of looking abroad summer and winter, with free gaze, from some mountain-side, while my eyes revolve in an Egyptian slime of health,—I to be nature looking into nature with such easy sympathy as the blue-eyed grass in the meadow looks in the face of the sky." Mrs. Brown and others who knew Thoreau well could empathize with his strain of savagery, for as he drew further into nature, they could see how much it opened him to the human. To Mrs. Brown, who, despite her affection for Thoreau, felt that human nature rather than nature held the key to the heavenly kingdom, he pleaded, "Why won't you believe that mine is more human than any single man or woman can be? that in it, in the sunset there, are all the qualities that can adorn a household, and that sometimes, in a fluttering leaf, one may hear all your Christianity preached." This summer he heard celestial sounds coming from every corner of Concord's landscape. As usual, he answered with his own melody; sailing on the north branch of the Assabet one August night, his flute "fell from note to note as a brook from rock to rock." Though he had a repertoire of popular tunes for the parlor, out of doors he only improvised—or more accurately, played what he heard coming to him.[109]

More music—in the form of inspired verse—was reaching Thoreau's ears in the summer and fall of 1841 than at any other period of his life. Thoreau heard poetry "rustle around me as the leaves would round the leaves of Autumnus himself." He finished his longest poem, "The Mountains in the Horizon" this summer, and it was followed by poems inspired by the sounds of cocks crowing, Sabbath bells, the vireo, falling leaves. Two poems he entitled "Inspiration"—the long one describing how the Muse speaks to him, and a four-line prayer to her:

> If thou wilt but stand by my ear,
> When through the field thy anthem's rung,
> When that is done I will not fear
> But the same power will abet my tongue.[110]

Half a dozen of these poems were prayers, the most stunning published as "To the Maiden in the East" in the October 1842 issue of the *Dial*. Thoreau biographer Frank Sanborn in 1906 guessed that Mary Russell Watson of Plymouth was the subject of the poem, because Thoreau sent her a copy of it. Whether readers of the *Dial* had similarly lost the ability to recognize mystical poetry addressed to a spiritual being, it seems unlikely that anyone other than Thoreau knew her true identity:

Low in the eastern sky
Is set thy glancing eye;
And though its gracious light
Ne'er riseth to my sight,
Yet every star that climbs
Above the gnarled limbs
  Of yonder hill,
Conveys thy gentle will.

Believe I knew thy thought,
And that the zephyrs brought
Thy kindest wishes through,
As mine they bear to you,
That some attentive cloud
Did pause amid the crowd
  Over my head,
While gentle things were said.[111]

At the end of November, Thoreau had taken a room in Cambridge with his old Harvard roommate Charles Stearns Wheeler, so that he might qualify as a "Resident Graduate" and thus receive borrowing privileges. His appetite was all for English poetry. Leafing through Thomas Warton's *History of English Poetry,* Alexander Chalmers's *The Works of the English Poets,* or Joseph Ritson's *Ancient Metrical Romances,* Thoreau would still not have come across a poem with the devotional character of his own "To the Maiden in the East." He would have had to go to Dante or the Song of Songs to encounter such a being as Sophia, who in pre-Christian times was known as Ishtar, Isis, Maat, Nut, Demeter, Persephone, Athene. In the twelfth century, in the School of Chartres, she was Natura, and some dim memory of Her lingered across the English Channel during Elizabethan times, where in Rosicrucian-inspired poetry She appeared as Diana.[112]

Margaret Fuller continued to find fault with Thoreau's poetry; in

October she rejected his long poem, "The Mountains in the Horizon," grudgingly admitting its "noble recognition of nature, two or three manly thoughts, and, in one place, a plaintive music." The poem surveyed the "solid stacks of hay"—Monadnock and the Peterborough hills to the north, the Wachusett Range to the west—"reposing yonder on God's croft," but once again, the poem was really a portrait of Thoreau resting on God's croft, and Fuller, the most ardent seeker after visions of all the transcendentalists, was blind to Thoreau's. His vision and dreams were increasingly centripetal, so that those horizontal mountains, but half a day's hike away, seemed as distant as the Rockies. God's croft was coming to be his croft: "I seem to see somewhat more of my own kith and kin in the lichens on the rocks than in any books. It does seem as if mine was a peculiarly wild nature—which so yearns toward wildness—I know of no redeeming qualities in me—but a sincere love for some things—And when I am reproved I have to fall back on to this ground. . . . Therein I am whole and entire. Therein I am God-propt." His reading of dozens of Robin Hood ballads was working on his desire to live in some sacred grove, and one particular place was already becoming the fateful center: "I want to go soon and live away by the pond, where I shall hear only the wind whispering among the reeds—It will be a success if I shall have left myself behind."

On Christmas Day some inner clock tolled *this* as the hour: "I don't want to feel as if my life were a sojourn any longer. . . . It is time now that I began to live." [113]

Sympathy, Act II: My Father's Cup

A week later, on the first day of the new year 1842, John Thoreau's inner clock struck the first bell of its last hours. While stropping his razor, he cut off a small piece of his finger, replaced the skin, and wrapped it with a rag. Eight days later, he discovered the skin had "mortified," and the next morning he woke with stiffening jaws. By evening, it was clear that lockjaw had set in, as John was convulsed by horrible spasms. Resigned to his imminent death, John said calmly to his family, "The cup that my Father gives me, shall I not drink it?" Henry came home from Emerson's to nurse his brother, but a day and a half later, John died in his arms. Eleven days later, Henry became ill, exhibiting all the symptoms of lockjaw, though he had not cut himself. On the third day of his sympathetic illness, he began to recover. That same evening, the twenty-fourth of January, Emerson's five-year-old son, Waldo, developed scarlet fever; three days later, he was dead.[114]

In the past year, Henry had spent almost as much time with Waldo as Emerson had. The previous summer, Waldo had played endlessly with a toy house decorated with something that he christened "interspiglions" and bearing a bell "louder than a thousand bells, that could be heard in all the countries," which he and Henry had built for his sister Ellen. At age five, Waldo had quite suddenly metamorphosed from a normal, unprecocious child to one who seemed to his mother "wiser and more angelic all the time."[115]

The morning after Waldo's death, Bronson Alcott's daughter, nine-year-old Louisa May Alcott, came down the Lexington Road to Bush to ask how Waldo was. A stricken Emerson replied, "Child, he is dead." Both he and Lidian were devastated. Emerson immediately wrote a series of mourning letters to friends, and eventually composed the great elegy "Threnody," as compensation for his immense loss. Thoreau was not so resilient. He did not take up his journal again until late February, and in his letters to Lucy Brown, Emerson, and Isaiah Williams he struggled mightily toward acceptance of John's death. Fate was a mystery that had long occupied both Emerson and Thoreau. Both men tended to view fate—in the sense of a deterministic course of events—as a weakened will's outlook upon life. Thoreau once impressed Emerson with his remark that "as long as a man stands in his own way, everything seems to be in his way, government, society, and even the sun and the moon and stars, as astrology may testify." As Thoreau recovered from the shock of John's death, and his will strengthened, his innate optimism and sense of control over his own destiny triumphed over any despair he may have felt initially at the brutal senselessness of such a loss. Thoreau ultimately drew strength from his knowledge of nature's rhythms, writing to Emerson that death is "a law and not an accident—It is as common as life. When we look over the fields we are not saddened because the particular flowers or grasses will wither—for the law of their death is the law of new life.... So it is with the human plant." [116]

But the timing of human death—especially the premature deaths of loved ones—was hardly a law that either Thoreau or Emerson or any of their contemporaries could even begin to describe. Emerson, always dubious of the "daemonological," still thought that the physiognomic sciences of palmistry, phrenology, and astrology "rest on a real basis. It is certain that there is a relation between the stars and my wedding-day, between the lines of my hand and works done by it, between the activity of my brain, and its outward figure; there is a relation, but how to find it." Emerson expressed honestly his faith in Nature as hieroglyph, but his frustration at its illegibility. Lidian, who had always had a strong interest in paranormal events, had what appeared to be a precognitive dream of Waldo's death. Shortly before their last child, Edith, was born, Lidian dreamed of a statue "so beautiful that the blooming child who was in the room looked pale and sallow beside it." After speaking to the child about the mystery of life, the statue "gave the most forcible picture of decay and death and corruption, and then became all radiant again with the signs of resurrection." Four days later Edith was born; less than three months later, Waldo was dead. [117]

Stargazing

Thoreau also was convinced that the stars played down into human life, and like Emerson, was much more apt to focus on the birth star and good fortune than the star that accompanied the angel of death. In the month and a half after the deaths of John and Waldo, he had been reading Sir Walter Raleigh and made a five-page extract headlined by the comment "Hear how Astrology comes recommended from the lips of Sir Walter Raleigh." Thoreau, who admired Raleigh above all of his other heroes, was intrigued by the shadowy adventurer's esteem for astrology. Raleigh called astrology "star-learning"; he thought the stars to be "of far greater use, than to give an obscure light, and for men to gaze on after sunset," and that they had an effect on the seasons just as the sun and moon did. He felt that God would never have given His mundane works—plants, stones, animals—great virtues without bestowing active powers upon the stars as well, and that those powers were meant to be discovered and employed by man. Like Thoreau, Raleigh had been struck by Origen's view that the stars were not causal, but emblematic, revealing the working of fate only as influenced by the human actors below. Thoreau underscored in his notebook Raleigh's repetition of a Latin adage that "A wise man assisteth the work of the stars, as the husbandman helpeth the nature of the soil." [118]

Chaucer—whom Thoreau had been reading extensively, along with Spenser, Raleigh, and Shakespeare, in the spring of 1842—gave Thoreau a great deal to think about regarding the working into human life of the starry world. Astrological allusions punctuated every one of the *Canterbury Tales*, and Thoreau often transcribed just the astrological stanzas of a number of the lengthy verses. The belief that "all is this ruled by the sight above," as he phrased it in "The Knight's Tale," was firmly held by Chaucer and seems to have been held by Thoreau, as well. While some of Chaucer's astrological knowledge would have seemed arcane to Thoreau, a great deal of it was part of every American rural household in the 1840s. Venus was the ruling planet of love, Mars of war and hatred, Jupiter of wishes. When in "The Man of Law's Tale" Chaucer notes that "Of voyage is there no election, / Not when a root is of a birth unknown," he was saying that the auspicious time for traveling was when the moon was in a mobile sign. A "roote of a birthe" is a primary datum from which a horoscope can be calculated—i.e., the exact time and place at which birth occurred. Chaucer says in this same tale that "the death of every man is written in the stars clearer than glass," if we could but read it:

> Some weak aspect of disposition
> Of Saturn, by some constellation
> Has given us this, although we had it sworn;
> So stood the heaven when we were born.

In Concord and every American village and city, where in just a generation the stars would begin to dim as gas and then electricity lit up the night sky, progressive thinkers belittled astrology as primitive superstition, but just beyond the villages, all of this star lore was vernacular wisdom. Much diminished, it still preserved in the main an ancient heritage of humankind's veneration of the zodiac and the planets.

In "The Knight's Tale," Chaucer gives for Saturn a more complete list of planetary influences than for any other planet: In the twelve houses of the zodiac, Saturn rules drowning, prison, strangulation, rebellion, discontent, poisoning, vengeance, ruin of buildings, cold maladies, treason, deceit, and pestilence. As with his use of alchemical knowledge, Chaucer sometimes feigned disbelief in astrology through his characters. In "The Franklin's Tale," the franklin says astrology is folly and "not worth a fly." Written about 1387, when Chaucer was just taking up astronomical study in preparation for his *Astrolabe*, the franklin's disbelief only underscores Chaucer's extensive knowledge of and respect for astrology.[119]

In these same months of the spring of 1842, stars shone out from Thoreau's journal. "The stars are God's dream—thoughts remembered in the silence of his night." Whenever Thoreau turned his thoughts explicitly toward the question of destiny, stars appeared. "My fate is in some sense linked with that of the stars, and if they are to persevere to a great end, shall I die who could conjecture it? It surely is some encouragement to know that the stars are my fellow-creatures, for I do not suspect but they are reserved for a high destiny." Despite some doubts about his own fate—"I do not know but my life is fated to be thus low and grovelling always. I cannot discover its use even to myself"— Thoreau usually felt himself fated to a "fair destiny." "We can only live healthily the life the gods assign us.... I must not be for myself, but God's work, and that is always good. I will wait the breezes patiently, and grow as Nature shall determine. My fate cannot but be grand so."[120]

Excursions

Thoreau's fate continued to be linked with Emerson. In April he had given Thoreau a set of recently published scientific surveys of Massachusetts flora and fauna, believing Thoreau to be just the person to review them for the *Dial*. Published in July 1842, "Natural History of Massachusetts" marked Thoreau's debut as an idiosyncratic, independent transcendentalist voice. Thoreau saw the study of natural science as another avenue of personal bravery, even if the reports he reviewed fell far short of heroic. Displaying "more labor than enthusiasm," the catalogs of fishes, reptiles, birds, mammals, insects, and plants were given short shrift—intermittent one-sentence summaries throughout the essay, and five dismissive sentences in the essay's penultimate paragraph. That final paragraph outlined Thoreau's alternative natural science in opposition to the Baconian method of reasoning from the specific to the general and testing by controlled experiment, which he called "as false as any other." "The true man of science will know nature better by his finer organization; he will smell, taste, see, hear, feel, better than other men. His will be a deeper and finer experience." Facts could flower into truths only by "direct intercourse and sympathy." The rest of the essay displayed Thoreau's sympathetic science, mixing his poetry, natural history observations, and philosophical reflections in a style that was absolutely unprecedented in American letters.[121]

Enthusiasm for Thoreau always connoted its Greek root—*en theos*, the "god within," and "Natural History of Massachusetts" found in every Massachusetts wood and field and stream the gods that had been overlooked by the legislature's surveys. Along with Minerva, Ceres, Nereus, and Triton, Thoreau attends to the lesser gods of nature. While from the report, one can learn that "there are about forty quadrupeds belonging to the State," Thoreau takes readers into beaver lodges and muskrat "cabins," puts them aflight with fish hawks and geese, and sets them swimming amid the "midnight economy of the fishes." Snakes and snapping turtles are painted with brighter colors than any watercolorist could muster. In support of his claim that "Nature is mythical and mystical always, and works with the license and extravagance of genius," Thoreau surveys "crystalline botany"—the parallel working of the formative forces in ice crystals and vegetative growth.[122]

Thoreau's ability to transcend the prosaic taxonomic catalogs rested on observations he made during long, leisurely walks to favorite Concord-area haunts. Without its walking trails, Concord would never have fledged transcendentalism. All the members of the Concord circle were great walkers; this summer, Margaret Fuller lived with the Emersons, and she walked often with Emerson, who, along with Thoreau, had as regular tramping companions Ellery Channing and Bronson Alcott. Alcott and Channing walked with Thoreau. Hawthorne walked with Margaret Fuller and Herman Melville. In September, Emerson and Nathaniel Hawthorne took a two-day, forty-two-mile walk to visit the Shaker community at Harvard, Massachusetts. The rhythmic pulse of walking and talking forged new friendships, deepened old ones, and created a community of the heart verging on the chivalric orders of old. Thoreau declared himself and his walking companions "not equestrians or Chevaliers, not Ritters or riders, but Walkers, a still more ancient and honorable class I trust."[123]

In May 1843, Thoreau made the longest excursion away from Concord—his Rome, he called it in a letter to Richard Fuller—of his life, to Staten Island, New York, to serve as tutor to the son of Emerson's brother William. As he stepped onto the wharf at Castle Gardens, a horde of cab drivers tried to get him—the great walker—to ride with them, but he ran their gauntlet and straightaway circumnavigated the island on foot. "Give me time enough and I might like it," he wrote to his parents. "All my inner man heretofore has been a Concord impression; and here come these Sandy Hook and Coney Island breakers to meet and modify the former; but it will be long before I can make nature look as innocently grand and inspiring as in Concord." Though he enjoyed visiting telegraph stations and Barnum's American Museum, and though he loved the sea and the novel flora of the island, the crowds always enervated him. To Emerson he wrote that "The pigs in the street are the most respectable part of the population. When will the world learn that a million men are of no importance compared with *one* man?" [124]

Before the winter solstice, he was back in Concord, his delight at being home again tempering any disappointment he may have felt in having had limited literary success in New York. In Concord he was lord—and friend—of all he looked upon. Two weeks after his return, he was skating on the Grass-Ground River after a fox; when it turned, sat down, and barked at him, he felt the act a personal revelation directed at him. On the same January day, he imagined himself imparting his vast human knowledge to an insect trying to hide from him, only to then wonder if some equally greater intelligence did not stand in similar relation to him. At the end of April, on a rowboat excursion on the Sudbury River with young Edward Hoar, son of Concord's squire, Thoreau's native intelligence slipped momentarily when, making a fire in a pine stump to cook fish chowder, the blaze escaped and ignited three hundred acres of woodland. In July he climbed Mount Monadnock and then Saddleback (now Greylock) on his own, then met Channing for a walk west from the Berkshires to the Hudson River and a boat trip south to the Catskills. Shortly after this trip, Isaac Hecker— who, following a stint at both Brook Farm and Fruitlands, had come to board with the Thoreaus in Concord—proposed a European pilgrimage to Thoreau. In turning down the proposal, Thoreau explained to Hecker that he "constantly return[ed] from every external enterprise with disgust to fresh faith in a kind of Brahmanical Artesian, Inner Temple life."[125]

Toward the end of March 1845, Thoreau borrowed an axe and, with Emerson's permission, began to cut down some tall white pines on Emerson's land bordering Walden Pond. Though snow fell on a few of the days while he cleared the site for the cabin he planned to build there, he noted that the pond was completely free of ice by April Fool's Day.[126]

The three and a half years leading up to his move to Walden were truly "excursions," in the original Latin sense of deviating from a direct course. They also set his course for the seminal experience of his life. But the truly decisive movement Thoreau made in those years and in years to come was his characteristic pulse of heart and mind toward "the love that moves the stars." This movement was subtle enough that it often went undetected and unappreciated by Thoreau's peers, even Emerson. Both he and Fuller were underwhelmed by two essays published in the fall of 1843 in the *United States Magazine and Democratic Review*. "The Landlord" is Thoreau's tribute to the art of hospitality. The warm welcoming of strangers into one's household was second nature to Thoreau, whose own childhood home had been run by his mother as a boardinghouse. Throughout his journals, many of the most moving moments are scenes of hospitality given or received. In the America of Thoreau's youth, it was still common courtesy to offer traveling strangers bed and board for the night, but Thoreau always treated such hospitality as an uncommon kindness worthy of the highest praise. Thoreau concludes his essay "The Landlord" by ranking the tavern higher than the church, because it is the place where prayers take effect, and his constant capitalizing of "Landlord" hints that the model landlord is Jesus Christ.

Nothing comes between men more than the machine, which forever promises to deliver humanity from labor into leisure and thus liberate the latent love in his heart. Thoreau—a Yankee tinkerer completely comfortable around cranks and camshafts—keenly felt the falseness of that promise and voiced his dissent against the technological utopianism of his age in a review of German immigrant J. A. Etzler's 1842 mechanical manifesto, *The Paradise Within the Reach of All Men, Without Labour, by Powers of Nature and Machinery*. In this "Address to All Intelligent Men," Etzler far exceeded Fourier's wild schemes for rationalizing human society, proposing that in a single decade, by the mechanical harnessing of Nature's forces, all men might live in luxury. Mountains would be leveled, lakes and swamps drained, valleys lowered, canals dug, and palaces built, as machines effected a "life of continual happiness." [127]

Appalled at the "gross labor" already performed by the latest magnetic, electric, and steam engines, Thoreau offered a new motive power. When Etzler predicted that soon "Any member may procure himself all the common articles of his daily wants, by a short turn of some crank, without leaving his apartment," Thoreau countermanded with a call to turn the "crank within." "Suppose we could compare the moral with the physical, and say how many horse-power the force of love, for instance, blowing on every square foot of a man's soul, would equal.... Love is the wind, the tide, the waves, the sunshine. Its power is incalculable." [128]

In the spring of 1843, the stars were again on Thoreau's—and all America's—mind. In March, a brilliant comet appeared in the western sky below Orion, with a tail estimated to be 108 million miles long. So bright that it could be seen in daylight, it was widely interpreted as a harbinger of the Second Coming of Christ. After years of peddling chronologically imprecise apocalyptic sermons, prophet William Miller had in 1840 in Boston begun asserting the date as between 1843 and 1844, and early in 1843 he revised this to the exact date of the third of April. On Howard Street in Boston the Millerite Tabernacle, a circular temple over one hundred feet in diameter, capable of holding thousands, was still being constructed when, two days after April Fool's Day, the earth, instead of bursting into flame, continued bursting into spring green. The great crowds gathered on Boston Common to watch the faithful taken up were as disappointed as Miller's followers. Miller was only one of many End Times prophets of the day: A converted Jew in Palestine named Joseph Wolff, well known in England, predicted 1847 for the arrival of the Advent. Harriet Livermore, daughter of a United States Congressman from Massachusetts, had been preaching throughout America—including four appearances before Congress and large attendant crowds—the incipience of the Rapture for several years. Each of these celebrated eschatological evangelists spawned dozens of enthusiastic imitators. America was awash in a sea of millennial expectation. In thousands of homes one could find elaborate charts of human history plotting the rhythmic unfolding of civilizations' wars, famines, and plagues from Old Testament times to the present. Unlike the moon or the planets or even the distant stars—and despite the scientific deduction of Halley's Comet's seventy-six-year period, Encke's Comet's three-and-a-half-year period, and Biela's Comet's seven-year period—comets were still mostly considered "excursions," seemingly erratic and errant intruders through the concentric elliptical paths of the steady planetary wanderers. Arrythmic phenomena, they lent themselves to interpretation as God-sent signs from the heavens.[129]

Thoreau never caught the millennial fever, but the Great March Comet of 1843 did not pass over his head without setting him musing about humanity's fate among the stars. In his poem "To the Comet," his "sincerity" surpassing the "pretence of optic glass," he addresses his questions directly to the celestial visitor:

> Runner of the firmament
> On what errand wast thou sent,
> Art thou some great general's scout
> Come to spy our weakness out?
> Sculling thy way without a sail,
> Mid the stars and constellations,
> The pioneerer of a tail

Through the stary nations.
Thou celestial privateer
We entreat thee come not near.[130]

If there was in his poem a note of doubt about the particular apocalyptic message brought by the comet, Thoreau still intuited its import. A few months later he affirmed his belief in the starry script, and whatever errors hopeful prophets might make in their calculations about the fateful interaction of sidereal and earthly time, Thoreau assumed that the planets and stars conveyed a transcendental truth. "I think that the mythological system interwoven as it is with the astronomical, points to a time when a grander and mightier genius inhabited the earth than now. There is a grandeur and perfection about this scheme which match with the architecture of the heavens themselves."[131]

"The Respectable Folks"

In the spring of 1845, Thoreau was feeling within himself another cosmic rhythm: the seven days that make up a week. He had settled on a seven-day structure to enact the telling of the mythical journey he and his beloved brother had made almost six years before. Critics have made much of Thoreau's compression of his two-week journey with John into a single week, and of the elimination of John from the narrative—he vanishes to become the anonymous other person making up the book's "we"—but Thoreau employed much greater authorial sleights-of-hand than these as he composed *A Week*. Just three paragraphs into the book, after a paean to the generations of Concord farmers who have etched their lives into the land, appears this poem:

The respectable folks,—
Where dwell they?

They whisper in the oaks,
And they sigh in the hay;
Summer and winter, night and day,
Out on the meadow, there dwell they.
They never die,
Nor snivel, nor cry,
Nor ask our pity
With a wet eye.
A sound estate they ever mend
To every asker readily lend;
To the ocean wealth,
To the meadow health,
To Time his length,
To the rocks strength,
To the stars light,
To the weary night,
To the busy day,
To the idle play;
And so their good cheer never ends,
For all are their debtors, and all their friends.[132]

The published text picks up directly after this poem with the physical description of the river, saying nothing more of the "respectable folks," whom Thoreau seems to intend to be the solid citizens of Concord since the Revolution. *A Week* went through two more drafts, and Thoreau excised the following lines: "Such is the race which has long had a foothold in this land, and which these vagrant immigrants shall never displace. And yet there is room for all."[133] Clearly Thoreau's poem refers not to Concord's "respectable folks," for these whisperers in the oaks who are out in all seasons, who never die, and impart to the landscape "sound estate," precede the tenure of the "vagrant immigrants"—i.e., Concord's citizens. Thoreau knew the proper etiquette for addressing these folks, who wished above all to be noticed by humans, and yet could not abide being spoken of publicly, so he deferred to their wishes and called them "respectable." He knew well that they were immortal and that they were also somehow stoic, never crying nor seeking pity, even though their immeasurable gifts—of oceanic abundance, terrestrial vitality, geologic fortitude, stellar luminosity, even time itself—went completely unacknowledged by humankind. Though all of Concord's—and America's and the wide earth's—inhabitants were their debtors, they were these mysterious folks' friends only unconsciously.

Thoreau left in a clue to the identity of the respectable folks, this line that introduces the poem—"As yesterday and the historical ages are past, as the work of to-day is present, so some flitting perspectives, and demi-experiences of the life that is in nature are in time veritably future, or rather outside to time, perennial, young, divine, in the wind and rain which never die"—but it is a contrarian clue, as it seems to allude to the men "who were out in '75 and 1812," Concord's yeomen. This sentence lifts the poem up out of the prosaic, however, since it says that it will give "flitting perspectives," "demi-experiences" of a perennial reality—surely something more extraordinary than Concord farmers scratching the soil.

A second poem written while Thoreau was bringing together his thoughts to compose *A Week* gives a little more help. In the "Long Book," directly following draft lines that would become the last sentence of the book ("And now our boat was already grating against the bulrushes of its native port . . ."), appears a poem containing these lines:

> In concord, town of quiet name
>> And quiet fame as well,
>
> Ive seen ye, sisters, on the mountain side
> When your green mantles fluttered in the wind
> Ive seen your foot-prints on the lake's still shore
> Lesser than man's, a more ethereal trace,

I have heard of ye as some far famed race—
Daughters of gods whom I should one day meet—
I reverence your natures so like mine
Yet strangely different, like but unlike
Thou only stranger that has crossed my path
Accept my hospitality—let me hear
The message which thou bring'st
    Made different from me
    Perchance thou'rt made to be
    The creature of a different destiny.
I know not who ye are that meekly stand
Thus side by side with men in every land.
Reveal but that which ye can now tell
Wherein ye are not I, wherein ye dwell
Where I can never come.
What boots it that I do regard ye so
Does it make suns to shine or crops to grow?
What boots that I never should forget
That I have sisters sitting for me yet
And what are sisters
The robust man who can so stoutly strive
In this bleak world is hardly kept alive.
And who is it protects *ye* smoothes *your* way
Ye children of the moon in placid nights
Vaulted upon the hills and sought this earth.
When did ye form alliance with our race[134]

Beginning with an ecstatic Nature experience, it becomes declarative that "in concord" (the lowercase *c* allowing him to give both the location of his experience and his inner emotional state at the time) Thoreau has seen diminutive green-clad women on the mountainside, who have left tiny footprints along the lakeshore. They too are of a "race," like men, but also unlike them, of a different destiny. Like the folks of the first poem, these sisters seem unappreciated, giving of themselves but never receiving like courtesy from human beings. Thoreau offers hospitality to these "children of the moon in placid nights." Thoreau has the perfect attitude toward them, the one that all authors have prescribed to the fairy world: an attitude of deference as well as reverence, not using their name, not asking anything from them—indeed, an attitude of true hospitality and even concern for who takes care of them while they seemingly take care of us. He seems to know that he lives by their grace.

Reading Chaucer this year, Thoreau had transcribed the opening stanza of "The Wife of Bath's Tale," which tells of how in King Arthur's time, "all this wide land was full filled of faerie," how "many hundred years ago" the elf-queen and her "jolly company" would dance on green meads. "But now no man can see the elves, you know," the narrator had lamented, due to the "limiters and other holy friars," whose activities had driven them away. Chaucer was satirizing the sort of Christianity that rather than respect and honor the fairies, had banished them from their old haunts. For as long as the fairies had been "going away," vanishing from human sight, there had always been individual seers who could catch glimpses of them and report on their activity. Thoreau was—at least up until his twenty-eighth year—such a seer. The depth and intensity of his at-homeness in Nature both was given by and invited in the Nature beings—the fairies. By an act of hospitality—the transformation of a stranger into a close friend—Thoreau had brought Concord's Elysian Fields into view. Though he hid his visions from his peers by voicing them in verse and then enveloping them in double entendre in *A Week*, Thoreau shared his visions with one group of Concord citizens—the children. Thoreau played Pan to a generation of Concord children, whose memories of him emphasize his ability to imaginatively engage them through his use of fairy stories.

Edward Emerson, in his reminiscences of Thoreau, instinctively employed fairy imagery. Defending Thoreau from those who thought him aloof, Edward said that Thoreau merely could see "The beautiful hanging gardens that rocked in the morning wind / And sheltered a dream of Faerie and a life so timid and kind." Edward claimed that "many a boy and girl owed to him the opening of the gate of this almost fairy knowledge." Speaking of Thoreau's storytelling to the children, he likens Thoreau to "a True Thomas of Ercildoune returned from his stay in Faerie with its queen's gift of a 'tongue that shall never lie.'" In 1849, when Edward's sister Ellen was ten years old, Thoreau wrote her a letter recalling when he lived with the Emerson family the kinds of books that he and Ellen would look at: "You love to read or write a fairy story, and that is what you will always like to do, in some form or other. By and by you will discover that you want what are called the necessaries of life only that you may realize some such dream." Thoreau confessed to Ellen that his own task was to bring faerie into his adult world: "I suppose you think that persons who are as old as your father and myself are always thinking about very grave things, but I know that we are meditating the same old themes that we did when we were ten years old, only we go more gravely about it." All of their lives, the Emerson children (and Thoreau and Emerson and the rest of Concord) referred to the little pond about halfway on the walk from Bush to Walden as Fairyland Pond and the surrounding dell as Fairyland. For the children and Thoreau, fairyland was not something just from picture books.[135]

Julian Hawthorne, who met Thoreau in 1852 at age seven, recalled that while walking with him as a boy, Thoreau would "indicate the invisible to me with a silent nod of the head." Thoreau once took Julian to a brook-bisected meadow "treasure house" and then left him alone, "too shy to companion me there." Thoreau knew well the ways of the faerie world, respected their reserve, and did his best in shepherding the children of Concord toward the places and situations where they might meet these respectable folks. As fascinated by faerie as his adult peers may have been, Thoreau would never have spoken up at a Concord

Lyceum meeting of his own personal encounters with these beings of Nature. America was at this moment furiously denying the existence of Nature's beings, and her being-ness. Keeping his relationship with the fairies secret preserved the sanctity of the friendship, and could, Thoreau believed, even preserve their very existence in the gossamer landscape just beyond the visible.[136]

CHAPTER 3

Prodigies and Wonders

Shams and delusions are esteemed for the highest truths, while
reality is fabulous.   —*Walden* (95)

"The Creature of a Different Destiny"

The morning after Independence Day in 1845, Thoreau wrote in his
journal, "Yesterday I came here to live." His humble understatement
masked the declaration's double entendre, for coming to "live" at
Walden was in no way a change of address, but an intensification of Thoreau's journey of self-discovery. For the mythic hero, a life lived without
total dedication to heroic goals was death: "I went to the woods because
I wished to live deliberately, to front only the essential facts of life, and
see if I could not learn what it had to teach, and not, when I came to die,
discover that I had not lived. . . . I wish to meet the facts of life—the vital
facts, which were the phenomena or actuality the Gods meant to show
us,—face to face, And so I came down here. Life! Who knows what it
is—what it does?" Though in later years when he lectured or wrote
about his "experiment" at Walden, he would say that it was an "accident"
that it began on the Fourth of July, he knew full well that he was en-
acting a myth, and that mythic acts demand mythic timing. On his
fourth day at Walden, sitting on the stoop of his cabin, contemplating
the pitch-pine sentinel that had not succumbed to his axe, Thoreau
fancied himself a "fellow-wanderer and survivor of Ulysses." A week
later, on his twenty-eighth birthday, he made no entry at all, perhaps

because he was so keenly occupied with the vocation of living. But on the fourteenth of July, he gave voice to the conviction that stands behind the triumphs of all heroes: "Sometimes, when I compare myself with other men, methinks I am favored by the Gods. They seem to whisper joy to me beyond my deserts, and that I do have a solid warrant and surety at their hands, which my fellows do not. I do not flatter myself, but if it were possible *they* flatter me. I am especially guided and guarded." [137]

Thoreau shared his sense of being divinely favored with all America, whose destiny was manifesting apace. On March 1, just weeks before Thoreau had begun clearing the lot for his cabin, President John Tyler had signed a bill annexing northern Mexico to the United States. If there were Americans who were discomfited by their nation's aggressive acquisitiveness, they were far outnumbered by those who believed that God's especial providence for the United States equated to territorial expansion. The same week that Thoreau moved into his cabin, influential editor and Democratic leader John L. O'Sullivan—who in 1843, at Nathaniel Hawthorne's prompting, had invited Thoreau to write for his magazine, the *United States Magazine and Democratic Review*—published an editorial championing America's right to encompass the entire continent, calling it "our manifest destiny." O'Sullivan looked to nature as the model for America's prodigious physiology: "It is right such as that of the tree to the space of air and the earth suitable for the full expansion of its principle and destiny of growth." [138]

Thoreau already was coming to understand that the growth of trees was a rhythmic, almost musical process, and although he could confide to his journal that "Next to us the grandest laws are being enacted and administered," he could not fully see how his own biography exemplified grand laws of cosmic rhythm. Thoreau's life demonstrated Martin Luther's aphorism that "The seventh year always transforms man. It brings about a new life, a new character, and a different state." In his twenty-first year, Thoreau had met his destiny in a sort of stepwise fashion, encountering in the spring of 1837 first the transformative essay

Nature and then its author, who in turn, just three months into his twenty-first year, had set Thoreau upon a task that was to become his greatest life's work—the keeping of a journal. Just days after Thoreau's twenty-first birthday, Emerson had concluded his Divinity School address with a plea for the American hero yet to come: "I look for the new Teacher that shall follow so far those shining laws that he shall see them come full circle; shall see their rounding complete grace; shall see the world to be a mirror of the soul; shall see the identity of the law of gravitation with purity of heart; and shall show that the Ought, that Duty, is one thing with Science, with Beauty, and with Joy." At that moment Emerson, almost exactly twice seven years Thoreau's senior, hardly could know that he would eventually provide the land upon which the anticipated new teacher would harmonize Duty, Science, Beauty, and Joy.[139]

At Walden, Thoreau would fully live the truth he had uttered years before: "Surely joy is the condition of life." During Thoreau's life, that perennial condition always intensified at rhythmic seven-year intervals. His ecstasies grew stronger, his sense of his own heroic destiny more intense on or around the day of the septennial anniversary of his birth. The feeling of being specially "guided and guarded" was conveyed to him by the elemental world, the fairies who were just now fading from his view. Of all human emotions, joy passed most fully and fruitfully across the membrane separating the visible and invisible worlds, and Thoreau and his sister sylphs and undines experienced at seven-year intervals a particularly intense celebration of life's majesty. Born in the seventh month of the year, the rhythm of the seven was seemingly inscribed into Thoreau's most significant experiences and tasks: It took seven years for him to complete *A Week on the Concord and Merrimack Rivers*, the book whose seven chapters echoed the archetypal rhythm of the seven days of the week; his masterwork *Walden* would in seven years undergo seven revisions before publication. Other critical moments in Thoreau's life—such as the tragedy of John's death and also the first articulation of the desire to live at Walden—occurred at the exact midpoint of the seven-year periods. Thoreau's move to Walden Pond on the eve of his twenty-eighth birthday would be a destiny event that would ripple through the rest of his life and down through time into the hearts of Americans and people from all over the planet.

If Thoreau was not conscious of the working of this septennial rhythm in his own life, he was well acquainted with it from historical sources. Shakespeare's verse in *As You Like It* that begins with the famous lines "All the world's a stage . . ." continues with the less often remembered lines unfolding the archetypal human life in seven ages—the infant, the schoolboy, the lover, the soldier, the justice, the pantaloon, and the second childhood. Thoreau was familiar with a number of classical authors who spoke similar truths. Philo of Alexandria in the sixth century A.D. taught that "the ages of man from infancy to old age, which are measured by periods of seven years, show very clearly the perceptive force implanted in the number seven. For in the first septennial the teeth come forth. In the second we arrive at puberty. In the third we show signs of a beard. In the fourth we acquire the force of strength . . ." Julian Pollux, writing in the second century A.D., confirmed this rhythm as one taught by Greek philosophers for generations. "Hippocrates says there are seven ages. His words are: 'In the nature of man there are seven periods which are called ages: the infant; the boy; the youth; the young man; the man; the elderly man; the aged man . . .'" Even as nineteenth-century natural science grew more materialistic, it continued to acknowledge the working of rhythm in Nature. In the 1840s, Dr. Thomas Laycock published a series of studies in the British medical journal *Lancet* in which he described how, "from the Larva or Ovum of a Minute Insect up to Man," periodicity ruled. He concluded that "in animals, changes occur every three and a half, seven, fourteen, twenty-one, or twenty-eight days, or at some definite number of weeks." Laycock also noted how pronounced peaks or valleys in the progress of the illness almost always marked the seventh and fourteenth days of fevers.[140]

Sevens played throughout the lives of chapbook heroes and fairy tale characters, most famously Thomas the Rhymer, whose seven-year bondage by the Faerie Queen ended simultaneously with his being given the gift of prophecy. Though clairvoyance for the fairy world had mostly vanished among the modern peoples of the nineteenth century, even in England, western Europe, and North America, this and other atavistic forms of consciousness survived in children, but tended to end in or around the seventh year, at about the time of the eruption of the permanent teeth. Thoreau clearly kept an episodic clairvoyance for the faerie world into his adult years, but his last recording of a faerie encounter came at almost precisely age twenty-eight. In late July, he wrote this poem in his journal:

> Tell me ye wise ones if ye can
> Whither and whence the race of man
> For I have seen his slender clan
> Clinging to hoar hills with their feet
> Threading the forest for their meat
> Moss and lichens and bark & grain
> They racke together with might & main
> And they digest them with anxiety & pain.
> I meet them in their rags and unwashed hair
> Instructed to eke out their scanty fare
> Brave race—with a yet humbler prayer
> Beggars they are aye on the largest scale
> They beg their daily bread at heavens door
>   And if their this years crop alone should fail
> They neither bread nor begging would know more.
>   They are the Titmans of their race
>   And hug the vales with mincing pace
>   Like Troglodites, and fight with cranes
>   We walk 'mid great relations feet
>   What they let fall alone we eat
>   We are only able

to catch the fragments from their table
    These elder brothers of our race
    By us unseen with larger pace
    Walk o'er our heads, and live our lives
    embody our desires and dreams
    Anticipate our hoped for gleams
    We grub the earth for our food
    We know not what is good.
    Where does the fragrance of our orchards go
    Our vineyards while we toil below—
    A finer race and finer fed
    Feast and revel above our head.
    The tints and fragrance of the flowers & fruits
    Are but the crumbs from off their table
    While we consume the pulp and roots
    Some times we do assert our kin
    And stand a moment where once they have been
    We hear their sounds and see their sights
    And we experience their delights –
    But for the moment that we stand
    Astonished on the Olympian land.
    We do discern no traveller's face
    No elder brothers of our race.
    To lead us to the monarch's court
    And represent our case.
    But straightaway we must journey back
    retracing the slow the arduous track
    Without the privilege to tell
    Even, the sight we know so well.[141]

This slender, unseen (except by Thoreau) forest-dwelling "race of man" is brave, immortal ("elder brothers" walking "with larger pace"), and in some sort of economic relationship with human beings. Just like the "respectable folks" of his earlier faerie poem, there is something similarly "ambrosial" about their existence that is then passed on to man. Thoreau this summer had been reading Joseph Ritson's Robin Hood ballads; in one there had been mysterious, troglodytic creatures who also fought with cranes. New characteristics are given as well: they are "slender," "Titmans"—runts of their race, a race that seems to be both human and divine, as they dwell in an "Olympian land." The last lines confess that he is not licensed to speak of the elder brothers, and yet if the poem itself does not answer the mystery, perhaps the context from Thoreau's journal can. In the journal entry enclosing the poem, he invites "the illiterate and scornful rustic" to "listen . . . to the fames of godlike men—which yet as it were form an invisible upper class in every society." He goes on to muse about a Sops in Wine apple that he had been carrying, and its ambrosial smell seems to Thoreau "a friendly trick of some pleasant daemon to entertain me with." Directly following the poem, the entry continues: "In my father's house are many mansions. Who ever explored the mansions of the air—who knows who his neighbors are. We seem to lead our human lives amid a concentric system of worlds of realm upon realm, close bordering on each other— where dwell the unknown and the imagined races—as various in degrees as our own thoughts are. A system of invisible partitions more infinite in number and more inconceivable in intricacy than the starry one which Science has penetrated." From his descents into faerie, Thoreau knew that he would have neighbors round his cabin, even after James Collins and the other Irish railroad workers had departed, and even after his own ability to perceive the "respectable folks" had dimmed.[142]

In his second poem telling of his having met fairies, Thoreau declared that they were "creatures of a different destiny." So was he. For some reason, he had been afforded a glimpse of the Otherworld into full adulthood. He was hardly alone in this, but in the early nineteenth century, adult ability to perceive the fairy world was typically restricted to uneducated rural folk. Among Thoreau's scientifically sophisticated peers, it was safe to show an interest in the "second sight" of New England cunning men and women, or of simple Irish peasants, but to claim such clairvoyance for oneself was surely beyond the pale. Thoreau's curiosity and honesty demanded that he report his encounters with these ethereal beings, but his inner compass guided him to an understated, cryptic form of reporting.

If Thomas the Rhymer's Otherworld "bondage" was an image of the capacity to perceive faerie beings, his release and accompanying prophetic gift was an image of a universal human process—the maturation into a new form of clairvoyance. In perfect rhythmic fashion, with his move to Walden Pond, Thoreau was living out that mythic tale of humanity's dance between the greater Gods above and the lesser gods below. Age twenty-eight had for centuries in Western legend and folklore been thought of as the "noon" period of life, when the individual had to learn to heed his own inner voice, having in the previous seven years since age twenty-one gone forth into the world to acquire outer experience that might be turned into inner knowledge. Like Parsifal at the Grail Castle, Thoreau at age twenty-eight was faced with the challenge of asking the right question, of realizing what his mission on Earth was to be, and then of dedicating himself to the task of authoring his own destiny.

Building Temples

It was fitting that a man whose days were so marked by rhythm should be graced with the rhythmic visitation of gods of all stature. At Walden, even more than he had up to this point in life, Thoreau lived to the rhythms of both the natural world and the spiritual world, feeling their pulse. His daily routine in his new home was rhythmic: "After hoeing, or perhaps reading and writing, in the forenoon, I usually bathed again in the pond, swimming across one of its coves for a stint, and washed the dust of labor from my person, or smoothed out the last wrinkle which study had made, and for the afternoon was absolutely free." Far inland from the regular rhythms of the sea, Thoreau in his leisurely life at Walden of walking, swimming, paddling, thinking, and praying became a being of rhythm. He spoke rhythmically to the gods in a series of poems composed this summer.

> I make ye an offer,
> Ye gods, hear the scoffer,
> The scheme will not hurt you,
> If ye will find goodness, I will find virtue . . .
> If ye will deal plainly,
> I will strive mainly,
> If ye will discover,
> Great plans to your lover,
> And give him a sphere
> Somewhat larger than here.

In another poem he describes the "great friend" whose "native shore is dim," and in "The Hero," makes a prayer that he be given by this unnamed friend "some worthy task." The task he outlines—essentially to live authentically into the soil below him and "forever to love and to love and to love"—is the very one that he took up with the move to Walden.[143]

A more mundane task Thoreau took up was the accounting of his experimental economy at the pond. In late fall he worked on what would become the first section of *Walden*, a wry critique of his fellows' failure to live lives of higher purpose, followed by a legerdemain ledger of his cabin's construction. Thoreau was a man who loved to count and measure, and although he says that he gives the details to highlight how removed most people are from the making of their own homes, it is clear that he loves listing that the boards cost him $8.03½; the laths, $1.25; second-hand windows, $2.43; a thousand old bricks, $4.00; hair and lime for plaster, $2.71; nails, $3.90; hinges, screws, and latch, 24¢; chalk, a penny. The whole edifice cost $28.12½, comparing quite favorably with the $30 per year rent Harvard College collected from its students for a room of similar size.[144]

Visitors to Thoreau's cabin saw a rude, but clean and tidy, spare structure with the barest of furnishings, and almost all failed to see the magnificent temple he had built in the invisible world hovering about the pond. He and other lovers of the pond's beauty and tranquility—Emerson and his family, Channing, and many other Concord residents—had over the years constructed out of their devotion a cathedral housing a host of benevolent entities. Traditional tales of the faerie world always pictured them as dancing or singing, two of Thoreau's other favorite activities. The music of the spheres that he so frequently heard at Walden was the echo of the movement in rhythm of the invisible beings attracted to the airy mansion of the pond's environs by the beatific thoughts and emotions felt there. Thoreau had built this temple not only by his diurnal haunting of the pond, but also by his nocturnal dream sojourns there. A month after coming to Walden, he recalled his first visit to the pond at age five: "That woodland vision for a long time made the drapery of my dreams. That sweet solitude my spirit seemed so early to require that I might have room to entertain my thronging guests, and that speaking silence that my ears might distinguish the significant sounds. Some how or other it at once gave the preference to this recess among the pines . . . as if it had found its proper nursery." Reading about the temples of ancient Egypt, he scolded himself to "let those columns lie," and worship instead at the temple he knew himself to be building at that very moment, dwelling in the modest cabin:

> This is my Carnac, whose unmeasured dome
> Shelters the measuring art and measurer's home,
> Whose propylaeum is the system high
> And sculptured façade the visible sky.[145]

Unadorned by a single graven image, cluttered with no relics or statuary, fronted by no massive portal, and bearing no towering steeple or spire, Thoreau's Walden temple yet presented more beauty than the eye might imagine, and had a thousand entrances of the most splendid form. Divinity leaped from every niche and transept of the Walden woods, while a cathedral choir was ever singing ethereal hymns. Working on the manuscript of *A Week*, Thoreau was composing holy scriptures for his time, not sermons but myths and fables, letting the myths and fables of past times buoy him as the Concord and Merrimack had borne him and John. Recognizing the ancient myths as "hints for a history of the rise and progress of the race," Thoreau expected no less of his own day, when "other divine agents and godlike men will assist to elevate the race as much above its present condition."[146]

While Concord transcendentalists saw unadorned Nature as a temple that might elevate the human being, other Americans built more traditional temples. In November 1845, as Thoreau was getting ready for winter by building with secondhand bricks a chimney for his cabin, followers of the Mormon prophet Joseph Smith were finishing construction of the main section of the temple at Nauvoo, Illinois. Devoted Mormon "Saints" had tithed their labor to quarry, haul, and lay up the massive limestone blocks quarried from a site on the Mississippi, while Mormon women donated precious heirlooms to raise funds and prepared food for the laborers. The frontier town of Nauvoo was essentially founded to carry out construction of the temple, which was to be 128 feet long, 88 feet wide, and 165 feet high to the top of the spire. Having begun just a few months after Joseph Smith, in January 1841, received the revelation to build the temple, the Nauvoo Mormons had been guided throughout the construction by Smith's continuing divine revelations, both as to temple architecture and as to the rituals and rites that would be carried out among the elect once the temple was finished. Ever since receiving the Book of Mormon on a set of buried gold plates from the angel Moroni at Hill Cumorah in Palmyra, New York, in 1828, Joseph Smith had been a fount of odd apocalyptic revelation, but while other American prophets, such as William Miller, saw their flocks disperse as their revelations flopped, Smith's following grew steadily throughout the 1830s and 1840s.

Smith promulgated the Book of Mormon as a sacred canonical text, a new dispensation of truth that God delivered to humankind through the angel Moroni to him, the prophet. Smith's followers saw the Book of Mormon as God's third and final dispensation, signaling the fulfillment of John's Book of Revelation. The Book of Mormon identified Joseph Smith as the one who—aided by revelations from God—would prepare the way for Christ's Second Coming. After armed conflict in 1839 with neighbors in Missouri, Smith and nearly fifteen thousand followers fled to Commerce, Illinois, which they purchased and renamed Nauvoo. By 1844 Nauvoo had become the largest city in Illinois, an independent municipality with its own court system and militia. Smith's church was an elaborate hierarchy supposedly modeled on the ancient Hebraic church, with Smith the sole authority for receiving direction from God. In 1844, after revealing God's plan for organizing the Kingdom of Heaven on earth with himself as king, Smith declared his candidacy for president of the United States. This was only the latest of Smith's outrageous "revelations" guaranteed to anger "Gentiles"—both Christians and nonbelievers. In 1838 he had revealed that Adam had lived in the area that became western Missouri. In August 1839, he had declared that angels have flesh and bones. In April 1840, he preached that God was once a man. In 1841 he said that God also was made of flesh and bone, and that the earth had been formed out of other planets that had broken apart. In 1842 Smith's newspaper, *Times and Seasons*, printed a "translation" from a purported Book of Abraham that Smith had written, which said the Elohim lived near the star Kolob, and Smith also introduced the doctrine of plural gods. In 1843, Smith, who had thirty-three wives at the time, announced a divine revelation in favor of plural marriage. A few months later, he advocated decapitation or throat-cutting for certain crimes and sins. By 1844, church population was over twenty-five thousand, and the Mormon Legion, Smith's private army, had over three thousand men. The United States Army had but eight thousand troops. If not elected, many feared that Smith would seize the presidency by force.

Smith—who had been arrested nearly as many times as he had wives, for crimes including murder, high treason, burglary, arson, and larceny—was jailed with his brother Hyrum and two other Mormon leaders in Carthage, Illinois, for having ordered the destruction of the printing press, offices, and records of a Nauvoo newspaper critical of Smith's teaching polygamy and polytheism. On June 27, 1844, a mob of over two hundred fifty black-faced militiamen stormed the jail and killed Smith and his brother. Firing a gun smuggled to him by a confederate, Smith managed to kill two and wound another of his assailants. To his last breath, the prophet acted as he had throughout life—violently, and with the aid of magic. Just before his death, Smith made the Masonic sign of distress, then clutched at the Jupiter talisman around his neck. The talisman was a coveted symbol of personal power for Smith, for Jupiter was the ruling planet of his birth year. He had fashioned it of silver according to instructions in Francis Barrett's 1801 *The Magus*, a manual of magical techniques. Smith believed his talisman gained him both riches and power, including the love of women, all by the invocation of demon intelligences through the use of planetary forces.[147]

Like all temples, the facade of the Nauvoo Temple incorporated symbolic images designed to address and summon supernatural powers. Smith's visions included the erection of thirty "sunstones"—two-and-a-half-ton limestone blocks engraved with a radiant sun god—atop columns. The sunstones were said by Smith to represent the "Celestial Kingdom" seen in his vision. Thirty moonstones and thirty starstones topped other columns. Eleven large inverted pentagrams adorned doorway lintels. The weather vane atop the temple spire was in the form of a flying angel holding a trumpet in one hand and the open Book of Mormon in the other. Directly above the angel was the Freemasonic compass and square. Smith taught that the temple's astronomical symbols represented the glorious blessings performed within the temple walls. The temple ceremonies, like the symbols outside, were faithful imitations of Freemasonic rituals, which Smith and other Mormon elders had learned as members of the local lodge. At Nauvoo, the candidate for the temple "endowment" was given a secret sign by the presiding Saint: As they shook hands, the ball of the thumb was placed between the two upper joints of the forefingers. In Freemasonic ritual this was known as the Grip of the Entered Apprentice. Two more secret grips followed, corresponding to Freemasonry's Pass-grip of the Master Mason and the Sign and Due-Guard of the Master Mason. The candidate then placed his right hand under the left ear and drew it across the throat, after which the left hand was brought to the right shoulder, then quickly drawn across the breast, both gestures symbolic of the mortal penalty the candidate would pay should he reveal the nature of the ceremony.[148]

Those undergoing the Temple Endowment at Nauvoo also were anointed with oil; they were given a special garment with special stitches sewn into the breasts, navel, and knee; they were given a secret name, to be told to no one—except for female candidates, who were to tell their husbands their secret name; they witnessed an elaborate drama in which a black-clad Lucifer at one point instructs them to don green aprons, symbolic of the planet Venus, the Morning Star. Along with the ritual grips and tokens, these were all *magical actions*, causing very specific effects on both the candidates and the spiritual world. Though the Mormon temple initiation shared characteristics with the white magical activities of alchemy, Rosicrucianism, and other Christian initiatory paths, its character was essentially that of a black magical rite. The inverted pentagrams and stars on the temple facade were a clue to the perversion of magical ceremony within. The ritual grips were based on ancient knowledge of the body's meridians and pressure points. The pressure applied at the hand flowed back energetically to the nipples, where stitch marks on the temple garment led to the heart and then down to the navel. The temple candidate, in performing the Patriarchal Grip, unknowingly awakened latent sexual energies that produced distinct alchemical changes in his body, soul, and spirit. The third grip, the Sign of the Nail, was designed to stimulate an individual's hatred and rage, in order to augment the power of black magical action. The exactness required of all initiates assured the proper necromantic effect.

The initiation concluded with the candidate being conducted around the outside of the temple, past the inverted pentagrams and images of the sun god Baal, the stars, and the phases of the moon. At the Nauvoo Temple, the moon goddess Diana was the consort of Lucifer, the sacred god of Mormonism, and the fount of earthly wealth and power. Though the temple saw only six weeks of use before the Saints were run out of Nauvoo, over five thousand endowments were performed there. Smith's Halloween religion moved west and reached new heights of earthly prosperity; more and bigger temples arose throughout the Great American Desert. Back in Concord and Boston (where there had been great success in gaining Mormon converts) the newspapers continued to report on the Latter-Day Saints, but the spiritual politics were always masked by the mundane conflicts. Citizens from the Palmyra area who had known Joseph Smith as a young money-digger and necromancer spoke up about America's fastest growing religion's origins in grave-robbing, animal sacrifice, and demonic invocation, but Joseph's treasure-guarding toad was transformed into a white salamander, the Luciferic demon Moroni into an angel, the pugilistic and pugnacious wannabe wizard into a Sainted Prophet. No one seemed to notice that *moorman* was the Scottish term for someone in charge of cattle in waste ground, or that Mormo was an archaic name for a spirit who terrified children (antebellum dictionaries gave Mormo as "bug bear; false terror"). In the early years after his encounter at Hill Cumorah, Smith referred to the angel messenger interchangeably as both Moroni and Nephi, the latter being a "departed spirit called out by Magicians and Necromancers."[149]

The Nauvoo Temple was the inversion of the holy orders Thoreau was conducting at Walden Pond. If America was the site of spiritual warfare, a reflection of a heavenly battle, the dark powers seemed surely to be winning. In Bronson Alcott's Temple School (so-named because it was located in a former Masonic temple in Boston), the children circled their chairs around Alcott to have deep heartfelt conversations on the Gospels. On one occasion, Alcott had a student hit *him* each time that student misbehaved, bringing the boy to remorseful tears and better conduct. Yet the school had closed after salacious rumors flew about his teachings on the virgin birth. By 1847, when the second Mormon prophet, Brigham Young, arrived at Salt Lake and church membership approached fifty thousand, Fruitlands, Brook Farm, and dozens of other intentional communities of the idealistic 1840s—all devoted to building temples of Duty, Science, Beauty, and Joy—had all gone fallow. Transcendentalist fields lay unplowed and their haylofts and silos empty, while the Halloween religion made the desert bloom into a Paradise on Earth worthy of Etzler's visions.

In late summer of 1845, on his way to go fishing at Fair Haven Bay on the Sudbury River, Thoreau was surprised by a sudden thunderstorm and sought shelter at the hut of an Irish laborer by the name of John Field. Huddled beneath the hut's one sound section of roof with Field, his wife, children, and chickens, Thoreau struck up a conversation comparing and contrasting their lots in life. Thoreau sought sympathetic relation with the hardworking Irishman but was stymied by Field's narrower vision of life's possibilities. As the rain stopped and he went on his way, Thoreau heard the voice of his "genius" saying "from the western heaven":

> go fish & hunt far & wide by day—and rest thee from care before the dawn, and seek adventures. Let the noon find thee by other brooks— and the night over take thee every-where at home. Lead such a life as the children that chase butterflies in a meadow. There are no larger fields than these—no nobler fames—no more extended earth. With thy life uninsured live free and forever as you were planted. Grow wild and rank like these ferns and brakes—which study not morals nor philosophy. Nor strive to become tame and cultivated grass for cattle to

eat—these bull rushes . . . Let the thunder rumble in thy own tongue—
what if it brings rain to farmers' crops that is not its errand to thee—
take shelter under the cloud, while they flee to carts and sheds. Enjoy
the dominion—and name anew the fowl and the quadruped and all
creeping things. Seek without toil thy daily food—thy sustenance—is
it not in nature?

Here were a doctrine and covenant far different from the ones offered by the Mormon prophet or any of America's other contemporary
temple builders. Thoreau knew that it was from "want of confidence in
the gods men are where they are." In America there was also a surfeit of
confidence in false gods, whose voices were increasing in number.[150]

Sympathy, Act III: Somnambulism

By the end of March 1846, as song sparrows and blackbirds were joined
by the first robins and the spring rains drove the ice from the pond,
Thoreau had finished his first draft of A Week, and was largely carrying
out the daily communion that supported his ethereal temple. Morning
was the most important time of worship: "I get up early and bathe in the
pond—that is one of the best things I do—so far the day is well spent."
These ablutions were the return blessing for the one that he received
each morning upon waking. "The morning brings back the heroic
ages . . . All memorable events in my experience transpire in morning
time." The Auroral atmosphere was not confined to dawn, but was
available at any moment that one attended to one's Genius. Thoreau expected of himself and wished for all this perpetual dawn, an awakening
to the divinity within, even "in our soundest sleep."

Thoreau knew something about sound sleep, having been troubled
since his teen years by narcolepsy. During his sojourn on Staten Island,
he had undergone a particularly persistent episode, and his letters home
referred to "the demon that is said to haunt the Jones family, hovering

over their eyelids with wings steeped in juice of poppies." His uncle Charles suffered from the illness, falling completely asleep in the midst of shaving or other daytime activity. Thoreau complained of it coming on mainly while he was reading or writing. He also spoke on one occasion of being "somnambulic at least—stirring in my sleep; indeed quite awake." [151]

"Somnambulism" was the most common term used in the 1840s for the state of consciousness produced by mesmerists. It had first come to wide public attention in America in the summer of 1837 when Frenchman Charles Poyen and his invalid mesmeric subject Cynthia Gleason made lecture tours in the Northeast, including spectacular successes in Boston and Providence. In his public demonstrations, Poyen found that about half of the audience would succumb quite readily to the somnambulic state, which entailed much more than mere sleepwalking. Most of the people who came to such demonstrations did so to see their friends and neighbors transformed before their eyes. About 10 percent of the subjects attained "sympathetic rapport" with the mesmeric "operator"; it was not uncommon for this group to perform spontaneous feats of clairvoyance, locating lost objects, describing distant events, and telepathically reading the minds of audience members. By 1845, hundreds (in 1843 there were estimated to be two to three hundred in Boston alone) of mesmeric wizards circulated throughout America, and mesmeric demonstrations became an integral part of most stage magic performances. The seeming novelty of the somnambulic state obscured at least thirty years of earlier fascination with the mysteries of sympathetic sleep as it occurred naturally in individual "somnambulists." In 1808, fourteen-year-old Rachel Baker of Marcellus, New York, gave lengthy theological lectures while asleep, far beyond her abilities while in a waking state. Most of the adult members in Poyen's audiences recalled Jane C. Rider, a Springfield, Massachusetts, domestic who in June 1833 became a national celebrity through journalistic accounts of her spectacular somnambulism. While completely unconscious, her eyes shut tight, she would set the table, skim milk, slice bread, and cook a full breakfast. She could thread a needle in total darkness and, with her eyes wrapped in bandages, discern the dates of coins held at a distance. During her most acute episodes of somnambulic prowess, Rider wrote beautiful poetry and prose, sang tunefully, and became a gifted mimic. She trounced her physician in backgammon, and for the stream of folks seeking lost treasures, easily pronounced their whereabouts. Rider's and other cases of the 1830s and 1840s, such as Canada's Stanstead Somnambulist—challenged all existing theories of human sensory functioning. Physicians were puzzled at the paradoxical eclipse of certain senses while others became so highly developed; they were particularly fascinated by a number of somnambulic subjects who gave exact and effective medical diagnoses and treatments while in trance, for patients who did not even have to be in the same room.[152]

Both physicians and the lay public attributed the miraculous powers of somnambulists to their capacity for "sympathy" with both their own essential selves and with the higher selves of others. The pervasiveness at the time of sympathy as an explanatory concept for a diversity of human relations could be seen in Adam Smith's *Theory of Moral Sentiments* (1759), which held sympathy—the willful emotional identification between individuals—as a fundamental creator of social bonds and a safeguard against self-interested behavior. Just below the surface of this Enlightenment notion lay the older, occult view of sympathy as a powerful primal force of Nature. *Sympathy* denoted the mutual attraction among all manner of bodies, both earthly and celestial. By the affinity coursing through all things, the most distant parts of the universe might be drawn together. The astrological relation between zodiacal constellations, the planets, and human beings; the possibilities for alchemical transmutation of elements; and the mysterious relation between body and soul, soon to be collapsed by nineteenth-century psychology into "mind"—all operated upon the principle of sympathy. In antebellum America, vitalistic biological theories—which were held as widely by natural philosophers and the earliest professional life scientists as were mechanistic theories—universally rested upon the notion of sympathy. Physical science was equally enamored of sympathetic (and antipathetic) forces, accepting them as operative in the phenomena of gravitation, electromagnetism, and chemical reactions. In his 1838 *The Tongue of Time, and Star of the States: A System of Human Nature, with the Phenomena of Heaven and Earth,* Dr. Joseph Comstock—who attended somnambular patients throughout the 1830s—easily mixed alchemical, astrological, and magical terminology with the Enlightenment language of Bacon and Locke. Prior to 1845, it was still possible for American scientists to blend occult—and hence nonmaterialist—explanations with naturalistic ones in their attempt to explain Nature's most profound mysteries.

The clairvoyance demonstrated by these somnambulists sometimes extended beyond earth to other planets. In 1837 a Rhode Island girl named Loraina Brackett was struck on the head, suffering blindness and impaired speech. Treated by a mesmerist, she traveled in trance across Long Island Sound to his home, which she described in perfect detail, down to the pictures on the walls. Miss Brackett then began to narrate while asleep her journeys to the moon, Mars, Saturn, and even the Sun. Such extraterrestrial travel was known to Swedenborgians, who read avidly of the Swedish seer's visits to other planets and the wild descriptions of their inhabitants.

Given their intense interest in connecting heaven and earth, their predilection for ecstatic experience, and their cultivation of sympathetic relations both within society and between society and nature, the transcendentalists were fascinated by somnambulic phenomena. Margaret Fuller had gone to Loraina Brackett in Providence seeking—and getting—relief for her migraine headache. Fuller's *Summer on the Lakes, in 1843* (1844) included an entire chapter devoted to a review of the case of Frederica Hauffe, the Seeress of Prevorst, whose somnambulic state seemed to illustrate the promises and possibilities (and perils) of extracorporeal life. Fuller detailed the extraordinary clairvoyance—for angels, demons, and ghosts, as well as humans—and uncanny gifts of this frail peasant woman, who died at age twenty-nine. In her trance state, which in her final years of life was much more common than waking consciousness, she could diagnose her illness and that of others, and would have intense sympathetic reactions to gems and minerals, flowers, and people, whose moral qualities acted immediately and physically upon her. When completely debilitated, she drew vitality from healthy persons but lost vigor in the presence of weak or ill persons. She saw herself often from a perspective out of her body. Emerson did not share Fuller's—or his wife's—enthusiasm for the Seeress's or other homegrown somnambulists' style of seership, which he felt suffered from the same sort of banal literalism that plagued Swedenborg's visions. Though Emerson recognized Frederica's and Swedenborg's path (as well as that of Porphyry, Plotinus, Böhme, George Fox, and other mystics) of "getting out of the body to think" as "difficult, secret, and beset with terror," and though he himself had a great impulse toward ecstatic experience, he rejected their revelations. In declaring "this age is Swedenborg's" and including Swedenborg as one of the subjects of his work *Representative Men*, Emerson acknowledged the Swedish seer's capacity to see the divine in nature, but he eschewed his particular conceptions of heaven and hell. Emerson detested the taxonomic detail in Swedenborg's visions of all too literal otherworld heavens—"A man should not tell me that he has walked among the angels; his proof is that his eloquence makes me one"—and found his Inferno claustrophobic, preferring to Swedenborg's proposition that pure evil did everywhere and always exist the comforting philosophy that evil is but good in the making. Emerson, despite his thirst for transcendence and respect for his own personal daimon, ultimately consigned Swedenborg and less cultivated somnambulists to the dustbin of demonology. "Mesmerism is high life below stairs, or Momus playing Jove in the kitchens of Olympus," he declared. "It is a low curiosity or lust of structure, and is separated by celestial diameters from the love of spiritual truth.... Demonology is the shadow of theology."[153]

Still, Emerson did not let the vulgar excesses of somnambulic ecstasies keep him from traveling with Hawthorne to the Harvard Shaker settlement, where much of the community's religious experience centered on trance speaking and dancing. Shakers shared with somnambulists the faculty of prophecy, speaking in unknown tongues, and holding communication with the spiritual world. Mother Ann Lee's founding visionary episodes had been singular and nonsomnambulic in character, but in 1837 ecstatic somnambulism became epidemic in Shaker communities. The bulk of the Shaker brethren who fell into trance exhibited classic forms of demonic possession, the sort that in the seventeenth century would have led to accusations of witchcraft. An individual would suddenly be sent spinning like a top, not at all dizzy, continuing for an hour or more. Others would shake violently or skip around the room, wholly involuntarily. After falling to the floor unconscious, they would rise and detail what they had seen and heard while in trance. Some visited with members of a cast of illustrious historical characters: George Washington, General W. H. Harrison, William Penn, the Marquis de Lafayette, Napoleon Bonaparte, and more ancient ones—Saint Patrick, Samson, Alexander the Great, Nero, Saint John, King David. Then there were native spirits—Mohicans, Mohawks, Delaware, Shawnee, Seminole, Cherokee, Chickasaw, Choctaw. All assured the Shakers that Americans were a chosen people. Other spinning somnambulists returned to consciousness with instructions for the dances—Winding March, Lively Line, Double Square, Mother's Sister, Celestial March—for which the Shakers were celebrated.

Thoreau's opinion of mesmerism likely squared with that of the German *Naturphilosophes*, who understood the phenomena of magnetic rapport as evidence for their conviction that a vital force permeated Nature, including man. In his notes on J. B. Stallo's *General Principles of the Philosophy of Nature* (1848), Thoreau quotes Stallo: "The magnetized subject has merely been laid to the breast of the telluric parent—has been forced back to the state of impersonality, so that all the channels of direct cosmic emanations, which the waking subject, in distinguishing self from without, closes up, are laid open afresh." [154]

Thoreau was always far too immersed in the beauties of life in the body to concern himself with exotic travels out of the body, and yet he was in his own way an experienced astral pilot. A great deal of his enthusiasm for morning came from the ambrosial quality he carried into the waking state from his nighttime dream world. During dreaming sleep, Thoreau felt the heavenly hierarchies close around him, even within him. This communion with the angelic world formed the basis of his theory of dreams:

> A part of me which has reposed in silence all day, goes abroad at night, like the owl, and has its day. At night we recline, and nestle, and in fold ourselves in our being. Each night I go home to rest. Each night I am gathered to my fathers. The soul departs out of the body, and sleeps in God, a divine slumber. As she withdraws herself, the limbs droop and the eyelids fall, and nature reclaims her clay again. Men have always regarded the night as ambrosial or divine. The air is peopled then— fairies come out.[155]

Day or night, sleeping afforded humans commerce with the spiritual world, but that world was peopled with as many baneful as blessed beings. Once the individual ego departed the body, it was open to invasion by deceiving spirits, mischievous elementals intent upon delivering spurious revelations. This demonological knowledge was preserved in a few of the modern grimoires in Alcott's library, but the "Enlightenment" occulting of the spiritual world had by the 1840s especially marginalized the night side of nature and man. Enlightened Americans already saw the Salem witchcraft trials not as a response to virulent demonic attack but as the supreme example of human gullibility and folly. Comstock's *Tongue of Time*, for example, though borrowing from occult thought some of its holistic explanatory notions of Nature, dismissed Cotton Mather's perspective on New England witchcraft as superstitious and silly.

Thoreau when asleep—as when awake—seemed always to walk

only with angels, never with demons. Joseph Smith, greedy for earthly treasures of gold and silver, sold his soul and thus bound demonic entities to him, while Thoreau, ever hungry for heavenly wealth, drew toward himself only good and guardian spirits. Unbidden but by his pure and lofty thoughts, these spirits left tokens of gratitude for him. All his life his most desired treasures came to him fortuitously, repeating the magic of Tahatawun's arrowhead. Though grateful for the gifts, Thoreau never quite understood whence they came. In the summer of 1842, intent upon going to Hawthorne's home to borrow his music box, when he arrived, before speaking of it, Hawthorne's wife, Sophia, offered to lend it to him. A year later, eager to go to hear another neighbor's instrument, a parcel arrived in the mail—a music box, sent to Thoreau by Richard Fuller as thanks for Thoreau's tutoring and friendship. "I think I must have some Muses in my pay that I know not of, for certain musical wishes of mine are answered as soon as entertained." On earth, there was nothing Thoreau loved better to find than arrowheads, flowers, and melodies; all three flowed to him effortlessly. He intuited that this powerful working of desire operated between men as well: "I know of no rule which holds so true as that we are always paid for our suspicions by finding what we suspect.... Our suspicions exercise a demoniacal power over the subject of them. By some obscure law of influence when we are perhaps unconsciously the subject of another's suspicion, we feel a strong impulse, even when it is contrary to our nature to do that which he expects but reprobates." Suspecting always angels above and the angelic in man below, Thoreau found them. The demons would have to find a foothold elsewhere.[156]

A Night in Jail

In April 1846, meditating on what the essential nature of the birds, the pines, and the pond might be, Thoreau confessed to his journal his own: "I silently smile at my incessant good fortune. . . . The elements are working their will with me." He had been pondering the not so fortunate fates of vanished neighbors at Walden Pond. The pent road just a few paces from his cabin door was one of the few visible signs of a whole community of people who once made their home where he made his. This spring he was poking about both in conversation with elder Concordians and along the abandoned road for stories of these "former inhabitants." He tasted the wild fruit from the derelict orchard of ex-slave Brister Freeman, whose wife Fenda told fortunes. In an oak copse near his cabin, he found bricks from the chimney of Zilpha, a black conjure woman whose home and pets English soldiers set afire during the War of 1812. Just across from his bean field was the cellar hole of yet another ex-slave, Cato Ingraham; it was now filled with sumac and goldenrod. Thoreau also learned of Wyman the potter, whose kinship with Thoreau across the ages was founded in their both being squatters of a sort.

Not a single long-settled town in America nor even the newly settled places of the American West lacked this liminal geographic zone, where the poor and the outcast found homes at society's edge. Wyman's tenement had become the home of Hugh Quoil, an Irish "man of manners" who worked digging ditches, suffered from delirium tremens, and died "in the road"—a particularly ignominious fate—just after Thoreau came to live at Walden. Thoreau's tenancy at Walden Woods represented a third generation of marginality on the pond's shores, a self-conscious reinhabitation of a rejected place, by a social outcast who felt at home anywhere, but at Walden more than anywhere. Coming upon Quoil's tenantless house before townsmen anxious of its reputation as "an unlucky castle" destroyed it, Thoreau was affected by the sight of Quoil's old clothes curled up on his plank bed, his broken pipe upon the hearth, scattered playing cards upon the floor. No sentimentalist, Thoreau looked upon the bramble- and sumac-filled cellar holes of Hugh Quoil and the other former inhabitants of the marginal lands flanking Walden Pond as mysterious lessons regarding destiny. He neither condemned nor lauded the lives led there but was bound to them by their very humanity.[157]

Thoreau's capacity for empathy had moved him for the past six years to refuse to pay his poll tax, which he viewed as supportive of a government that permitted slavery. The moral imperative for tax resistance had heightened since the beginning of May, when the United States declared war on Mexico. In July, as a member of a huckleberrying party, he had met with Sam Staples, Concord's constable and overseer of local tax collection. Asked by Staples to pay his delinquent tax, Thoreau refused and was escorted to the town jail. Without informing him, someone (most likely his aunt Maria) paid the tax, and he was told in the morning that he was free to go. In a second act of civil disobedience, Thoreau refused to leave his cell, and Staples ended up throwing him out. His small act went largely unnoticed at the moment, but the hours spent behind bars became the seed experience for a lecture and essay years later that would reverberate through the centuries.

Thoreau's friend George Melvin, Concord's veteran fur trapper, once told him a tale of a muskrat he had caught in a trap, who had but one leg, the other three having been chewed off during previous encounters with steel leg-hold traps. The muskrat was for Thoreau but another illustration of a supreme law: "Only courage does anywhere prolong life, whether of man or beast." Thoreau found no courage in the action of either his government or its military men in their imperial war upon Mexico. The American soldier was no better than the leg-hold trap, an unthinking killing machine set in motion by ruthless commanders. Thoreau was more like the muskrat, and would if necessary have sacrificed his own limbs to wage moral war against transgressors upon freedom, even when that freedom belonged to an unseen confrere.[158]

Learning of his friend's incarceration, Emerson pronounced it "mean and skulking" and wrote in his journal, "The Abolitionists denounce the war and give much time to it, but they pay the tax. . . . Don't run amuck against the world. As long as the state means you well, do not refuse your pistareen." Thoreau's defiance was characteristic of both his conviction and his capacity for communion. Enslaved African Americans and embattled Mexicans alike were felt by Thoreau to be close companions; any trap set for them was set for him, as well. That solidarity was reflected in the fact that, a week after his night in jail, the antislavery society of Concord held its annual meeting on the doorstep of Thoreau's cabin, commemorating there the emancipation of slaves in the West Indies.[159]

Contact!

In late August, Thoreau left Walden for Bangor, Maine, to meet his cousin George Thatcher for a trip into the Maine woods. On a night steamboat from Portland to Bangor, Thoreau was sent by the speed and noise of the steamer into a dreamlike state that made the trip seem to him "utterly unreal." His sensitivity suggests how much the average American at midcentury was still adjusting to the acceleration in travel time brought by steam power.

At Old Town, on the Penobscot River, the Indians and their settlement appeared shabby and forlorn to Thoreau's New England village aesthetic. Though once "a powerful tribe," he thought "a row of wigwams, with a dance of pow-wows, and a prisoner tortured at the stake" would present a more respectable picture than what he saw. Upriver at Lincoln, seeking an Indian guide for their trip to Mount Katahdin, which he spelled Ktaadn, Thoreau's expectation of noble forest-dwelling natives was satisfied. Landing by canoe on the island shore, his first sight was of a Penobscot girl singing in her native language as she washed clothing on a rock in the river. A toggle-tipped wooden salmon spear lay nearby, and a dozen wolfish hounds appeared as they walked to the nearest house to make inquiries. Led to Louis Neptune, Thoreau recalled him as the same man who had led Emerson's brother-in-law, Charles T. Jackson, up Katahdin in 1837. To the adventurers' proposal of the trip, Neptune replied, "Ye! Maybe you carry some provision for all—some pork—some bread—and so pay. Me sure get some moose." After Neptune failed to meet them upriver at the post of "Uncle George" McCauslin, a trader to the logging camps, they went on to Katahdin with McCauslin as guide, joined by Tom Fowler and his brother, who poled their bateaux skillfully upstream through dangerous rapids. "I, who had some experience in boating," Thoreau admitted, "had never experienced any half so exhilarating before." Their first night out, they paddled four miles by moonlight across North Twin Lake, and made camp near its outlet in a spot known to McCauslin from his lumbering days. Sparks from the campfire set their canvas lean-to burning, so they turned it into a ground tarp and propped the bateau up as their shelter. The men lay their heads below the boat, feet toward the fire, and stayed awake talking about astronomy and "the most interesting discoveries in that science." [160]

Stepwise up a series of lakes and falls—Ambejijis, Passamagamet, Katepskonegan, Aboljacarmegus, Sowadnehunk, and Aboljacknagesic—the party progressed to the base of the mountain. As they made camp in the late afternoon, Thoreau attempted a solo summit ascent and "slumped, scrambled, rolled, bounced, and walked" over the krummholz just below timberline. He returned to camp without making the top, and the next day the whole party set out for the peak. Thoreau quickly outpaced the others and entered the clouds shrouding the summit all alone, the better to feel the Promethean powers of the elements there. "It was vast, Titanic, and such as man never inhabits." Thoreau rejoined the others for the descent; at one point Tom Fowler shimmied up a spruce tree to scout for the best route and spied a promising pond and meadow and beyond it open land. Coming out into the burned-over scrubland, Thoreau was overcome with the sense of Nature's awful savagery: "Man was not to be associated with it. It was Matter, vast, terrific—not his Mother Earth that we have heard of, not for him to tread on, or be buried in.... There was there felt the presence of a force not bound to be kind to man." The Penobscot knew Katahdin's summit as the dwelling place of the forbidding monster Pamola and thus avoided this and other high mountain summits. This invisible astral demon, not the charred, stunted trees and naked rock, created a kind of terror in Thoreau that he had never felt before. "What is this Titan that has possession of me? Talk of mysteries!—Think of our life in nature,—daily to be shown matter, to come in contact with it,—rocks, trees, wind on our cheeks! the *solid* earth! the *actual* world! the *common sense! Contact! Contact! Who* are we? *where* are we?" As surely as he had felt the presence of benign elemental creatures at Walden, tamed from centuries of contact with human beings and particularly domesticated by Thoreau's worshipful approach to them, on wild Katahdin he met their antithesis, a *demonic*—not *daimonic*—dragon inhospitable to man.[161]

On the trip back, at Tom Fowler's house at the junction of the Millinocket and Penobscot, they encountered Louis Neptune and a fellow Indian on their way finally to hunt moose farther north. They had, Thoreau judged, been delayed by a "drunken frolic" and now appeared as "sinister and slouching fellows." This disappointment in finding degraded as well as dispossessed aboriginal men did not distract Thoreau from the realization of just how new and unexplored a place America still was in 1846. "We live on the shores of a continent even yet, and hardly know where the rivers come from which float our navy." This trip to Maine in the midst of his colonial experiment at Walden gave him a new and not altogether welcome experience of Nature, whose face he now knew could be fiendishly unfriendly.[162]

Neptune

A week after Thoreau returned from Maine, unbeknownst to anyone in America, an eighth planet was added to the seven that he and his camp mates spoke of while beneath their upended bateau on the bank of the Penobscot. News of Neptune's discovery did not reach the United States until October 20, 1846, when the steamship *Caledonia* docked at

Boston and brought the news from across the Atlantic. The very next evening, William Cranch Bond and his son George Phillips Bond endeavored to find the new planet with the small refracting telescope at the Harvard College Observatory. Before news of the discovery reached other American cities (this was just before the erection of intercity telegraph lines), the Bonds had sighted Neptune, and Thoreau's old Harvard professor, Benjamin Pierce, quickly calculated that Neptune was not the planet that had been predicted by French astronomer Urbain Leverrier and English astronomer John Couch Adams. Pierce's announcement set off a chauvinistically charged debate between European and American astronomers about the power of predictive theoretical science, at the moment when American science was on the threshold of coalescing into a mature national community. The Smithsonian Institution was founded this year, which would also see the establishment of America's first scientific schools, at Yale and Harvard. American astronomy was just reaching a critical stage, as ten observatories had been established in the previous fifteen years, and the *American Nautical Almanac* would soon begin publication; 1846 was a signal year for seeing more clearly into the cosmos.[163]

If in 1846 one perused the pages of America's oldest scientific journal, the *American Journal of Science*, one found that the hottest topics of scientific investigation were animal magnetism, galvanism, electricity, and terrestrial magnetism. The same newly discovered powers dominated the columns of the popular periodicals, including the *Concord Freeman*. The previous winter, it had carried a report about a Natick, Massachusetts, woman who after being mesmerized, described in accurate detail the unsolved murder of a local man five years before, and gave the location of the pond where his body had been deposited. A month later, Concord's Unitarian church hosted L. H. Whiting, "discoverer of the Philosophy of Clairvoyance," for a series of lectures on "Phreno-Magnetism," including a surgical demonstration showing its utility as an anesthetic. Serial fiction also found mesmerism a useful plot device; in "The Jealous Wife, or Mesmerism Proved," after opening with a mock testimonial hailing mesmerism as "a great science . . . a key to unlock every mystery worth knowing," a charlatan mesmerist is run out of town. The paper's attitude toward mesmerism was flippantly skeptical; noting the last lecture of Whiting's series, the editor promised "rare sport may be expected." [164]

The mocking of mysteries both scientific and spiritual was common sport in the 1840s, and no mystery came in for as much mockery as mesmerism. A key agent of disenchantment was the popular theater, where magicians quickly incorporated the latest mysteries into their stage routines. Urban opera houses and Masonic temples would frequently host earnest mesmeric lecturers on one evening, and debunking prestidigitators the next. At halls throughout the Northeast, Signor Blitz, Signor Vivaldi, and dozens of other pretend Persian or Hindoo or Egyptian fakirs, along with demonstrating automata and electrical phenomena, invariably made displays of mesmeric fascination part of their acts. In Boston in 1843, while a lecture series on animal magnetism was being conducted at the Masonic temple, across town at the Boston Museum, "Dr. Guy, Corresponding Secretary of the RMBC, Fellow of the UCS, Member of All Learned Societies East of Bangor and Professor of Everything," was giving a "diffuse lecture" on the same subject. Any occult power that mesmerism might at first have seemed to possess was quickly drained away by the lampooning and sleight-of-hand duplicity, which threw all authentic phenomena into question. [165]

Among the Concord circle, Thoreau was perhaps the least interested in mesmeric revelations. Emerson's notebooks and a number of his essays show that he often read about mesmerism (in *Nature,* Emerson even considered mesmerism as one of a number of hopeful signs of some "in-streaming power"), which he came to believe was entitled "only to a share of attention, and not a large share." Alcott was fascinated by all forms of fascination, and was particularly taken with the somnambulic revelations of Andrew Jackson Davis, the Poughkeepsie Seer. Orestes Brownson met many leading mesmerists and learned to perform magnetic passes on others. Margaret Fuller—Emerson,

Hawthorne, and others were convinced of Fuller's power of "magne-tizing" others—saw mesmerism as a harbinger of "future states of being," and had successful treatments for back pain with a French phy-sician who practiced a form of mesmerism he called "psychodunamy." On one occasion Fuller attempted to get Emerson to attend a demon-stration at James Freeman Clarke's by Anna Parsons, a member of the Brook Farm community who practiced "psychometry," a form of mes-meric trance state in which she would put letters to her forehead and give vivid images of the thoughts and emotions of the writer. The week before inviting Emerson, Fuller had given Parsons a letter to her from Emerson, in which he had enclosed a new poem he had written. The "inventor" of psychometry, Joseph Rodes Buchanan, had put Parsons into trance and given her the letter, which immediately brought a serene look to her face. "The writer," declared the entranced Parsons, "is holy, true, and brave." Asked by Buchanan if he would fight for the Greeks, Parsons replied, "He does not fight with weapons; he has arms of his own." She went on to say that the writer was "not perfect though; there is something wanting." Finding it difficult for her to be more specific in her criticism, Buchanan suggested that he magnetize her "organ of self-esteem." Parsons then said: "You cannot get me so high up that I can overlook him. I might many, but not him." Fuller told Emerson that the most profound insight the sleeping Parsons had about his character was when she finally replied to their questions with the statement that "If he could sympathize with himself, he could with every one." [166]

Fuller and the Clarkes were most impressed when Buchanan placed her hand on the poem, "The Humble Bee." While they imagined that Parsons could perhaps have derived her images of the unknown corre-spondent from "sympathy" with images of Emerson in their own minds, they had not read the poem, so could not be the source of her images. Silent for some time, Parsons then became upset when Clarke broke into her trance with his question but answered that she had been lying down in sweet grass in a country place. Emerson's poem described a "humble-bee" (bumblebee) luxuriating amid violets, columbine, and clover. Emerson declined the invitation to personally witness Parsons's somnambulic clairvoyance. "The idea which I approach and am magnetized by," he wrote, "is my Country." Yet Emerson knew full well the efficacy of the magnetic relation; his success as a lecturer depended wholly upon it. Discussing Emerson's Boston lecture given the same week as the invitation to hear Parsons, Thoreau voiced his distrust of the charismatic art of the orator, saying, "To me it is vegetation, the pullulation and universal budding of the plant Man." [167]

No one distrusted the gravitational pull of the mesmerizer more than Nathaniel Hawthorne. When, shortly before their marriage, Sophia had gone to her father's dental assistant for a mesmeric session to relieve her debilitating headaches, Hawthorne was horrified. He filled his fiction with mesmeric agents and mesmerized subjects: In a short story called "The Hall of Fantasy," he lampoons the mesmeric theorist Robert Collyer (in 1841 Collyer drew crowds of five hundred to a thousand people for his lectures in Boston and New York). In his novels—*The Scarlet Letter, The House of Seven Gables, The Blithedale Romance, The Marble Faun*—characters meet tragic ends after having fallen under mesmeric spells cast by actual mesmerists or by particularly hypnotic individuals in their lives. As America's master of gothic fiction and an eloquent critic—in stories like "The Birth-Mark" and "Rappaccini's Daughter"—of the Faustian attempt to penetrate nature's secrets, Hawthorne was drawn irresistibly toward mesmerism as an agent of Promethean but altogether dark and dangerous power. "It seems to me," thought Hawthorne, "that the sacredness of an individual is violated by it . . . [it is] an intrusion into the holy of holies." Like the counterfeiters whose crimes were constantly being recounted in the *Concord Freeman* and all American newspapers, the mesmerizer stealthily acquired power over society's open and honest subjects, introducing a note of doubt into all human commerce. Somnambulic clairvoyance collapsed the bounds between public and private, and even the innocent mesmerized subject could enter psychic spaces where he or she had not been invited. [168]

Hawthorne, Emerson, and Thoreau intuited that mesmerism was a revolt against the gods, an unholy alliance with a dark power of Nature. Thoreau, with his keen interest in mythology, was aware that before Neptune was chosen as the name of the new planet, many preferred the name Atlas, the Titan who for his role in the revolt against the gods was obliged to support the heavens with his head and hands. The sea, Neptune's domain, was still in the mid-nineteenth century a dark and mysterious part of Nature, so perhaps it was a fitting name for the new planet, whose discovery coincided with modern man's attempt to see through the murky depths of Mother Nature. The Neptunian decade of the 1840s was a Sargasso Sea of foggy, misty, somnambulic dreaminess, marked by the Opium Wars in the Far East and the Mormon wars in the Midwest. Despite the seeming clarity promised by astronomy, telegraphy, Morse code, and an explosion of fact in the sciences, a thick cloud of illusion hung over America.

Thoreau's remove to Walden was a singular effort from within Neptunian America to see the world true, and the journals he kept while there became gospels instantly because his fellow citizens had fallen so far away from reality. "Shams and delusions are esteemed for soundest truths," Thoreau lamented, "while reality is fabulous. If men would steadily observe realities only, and not allow themselves to be deluded, life, to compare it with such things as we know, would be like a fairy tale and the Arabian Nights' Entertainments." The theatrical thaumaturgies of the day were only the most obvious of illusions: "By closing the eyes and slumbering, and consenting to be deceived by shows, men establish and confirm their daily life of routine and habit everywhere, which still is built on purely illusory foundations. . . . I perceive that we inhabitants of New England live this mean life that we do because our vision does not penetrate the surface of things. We think that that is which appears to be. If a man should walk through this town and see only the reality, where, think you, would the 'Mill-dam' go to? If he should give us an account of the realities he beheld there, we should not recognize the place in his description." By "the perpetual instilling and drenching of the reality" surrounding him at Walden, Thoreau escaped imprisonment in the hall of mirrors that his fellows erected. While millennial ecstatics peered into a futile future, Thoreau set his sights underfoot and found the eternal present. "Men esteem truth remote, in the outskirts of the system, behind the farthest star, before Adam and after the last man. In eternity there is indeed something true and sublime. But all these times and places and occasions are now and here. God himself culminates in the present moment, and will never be more divine in the lapse of all the ages." [169]

On October 19, 1846, the day before the arrival of the news of Neptune's discovery, a Boston doctor named William Morton rejected his patient's request for mesmeric anesthesia, which had become the safest and most effective form of anesthetic, and instead applied ethyl ether before removing the patient's tumor. The success of this operation dealt the death blow to mesmerism as a therapeutic agent, since its full extinguishing of consciousness without provoking somnambulic lucidity meant that dentists and physicians would not have to confront the philosophical question of mesmeric anesthesia's puzzling side effect—clairvoyance. Ether was preferable to surgeons and dentists because they believed it could be controlled through fully material—i.e., chemical—means; this preference persisted despite the fact that no patient ever died from the administration of mesmeric anesthesia, while scores of patients died from improper use of ether anesthetic. The triumph of ether over mesmeric anesthesia was an important event in walling off from full investigation the nature of the medium—universally conceptualized as a fluid by antebellum investigators—that permitted the remarkable feats of the somnambulic state. With its adoption as a chemical for extinguishing consciousness, the "ether" took one step closer to a fully materialist explanation, away from its actual nature as a nonphysical, nonspatial dimension through which physical phenomena manifest. In banishing the phenomena of mesmerism from open investigation, nineteenth-century American scientists closed their eyes, sleepwalking in the face of the animating power of nature. The exclusion of the history of mesmerism from contemporary history of science attests to the triumph of mechanistic and materialistic theories of nature.[170]

At Walden, Thoreau was mythologizing Nature and Self at the very moment when modern materialist science made it all but impossible to appreciate the deep truths of ancient myth. The advent of academic interest in mythology came just as the understanding of myth as the record of ancient clairvoyance of spiritual realities disappeared. Even though the name of a Roman god was used, the naming of Neptune as the eighth planet marked the death of mythology. Thoreau knew from his reading in classical mythology the association of the principal gods and goddesses with the planets, and the qualities and capacities shared by both: Venus ruled the emotions; Mercury was the quicksilver messenger, the agent of communication between heaven and earth; the warrior god, Mars, represented power in both battle and in less martial aspects of life; stately Jupiter inspired humans to elevate themselves toward the essential in life; and Saturn—Kronos in Greek—was the archetypal timekeeper, the bearer of cosmic memory in its leisurely twenty-nine-and-a-half-year orbit round the Sun. The ancient sages had no knowledge of the outer planets, including Neptune; they lay wholly outside human consciousness and physiology until the modern materialistic "Enlightened" mind was fully matured.

Thoreau was born with Neptune in opposition to the moon, a configuration that seemed to suggest that he was born with the potential to summon the moon forces to overcome and thus redeem the potentially adverse power of the eighth planet. As antebellum America descended into a maelstrom of illusions and humbug, Thoreau saw clearly. In early December, stimulated by reading Goethe's autobiography, he realized that "no method or discipline can supersede the necessity of being forever on the alert." To become a seer, he told himself, he must keep his eye "constantly on the true and real." As always when articulating his sense of his own personal destiny, he used the language of the stars: "Every mortal sent into this world has a star in [the] heavens appointed to guide him—Its ray he cannot mistake—It has sent its beam to him either through clouds and mists faintly or through a serene heaven—He knows better than to seek advice of any. . . . Astronomy is that department of physics which answers to Prophesy the Seer's or Poet's calling. It is a mild a patient deliberate and contemplative science. To see more with the physical eye than man has yet seen to see farther, and off the planet—into the system."[171]

"A History of Myself"

Portraying reality to one's neighbors during such an era as the 1840s was a tricky business, but Thoreau was a born trickster and up to the task. During his first winter at Walden, he had anchored himself in the real by conducting a survey of the pond with compass, chain, and sounding line. Local folklore held Walden Pond to be bottomless, a convenient myth for Thoreau simultaneously to debunk physically and prove philosophically. With the solid, sixteen-inch-thick ice beneath his boots, he could easily sound any spot below from the ice roof above, sometimes dropping his pound-and-a-half stone and attached cod line down through holes made by ice fishermen, and more often through cuts he had made with his axe. Thoreau—whose techniques permitted him such accuracy that he could calculate the variation of the bottom depth over each hundred feet within three or four inches—delighted to find a fractal symmetry in the submerged topography. Mapping out his data, he discovered a "remarkable coincidence"—the pond's greatest depth (at 102 feet, the deepest pond in Massachusetts, even if not bottomless) lay at the exact intersection of the lines of greatest length and breadth. Other topographic laws and formulas disclosed themselves—such as how coves come to have bars at their mouths—and these rippled out under Thoreau's attention to become laws by which the human being could also be mapped and measured: "Such a rule of the two diameters not only guides us toward the sun in the system and the heart in man, but draw lines through the length and breadth of the aggregate of a man's particular daily behaviors and waves of life into his coves and inlets, and where they intersect will be the height and depth of his character." [172]

The second winter at Walden saw a whole army of ice experts descend on the pond for two weeks. Local baron Frederic Tudor—whom Thoreau anonymously accused of taking off "the only coat, ay, the skin itself" of Walden Pond in order to cover each one of his half million dollars with another—purchased the rights to harvest the ice from Emerson and the Fitchburg Railroad, and under Yankee overseers, set a hundred Irishmen cutting the pond ice into cakes. Thoreau loved watching the "merry race" of ice-cutters at work, and they invited him to saw with them. He in turn invited them into his cabin to dry off after their frequent spills in the pond. Harvesting an acre—equal to one thousand tons—a day, the ice-cutters laid up a hill thirty-five feet high. Covered with an insulating layer of hay, it came to resemble a "venerable moss-grown and hoary ruin ... the abode of Winter, that old man we see in the almanac." The pond's owners miscalculated the market; not even the 25 percent of the ice projected to be sold ever left the pile, which did not completely melt away until September 1848. [173]

Thoreau well knew the price of hawking wares unwanted by men. This winter and spring, Emerson recommended Thoreau's "book of extraordinary merit"—*A Week on the Concord and Merrimack Rivers*—to four different publishers; each turned it down. While men declined to drink at his literary well, he thrilled to imagine the "sweltering inhabitants of Charleston and New Orleans, of Madras and Bombay and Calcutta" imbibing the waters of his literal well, as they quenched their thirst on melted Walden ice. Reading this winter the *Bhagavad Gita* as he composed his own *gita*—the first draft of *Walden*—he imagined the pure Walden water mingling with the sacred water of the Ganges, then being wafted past "the Hesperides ... the periplus of Hanno, and, floating by Ternate and Tidore and the mouth of the Persian Gulf," finally landing in "ports of which Alexander only heard the names." [174]

This January and February Bronson Alcott came every Sunday to visit Thoreau at the pond, and experienced perhaps more closely than anyone Thoreau's inner state of grace. "So vivid was my escape from the senses while conversing with Henry today that the men, times, and occupations of coming years gave me a weary wish to be released from this scene and to pass into a state of noble companions and immortal labors." As a fellow mystic, Alcott knew what Thoreau was up to, but communicating the nature of his experiment to the general public was a greater challenge. At two successive meetings of the Concord Lyceum in February, Thoreau presented "A History of Myself." A less than electrifying lecturer, Thoreau was still an extraordinary talker, and his best friends commented on how closely his talk resembled his writing—the puns, witticisms, riddles, chestnuts, and overall verbal virtuosity of his best prose were the stuff of his everyday conversation. The stern and steely note with which Thoreau greeted his lyceum listeners—"I have traveled a good deal in Concord . . . and the inhabitants have appeared to me to be doing penance in a thousand remarkable ways"—cleared the air, set up a friendly opposition, and warned everyone that he would speak frankly.[175]

Telling his fellow Concordians that the conscious penance they performed was greater than the twelve labors of Hercules, that they began digging their graves as soon as they were born, that they lived lives of quiet desperation, it is a wonder that he was invited back for the second lecture. But they recognized his relentless wake-up call as one directed at all America, not just at them, and they felt too his irrepressible good humor, the sense of prospect and possibility that stimulated such stinging critique. The lyceum audience got to feel in the flesh what every awake reader of *Walden* would feel—that the parables of two fish on one hook; birds under water; fish in the sky; lost hound, horse, and dove; and melting ice cakes in the village street all were calculated to offer resurrection and redemption to those who would make the effort. Thoreau's history of himself (surely a history of every self) openly pilfered his good public's nostrums—their economic assumptions, their treasured mobility, their Bibles and other good books, their philanthropy—and left them with a greatly enlarged sense of their own destinies. While other transcendentalists talked of the Hermetic maxim "as above, so below," Thoreau performed it as a daily rite. When it came time to speak of his experiment, he could not help—like Hermes Trismegistus and all the ancient sages—but use the language of the birds. "If I should attempt to tell how I have desired to spend my life in years past, it would probably surprise those of my readers who are somewhat acquainted with its actual history; it would certainly astonish those who know nothing about it. I will only hint at some of the enterprises which I have cherished." He asked pardon for his obscurities, then doubled their darkness, always subtly leading listeners toward a light they themselves had to supply. Therein lies the alchemical action of *Walden*—to read it is a spiritual labor, a pilgrimage, which, even after we stop walking/ reading, goes on apace at night when our daimones are fully awake.[176]

All of Thoreau's punning, his fascination for doubleness, for mystery, was silent encouragement for each member of his audience to reach for a poetic, mythic understanding. There is a beautiful symmetry between Thoreau's predilection for punning and his "hiding" his Truth, doubling it, never doubting it, but in fine Fool fashion, keeping that quality he loved in his engagement with landscape—a certain indistinctness, indeterminacy, even benign illusion. That is the beauty of a pun: it deceives and enlightens all at once. It is a gift offered also with no guarantee of acceptance or even recognition on the part of the hearer. God does this with Creation, offers it up freely and takes the chance that we may not get the joke. Indeed, few do, and Thoreau is the one American of his era who consistently brings this to the attention of his neighbors. Thoreau does the same with his literary creations, which are grandiose puns almost sure to be mistaken or ignored. This is the Holy Fool, who can count on being misunderstood, ignored, or more likely, ridiculed. It takes a Fool to know a Fool, so it is no surprise that Alcott became at Walden his most faithful visitor.

Visitors were a large part of Thoreau's life at Walden Pond, becoming the subject of two chapters in *Walden*. America's predilection to see

Thoreau as a failed and faithless hermit for his sociality—irked more by his trips to town than the hosting of friends and strangers at his cabin—demonstrates both its lopsided national myth of individualism and its failure to recognize a higher form of hospitality. Saying that he had "more visitors while I lived in the woods than at any other period of my life," Thoreau mentioned "children come a-berrying, railroad men taking a Sunday walk in clean shirts, fishermen and hunters, poets and philosophers, in short, all honest pilgrims." In the "Visitors" chapter in *Walden*, he focuses on the Quebecois woodchopper Alec Therien, but a more cryptic visitor appears in other places in the book. "I have occasional visits in the long winter evenings . . . from an old settler and original proprietor, who is reported to have dug Walden Pond, and stoned it, and fringed it with pine woods; who tells me stories of old time and new eternity . . . a most wise and humorous friend, whom I love much, who keeps himself more secret than Goffe or Whalley; and though he is thought to be dead, none can show where he is buried." Later on he mentions the "ancient settler" again, "who remembers so well when he first came here with his divining rod, saw . . . the hazel pointed downward, and he concluded to dig a well here." Even without his telltale double entendre of the "divining rod," Thoreau clearly is speaking of God, who comes in winter while he is most solitary.[177]

And yet it is in a chapter called "Winter Visitors" that Thoreau most vividly describes a pair of visitors, one a "poet" and the other "one of the last of the philosophers." Critics assume Ellery Channing to be the unnamed poet, and Alcott the philosopher, and indeed, if one compares Thoreau's journal notes about Alcott to the passage in *Walden*, they are nearly identical in some places. This philosopher was given to the world by Connecticut and "peddled her wares"—Alcott was from Connecticut, where he had worked as a peddler. The entry—"When Alcott's day comes Laws unsuspected by most will take effect"—becomes in *Walden* "But though comparatively disregarded now, when his day comes, laws unsuspected by most will take effect, and masters of families and rulers will come to him for advice." This philosopher is "a true friend of man," "an Old Mortality, say rather an Immortality," "the sanest man, . . . the same yesterday and tomorrow." This last phrase— modeled after the New Testament (Hebrews 13:8)—gives away the philosopher's identity as Christ. "I do not see how he can ever die; Nature cannot spare him." The poet, "actuated by pure love"; the hermit, seemingly Thoreau himself; and the philosopher constitute a Trinity, not three mortal visitors, not three aspects of Thoreau, but Father, Son, and Holy Spirit, whose presence "expanded and racked my little house . . . opened its seams so they had to be calked with much dullness thereafter to stop the consequent leak." Alternately calling the poet "the old settler I have spoken of," Thoreau confirms the hidden message that the "little house" is his own self, "expanded and racked" by the holy presence of the threefold God.[178]

In *Walden*—a sacred book whose every word was scrutinized seven times over, which has not a single sentence out of painstakingly chosen place—Thoreau even put the book's only illustration in service to his higher purpose. A "reduced plan" showing the depths of Walden Pond and two topographic profiles accompanies the chapter "The Pond in Winter." In characteristically careful fashion, Thoreau noted the location of the Fitchburg Railroad, his cabin, and two nearby hills and listed the area, circumference, and greatest length and depth of the pond. Though he never draws attention to it in the text, the two cross-sectional lines describe a perfect cross of about the proportions of the Christian crucifix. Thoreau's *gita—Walden*—immortalized Walden Pond as an emblem for Truth, and his survey echoed this in its mapping of a universal law of Nature—that this intersection marked a pond's greatest depth. Strict draftsman that he was, he could in full faith inscribe these two axes upon the outline of the pond.

Thoreau's repugnance for the Church never affected his devotion to Christ. In *A Week* he had said, "Christ was a sublime actor on the stage of the world. He knew what he was thinking when he said, 'Heaven and earth shall pass away, but my words shall not pass away.' I draw close to him at such a time." Thoreau identified with Christ the fellow heretic and Fool not only as a historical figure but as a living presence whom he had experienced intensely in the dark of winter in his Walden cabin. "It is necessary not to be a Christian, to appreciate the beauty and significance of the life of Christ," Thoreau declared in the Sunday chapter of *A Week*.[179]

From his long love of Virgil's *Georgics* and other classical writers, Thoreau knew well the rhythms of both the Roman farmers and the gods that attended them. In *Walden*, when he wished to criticize the desacralized agricultural practices of Concord's farmers, he accused them of sacrificing "not to Ceres and the terrestrial Jove, but to the infernal Plutus rather." Thoreau knew Saturn as the principal ancient Roman god of agriculture, another of the celestial beings thought to regulate the patient patterning of planting and harvesting, and he was aware of the planet Saturn's twenty-nine-and-a-half-year orbital period. The ancients knew that the more advanced the human being, the more faithfully that person's lifetime affirmed universal spiritual laws, including the laws of cosmic rhythm. Jesus Christ's life would be expected to dramatize the Saturn rhythm, the longest and most majestic of the planetary rhythms. The cycle of Saturn, Lord of Time, marks a turning point when destiny comes sharply into focus, demanding inner and outer changes in each individual. Jesus of Nazareth at thirty underwent the most dramatic change of any human being, as his body became the vehicle for the Son of God's descent into man. Other avatars' biographies show the same Saturn rhythm operating in them: Zarathustra received his revelations from the archangels at age thirty, when he began his prophetic mission; Siddhartha's great renunciation of his princely life took place in his thirtieth year. Thoreau at age thirty finished his self-imposed isolation at Walden Pond.

In the fifth draft of *Walden*, penned in 1853, Thoreau added a parable to the Conclusion about "the artist of Kouroo," a man whose single-minded devotion to carving a perfect walking staff allows the world and all Time to pass away, so that, upon carving the finishing stroke, "it expanded before his eyes into the fairest of all the creations of Brahma."

Sounding like a tale straight out of Hindu scripture, it was instead Thoreau's autochthonous parable of his experience in fashioning his perfect staff—*Walden*. Standing outside the body of the book as commentary upon its creation, in the middle of a series of paragraphs so ethereal that they seem to take flight, it ultimately yields to yet another parable, added in the penultimate draft. "Every one has heard the story which has gone the rounds of New England," he says, of the tale of a "strong and beautiful bug" which hatches out of its "well-seasoned tomb" in a sixty-year-old oak table, "hatched perchance by the heat of an urn." Though everyone may have heard this bit of regional folklore, only Thoreau turned it into a myth of human resurrection: "Who knows what beautiful and winged life, whose egg has been buried for ages under many concentric layers of woodenness in the dead dry life of society, . . . may unexpectedly come forth from amidst society's most trivial and handselled furniture, to enjoy its perfect summer life at last!" In two summers and their brethren seasons of 1845 to 1847, Thoreau had divined his life and, in the process, divined life for all Americans. "Only that day dawns to which we are awake," concludes *Walden*'s conclusion. "There is more day to dawn. The sun is but a morning star." Like the sleeping larvae—and like the life of Christ—Thoreau knew, his true book would lie dormant, to "unexpectedly come forth" before "the astonished family of man" at some future date.[180]

Farewells

On September 6, 1847, two years, two months, and two days after arriving at Walden Pond, Thoreau left, declaring that he had "several more lives to live." Emerson was about to embark on his second European tour and had invited Henry to come take up his old quarters at Bush, becoming the man of the house in Emerson's absence. In October he did so, staying for ten months. Even before he moved in, he was in Emerson's employ; in July and August, he and Alcott were building a summerhouse in a two-acre field east of Bush, where Emerson the previous fall had begun a grape arbor and orchard of plums, peaches, apples—thirty varieties, including one christened Thoreau, after its cultivator—pears, and even a dozen quince trees. Emerson's gardener, Hugh Whelan, made an agreement with Emerson to pay ten dollars a year to rent part of the Walden Pond lot, where Whelan intended to move Thoreau's cabin, enlarge it, and move in. The return to civilized life prompted Thoreau to finally reply to a form letter he had been sent in March from his Harvard class secretary, inquiring about graduates' activity: "I am a Schoolmaster—a Private Tutor, a Surveyor—a Gardener, a Farmer—a Painter, I mean a House Painter, a Carpenter, a Mason, a Day-Laborer, a Pencil-Maker, a Glass-Paper Maker, a Writer, and sometimes a Poetaster." While Emerson lectured to large audiences in Liverpool and Manchester and paid visits to Tennyson, Disraeli, Dickens, De Quincey, Wordsworth, Matthew Arnold, George Eliot, and other English notables, back in Concord Thoreau built closet shelves, weeded the garden, pruned the fruit trees, filled the wood box, and endlessly entertained the Emerson children.[181]

Emerson in England met George Stephenson, the engineer responsible for the modern railroad system; geologist Charles Lyell; Robert Chambers, author of *Vestiges of the Natural History of Creation*, the provocative pre-Darwinian survey of life; Richard Owen, the anatomist and paleontologist who established the Order Dinosauria and whom Prince Albert was about to put in charge of designing the dinosaur displays for the Great London Exhibition of 1851; and Charles Babbage, inventor of the calculating machine. Emerson met Michael Faraday, heard Frédéric Chopin perform, and went to see J. M. W. Turner's paintings.

Thoreau heard of all this in letters from Emerson; Thoreau's return letters were nearly oblivious to the momentous events transpiring in America. As 1848 began, gold was discovered at a new lumber mill on the American River, though it would be months before the news was reported in Yerba Buena—recently renamed San Francisco. No one believed the news at first, but by July, as Emerson boarded a ship home, crewmen on ships in San Francisco Bay were already deserting for the gold fields, and entire California towns emptied as their citizens rushed to Sutter's Mill.

In the spring, in between firm instructions to Lidian about Thoreau's tasks—manuring the orchard, planting ample crops of melon and corn and potatoes—Emerson complained that Henry did not write to him. Thoreau had found a new correspondent, Harrison Gray Otis Blake, of Worcester, Massachusetts, who wrote to Thoreau in March after reading his *Dial* article on the Stoic poet Persius. Blake had met Thoreau only once but had recognized the uniqueness and gravity of Thoreau's mission, and he drew forth from Thoreau frank elaborations of his philosophy of life. "Do what you love. Know your own bone; gnaw at it, bury it, unearth it, and gnaw it still. Do not be too moral. You may cheat yourself out of much life so. Aim above morality. Be not *simply* good— be good for something." The perfect faith of this advice was hard-won, for the gnawing at his own bone that Thoreau had done for two years at Walden, and over the next two years of efforts to publish *A Week* and *Walden*, was producing few results. In February 1849 he finally arranged for the publication of *A Week*, but the publisher insisted that Thoreau pay the cost of the book's production if it didn't sell. After it was finally published, on May 30, Horace Greeley's *New York Tribune* reviewed it on the front page, praising its prose over its intermittent poetry, and attacking its "misplaced Pantheistic attack on the Christian Faith." As anticipated by its author, *A Week* was thoroughly misread from the moment it appeared. Ironically, the most perceptive review came from James Russell Lowell, with whom Thoreau would later have a serious quarrel over an article he did for Lowell's *Atlantic Monthly* on his Maine woods journeys. Lowell's essay was actually a fervent lament against disenchantment, a plea for faith in an age of faithlessness. "We stick to the sea-serpent," he began, saying that this chimeric creature was the last link between Belief and Science, "interpreting between the age of the dragon and that of the railroad train." Lowell voiced respect for those who had seen the sea-serpent, against those moderns who "see nothing out of sight"—"materialists reporting things for other skeptics to doubt still further upon." Exploration had diminished rather than enriched the menagerie of human imagination:

> Year by year, more and more of the world gets disenchanted. Even the icy privacy of the arctic and antartic [sic] circles is invaded. Our youth are no longer ingenious, as indeed no ingenuity is demanded of them. Every thing is accounted for, every thing cut and dried, and the world may be put together as easily as the fragments of a dissected map. The Mysterious bounds nothing now on the North, South, East, or West. We have played Jack Horner with our earth, till there is never a plum left in it.[182]

Lowell thought that since the old class of voyagers was gone, the best thing to do was to "send poets a-travelling," bringing their fresh-eyed perspective to bear on the disenchanted world. "Mr. Thoreau is clearly the man we want. He is both wise man and poet," who "with the touch of his oar conjures back as much as may be of the old enchantment." Praising his "fine, intelligent paganism," Lowell thought Thoreau "holds a very smooth mirror up to nature." Lowell's sincere appreciation of Thoreau's enchanted view of the world was drowned out by a chorus of smugly self-righteous critics who found the book underwhelming: "The matter is for the most part poor enough" (*London Athenaeum*). "The bulk of the book consists of Mr. Thoreau's reveries that might have been written anywhere: they are rather flat and not of a kind of interest" (*London Spectator*). "It is interspersed with inexcusable crudities, with proofs of carelessness and lack of healthy moral discrimination, with contempt for things commonly esteemed holy, with reflections which may shock every pious Christian" (*Universalist Quarterly*). Even the less sanctimonious critics were mostly puzzled by the book. The *New York Evening Post* said that Thoreau "conducts his readers through a maze of reflections of almost desultory nature, often as agreeable as they are quaint, and sometimes running into a certain mysticism through which we do not always find it easy to follow him."[183]

Speaking true in America's great age of humbug ensured that Thoreau's "American book," as Alcott called it, would be greeted with the same sort of flippant cynicism that Thoreau had met when going beyond Concord to give his lecture "Life in the Woods." "Henry D. Thoreau of Concord had better go home and ask his mother if she 'knows he's out.'...To be frank with you, you are better as a woodsman, or say, a woodpecker, than as a cockney philosopher, or a city parrot, mimicking the voices of canaries or cat owls, of Emersons or Carlyles," wrote one Worcester paper, while another complained of his lecture's "constant struggle for eccentricity." Even readers of the printed lecture shared the press's brassy tone: The *New York Daily Tribune* published a letter from a "Timothy Thorough," which called Thoreau a "good-for-nothing, selfish, crab-like sort of chap."[184]

Even if he had been interested in hearing what critics had to say, Thoreau was deaf to them, for on June 14, the day after the first review of *A Week* appeared, his sister Helen died of consumption. After the funeral service, Henry rose and set a music box playing near Helen's casket, while everyone sat quietly and listened. Shortly afterward, he wrote a farewell poem affirming their continued love across the threshold:

> Where thy love followeth me
> Is enough society
> Thy indelible mild eye
>   Is my sky.
> Whether by land or sea
>   I wander to and fro,
> Oft as I think of thee
>   The heavens hang more low...
> I discover by thy face
> That we are of one race

Flowed in one vein our blood
Ere the sea found its flood
The worm may be divided
And each part become a whole,
But the nobler creature man
May not separate a span.

Seven years after their brother John's death, Helen's death similarly affected him, sharpening his sense of purpose in having received the gift of life while those he loved most had that gift taken from them. "We must act with so rapid and resistless a purpose in *one* direction," he wrote to Blake, "that our vices will necessarily trail behind. The nucleus of a comet is almost a star." [185]

Sometime between May and October 1849, Thoreau wrote a love letter, "A Sister," but its addressee was neither his sister Helen nor Sophia, nor Lidian Emerson, whom he loved—and often addressed—as a sister.

One in whom you have—unbounded faith—whom you can—purely love. A sweet presence and companion making the world populous Whose heart answers to your heart. Whose presence can fill all space. One who is a spirit. Who attends to your truth. A gentle spirit—a wise spirit—a loving spirit. An enlargement to your being. Level to yourself. Whom you can know A great heart An integral portion of God. The stream of whose being unites with your own without a ripple or a murmur. & they spread into a sea.

I still think of you as my sister. I presume to know you. Others are of my kindred by blood or of my acquaintance but you are mine. you are of me & I of you I can not tell where I leave off and you begin.— there is such a harmony when your sphere meets mine To you I can afford to be forever what I am, for your presence will not permit me to be what I should not be.

... My sister whom I love I have almost no more to do with. I shall know where to find her It is those whom I do not love who concern me—and make affairs for me. What can I ask of my sister that she will do only that she will never be less than she is, that so I may be more. Persevere. I have intelligence with her as often as I am her brother—& as long. I know her in spirit and in truth. I can more heartily meet her when our bodies are away I see her without the veil of the body. When I commune with her I forget to speak. An imbodiment of truth—of goodness of sincerity & love Why will we add to our farms & not add to our sky our heavens I may add a soul to mine.

When I love you I feel as if I were annexing another world to mine. We splice the heavens. Can there be a rich man who does not own a friend?

My sister, it is glorious to me that you live. Thou art a hushed music to me—a thousand melodies commingled and filling the air. Thou art transfigured to me, and I see a perfect being—O do not disappoint me.

Whose breath is as gentle and salubrious as a zephyr's whisper Whom I know as an atmosphere. Who art dear to me—A Sicilian atmosphere. Whom in thought my spirit continuously embraces. Into whom I flow Who is not separated from me.

Who art clothed in white Who comest like an incense. Who art all that I can imagine—my inspirer. The feminine of me. Who art magnanimous.

It is morning when I meet thee in a still cool dewy white sun light In the hushed dawn—my young mother—I thy eldest son—who art refreshing as the first breath of morning—who speakest above the breathing of the crickets with an Auroral breath. Whether thou art my mother or my sister—whether am I thy son or thy brother.

On the remembrance of whom I repose—So *old* a sister art thou—so newly hast thou recreated me. Who speakest never colored words—who art not possessed by a demon. Who dwellest in the morning light whose eyes are like the morning star Who comest to me in the morning twilight

This extraordinary hymn of praise is something beyond a paean to his Muse, more like the rendering of a mystical vision on the order of Dante's encounter with Beatrice. A few pages before this entry in his journal, Thoreau had been musing upon Jesus's "I Am" sayings from the Gospel of John. These little fragments—"He is 'the good Shepherd,' "'I and my Father are one' affirmed the divine," "He says of himself 'I am the resurrection & the life,' 'he that believeth in me,'" "'A new commandment I give unto you; that is to love one another,'" "'I am the way, and the truth, and the life; no man cometh unto the Father but by me'"—affirm that Thoreau embraced the Father principle of God. This anonymous song of joy to "A Sister" suggests that he had also experienced Sophia, the eternal Divine Mother principle lost almost completely from Western Christianity. Thoreau's vision had not been of the Virgin Mary, whose mystical presence had been expressed to thousands of devoted followers at Paris in 1830 and at La Salette in 1846 (and would again at Lourdes in 1858). His was a wholly solitary encounter with a sisterly—but magnificent—spiritual being, embodying divine wisdom as well as love. Having felt and seen this Sister so intensely, Thoreau could more easily say good-bye to his own sister Helen, for he knew she was going to a place of true Concord.[186]

"Some Infernal Influence"

In early October 1849, Thoreau and Ellery Channing planned an excursion to Cape Cod, where Thoreau wished to gather material for a lecture about the region. At Boston, they found that the steamer to Provincetown had been delayed by a violent storm, and in the streets they saw handbills headed "Death! One hundred and forty lives lost at Cohasset." Deciding to proceed to the Cape by way of Cohasset, they arrived two days after the brig *Saint John*, carrying immigrants from Galway, had hit an offshore rock and then broken up. They came upon a horrendous scene of mangled, swollen bodies—some covered up, but others fully exposed—of the drowned strewn along the shore. They continued by stage out through Barnstable, Yarmouth, Dennis, Brewster, and Orleans to Provincetown, where $15,000 was stolen from the Union Wharf Company safe during their stay. Thoreau learned on his next visit to Cape Cod that he and Channing had been among the suspects. For an inland village boy like Thoreau, the shipwreck and robbery added to the innate sense of the Cape's wild outlandishness. Reading up on the early exploration and colonial history of the Cape, he marveled at being able in six hours by train to reach the isolated reach of sand that pioneer explorers Thorfinn and Gosnold saw. He thought about the fishermen's wives of Truro looking out to see their husbands and sons twenty miles offshore, but being unable to call them with the dinner horn. He learned that on Miles Standish's expedition, a dozen men were sent ashore to fetch wood from a swamp that the natives called something the English sailors glossed as "shank painter"—the short rope and chain holding the shank and flukes of the anchor to the ship's side. From his reading, he knew the Pilgrims to be landlubbers like himself, and untrustworthy observers, given their state after the long ocean passage. "They exaggerated the fairness & attractiveness of the land for they were glad to get any land at all after that anxious voyage everything appeared to them of the color of the rose and had the scent of Juniper or sassafrass—They do not speak like navigators. . . . They looked at the land of the New World with infant's eyes, in describing the country described their own feelings & hopes." [187]

Two weeks after his return to Concord, between three and four on a Monday afternoon, a severe earthquake—or what was reported as an earthquake—shook Concord. Two loud explosions sent Acton and Concord people running from their houses and stores, expecting that the Sudbury powder mill had blown up. *Scientific American* reported that the shaking resembled "that produced by [the] rolling of something heavy in a room overhead," and commented that a similar event had occurred in the same location the previous year. While *Scientific American* and the *Concord Freeman* called this trembling an earthquake, many local people with longer memories and wider views of Nature attributed this to the evil spirits around Nashoba Hill and Nagog Pond. Thoreau had walked out to the area with Emerson the previous August, musing all the while about Tahatawan, Sarah Doublet, and the other Pawtucket Indians who once made their home there. Nashoba was the first inland reservation—known to the English as "praying towns"—in the Massachusetts Bay Colony, the site having been chosen by the General Court of Boston in 1654. The sachems from the area that would become Concord had proposed the land just to the east of Walden Pond, near Flint's Pond, but colonial authorities were uncomfortable with the savages living this close to English settlement, and designated the more remote area at Nashoba Hill. Laws meant to "civilize" the Indians governed daily life at Nashoba; Rule 2 required that "there shall be no more powwowing amongst the Indians." Anyone in Nashoba engaging in ceremonial activity—seen by colonial authorities as witchcraft—risked a fine of twenty shillings.[188]

Thoreau knew from his historical study as well as from local folklore that the Indians at Nashoba Hill had periodically heard strange rumbling noises in the area and that there was a tradition of the "Hind-diabolus"—a spectral demonic dog—at nearby Nagog. Native legend attributed the disturbances to the activities of "Hobbamocko," i.e., Obomakwit, literally "the Wanderer," a devilish spirit known to all the Algonquian-speaking native peoples of the Northeast. Obomakwit haunted other places in colonial Massachusetts, most famously a pond in Westborough, where "some infernal influence"—as Thoreau copied into his journal from his historical study—had for generations caused a whole range of human miseries and terrors. In English colonial and later American folklore, Obomakwit's nefarious doings there were immortalized in "The Devil and Tom Walker," a tale that by Thoreau's day had become formalized as a literary creation; in 1824 Washington Irving retold the story in *Tales of a Traveller, by Geoffrey Crayon*. While Westborough's Hobbamocko Swamp and Tom Walker would enter the national consciousness thanks to Irving—"the Devil and Tom Walker" became a popular saying of antebellum America—in Concord there were equally haunted landscapes. Such local toponyms as "Devil's Stairway" on Fair Haven Hill and "Devil's Bar" in Walden Pond reflected playful folklore about inexplicable landscape features, but other place names pointed to more disturbing origins. Thoreau was more given to locating the Devil in human nature than in an external being; walking with Channing in a haunted section of Sudbury, Thoreau's journal lightheartedly noted that the area was "where Old Nick lived, & you may see his cellar-hole & hollow orchard stumps." Though Thoreau saw the deserted dwellings as no more devilish than the abandoned "village" out near Walden Pond, Channing was spooked by the place. He wrote a poem about "a solitary town, where man was not":

> Soon did we enter with protracted dread!
> Like one who walks at midnight in a trance,
> And balconizing with the cats curvets,
> So stalked we silent on, terrified all!
> A mesmerized abyss, where mystic hands
> Had with soft passes put the place asleep,
> Then folded & gone on forgetting it.
>
> ... For though the eaves were rabbitted
> & the well sweep was slanted,
> Each house was not inhabited
> But haunted.[189]

In colonial times, the area was called Whipsuppenicke—"place of sudden death"—as only fifty Pawtuckets survived the plague brought by English settlers in 1674. But during King Philip's War, any place where the English encountered Indians could become a place of sudden death. In August 1675, after the Massachusetts General Court ordered that all native people be interned in camps, or else be shot on sight, the residents of Nashoba were told by Captain Mosely of the English militia to collect a few things—but no food—and then were marched eleven miles along the narrow Indian path to the English village at their former fields at Musquetaquid, the place the English now called Concord. While the Nashoba men were eventually taken to Deer Island in Boston Harbor to join other native prisoners—before being sold off into slavery—the women and children were taken to John Hoar, a colonist sympathetic to their plight. Hoar was required to hold the Nashoba villagers in a stockaded yard, but risked his life by returning to Nashoba to retrieve corn for the prisoners. After he returned from Deer Island, Mosely came after the other "tawny vermin," taking them forcibly from Hoar's protective care. This episode was the first "Indian removal," to be followed by countless others over the next two centuries as first the English and then America pursued their manifest destiny across the continent. A year later, three native women and three children who lived on Flint's Pond had ventured to the other side of Walden Pond, about one and one-half miles from their wigwams, while picking huckleberries. Colonial law specified that any native person who was more than one mile distant from his or her habitation of record could be killed, and so the Concord Militia slaughtered the huckleberrying party.[190]

Whether or not caused by colonial race atrocities, there were places about Concord that seemed altogether cursed. In the nineteenth century, the Acton neighborhood, once a Nashoba site, saw nine suicides and a murder between 1863 and 1893. Reminiscing on the history of the area's tragic fortune, Joseph Hosmer recalled that lightning had killed his nearest neighbor, and his own house and two trees had been struck as well. "Two of my nearest neighbors have hung themselves, and there is one place within rifle shot distance that I believe has been possessed by the devil.... Sometime in the 1840s the owner dropped dead in the field, and his wife cut her throat a year or two after. The next occupant and his son have suicided since, the man who owned it when I came here, shot himself, the man who cut hay the same season was killed on the field, and the man lived opposite was burned in his barn. I hired a piece of this land, ... and I almost [died] from inflamed lungs ... I am not very superstitious, but I shall not plant there next year.... There are some things in this world which are hard to understand, or account for."[191]

The day after the mysterious tremors, Thoreau learned that Tilly Holden, a farm widow who lived west of Fair Haven Bay, had the week before gone out to her barn to feed her twenty-eight hens, and found eight of them lying dead on the floor, their blood drained completely. The following Saturday the remaining twenty had been killed in the same way. Something weird was afoot and it was not confined to Concord; in Brooklyn, at three o'clock in the afternoon on Monday, October 29, 1849, meteorological observer Ebenezer Meriam reported an earthquake "of great energy," accompanied by lightning, thunder, and snow. "There was a lurid glow resting on the earth while this illumination continued, and it had a quivering, tremulous motion, and there was an invisible current in the lower atmosphere, and I could realize in my breathing that I was inhaling winged air." Meriam had been documenting weather patterns for decades and had witnessed many odd atmospheric events, often coinciding with each other. In 1846, on April 23, at two P.M., a snowstorm was active at Boston, yet at the same time the previous day the temperature had been 83°. In Albany, thermometers registered a 99° difference over a few weeks in April. On the morning of April 24, Meriam's "meteoric, electric, and magnetic wires were in an extraordinary state." Meriam received a letter from Judge Josiah Butler of South Deerfield, Massachusetts, dated April 15, 1847, reporting a series of earthquakes in that region. "I find that every shake has been proceeded or succeeded by a storm—generally a storm followed in proportion in severity to the violence of the shock." During the same period, there had been earthquakes accompanied by storms in Livingston County, New York, and in Chelsea and Newburyport, Massachusetts, where fires killed horses and half a dozen people. The year had opened with equally violent tempests and anomalous events: On January 14 an earthquake shook Rice Lake in Upper Canada, at the same time that a ship on the lake was struck twice by lightning, knocking down five men and disabling two of them. On the same day, ashes fell from the sky on the Faro Islands. Two weeks later, in Nova Scotia, a brilliant meteor that outshone the moon, then exploded, followed an earthquake. A few days after this, during a snowstorm in the same area, grubs fell to earth with the snowflakes, and "what is still more extraordinary for that season of the year, in that cold climate, great numbers of Robins appeared and fed upon these grubs or worms." In May, in Dumfries, Scotland, a shower of flies darkened the air for half a mile; the fallen flies covered a six-hundred-yard stretch of road. The same day, a red cloud of smoke formed over the city. In the midst of all this meteorological mayhem, *Scientific American* reported, astronomers had also discovered a new comet in the sky. A year later Meriam reported that the steamboat *Governor Marcy* had run aground on rocks on Lake Erie's shore, the sixth steamer wreck in two years, all of which were attended by earthquakes. Meriam was a fanatical observer, making atmospheric records from his "equilibrium wires" nineteen of every twenty-four hours. During peculiar states, he made observations every five or ten minutes. From January 1846 to June 1847 he had recorded fifty-four earthquakes.[192]

The October 1849 quake went unrecorded by Thoreau, whose journal was far from being the almost daily record of local phenomena that it would soon become, but he was certainly aware of Nature's "prodigies and wonders," these anomalous events whose inscrutability made them a favorite topic for the periodicals, including leading scientific journals of the day. In his "Fact Book," a massive compendium of natural history lore gleaned from hundreds of printed sources, there is a newspaper clipping inserted on a page of his notes from reading Kirby and Spence's *Entomology*: "A Shower of Flies. A recent number of the St. Louis *Democrat* says 'On the down trip of the steamer *Editor* in the Illinois, the other night at 9 PM, a shower or stream of the Mormon or Shad fly poured upon the decks to the depth of six inches, and it was a very difficult matter to shovel them overboard. They were so numerous as to put out the watchmen's light and envelope everything in midnight darkness. The trees along the shore look as if borne down by these

short-lived insects. The visitation is said to prognosticate a sickly season.'"
In *Walden,* Thoreau alludes to a number of "prodigies." An unnamed old
woodsman—perhaps George Melvin—told Thoreau about the time that
he had been duck hunting on the largely still-frozen Fair Haven Pond,
when, while hidden in the bushes awaiting his prey, he heard "a low and
seemingly very distant sound, but singularly grand and impressive,
unlike anything he had ever heard, gradually swelling and increasing."
There was then a "sullen rush and roar," and the man ran out, expecting
to find a huge flock of ducks had settled onto the water fringing the ice.
Instead, he discovered that the entire body of ice covering the pond had
vaulted forward, heaving up huge fragments of solid ice in a pile. There
was no note of ridicule in Thoreau's recounting of this curious incident;
he said about the man who told him the story that he was "a close observer of Nature, and seems as thoroughly wise in regard to all her operations as if she had been put on the stocks when he was a boy . . . [he
could] hardly acquire more of natural lore if he should live to the age of
Methuselah." Thoreau was amazed that this sage should express "wonder
at any of Nature's operations, for I thought that there were no secrets
between them." As freakish as the sudden eruption of ice seemed, it was
hardly singular; the *Concord Freeman* in 1846 had reported a similar
"Singular Phenomenon" from Missouri where lake ice had been thrown
up, "by agency of some subterranean power." *Scientific American* in 1847
reported the experience of a man who had been standing on the shore of
a perfectly calm Lake Ontario, with a very light wind, when he saw the
waters suddenly retract along a line 350 feet long, then surge forward
eight or nine times in a huge cone, making a "dreadful noise." The *Scientific American* editors speculated that volcanic activity was the cause. In
1848, *Scientific American* published a report from Newfoundland, where
the water inside Halifax harbor had suddenly risen and then fallen again
ten to twelve feet, leaving fishing boats high and dry. The surge continued at intervals all afternoon, yet no earthquakes (or volcanoes!) were
reported anywhere. When, in *Walden,* Thoreau notes that "sometimes it
has rained flesh and blood!," he alludes to yet another freak of Nature

episodically reported from around the world, and as likely to go uninvestigated by natural scientists, who preferred to discount any such reports as hoaxes or hallucinations.[193]

Among rural uneducated folk, all of these prodigies and wonders were still in the 1840s understood to be the meddlesome work of mischievous and malevolent invisible beings. Whether attributed to Old Nick or Old Scratch or the "good people," these sports of Nature were more honestly met by the unschooled than by Harvard professors or science magazine editors, who unconsciously cultivated a blind spot about such phenomena. The age's atmosphere of humbug, so wonderfully aided by Barnumesque displays of chimerical Feejee mermaids and ersatz animal magnetism, let America's nascent scientific establishment off the hook, as it could strike the same skeptical pose as the layman when confronted by things seemingly too weird to be true. While Emerson would fill his notebooks with paranormal tidbits all his life and would continue to lecture on "Demonology" right through the 1860s, Thoreau largely remained oblivious to the question of the meaning of such sports and wonders. As preoccupied by daimones as any man in America, he took almost no interest in their shadowy siblings, the *demons*. That was the province of Hawthorne and Poe. Thoreau was "haunted" to be sure, but only in the original sense of the word, whose Anglo-French root—*hanter*—meant "to frequent, or dwell." His style of haunting restored harmony to his natal landscape through his thoughts and deeds, and through the expectation of the deeds of one supreme daimon, Pan, the Lord of the elemental beings of Nature. His obliviousness to the demons was concurrent with an intense awareness of and clairvoyance for the daimones, and he was always well served by his naïveté regarding the darker denizens of the spiritual landscape. Ignorance of their existence, however, carried great danger for those who denied that *any* beings other than the physical roamed the Earth. When Concord was a frail and fledgling settlement of awkward alien Englishmen, battling what they perceived as the dark demons of the Pawtucket, Massachusett, Nipmuck, and other native peoples, scarcely a single event, meteorological or political, was *not* seen as the reflection of the activity of infernal or angelic agents.

Conversely, mid-nineteenth-century America, apart from its millenarian fringe, could not bring itself to see *any* signs from the heavens as "signs of the times." Flies and grubs did not fall in copious quantities from the sky. Earthquakes did not cause fireballs nor electrical storms. Lakes and oceans did not spontaneously have heaving fits. There was no such thing as Satan, and no place nor person could be "cursed." This was the stuff of Cotton Mather's deranged Calvinism, thought the scientific savants of antebellum America. Yet someone swept up the piles of flies, robins appeared in February to gobble the grubs, and Thoreau's most well respected observer saw heaps of ice instead of sitting ducks. Both *Scientific American* and hundreds of American newspapers ran these accounts under the heading "Singular Phenomena," but there was nothing singular about them at all. For all of their seeming eccentricity, there was something rhythmic and repetitious about these breaches of nature's laws. Their very newsworthiness was in the recognition by the reader of their *non*-singularity. More often than not, they had heard of just such a caprice having happened a few years ago in a neighboring town or state or country. P. T. Barnum could shout "Humbug!" from the top of his American Museum and be echoed by scientific committees convened from Harvard and Yale, but the reports kept coming in, and some careful observers, like Mr. Meriam of Broooklyn Heights, were pretty sure that things that couldn't happen were happening more often than ever before.

"An East Quarter Bargain"

Thoreau once told Blake that it was about November 1849 that he began to practice a daily habit of afternoon walks; if anything odd were to be falling onto or erupting from under Concord, Henry Thoreau was the man who was most likely to see it. His journaling habit was still intermittent, so even if nothing escaped his eye or ear, we have no complete record to apprise us of it. Sometimes his journal entries had the telegraphic style of his pocket notebooks where he listed short signifiers for later expansion and transcription. Inspired by a late fall ramble, Thoreau wrote this Whitmanesque itinerary:

> We have a saying an East quarter bargain i.e. a secret one—The Copper mines—the old silver mine now deserted—the holt—the great meadows—The Baker Farm—The Dam Meadows—The Eastabrooks Place—Jenny Dugan's—The Ministerial Lot—Fairy land—Sleepy Hollow—Laurel glen Talls Island The bog-iron mines—The old lime-kiln—the place where the cinnamon stone was found—Hayne's Island—I usually went across lots & some times I swam in the river holding my clothes up with one hand to keep them dry. & at last crawling out the other side like an otter or I forded broad deep & rapid streams on temporary Peruvian bridges which I constructed, by letting fall a rider across & using a steady pole . . .

These favorite places of Thoreau's were not in any literal geographic East Quarter of Concord but spread over the local landscape, punctuating the prosaic places with silent exclamations of poetic mystery. These were the liminal lands where even the adult imagination might find everything new again. It was no accident that copper, silver, and iron mines—dark excavations into the mineral earth—made his list, nor the old lime kiln, a giant alchemical retort fallen into romantic ruin. Islands and glens and hollows all were slightly closed spaces where the rest of the daylight world might be shut out a bit for the crepuscular space of the mind to widen some. Even the open expanses of land—the Dam Meadows and the Great Meadows—were liminal because they were so watery and hence sealed off from unamphibious explorers. The Holt was a little copse at a bend in the Concord River, in sight across the Great Meadows of Thoreau's birthplace on the Virginia Road. It too afforded a sense of secrecy, of enclosure from the all too obvious fields and forests of the rest of Concord. For Thoreau, an "East quarter bargain" was one he made with the wild places around him:

> How near to good is what is wild. There is the marrow of nature—there her divine liquors—that is the wine I love. A man's health requires as many acres of meadow as his farm does loads of muck. They are indispensable both to men & corn There are the only strong meats—We pine & starve and lose spirit on the thin gruel of society. A town is saved not by any righteous men in it but by the woods & swamps that surround it.[194]

Antebellum science sought to expunge "secrecy"—in the sense of the quiet cultivation of a mysterious sacramental relation to Nature—from its practices and findings. Science as it was developing in America in the 1840s was anything but wild, and Thoreau would make no east-quarter bargain with it. "The scientific startling & successful as it is, is always something less than the vague poetic—it is that of it which subsides—it is the sun shorn of its beams a mere disk. . . . Science applies a finite rule to the infinite.—& is what you can weigh & measure and bring away. Its sun no longer dazzles us and fills the universe with light." To approach the places Thoreau loved, one went on one's knees, "cross lots" to be sure, and if necessary holding one's clothing aloft above the water. And you told only the closest of confidants of your destination or risked disenchanting it. The same rules applied when one practiced scientific inquiry: go on your knees, by a route of your own making, immersing yourself as fully as possible in the phenomenon, and tell only a few what you find. Thoreau's journal served as his publication of record, a perfect "holt" where he could disclose his findings without risking the dimming of his inner light. In early January 1850, that light seemed to be brightening:

> Seeds beginning to expand in me, which propitious circumstance may bring to the light & to perfection. If I look within all is indistinct

as the night—unless there is a faint glimmer & phosphorescence, a sort of boreal light—there—and perchance there is heard the breathing of crickets under the sod—and as the darkness deepens I may see some twinkling stars. I know not whether it is the dumps or a budding extacy—Were they too many slap jacks or is it the incoming God?

It is soil good for any thing to grow in. It is the excess of—vitality— It was the noiseless visitation of some spirit—[195]

The visitation of spirits was all the rage at the moment in America. On Sunday, March 10, a few days after Thoreau lectured at the Lincoln Lyceum about his Walden bean field—a masterfully disguised sermon showing transcendental experience to be as substantial as beans— Reverend Eliakim Phelps of Stratford, Connecticut, returned with his family from church to their sprawling mansion on Elm Street and found all the doors and windows open. Inside, they found the furniture knocked over, dishes smashed, books, papers, and clothing scattered all over. They had not been robbed; Rev. Phelps found his gold watch, silver heirlooms, and even loose cash undisturbed. In an upstairs bedroom, a sheet was spread over a bed, and Mrs. Phelps's nightgown was laid out upon it. At the bottom a pair of stockings were stretched out, and the arms of the gown were folded across the chest, like a corpse.

Later, while the rest of the family returned to church for the afternoon service, Rev. Phelps hid in his study with a pistol, hoping to catch the intruders should they return. After some time he went downstairs and, entering the dining room, found a circle of eleven effigies of women, kneeling or standing in prayer, some holding Bibles. Articles of the family's clothing had been stuffed with rags and other materials from around the house to create the dummies, which had been put in place during the brief period while Phelps was standing guard. Over the next few months, twenty more mock women would appear out of the blue. They would be joined by leaping umbrellas, silverware, books, and other household objects; bedding sailing off of beds; food and clothing dropping out of nowhere onto the breakfast table while the family ate. Friends and other visitors to the house watched as these objects fell at impossibly slow speeds, or changed course in midair. By the end of April, the disturbances had turned quite nasty: screams and odd sounds were heard each night; silverware was mangled; windows were broken; the children's limbs were jerked about violently and welts appeared on their skin. Rev. Phelps's son was hit with a barrage of small stones. Later, in front of a dozen witnesses, the boy vanished, and was later found tied up and suspended from a tree in the yard.

A week before the odd visitation, Rev. Phelps and a friend had been discussing spiritualism and decided to hold a séance, at which they produced knocking and rapping sounds, just as the Fox sisters had on April Fool's Eve in 1848 in Hydesville, New York. Following their lead, Phelps decided to try communicating with the spirit by a system of telegraphic raps, and he soon ascertained that his resident poltergeist was a tormented soul in hell. When Phelps asked how he might help, the spirit asked Phelps to bring him a piece of pumpkin pie. Asking again, the invisible trickster asked instead for a glass of gin. When the exasperated minister finally asked why the spirit was making such mischief, it replied, "For fun." It went on to give an elaborate tale of having been a law clerk in Philadelphia who had been convicted and jailed for fraud. Like the Hydesville "spirit," who claimed to have been a peddler murdered by previous occupants of the Fox house, the Stratford spirit's information was frequently false, and yet all were puzzled as to how the disembodied intelligence could exist at all.[196]

Both the Hydesville and the Stratford specters, and thousands of others who manifested throughout America, claimed and were believed to be spirits of the dead and, despite the rude, lewd, and downright demonic nature of much of their communications, became venerated by millions eager for proof of life after death. The faithful turned a blind eye to the fact that Kate Fox's first words to the pioneer poltergeist at Hydesville were "Do as I do, Mr. Splitfoot!" (i.e., the Devil), or that that first manifestation had commenced on the eve of the most favorable day of the year for elfin activity. Clergymen who suggested that the spirits were devils in disguise were ignored or ridiculed. Their congregations—and often they themselves—had long since ceased believing in the active presence of nonhuman spiritual beings within the spiritual world. They reasoned that these phantasmic folk must be spirits of the dead, and the more physical their manifestations—moving tables, playing musical instruments, oozing ectoplasmic limbs, producing bouquets of flowers, and other such corny parlor tricks—the more credence that belief was given.

Concord—for all its transcendentalist enlightenment—was not immune from the rapping mania. Women were most enthusiastic, and as with mesmerism, women acted more often as mediums than did men; Lidian Emerson, Sophia Hawthorne, and Elizabeth Palmer Peabody visited spiritualist mediums, but Bronson Alcott, Orestes Brownson, and many of the male Brook Farm veterans at least flirted with spiritualism. Augustus Merrick, whose sister was president of the Concord Ladies' Anti-Slavery Society, visited Boston mediums regularly, and in 1853 he organized a "spirit circle" at Concord.

Thoreau was as damning in his estimation of spiritualism as he was of materialism, writing to his sister Sophia:

Concord is just as idiotic as ever in relation to the spirits and their knockings. Most people here believe in a spiritual world which no respectable junk bottle which had not met with a slip—would condescend to contain even a portion of for a moment—whose atmosphere would extinguish a candle let down into it, like a well that wants airing—in spirits which the very bullfrogs in our meadows would blackball. Their evil genius is in seeing how low it can degrade them. The hooting of owls—the croaking of frogs—is celestial music in comparison. If I could be brought to believe in the things which they believe—I should make haste to get rid of my certificate of stock in this & the next world's enterprises, and buy a share immediately in the

Immediate Annihilation Company that offered—I would exchange my immortality for a glass of small beer this hot weather. Where *are* the heathen? Was there ever any superstition before? ... Consider the dawn & the sunrise—the rainbow & the evening—the words of Christ & the aspirations of all the saints! Hear music? See—smell—taste— feel—hear—anything—& then hear these idiots inspired by the cracking of a restless board—humbly asking "Please spirit, if you cannot answer by knocks, answer by tips of the table."!!!![197]

Surely the most important year in the growth of American spiritualism was 1850, for by then the publicity generated by the Hydesville and Stratford poltergeists caused an explosion of mediumistic phenomena from coast to coast. "Experimental" spiritualist circles formed in Boston (where there was estimated to be over a thousand mediums by 1850), Philadelphia, Providence, all the major cities in New York state, and all the New England states, as well as in Cincinnati, Memphis, Saint Louis, California, Oregon, and Texas. Fittingly, spiritualism's advent had been prophesied by America's most famous mesmeric somnambulist, Andrew Jackson Davis, who had begun dictating in trance his eight-hundred-page compendium, *The Principles of Nature, Her Divine Revelations and a Voice to Mankind,* in 1845. Published in 1847 (and going through thirty-four editions in the next thirty years), it included among its revelations that the truth of a world of spirits would "ere long present itself in the form of a living demonstration. And the world will hail with delight the ushering-in of that era when the interiors of men will be opened, and the spiritual communion will be established." While Davis gave no exact date for the arrival of the event, Shaker somnambulists in the 1830s had made a similar prediction for the year 1848 and also prophesied that America would see an extraordinary discovery of material wealth to accompany the spiritual wealth. The discovery of gold at Sutter's Mill came only two months before Kate Fox taught Mr. Splitfoot to speak in raps.

Davis's *Principles of Nature* presented a muddy, grandiose-sounding cosmogony in its first section, a damning review of the Old Testament and a rejection of the divinity of Christ in the second, and a program for a Fourierist-style socialism in the third. Some of Davis's cosmic pronouncements seemed to come from a true clairvoyance: In advance of the discovery of Neptune and Pluto he spoke of eighth and ninth planets, and his descriptions of Uranus's composition accorded with later findings. He also seemed to know about the galactic center long before its discovery. But the bulk of his book delivered wild descriptions of inhabited planets, pop versions of Swedenborg's otherworldly visions. Saturn he described as inhabited by a more advanced race of humanity, while on Venus and Mars, the inhabitants were more primitive than on Earth. By 1850, when the Phelps spirit story was grabbing headlines across America, Davis was the most famous authority on spiritualism in the nation, and he made a visit to Stratford to investigate. Davis lent his authority to the genuineness of the activity, and stated that the outbreak was caused by "vital radiations" from the Phelps children, whose "magnetism" caused objects to be attracted to or repelled from them.

As time went on, the public demanded more rigorous examinations of spiritualist phenomena, and investigative panels were convened at regular intervals, all of which routinely branded the spirits as humbug. In 1857 Boston newspapers offered a prize of $500 for the successful production of physical phenomena, choosing as judges three Harvard scientists—astronomer Benjamin Pierce, chemist Eben Horsford, and zoologist Louis Agassiz. They oversaw séances with the Fox sisters and other leading mediums, and pronounced in their final report that "any connection with spiritualistic circles, so called, corrupts the morals and degrades the intellect." The Harvard panel was a direct outgrowth of the furor over divinity student Frederick Willis, who in 1855 spontaneously began to produce visions, trances, premonitions, raps, and telekinesis in his dorm room. When friends invited him to sit at a séance circle, he immediately generated voices who claimed to be spirits of the dead. By the spring of 1857, the president of Harvard sent Willis a letter leveling various charges of immorality at him. Noted Unitarian minister, abolitionist, and spiritualist enthusiast Rev. Thomas Wentworth Higginson became interested and investigated Willis's case, then wrote to Harvard defending Willis.[198]

Thoreau knew Willis, who in July 1847 had come with the Alcott family to visit Thoreau at Walden. Henry took the nine-year-old Willis and the four Alcott children out on the pond in his boat, playing his flute to them while they drifted a little way from shore. He then lay down his flute and told them stories of the Indians who once lived by the pond and of the great mysteries that now dwelled there. Willis remembered Thoreau suddenly interrupting himself to speak of the wonders of the white pond lily, then rowing the children over to where they could pick some of the flowers. Walking back to the cabin, Thoreau said to Willis, "Boy, you look tired and sleepy; remember, sleep is half a dinner." Willis and the Alcott children had the privilege that afternoon of sharing in one of Thoreau's many east-quarter bargains.[199]

In America, every day of the year became April Fool's Day for the liberated sprites and poltergeists. The Stratford shenanigans were just a small sampling of their kaleidoscopic circus of tomfoolery. Puritanical matrons manipulating Ouija boards were made to utter the foulest of oaths. Greedy fortune hunters were promised gold and silver in a thousand secret locales. Would-be prophets were tantalized with authentic tidbits of advantageous foreknowledge, then sucker-punched with ersatz revelations guaranteed to be passed on to the multitudes. Earnest seekers of spiritual truths were hoodwinked with bizarre celestial untruths; the planetary fantasies of Andrew Jackson Davis were repeated in a hundred varieties by unsuspecting spiritualist mediums. Masquerading elementals donned the personas of every historical celebrity imaginable, from George Washington to Alexander the Great, proclaiming all sorts of twaddle as the most sacred scripture.

The Frankenstein monster of spiritualist manifestations was an east-quarter bargain made by America just at the moment when her own national science was maturing into a daylight endeavor capable of penetrating nature with new power. Transcendentalism, like European Romanticism, was an antidote to the seductive dangers of both Mammon, the materialist mind-set, and Lucifer, the unmoored angel of light whose promise of knowledge glimmered blindingly from the temples of Spiritualism, Mormonism, and Freemasonry. Thoreau's martial attitude, his sense that he was doing daily battle with a godless adversary, was as much historical reality as personal myth. His hermitage at Walden Pond was the hallmark of a new era in the evolution of human consciousness, wherein each and every individual meets his nemesis in the physical world, whose Siren song promises that it will fulfill all his heart's desires. Idealistic young American squires and lads embarking upon their Grail quests could no longer count on joining others in hopeful apprenticeship to sage Knights. The mystery school was now the world, where each individual human heart and mind was compelled to discover Truth amid a bewildering hall of mirrors. On the verge of his thirty-third birthday, Henry Thoreau had passed a whole series of tests and was ready for the highest of initiations.

CHAPTER 4

A Turning Point in Time

In Adam's fall
We sinned all.
In the new Adam's rise
We shall all reach the skies.
—*Journal*, February 12, 1851

Measuring

For one who was chronically accused of having his head in the clouds, Thoreau was the most exacting of men. His second manuscript journal volume, in May 1850, opens with his enthusiastic reflections upon his reading in the Hindu Vedas, then immediately turns to condemn the restricting dimensions of men's shoes: "A wise man will wear a shoe wide and large enough, shaped somewhat like a foot, and tied with a leather string, and so go his way in peace, letting his foot fall at every step." He also complained that he couldn't get clothes fashioned to the proper form. Thoreau's expectation of precision from others stemmed from his relentless requirement of accuracy in himself, a quality that found vocational expression in his work as a land surveyor. Having first advertised his services in 1848—"Areas warranted accurate within almost any degree of exactness" boasted his broadside—the spring of 1850 saw Thoreau busy with boundary work. In March he surveyed two lots owned by Emerson and acted as Emerson's attorney in a boundary dispute with a neighboring landowner. In April and May, along with more work for Emerson, he surveyed half a dozen other parcels; his reputation was impeccable, and in following years, he would do surveys for Concord's solidest citizens. County commissioners sought him out for road surveys; the selectmen of Concord and neighboring towns hired him to perambulate their borders; the Mill Dam Company employed him to determine the bounds of Concord's most valuable real estate; and in 1856, he went to Perth Amboy, New Jersey, to lay out house lots for Marcus Spring's soon-to-fail Fourierist commune. Thoreau's penchant for measuring was so strong that he notched twenty-four inches on his walking stick so that he always had a measuring rule at hand.[200]

"How many new relations a foot-rule alone will reveal," Thoreau wrote in A Week on the Concord and Merrimack Rivers, "and to how many things still this has not been applied! What wonderful discoveries have been, and may still be, made, with a plumb-line, a level, a surveyor's compass, a thermometer, or a barometer!" In Maine, with no standard yardstick available, he once measured a moose hide by tying knots in a canoe painter, later converting this into lengths of his umbrella, for final calculation against a ruler. (He went to such lengths, he said, "because [he] did not wish to be obliged to say merely that the moose was very large.") He and Channing, whose walks frequently found them stopping to tie their shoes, agreed that one could use the longevity of a shoelace as a unit of measure. To sound a river's depth, Thoreau recommended a heron's leg, since it had already measured every margin of riparian shoreline.[201]

In early May, in Haverhill to survey house lots, Thoreau visited the site of the Hannah Dustan homestead. In A Week, reflecting on his stop upon the Merrimack River island where Dustan and two fellow English captives had killed and scalped their Abenaki captors, Thoreau had transformed this bloody colonial encounter into a myth of redemption by imagining generations who had eaten apples from the tree upon whose trunk Dustan's infant's brains had been dashed out. A century and a half after the event, Thoreau found no apple tree nor house, just a three-foot-deep dimple in a cornfield marking the cellar hole. Still there were other things to be surveyed: He counted the number of ships in port (fourteen); the dimensions of windows in the old garrison house (two and a half feet long by one foot wide); a buttonwood tree on the bank of the Merrimack, said to have been one of twenty set out in 1739 (thirteen feet eight inches in circumference at three and a half feet off the ground). In the midst of all this measuring, he coined a new unit of measure for use in recording his travels—the "'itinerary distance' between two points." [202]

Thoreau didn't professionally survey a cemetery until 1854, when he laid out the lines of Concord's new Sleepy Hollow Cemetery, but his historical investigations frequently found him walking among the dead in their places of final rest. At the end of May, he visited an old graveyard in Lincoln where lay five British soldiers struck down at the Concord Fight in 1775, and he heard from the grandson of the man who buried the soldiers that one man had leaped up erect out of the ranks upon being shot. Thoreau's informant even had seen the bullet hole through the soldier's skull, after a phrenologist had secured permission from the selectmen to perform a postmortem characterological analysis of the two grenadiers' skulls. Thoreau loved all sorts of inscriptions, not just for the historical data they offered, but for their dimensional expression. In this same graveyard, he found the headstone of a runaway slave, and he transcribed the exact words line by line as they appeared on the stone. When he noted in his journal the text of an old trade sign of a Haverhill tailor and barber, Thoreau lettered it exactly as it appeared on the sign. He thought about the way Massachusetts farmers marked natural topographic and vegetative divisions with their fences and noted how these made fields appear larger than their actual extent. Time was as finely divided as space for Thoreau, whose inner almanac recognized hundreds of seasons unmarked on the standard calendar. About the twentieth of May, farmers drove their winter barn–bound cows to pasture for the first time. About the first of June, the buttercups blossoming marked the beginning of summer and the first cut of hay. [203]

Erratic events also had their seasons, though undetected by Thoreau. On May 31, after reflecting about the memorable occasion farm boys often experience in the fall—when, after driving their fathers' cows to distant pastures for the summer, they discover that the calf they haven't seen all summer now as a heifer still recognizes them—Thoreau suddenly wrote, "I once set fire to the woods." In the most matter-of-fact fashion, he detailed the unfolding of the catastrophe that had happened in April 1844, when he and Edward Hoar, son of Concord's squire Samuel Hoar, had been out on a rowboat excursion on the Sudbury River. Thoreau had made a fire in an old stump to cook a catch of fish into chowder, and sparks had set nearby dry grass on fire. The fire quickly spread to the dry scrub oak, huckleberry, and sweet fern chaparral on the sandy plain nearby, and eventually burned 100 to 150 acres. After running a couple of miles to alert a number of local men to the fire, an exhausted Thoreau found a perch on Fair Haven Cliffs and watched the conflagration. When the flames threatened to encircle his lookout, he descended and joined the group of men who were digging firebreaks and setting backfires to stop the blaze. The same evening he walked in the dark through the burned lands to the stump where he had first kindled the fire. Scattered over the blackened grass he found "the now broiled fish—which had been dressed." [204]

Thoreau's retrospective was full of this nonchalance about the incident, reflecting what he apparently felt at the time. The "shame and regret" he felt at the moment when the fire began quickly passed: "It has never troubled me from that day to this more than if the lightning had done it. The trivial fishing was all that disturbed me and disturbs me still." Instead of guilt, he felt anger for those who condemned him, while enjoying the great sport of fighting the fire. He belittled the farmer who owned some of the burned land; during the fire, Thoreau had led this man to the spot, and now he needed to ask Thoreau directions to get back home across his own land. Thoreau felt anger for the townspeople who thought him a "damned rascal" for setting fire to the woods. He protested privately in his journal that the railroad engine had since 1844 twice set fire to the same area and beyond. Ultimately he found the regenerating vegetation a "cheering and inspiring sight." Because it would be another decade before Thoreau himself would discover that the forest type growing in the location was itself the product of millennia of fire, he couldn't congratulate himself as an agent of ecological restoration, but he did claim that forest fires were advantageous to both nature and man. He noted that by destroying underbrush they favored the "larger and sturdier trees," which in turn made walking in recently burned woods much easier. The berry crop that arrived in two or three years after a burn was a boon to both birds and people. Thoreau speculated—with good reason—that New England's "noblest natural parks" were a consequence of "this accident." [205]

Biographers have psychologized the 1850 journal retelling of the fire in Concord's woods as motivated by Thoreau's lingering sense of guilt, but Thoreau clearly felt no guilt at all about his having set the fire. What Thoreau said about the rejuvenating effect of a fire—"it sweeps and ventilates the forest floor, and makes it clear and clean"—was equally true about his meditation upon it so many years after the fact. There was an alchemical aspect of this particular accident for Thoreau, as if in telling the story of the fire he burned away the dross of his old personality to leave behind a green and growing self. Ecologists and historians—in minutely detailing the meteorological conditions in the months leading up to the fire, the soil and vegetation growing on the site, and the lay of the local hills, which created a "fetch" that tunneled the light southwest wind that spread the fire so rapidly—have "explained" the fire but left unexplained Thoreau's singular role in igniting the event. Thoreau's account notes that they had forgotten matches and had borrowed some from the shoemaker who lived along the river. This last minute bit of luck underscores the contingency of the whole episode, and yet there is still a distinct hint of purposefulness at the heart of this accidental event. That denial of contingency was echoed by Thoreau's intense rumination upon this incident over six years after it occurred. The timing of his looking back upon the event is another expression of the septenary rhythm in human biography. Luther's aphorism—"The seventh year always transforms man"—applies not only to the rhythm beginning at birth, but for certain seminal events distributed throughout an individual's life. The 1844 "accident" needed seven years' incubation in Thoreau's soul before it could emerge as an exact and exacting measure of his own character. Only four days after reliving the 1844 fire through his writing about it, Thoreau spent a couple of days in Lincoln fighting a forest fire, learning how critical systematic and precise action was to preventing its spread. The experience left him certain that the circus of hundreds of untrained and unequipped men who typically showed up at a fire should be replaced with a company of forty or fifty men with access to rakes, hoes, and shovels and captained by officers who at the outbreak of a fire could convey the men and tools by wagon to the site. He assigned a key role to the fire company's drummer, who could convey signals through the smoky confusion by the beat of the drum. When someone responded to Thoreau's idea by saying that he would join up if "some delicious music" were substituted for the drum, Thoreau entertained the thought, saying that it might do well to refresh the weary firefighters upon their return. "Music is the proper regulator," he concluded. A musical, rhythmic pulse moved through Thoreau's life, wholly unheard by his contemporaries.[206]

An Actual Button

Thoreau found nothing particularly heroic or villainous in his having set ablaze a section of the Concord woods. The heroic ideal was still very much alive for him this spring, as he read Humboldt's account of Columbus. "The heroes and discoverers have found true more than was previously believed," wrote Thoreau, "only when they were expecting and dreaming of something more than their contemporaries dreamed of, when they were in a frame of mind prepared in some measure for the truth." The same day that he recorded his proposal for local fire brigades—in his mind, mere municipal institutions unmarked by heroic heraldry—Thoreau intimated his heroic ideal: "There [are] as many strata at different levels of life as there are leaves in a book. Most men probably lived in two or three. When on the higher levels we can remember the lower levels, but when on the lower we cannot remember the higher." To live always at the higher levels, elevated above the ephemeral concerns of the animal man, demanded a heroism unsung and unseen by modern men and women. Thoreau expected and dreamed of something more than his contemporaries; their disinterest in and disdain for him confirmed it. His own sense of striving felt somewhat attenuated this spring: "My imagination, my reverence and admiration, my sense of the miraculous, is not so excited by any event as by the remembrance of my youth. Men talk about Bible miracles because there are no miracles in their lives." If at age thirty-two he was less immediately living a life in the lap of the gods, still the memory of the gods stayed with him, seemingly contradicting his rule of thumb about levels of life: "We inspire friendship in men when we have contracted friendship with the gods. When we cease to sympathize with and to be personally related to men, and begin to be universally related, then we are capable of inspiring others with the sentiment of love for us.... We hug the earth—how rare we mount! how rarely, we climb a tree! We might get a little higher methinks.... Shall not a man have his spring as well as the plants? The halo around the shadow is visible both morning and evening." Thoreau knew that the human being is *always* divine, no matter how fully he might forget it.²⁰⁷

Of the men of the Concord circle, though, Thoreau clearly most closely resembled Victorian ideals of the heroic male. Alcott was a bumbling, frail fellow, full of faith but altogether lacking in manly vigor. The physically fit Channing—Thoreau's favorite walking companion—was a bit of an idler, a failure as husband and father. Even Emerson fell short; in good health, fond of exercise out-of-doors, he was all brain and no brawn, relying on Thoreau or hired men to execute the physical tasks around his own household. Countless times during their friendship, Emerson sent Thoreau to carry out errands from which Emerson's elevated position insulated and isolated him. On July 22, having learned that Margaret Fuller had died in a shipwreck at Fire Island, New York, Emerson dispatched Thoreau to the scene of the accident to gather what news he could and to search for any manuscripts that might have survived the accident.

Margaret Fuller had been living in Europe since August 1846, when, commissioned by *New York Tribune* editor Horace Greeley, she had crossed the Atlantic with Marcus and Rebecca Spring and their son. Fuller and the Springs shared with Greeley an intense commitment not only to abolitionism, feminism, prison reform, and urban philanthropy, but to European social revolution, and her articles for the *Tribune*, though reporting on rural landscapes and ruined castles along with her encounters with European literati living and dead, shared a common Romantic thread of lionizing the common man. Many if not most of the writers Fuller met while living in Europe—Harriet Martineau, Giuseppe Mazzini, William and Mary Howitt, George Sand, Adam Mickiewicz, Pierre Jean de Béranger, Félicité de Lamennais—played significant roles in promoting revolutionary causes and activities. In 1847 in Rome, having become separated from the Springs while at a vespers service at Saint Peter's Basilica, she was rescued by a gallant Italian named Giovanni Angelo Ossoli, a republican from an old family that had for generations served the pope. The daimonic Margaret Fuller, at home kept always from full expression by Boston convention, in Rome with Count Ossoli plunged passionately into politics and love. At the end of Carnival week in 1848, having just heard the news of the simultaneous revolutions in Paris and Vienna, she had stood with Adam Mickiewicz— soon to be known as the "Dante of Poland" for his leadership of the Polish Legion during revolutionary fighting in Florence—while Romans cried *"Miraculo! Providenza!"* and then dragged Austrian arms into the street and burned them.[208]

By the time that she boarded the *Elizabeth* in Livorno in May 1850 to return to America with Ossoli, Fuller was carrying with her both their two-year-old son (and to supply the not yet weaned boy's needs, a goat, a small flock of poultry, extra baby linen, and a medicine chest) and the manuscript of the book she had written about the revolution in Rome. The *Elizabeth* was a new vessel commanded by a captain from Maine; her cargo included 150 tons of Carrara marble and Hiram Powers's statue of John Calhoun. The ever superstitious Margaret had always been nervous about the sea, but despite her confidence in the captain (whose own faith was shown by the fact that his wife was sailing with him), she saw evil omens everywhere. The *Westmoreland*, carrying another of Powers's sculptures, had recently been wrecked; a Paris acquaintance died just before visiting Margaret, and on the same day, the steamer on which she had originally booked passage sank. She and Ossoli spent their last evening in Florence with Robert and Elizabeth Browning, who were as superstitious as Margaret, and after mentioning an old prediction that Ossoli should fear death by water, Elizabeth was shaken when she read the inscription in the Bible the Ossolis brought as a gift to the Brownings' son from the infant Angelino: "In memory of Angelo Eugene Ossoli." Then, after a week at sea, the captain became ill and ten days later died of smallpox while the ship was anchored at Gibraltar. The ship was quarantined, and no one appeared ill, but after two days at sea Angelino came down with a fever. "It is vain by prudence to seek to evade the stern assaults of Destiny, I submit," wrote Margaret to Marcus Spring.[209]

The boy recovered, the rest of the voyage was uneventful, and Margaret felt unusually well but for occasional back pain. Just before dawn on July 19, the *Elizabeth*, having been driven north along the New Jersey coast under hurricane-force winds, slammed into a sandbar off Fire Island. When Thoreau arrived on the twenty-fourth, much of the ship could still be seen hung up where it had struck. Thoreau heard from eyewitnesses how, while lifesaving crews stood helplessly upon shore, their mortars and surf boats ineffectual against the gale winds, Margaret sat "with her back to the foremast, with her hands on her knees, her husband and child already drowned. A great wave came and washed her aft." Sailors had buried Angelino in the dunes, and all that was found of Margaret and her husband were a broken desk holding no valuable papers, a black leather trunk full of books, and Ossoli's carpetbag and one of his shoes. Thoreau wrote to Emerson that he would go ahead to Patchogue, since this was where most of the wreck-pickers had come from. Greeley's newspaper reported that there had been massive plundering of flotsam from the ship even while Fuller and others waited on deck for rescue. As many as a thousand people scoured the beach the day after the wreck, and rumors circulated that pilferers buried bodies in the sand after stripping clothing and jewelry from the corpses. Margaret Fuller's plundered clothing was later discovered in someone's Patchogue home.[210]

Thoreau was no stranger to Margaret Fuller, having worked with her on the *Dial*, having tutored her brother Richard, and having as best friends both Fuller's brother-in-law Ellery Channing and her closest male friend, Emerson. But while Emerson, James Freeman Clarke, William Henry Channing, and others celebrated her passionate life and her inexhaustible capacity for friendship, the passionate celebrator of friendship Henry Thoreau showed no such loyalty. In a letter to Harrison Blake shortly after he returned from Fire Island, Thoreau's tone is so cold and distant that he appears to have no feeling of grief whatsoever for Fuller and her family. "I find that actual events, notwithstanding the singular prominence which we all allow them, are far less real than the creations of my imagination. They are truly visionary and insignificant,—all that we commonly call life and death,—and affect me less than my dreams.... I have in my pocket a button which I ripped off the coat of the Marquis of Ossoli, on the seashore, the other day. Held up, it intercepts the light,—an actual button, and yet all the life it is connected with is less substantial to me, and interests me less, than my faintest dream. Our thoughts are the epochs in our lives: all else is but as a journal of the winds that blew while we were here." This detachment is followed by a series of injunctions that suggest that Fuller's death, like the other losses Thoreau had sustained in his life, only redoubled his commitment to living nobly and well. "Do a little more of that work which you have confessed to be good.... Do not entertain doubts if they are not agreeable to you. . . . Do not read the newspapers. . . . Do not engage to find things as you think they are. Do what nobody else can do for you." The tragedy of the shipwreck only bound Thoreau more tightly to a faith in the triumph of the individual will. Months after the event, he told a bit more of the story of finding Giovanni Ossoli's coat. At Patch-ogue, a lighthouse keeper asked by Thoreau about possible remains or remnants of the Ossoli party had sent him a mile or two down a beach to a spot that he said was marked with a stick covered with a cloth. Expecting that it would be difficult to locate so small an object amid the vast expanse of sand and sea, Thoreau was stunned to find that "it was as conspicuous on that sandy plain as if a generation had labored to pile up a cairn there." The stick and the button were as much tokens of the significance—indeed, the necessity—of the isolated individual soul as they were emblems of the insubstantiality of the material world.[211]

An Ambrosial Summer

Homebody Henry Thoreau's summer of 1850 was book-ended with exotic excursions: Around the summer solstice he had made a second trip to Cape Cod, this time to Provincetown by steamer, and a few days after the equinox, he set out with Ellery Channing for Quebec. "What I got by going to Canada was a cold," declared the underwhelmed Yankee upon his return from Canada. His finest traveling this summer as in every summer was in Concord, whose jumble of hills and brooks and swamps and meadows offered as fine a landscape as the Falls of Mont-morency and the Plains of Abraham. The historical pageant that un-folded through Canada's colonial past had nothing on Concord's idiosyncratic annals, which for Thoreau were brought before his mind's eye on every walk. Americans this summer were reading Long-fellow's epic poems in his new collection *Seaside and Fireside*; Thoreau composed his own miniature epic set on the Old Marlborough Road leading from Jenny Dugan's Desert near the Nut Meadow Brook southwest into Sudbury—a land where they "once dug for money," the former abode of local legends Martial Miles, Elijah Wood, Elisha Dugan, and the Irishman Quin. It was dotted with "great guide-boards of stone," and Thoreau thought one might "go round the world by the Old Marlborough Road." By the Old Marlborough Road and all of Concord's other byways, Thoreau went right round the world to otherworlds:

> It is a real place,
> Boston, I tell it to your face.
> And no dream of mine
> To ornament a line
> I can not come nearer to God & Heaven
> Than I live to Walden ever.
> It is a part of me which I have not prophaned
> I live by the shore of me detained....
> I am its stoney shore
> And the breeze that passes o'er
> In the hollow of my hand
> Are its water and its sand;
> Its deepest resort
> Lies high in my thought

One poem composed this summer spoke of "Icarian thoughts returned to ground," and "going to heaven the long way round," while another pair considered the fall-blooming Roman wormwood, *Ambrosia elatior* (known more commonly as hogweed or bitterweed) as a reminder that "We trample underfoot the food of gods / & spill their nectar in each drop of dew." "'Tis very fit the ambrosia of the gods / Should be a weed on earth," Thoreau declared in the other *Ambrosia* poem, "For the gods are simple folks and we should pine / upon their humble fare." [212]

Though he made them out to be as commonplace as the wormwood, pigweed, amaranth, and polygonum that filled the fields at this season, the gods Thoreau knew still could send him to his knees in awe. In a place "not Mr. Bull's swamp . . . a far faraway field on the confines of the actual Concord where nature is partially present," Thoreau on All Hallows Eve once again met the goddess "clothed in white."

> Thou art a personality so vast & universal that I have never seen one of thy features . . . love makes fragrant all the atmosphere—It is because of nothing which he has done—or I—Someone has done it for us. My dear, my dewy sister—let thy rain descend on me. I not only love thee, but I love the best of thee; that is to love thee rarely. I do not love thee every day. I love thee on my great days—Thy dewy words feed me like the manna of the morning. I am as much thy sister as thy brother— Thou art as much my brother as my sister. It is a portion of thee & a portion of me which are of kin. Thou dost not have to woo me—I do not have to woo thee. O my sister! O Diana—thy tracks are on the eastern hills—Thou surely passed that way I, the hunter, saw them.— in the morning dew—my eyes are the hounds that pursue thee. Thou canst speak, I cannot. I hear & forget to answer I am occupied with hearing.—I awoke and thought of thee—thou wast present to my mind. How camest thou there? Was I not present to thee likewise?

A couple of weeks later, he was still haunted by this visionary encounter, noting that "We walked in so pure and bright a light, so softly and serenely bright, I thought I had never bathed in such a golden flood, without a ripple or a murmur to it. The west side of every wood and rising ground gleamed like the boundary of Elysium." The two pages preceding this entry, and four pages preceding the October 31 vision, were torn out, suggesting that both entries are fragments of longer reflections upon this experience, which were perhaps so intensely personal that Thoreau decided to keep them private. "Diana"—the same being as the "Maiden in the East" whom he met the summer of 1841, and the "Sister" of his summer 1849 vision—left her tracks not only upon the eastern hills, but upon the highest summits of Thoreau's soul. While other American visionaries—most notably at the moment, Andrew Jackson Davis, who continued to pour forth Swedenborgian tableaux of celestial creatures in his 1850 tome *Philosophy of Spiritual Intercourse*—shouted their raptures to all who would listen, Thoreau kept his share of an east-quarter bargain, preferring to secret this spiritual gold so as not to diminish its luster. He also remained fully grounded in plebeian verities. Directly following his reminiscence of his Elysian walk, he wrote in his journal: "Some circumstantial evidence is very strong, as when you find a trout in the milk." Thoreau continued this year to find strong circumstantial evidence of a divine world—as plain as the yellow *Ambrosia* pollen that dusted his shoes on his September walks. But as his poem noted, while his "honest shoes" perennially bore the marks of his ambrosial adventures, when he went to town he saw no "morning dew" on the shoes of his fellows, only "Gallic gloss." Concord and all America with it were so preoccupied with pasture hay or Main Street that the Old Marlborough Roads to higher pastures went untrodden by any shoes.[213]

A Record of My Love

Anyone wishing to chronicle Thoreau's thoughts and actions on a daily basis before November 16, 1850, cannot rely on his journal, for missing pages and dates outnumber the remaining dated journal leaves. Prior to this date, Thoreau rarely gave date headings to his entries; in 1850, only seven journal entries are headed by dates before November 16. For those eleven months of the year, just another dozen or so dates occur at all in the body of the journal entries. After November 16, Thoreau almost never missed a daily entry, and assumed the habitual practice of heading each day's journal entry with the date. Beginning with this November 16 entry, Thoreau's journaling practice transforms entirely, becoming a laboratory for phenomenological perception and description. Whereas previously he had on dated days typically taken up individual questions, told single discrete stories, or noted particular places or people, and in undated entries separated subjects from one another slightly, now a single day's reflections would come cascading one upon another, alternating between diurnal or seasonal arcana and perennial philosophical discussions. November 16 opens with Thoreau's report that he has found three arrowheads while out walking, then declares that he regards the tiniest tributary brook with the same awe he would feel for the Orinoco or Mississippi; his next paragraph claims that it is always the wild element in literature that is most compelling; he discovers that cranberries are fine fare as one crosses meadows, wonders what alarm a blue jay is sounding in some birch grove, muses on how he chooses his bearing when setting out on a walk, wrestles with his antipathy and sympathy toward friends, confesses that the scream of a cat whose tail was caught by a closing door drove off celestial thoughts, asks why shrub oaks keep their leaves all winter, observes black walnut trees heavy with nuts and birches bare but for their catkins, notes the late autumn burst of blossoming by spring herbs, hears cows running scared in the woods, asks what salvation there might be for men who are afraid of the dark if "God is silent and mysterious," discovers that some of our brightest days are ones when the sun is not shining, comments that land where trees have been cut off and are rejuvenating is called "sprout land," questions whether the partridgeberry shouldn't be called "checkerberry," laments the loss of wild apple trees, and closes with this extraordinary—though for Thoreau altogether ordinary—declaration:

> My Journal should be a record of my love. I would write in it only the things I love, my affection for any aspect of the world, what I love to think of. I have no more distinctness or pointedness in my yearnings than an expanding bud, which does indeed point to flower and fruit, to summer and autumn, but is aware of the warm sun and spring influences only. I feel ripe for something, yet do nothing, can't discover what that thing is. I feel fertile merely. It is seedtime with me. I have lain fallow long enough.

Notwithstanding a sense of unworthiness which possesses me, not without reason, notwithstanding that I regard myself as a good deal of a scamp, yet for the most part the spirit of the universe is unaccountably kind to me, and I enjoy perhaps an unusual share of happiness. Yet I question sometimes if there is not some settlement to come.

With this entry, he had already begun practicing his intended goal for his journal: The string of reflections is punctuated with "I love to pause in mid-passage" (crossing fences); "I love my friends"; "I love nature, I love the landscape." "I love" hereafter becomes one of the journal's most characteristic expressions.[214]

Thoreau had always had a keen sense of seasonality, of turning points in time marking transformation and change, but after November 16, 1850, it becomes the main leitmotif of his journal. The following day, November 17, he finds in a field of winter rye what he at first takes to be a smooth white pebble, but as he picks it up, it breaks, and he finds it is a snapping turtle egg. "The little turtle was perfectly formed, even to the dorsal ridge, which was distinctly visible." Seeing into biological form as it unfolds in time becomes the central quest of Thoreau's life after this November, and the daily logging of observations in his journal is his main method for accomplishing that quest. Two days later, he breaks off a shrub oak leaf, and finds the cambium layer still green, inspiring a diligent search for life in warm, south-facing places. This marks the beginning of his search for precise moments in the stages of plant growth, when time stands still for an instant as what for weeks or months had been stem and leaf suddenly erupts into flower, or for days had been flower metamorphoses into seed. A parallel mystery struck him as he watched wheeling flocks of migrant birds: "Now . . . you will see flocks of small birds forming compact and distinct masses, as if they were not only animated by one spirit but actually held together by some invisible fluid or film, and will hear the sound of their wings rippling or fanning the air as they flow through it, flying, the whole mass, ricochet like a single bird, or as they flow over the fence." What was the "invisible fluid" that allowed the flock to act as one body? What invisible agent guided so precisely the embryonic form of the snapping turtle or signaled plants when to leaf out, flower, and fruit?[215]

Nineteenth-century life science's attempt to discover the nature of this "invisible fluid" had largely been derailed by the taint of mesmerism and its attendant charlatanry, and so successful was the mechanistic model that replaced the romantic biology being forged by Thoreau and others that a century and a half later, no acceptable scientific language exists with which to speak about the formative forces that fascinated Thoreau. Despite the popularity with nonscientists of Carl von Reichenbach's theory of "odic force," the *ether*—the most popular term at the time for the medium in which these postulated subtle forces operated—was already by 1850 conceived of by the scientific community as a physical agent. Orthodox nineteenth-century biology progressively moved away from explanations built upon archetypal forms or invisible forces. Though undoubtedly acquainted with Reichenbach's and other vitalist theories, Thoreau never explicitly discussed them. He was content to observe and chronicle the rhythmic movement of the invisible fluid.

Though he criticized himself for lying fallow, his life was also unfolding according to some mysterious fluidic rhythm. Up until November 16, 1850, Thoreau's destiny had been to craft an authentic life in the face of a society growing less and less authentic, and he did this principally by attending to the divinity within and around human nature. Now, almost at a single stroke, he would become America's premier chronicler of Nature, specifically by attending scrupulously to its rhythmicity.

Thoreau still considered himself blessed, his only reservation being that he had not accomplished some as yet undefined task. A couple of weeks before, he had had a long discussion with Emerson during which Emerson maintained that America, unlike England, was not yet prepared to realize its destiny, as it "want[ed] a fortnight's more sun." Thoreau disagreed, saying that the English were "mere soldiers . . . in the world," whose role in world history was "winding up." America, Thoreau believed, was to be a "pioneer . . . unwinding his lines." Within the body of that pioneering republic, Thoreau was a pioneer unwinding the lines of his destiny in a rhythm that could be seen only long after his last waves had beat upon the shore.[216]

A Saunterer in Life

This summer Thoreau's family had moved into the "Yellow House" on Main Street, and Thoreau had taken up residence in the finished attic room. His writing energy this year was poured into his journal; he published nothing, wrote few letters, and gave only four lectures. He took a hiatus from revising *Walden*, adding nothing to the manuscript until the beginning of 1852. The journal now more faithfully than ever records the daily juxtaposition of the sublime and the mundane, in the process humbling heaven and elevating earth. "It is a common saying among country people that if you eat much fried hasty pudding it will make your hair curl," Thoreau says, then confesses that his own considerable experience contradicts this belief. Concord's dirt farmers amaze him with their perspicacity; Horace Hosmer discovers in his cranberrying a new variety undetected by professional botanists. Alex Therien tells him of catching trout in a box trap and of carving pine logs into sap buckets and sumac and white ash branches into spouts. A Mr. Gleason directs him to a Norway (red) pine—Thoreau has never seen one before—behind Joe Meriam's house. He composes a beautiful poem for Johnny Riordan, an Irish boy living in a shanty. Pained by the deprivation of the boy's indigent home, he celebrates his simple faith:

> My mother does not cry,
>   And my father does not scold
> For I am a little Irish boy,
>   And I'm four years old . . .

> And if my feet ache
> I do not mind the cold,
> For I am a little Irish boy,
> And I'm four years old.[217]

The simplest scenes send Thoreau into ecstatic states where, instead of leaving his body and the earth, he enters more deeply into them. Walking between Conantum Cliffs and Fair Haven Bay just after the last witch hazel blossoms have gone by, Thoreau comes upon a place where a white pine woods meets a shrub oak hillside, and feels it "far away, yet actual and where we have been," like the dreams of his youth. Feeling "a certain flash as of hazy lightning, flooding all the world suddenly with a tremulous serene light," he walks on, and all that he looks upon overwhelms him with its absolutely unquestionable fitness:

> I did not see how it could be improved. Yet I do not see what these things can be. I begin to see such an object when I cease to *understand* it and see that I did not realize or appreciate it before, but I get no further than this. How adapted these forms and colors to my eye! A meadow and an island! What are these things? Yet the hawks and the ducks keep so aloof! and Nature is so reserved! I am made to love the pond and the meadow, as the wind is to ripple the water.

This moment of ecstatic participation was fleeting but unforgettable. Eleven weeks later he spoke of this episode again, repeating almost verbatim the words he wrote in November but expanding the "I" to "we," turning his singular experience into a general epistemological law: "We shall see but little if we require to understand what we see."[218]

Thoreau went to see a group of Indians—he does not identify them, but it may have been a band of Penobscot, Passamaquoddy, or perhaps even Abenaki, down from Canada to visit old haunts—camped in tents along the Concord River in late November, and his notes are direct reportage, free of the simultaneous sentimentalizing and censuring of his previous thinking about Indians. They showed him a set of moose antlers, told how they fashioned a papoose cradle out of the broadest section, and also used them to divine future events. He noted that caribou horns in their tents had been gnawed by mice and that the Indians estimated the population of moose to be about the same as it had been fifty years before. The Indian hunters demonstrated moose, caribou, and deer calls with a birch bark horn, showed him their fishing spears, birch bark buckets, sleds, and canoe. Thoreau rarely and rudimentarily sketched what he saw, but the ingenuity of the Indian devices compelled him to make a set of small drawings, particularly of their animal traps. With no editorial commentary at all, he describes a little device they had, of stick, string, and leaves, called an *ar-tu-e-se*, which they used to "make the clouds go off the sun." Since his trip to Canada in September, he had embarked on an ambitious program of reading in the literature of early exploration of North America, and this had quickly become a systematic research effort to understand the "red face of man."[219]

Winter's snows shut up Concord's cows, so cowherds—and "cowards"—vanished from remote pastures and hills, but Thoreau kept up his daily walks, appreciative of the extra solitude brought on by winter. Winter's bareness afforded all manner of revelation unavailable in the green months; shrubs and trees inconspicuous at other seasons now leaped out in full silhouette; frozen ponds could be traversed easily, and Thoreau discovered new plants like sweet gale and panicled andromeda on islands previously unexplored; sour, inedible crabbed apples after repeated freezing and thawing were full of sweet cider; wind patterns could be studied from the humping and hollowing of snow, and the winter deposition of sand and stones from cut banks was revealed to leave lines of demarcation as pronounced as the pine pollen which ringed Walden Pond in summer. New walks could be traced out, like the path following the line of bare ground or snow just between the high water mark and the present water line of wet meadows.

Winter's highlighting of essentials was conducive to poetry. In February 1851 Thoreau wrote four poems reflecting on the meaning of his own life and of life for all who were given the gift of it. Comparing his life to "a stately warrior horse," Thoreau asks when the horseman's "rambling head and neck" will meld with "that firm and brawny beast." He overcomes his hesitancy about his destiny, declaring "my unresting steed holds on its way," and then the steed becomes a ship with "expanded sail," and an eagle with "unwearied wings," all tropes of triumph. Another poem allows that while moon, brook, and meteors move "without impediment, ... No charitable laws alas cut me / An easy orbit round the sun," his current never "rounds into a lake," nor does his life "drop freely but a rod ... as Meteors do." A third poem gives thanks for this very fact, that by aiming at "the splendid heights above," he inevitably must fall along the way. Out of this richly textured life he lifts the image of an "unanxious hen" bragging of a new laid egg—"Now let the day decline / They'll lay another by tomorrow's sun." The last poem—"Manhood"—though taking as its subject other men, is pure Thoreau. Beginning "I love to see the man ... as yet uninjured by worldly taint" and continuing "But better still I love ... " him who "proudly bears his small degen'racy." Thoreau at thirty-three had seen enough of life to know that its nobility lay in the fight against mere fatedness, that "man's eminence" sprang from his undying resolve to make his own fate. The brave man was finally he who, though struck down repeatedly, never lost sight of his high goal.[220]

Such sentiments would seem to put Thoreau at the center of the human community, but he was still a marginal man for all his poetic wisdom about life. (This summer, telling of how the jailer, Sam Staples, spoke to him as if he were an errand boy, Thoreau owned how "there is some advantage in being the humblest, cheapest, least dignified man in the village, so that the very stable boys shall damn you.") Indeed, it was his wisdom that put him on the outs. "Almost all that my neighbors call good I believe in my soul to be bad," the contrarian Thoreau declared. "If I repent of anything, it is of my good behavior. ... I hear an irresistible voice, the voice of my destiny, which invites me away from all that." That voice was eloquently loquacious in this annus mirabilis, speaking to Thoreau at all hours and places. Going into the cellar to bring up firewood, he heard a voice speak "a commonplace suggestion," and at first took it to be his own, then realized "it was the voice of a god who had followed me down the cellar to speak to me." The voice of his genius spoke a familiar dialect: "Improve your time," it hinted one July morning as he awoke. His own voice was in harmony with the unbidden voice of his genius: "There is no account of the blue sky in history. Before I walked in the ruts of travel; now I adventured." Walking continually carried him to such high escapades that he confidently claimed a genius for sauntering, then playfully reinvented that word's origins from its associations with the pilgrims of the Middle Ages, going *à la Sainte Terre*. A saunterer was a "Holy-Lander" like himself, while any who walked with less lofty destinations in mind were "mere idlers and vagabonds." [221]

Thoreau's high ideals continued to ostracize him from the opinions and activities of his neighbors. At the end of March, runaway slave Thomas Sims was sent back to his owner by a Boston judge upholding the provisions of the Fugitive Slave Act. To appease the South for the admission of California as a free state, Northern legislators had passed this law mandating that federal marshals help slave owners recapture escaped slaves. The penalty for noncompliance was $1,000, and the law established a bounty system for federal commissioners deciding the status of suspected fugitives; the commissioners were paid $10 if they found in favor of the slave owner, $5 if in favor of the slave. In the decade after the law was enacted, 332 blacks were returned to slavery while only 11 were declared free. The Boston judge's action enraged Thoreau, who condemned all those complicit in this injustice, including the press, the Church, and the governor of Massachusetts. Coming but one week before the celebration of the Concord Fight, Thoreau found it outrageous that his neighbors would ring bells and fire cannon to celebrate the courage and the love of liberty of the few hundred men who assembled at Concord Bridge, but not one neighbor—save Daniel Foster of Concord, who protested on the Boston wharf—was mindful of the three million men, women, and children held in slavery. Upon hearing the celebratory bells and cannon of the Concord Fight anniversary, every "human and intelligent citizen of Concord," Thoreau declared, should have thought of the events of April 12, 1851, not April 19, 1775. "Of course it makes not the least bit of difference—I wish you to consider this—who the man was, whether he was Jesus Christ or another,—for inasmuch as ye did it unto the least of these his brethren ye did it unto him. Do you think *he* would have stayed here in liberty and let the black man go into slavery in his stead?" Thoreau was ashamed that all but a few friends of liberty would allow a law whose "natural habitat is in the dirt" to supersede the higher law.[222]

Hypoethral

The high moral standards Thoreau demanded of others he worked assiduously to practice himself. He was not puritanical, but loved purity, aspiring always to chasteness in all his personal relations. Finding himself impure by his own standards, he knew well that he was better than the "mass of men," who had "little love and reverence" for chastity. Reading in Hindu scripture this spring heightened his sensitivity to the possibility of a purer and higher life. He learned of the yogis and rishis who emancipated themselves from sensual desire and thereby made themselves available to divine thoughts. Thoreau took particular interest in the Hindu concept of Purusha, the Cosmic Man or *mahat* ("the great"), both conceived as a spiritual substance indwelling in the physical body but capable of returning to the "eternal body." "It is mysterious wisdom, the perpetual sacrifice made by the virtue of the *Yoga*, the fire which animates animals, shines in the sun, and is mingled with all bodies. Its nature is to be born and to die, to pass from repose to movement." Though different from the *akasha* of Hindu philosophy, which, with the concept of *prana*, constitutes much of what Western esoteric thought conceives of as the "etheric," Purusha appeared to Thoreau as a potential principle for linking heaven and earth.[223]

Out of the blue one day in June, Thoreau mused a little about his book *A Week on the Concord and Merrimack Rivers*, saying that its merit was its "*hypoethral* character," meaning that it was like Egyptian temples, "open to the heavens above, *under the ether*." In America, "under the ether" was coming to have an entirely different meaning, as dentists and physicians sent patients into unconsciousness with ethyl ether gas. Thoreau underwent the experience himself when he had a tooth extracted:

> By taking the ether the other day I was convinced how far asunder a man could be separated from his senses. You are told that it will make you unconscious, but no one can imagine what it is to be unconscious— how far removed from the state of consciousness and all that we call "this world"—until he has experienced it. The value of the experiment is that it does give you experience of an interval as between one life and another, a greater space than you ever traveled. You are a sane mind without organs, groping for organs, which if it did not soon recover its old senses would get new ones. You expand like a seed in the ground. You exist in your roots, like a tree in the winter. If you have an inclination to travel, take the ether; you go beyond the furthest star.

But for all this travel, Thoreau hardly recommended the trip. "It is not necessary for them to take ether, who in their sane and waking hours are ever translated by a thought, nor for them to see with their hindheads, who sometimes see from their foreheads; nor listen to the spiritual knockings, who attend to the intimations of reason and conscience." Thoreau was transcendental enough without the help of ether. "It is a certain faeryland where we live.... I wonder that I ever get five miles on my way, the walk is so crowded with events and phenomena." On a beautiful June night—"not too warm, moon not quite full, after two or three rainy days"—Thoreau walked to Fair Haven along the railroad. Accompanied by whip-poor-wills, nighthawks, and fireflies, he moved through different strata of air and approached the ecstasy of his youth: "Ah, that life that I have known! How hard it is to remember what is most memorable! We remember how we itched, not how our hearts beat. I can sometimes recall to mind the quality, the immortality, of my youthful life, but in memory is the only relation to it." [224]

The far-off faeryland of youth was still available to Thoreau in the dawn hours of each day. "My most sacred and memorable life is commonly on awaking in the morning. I frequently awake with an atmosphere about me as if my unremembered dreams had been divine, as if my spirit had journeyed to its native place, and in the act of reentering its native body, had diffused an elysian fragrance around." No contemporary came as close as this statement to an understanding of what transpires for the human being each morning as sleep yields to wakefulness. The native place to which Thoreau's spirit soared was the "Moon" world of Neoplatonism, known in Hindu metaphysics— perhaps the most elaborate in human history—as *kama* (desire), and soon to become known in Western esoteric literature as the "astral world." When Thoreau's astral body—the nonphysical emotional body intermediate between the etheric body and the ego or "I"—each evening flew back to its home in the astral world, it was restored to wholeness and harmony, and upon waking, a dim memory of that ambrosial condition lingered. More than most other men of his time, Thoreau's divine self was not left behind on the opposite bank of the River Lethe but followed him like the fog across the Musketaquid, so that he could "revolutionize" each day, becoming a wakeful creator rather than a somnambulic consumer at the creation. [225]

This June Thoreau was reading Charles Darwin's *Voyage of the Beagle,* his account of the five-year voyage around the Southern hemisphere that became the impetus for his theory of the origin of species by natural selection. Thoreau loved Darwin's eye for detail, so much like his own, which conjured before his imagination the most exotic scenes: an Argentinian gaucho sharpening his knife on the back of an armadillo before killing him, hail in Buenos Aires as large as apples, tree ferns in Van Diemen's Land six feet in circumference, icebergs in Patagonia, Darwin himself riding on the back of a Galápagos tortoise. Thoreau noted Darwin's theories of coral atoll formation, the greater variation in individual plants propagated by sexual rather than asexual reproduction, and Darwin's keen interest in the stunning diversity of the Galápagos fauna and flora. Struck by Darwin's contention that the only religious rite practiced by Tierra del Fuegians was the observation of silence during a feast on whale blubber, Thoreau concluded that "it suggests that even the animals have something divine in them and akin to revelation, some inspirations allying them to man as to God." [226]

Ascribing animality to the native peoples of those antipodal islands was a harsh—but typical—ethnocentric attitude, but Thoreau's statement suggests how convinced he was of the divinity of the human being, a conviction that Darwin's theory of evolution would soon do much to diminish. Man, Thoreau believed, was "the crowning fact, the god we know. . . . Who shall say that there is no God, if there is a *just* man." To him, these were not statements of faith, but of *fact*, as sound reportage of his experience as the *Voyage of the Beagle* narrative was of Darwin's. "We have the material of heaven here. I think that the standing miracle to man is man." That the author of these affirmations ever was accused of being a misanthrope is astonishing. Thoreau's acquaintance with the Galápagos Islands and Tierra del Fuegos of the astral world gave him the authority to speak with confidence about the nature of human divinity, an authority he found absent in most of his fellows. "I am struck by the fact that . . . though any knowledge of, or communication from, 'Providence' is the rarest thing in the world, yet men very easily regarding themselves in the gross, speak of carrying out the designs of Providence as nations. How often the Saxon man talks of carrying out the designs of Providence, as if he had some knowledge of Providence and His designs. . . . This 'Providence' is the stalest jest in the universe. The office-boy sweeps out his office 'by the leave of Providence.'" [227]

Thoreau's childhood longing to know what lay behind the stars had not abated; he still could not observe them without feeling them to be a physical manifestation of a higher invisible realm. Going with Anthony Wright out to the home of Perez Blood—who reminded Thoreau of Tycho Brahe—to see the night sky through Blood's telescope, he was irked by Wright's telling him of digging a grave for a former pupil of Thoreau's:

> I am astonished to observe how willing men are to lumber their minds with such rubbish—to permit idle rumors, tales, incidents, even of an insignificant kind, to intrude upon what should be the sacred ground of the thoughts. Shall the temple of our thought be ... a dusty, noisy, trivial place? Or shall it be a quarter of heaven itself, a place consecrated to the service of the gods, a hypoethral temple? ... it behooves us to preserve the purity and sanctity of the mind. . . . Even the facts of science may dust the mind by their dryness, unless they are in a sense effaced each morning, or rather rendered fertile by the dews of fresh and living truth. . . .
>
> Knowledge does not come to us by details but by *lieferungs* from the gods. What else is it to wash and purify ourselves? Conventionalities are as bad as impurities. Only thought which is expressed by the mind in repose—as it were, lying on its back and contemplating the heavens—is adequately and fully expressed. What are sidelong, transient passing half views? The writer expressing his thought must be as well seated as the astronomer contemplating the heavens; he must not occupy a constrained position. . . .

A few days later, Thoreau visited the Harvard Observatory, where he learned from William Cranch Bond that astronomers at the Smithsonian were attempting to catalog the stars, and that Harvard could not assist because its telescope was so small. Thoreau, as usual favoring the bodily senses over remote instrumental sensing of phenomena, was delighted to hear from Bond that useful observations of changes in stellar brilliancy and other facts might still be made with the naked eye.[228]

As the sun came round again this year to its same position beneath the stars as on July 12, 1817, when he had left his home in the stars to come to earth, Thoreau again was haunted by a Wordsworthian nostalgia for his childhood:

Methinks my present experience is nothing; my past experience is all in all. I think that no experience which I have today comes up to or is comparable with the experiences of my boyhood—And not only this is true—but as far back as I can remember I have unconsciously referred to the experiences of a previous state of existence.... Formerly, methought, nature developed as I developed, and grew up with me. My life was extacy. In youth before I lost any of my senses—I can remember that I was all alive—and inhabited my body with inexpressible satisfaction, both its weariness & its refreshment were sweet to me. The earth was the most glorious musical instrument, and I was audience to its strains. To have such sweet impressions made on us—such extacies begotten of the breezes. I can remember how I was astonished. I said to myself—I said to others—There comes into my mind or soul an indescribable infinite all-absorbing divine heavenly pleasure, a sense of elevation & expansion—and have nought to do with it. I perceive that I am dealt with by superior powers. This is a pleasure, a joy, and existence which I have not procured myself—I speak as a witness on the stand and tell what I have perceived. The morning and evening were sweet to me, and I led a life aloof from society of men. I wondered if a mortal had ever known what I knew. I looked in books for some recognition of kindred experience—but strange to say, I found none. Indeed I was slow to discover that other men had had this experience—for it had been possible to read books & to associate with men on other grounds.

The maker of me was improving me. When I detected this interference I was profoundly moved. For years I marched as to a music in comparison with which the military music of the streets is noise & discord. I was daily intoxicated and yet no man could call me intemperate.

With all your science can you tell how it is—& whence it is, that light comes into the soul?

His birthday only added to Thoreau's sense of unfulfilled promise: "Here I am 34 years old, and yet my life is almost wholly unexpanded. How much is the germ! There is such an interval between my ideal and the actual in many instances that I may say I am unborn." And yet he consoled himself with the belief that he was merely out of sync with grander rhythms:

> Methinks my seasons revolve more slowly than those of nature; I am differently timed. I am contented. This rapid revolution of nature, even of nature in me, why should it hurry me? Let a man step to the music which he hears, however measured. Is it important that I should mature as soon as an apple tree? aye, as soon as an oak? May not my life in nature, in proportion as it is supernatural, be only the spring and infantile portion of my spirit's life?

Hardly a man in America was as much at home upon the earth as Henry Thoreau; hardly a man felt as much that he was an orphaned angel, a fallen star. "The society which I was made for is not here," he lamented. "Shall I, then, substitute for the anticipation of that this poor reality? . . . Shall I with pains erect a heaven of blue glass over myself, though when it is done I shall be sure to gaze still on the true ethereal heaven far above, as if the former were not,—that still distant sky o'erarching that blue expressive eye of heaven?" As this thirty-third year of his life closed, Thoreau had clearly recapitulated the Fall, feeling the full force of his earthly incarnation while never losing sight of the stars.[229]

On July 21, the cosmic forces playing through Thoreau were so active that he made four separate entries for the day in his journal. At eight A.M., he tells how he yearns "for one of those old, meandering, dry, uninhabited roads which lead away from towns," where his "head [was] more in heaven than [his] feet . . . on earth." Paraphrasing John's Gospel, he requires that "it must simply be the way and the life, a way that was never known to be repaired, nor to need repair, within the memory of the oldest inhabitant." The way he speaks of is the Way, the unimpeded path of spirit and soul toward the Godhead. Finding the track of a bare foot in the dusty road moves him deeply, the nakedness restoring the possibility of authenticity in the maker. At nine A.M. on the Conantum Cliffs, after an indigo bunting flies past him toward its nest, a voice speaks to him: "Remember thy Creator in the days of thy youth. Lay up a store of natural influences— sing while you may before the evil days come—he that hath ears let him hear—see—hear—smell—taste—&c while these senses are fresh & pure." Then he hears "a kind of fine Aeolian harp music . . . in the hollow mansions of the upper air." When he asks who hears when "the quail, in- visible, whistles," he means to say that the harpist he hears is also invisible, and that *he* hears both the quail and the Aeolian harp, though one might be more easily discovered than the other. At ten A.M., he finds the white lily opened on the river, an emblem of his own faithful unfolding under the light of the sun, and at eight thirty in the evening, as villagers and farmers mingle in conversation and music can be heard from within the houses, he works out a formula for virtuous conduct in hopes that it might settle on society "like the morning dew." Soon Thoreau would be intent on creating a calculus for knowing just when the turning point came in the seasons of countless Concord phenomena, but in the midst of his close chronicling, he remained largely opaque to the calculus for his own inner seasons. What ethereal rhythms ran through his subtle body to make such a festival of this one July day?[230]

Harp Music

This culminating year in Thoreau's life saw a blossoming of his physical as well as his subtle body. He took to repeated skinny-dipping in Con- cord's ponds, and on his walks would strip down to his hat and carry his clothes above his head when he crossed a river. His walks grew longer, and he never complained of any illness. His senses, always acute, were more alert than ever. At Bear Garden Hill, southeast of Walden Pond on an August evening, he heard "the sound of a flute, or a horn, or a human voice." Thoreau's sense of hearing was exceptional; he frequently reported birdcalls, church bells, and human conversations heard over great distances, but this mysterious evening music—like the Aeolian harp he heard by day—was heard in Concord and almost in all America by Thoreau alone. Thoreau's hesitancy in identifying the source of the sound is understandable, as is his hesitancy to disclose overtly his own sense of what he was hearing. He offers a wonderful riddle instead:

> It is a performer I never see by day; should not recognize him if pointed out; but you may hear his performance in every horizon. He plays but one strain and goes to bed early. . . . He is Apollo watching the flocks of Admetus on every hill, and this strain he plays every evening to remind him of his heavenly descent. . . . He is highly related, I have no doubt; was tenderly nurtured in his infancy, poor hind as he is. . . . The elements recognize him, and echo his strain. All the dogs know him their master, though lords and ladies, rich men and learned, know him not. . . .

This music appears in two poems from 1851. In "Music," it bursts from "some azure chink in the dull clouds / Of sense," to rescue him from despondency over his "sin" of succumbing to a life of mere physicality. In "The Just Made Perfect," Thoreau mentions others who can hear the music:

> A stately music rises on my ear,
> Borne on the breeze from some adjacent vale;
> A host of knights, my own true ancestors,
> Tread to the lofty strains and pass away
> In long procession, to this music's sound
> The Just move onward in deep serried ranks,

> With looks serene of hope, and gleaming brows,
> As if they were the temples of the Day.

These just knights are spiritual beings who, like Thoreau, press forward toward "the Heart of hearts," "their great Commander," God, the master musician of the spheres. Thoreau clearly had the gift of hearing into some east quarter of the cosmos, where he caught strains of celestial music.[231]

What was true of hearing—that there were strains of sound unheard by most men—was doubly true of sight. Reading the *Annual of Scientific Discovery* for 1851, Thoreau thought the "astronomer is as blind to the significant phenomena, as the wood-sawyer who wears glasses to defend his eyes from sawdust. The question is not what you look at, but what you see." Yet even Thoreau worried that his appetite for natural detail, the appetite that waxed this year as his pursuit of poetry waned, kept him from seeing. "I fear that the character of my knowledge is from year to year becoming more distinct and scientific; that in exchange for views as wide as heaven's cope, I am being narrowed down to the field of the microscope. I see details, not wholes nor the shadow of the whole. I count some parts, and say, 'I know.'" Thoreau may have been practicing natural history now instead of writing poetry, but the poet was still his polestar. "The poet must be continually watching the moods of his mind as the astronomer watches the aspect of the heavens. What might we not expect from a long life faithfully spent in this wise—the humblest observer would see some stars shoot.... Catalogue stars—those thoughts whose orbits are as rarely calculated as comets. It matters not whether they visit my mind or yours—whether the meteor falls in my field or yours—only that it come from heaven." At the end of 1850, the Boston Society of Natural History had made him a member, and at the moment he was reading Augustus Gould's *Principles of Zoology* and George Cuvier's *The Animal Kingdom*, but Thoreau hardly aspired to these circumscribed provinces of knowledge. His practice was still thoroughly transcendental: "I am not concerned to express that kind of truth which Nature has expressed. Who knows but I may suggest some things to her. Time was when she was indebted to such suggestions from another quarter—as her present advancement shows. I deal with the truths that recommend themselves to me—please me—not those merely which any system has voted to accept." His territorial tone brooks no compromise: "You shall observe what occurs in your latitude, I in mine." "My profession is to be always on the alert to find God in nature," he told himself, "to know his lurking-places." [232]

Thoreau's "meteorological journal of the mind" found the higher aspects of the most mundane phenomena. Hornets' nests, leaves of rattlesnake plantain, carpenters laying new planking on Hubbard's Bridge, the relation of insects and birds to their host plants, a snake devouring a toad—encountered by Thoreau, all of these became revelations both about the things themselves and a host of other things and relations. In September, on the very day that the first telegraph messages were conveyed over the new line erected along the railroad, Thoreau heard its humming "as the sound of a far-off glorious life, a supernal life, which came down to us, and vibrated the lattice-work of this life of ours." Just a week before, he had been considerably less sanguine about the arrival of the new technology; watching the laborers erect the wire, he said it was "a work which admits of the greatest latitude of ignorance and bungling—and as if you might set your hired man with the poorest head and hands to building a magnetic telegraph. All great inventions stoop thus low to succeed, for the understanding is but little above the feet. They preserve so low a tone; they are simple almost to coarseness and commonplaceness." A week after the first transmission, the low invention had become for Thoreau one more celestial instrument:

At the entrance to the Deep Cut, I heard the telegraph wire vibrating like an Aeolian harp. It reminded me suddenly... of what finer and deeper stirrings I was susceptible, which grandly set all argument and dispute aside, a triumphant though transient exhibition of the truth. It told me by the faintest imaginable strain, it told me by the finest strain that a human ear can hear, yet conclusively and past all refutation, that there were higher, infinitely higher, planes of life, which it vibrated as it passed. I instantly sat down on a stone at the foot of the telegraph pole, and attended to the communication. It merely said: "Bear in mind, Child, and never for an instant forget, that there are higher planes, infinitely higher planes, of life than this thou art travelling on. Know that the goal is distant, and is upward, and is worthy of all your life's efforts to attain to." And then it ceased, and though I sat some minutes longer, I heard nothing more.[233]

The telegraph came late to Concord, considering how early its advent had been. In 1826, when Thoreau was just nine years old, a Concord resident named Harrison Dyer had strung a telegraph wire up Monument Street, to transmit the signal of his telegraphic device, which used a chemical medium—moist litmus paper—to record the signals. America at that moment was not yet ready for this infernal machine that could carry human thoughts through space in an instant. Dyer, continuing his early Concord experiments in Long Island, ended up fleeing the country to escape prosecution after he was accused of conspiring to carry on secret communication. Samuel F. B. Morse's interest in developing an electromagnetic telegraph, which eventually superseded all inventions based on a chemical method, was initiated when in 1832, on a transatlantic crossing, Morse met Dr. Charles T. Jackson and they discussed the experiments that Jackson had witnessed in France. By the time their ship had docked in New York, Morse had an elaborate set of drawings for a telegraphic system. Within the year, Jackson's sister would meet and marry Ralph Waldo Emerson and they would move to Concord. The world of antebellum American technology was so small that it seemed to allow even a little village like Concord a role in the creation of one of the century's most important innovations.[234]

It would be another decade before Samuel Morse sent the first intercity telegraph transmission, from Baltimore to Washington, D.C. On

May 24, 1843, Morse's question—borrowed from the Bible to express the awe and wonder of everyone—came pulsing in dots and dashes over the line: "What hath God wrought?" Whether wrought by God or man, the electromagnetic telegraph—as uniquely American in origin as spiritualism—was another Neptunian promise. Just as Neptune was being discovered in 1846, Michael Faraday came to the conclusion that magnetism is present in all matter. In the wake of Neptune's discovery, a wave of magnetized feeling swept over Europe, producing the 1848 revolutions, the mirror of America's magnetizing wave of spiritualism. While the planets of the ancient cosmos together contributed the qualities that constituted the Hermetic man, Uranus and then Neptune were never incorporated into the human being's evolution and so represented titanic adversarial forces. Neptune brought to earth the force of magnetism, which esoteric orders knew as essentially trapped sound, just as Uranus's force of electricity represented trapped light. Neptune's action within the human being's soul took place in the realm of sympathy and antipathy and in its highest manifestation offered the possibility of spiritual hearing, a true "telegraph" from earth to heaven, allowing communication between the gods and man. The fallen form of Neptune's action manifested in the so-called "Spiritual Telegraph" erected in the 1850s from the Atlantic to the Pacific coast—the network of magnetized somnambulic mediums who became the telegraph tickers for Beings bent on human destruction. In the same esoteric orders that introduced the phenomena of spiritualism, it was taught that in order to overcome the temptation of magnetized feeling, one must practice chastity. In Concord, at the epicenter of Neptune's penetration into American life, Thoreau in his thirty-third year had overcome the Neptune forces, singlehandedly forging a path for others to follow.

CHAPTER 5

"What You Commonly See Is but Half"

He knows no change who knows the true,
    And on it keeps his eye,
Who always still the unseen doth view;
    Only the false & the apparent die.

Things change, but change not far
    From what they are not but to what they are,
Or rather 'tis our ignorance that dies;
    Forever lives the knowledge of the wise.

———

When the toads begin to ring,
    Then thinner clothing bring
or Off your greatcoat fling

Nocturne

In mid-September 1852, Thoreau was perambulating the bounds of Concord with its neighboring five towns, just the sort of surveying work he enjoyed, for it brought him encounters with wild places and people. He complained afterward, however, that he felt "inexpressibly begrimed, my Pegasus has lost its wings, he has turned a reptile and gone on his belly. Such things are compatible only with a cheap and superficial life." While working as a surveyor, he still thought of himself as a poet. "The poet must keep himself unstained and aloof. Let him perambulate the bounds of Imagination's provinces the realms of faery, and not the insignificant boundaries of towns. The excursions of the imagination are so boundless—the limits of towns are so petty." His impatience with this task of circumscription and with those who had hired him to execute it—he compared the "select-men" to earthbound woodchucks—contrasted with the expansiveness he felt upon reading Elihu Burritt's *Geography of the Heavens*, an astronomical primer and accompanying celestial atlas that pioneered the use of star maps portraying the constellations at every month of the year. "Let the student go out in a clear evening, with one of these maps in hand, representing the heavens at that time, and he will see all the constellations and visible stars spread out before him, in the same order as they appear on the map; and he will have the satisfaction of seeing one bright star after another pass over his head which he can call by name." Burritt guaranteed that in two or three evenings' study, the stargazer would know the relative positions of all the constellations of the fixed stars better than the principal places on earth. Beginning with the North Star, Burritt walked his reader through Andromeda, Pisces, Cassiopeia, Cepheus, Pegasus, Aquarius, the rest of the Zodiac, and dozens of other, non-zodiacal constellations. Drawing on Virgil, Ovid, Hesiod, and other classical authors, Burritt concluded each chapter's enumeration of the longitude, latitude, and magnitude of a constellation's principal stars with concise synopses of the mythological lore associated with it.[235]

The discovery in 1821 by Champollion of a pair of zodiacs on the walls of an ancient Egyptian temple on the banks of the Nile, a star map demonstrating knowledge of the precession of the equinoxes, was considered by Burritt of greater import than all of Napoléon's conquests, but he dismissed the Egyptians' judicial astrology as the "hallucinations of a vitiated intellect." *Geography of the Heavens* also gave natural history lore for the zoomorphic constellations. Burritt related for Canis Minor tales of canine faithfulness; for Leo, he cited various authorities as to whether lions hunt alone or in pairs and groups; for Serpens he cited Pliny on the hundred-twenty-foot serpent that attacked the

Roman general Regulus's army on the banks of the River Bagrada, then noted the hundred-foot sea serpent of August 1817 on the Massachusetts coast; for the modern constellation Monoceros (it was unnamed by the ancients), Burritt quoted naturalists who reported that the unicorn—"said to exist in the wilds of Ethiopia, and to be very formidable"—when pursued by hunters, pitched itself off of the cliffs and landed on its horn, "so that it receives no damage thereby." [236]

All Burritt's empiricism did not keep him from seeing the stars as divinely appointed: "It is one of the wonders of creation, that any phenomena of bodies at such an immense distance from us should be perceptible by human sight; but it is a part of the Divine Maker's plan, that although they do not act physically upon us, yet that they should so far be the objects of our consciousness, as to expand our ideas of the vastness of the universe, and of the stupendous extent and operations of his omnipotence." Here Thoreau parted company with Burritt, for he continued to feel sidereal influences. This fall in particular, the moon affected him each time he went abroad by the full or nearly full moon to explore the night landscapes of both Concord and his own being. He wondered whether the moon combined with "the winds of heaven to produce those memorable high tides of the calendar which leave their marks for ages." He experimented with angles of perspective at night in the same way he did on his daytime walks. "To appreciate the moonlight," he advised, "you must stand in the shade & see where a few rods or a few feet distant it falls between the trees." Thoreau thought it a "milder day" made for fairies, "a quiet gentle folk invented plainly to inhabit the moonlight. . . . As moonlight is to sunlight so are the fairies to men." He also played with night's particular method of doubling, finding places where both his voice and vision were echoed, the "answering reflections"—"a dualism which nature loves"—suggested to him that "what you commonly see is but half." [237]

Thoreau loved the solitude he always found at night, which made it "less profane than day." He preferred moonlit nights not only for the relative ease of travel, but also because he could feel Diana's influence upon him then. "Moonshine"—his age's dismissive term for false notions—Thoreau defined instead as meaning that which men do not understand or are "abed and asleep to," as they were to the moon. July—when night presented such a cool contrast to day—was his favorite month for moonlit walks: In that month, he found whip-poor-wills in place of wood thrushes, fireflies for butterflies, crickets and frogs for singing birds. Shadows became more conspicuous than the objects that cast them, and he could detect variation in topography and vegetation where by day he found sameness. The dark senses—smell, touch, and hearing—took the lead at night, so that he smelled the swamp-pink in the meadow, felt subtle shifts in air temperature, and heard the tinkling of rills he never detected before. The man who famously declared in *Walden* that "Corn grows in the night" could do so because he had smelled, felt, and heard it doing so.[238]

The affinity felt by Thoreau—who was born just a few days past the new moon—for moonlight was more than just an idiosyncratic response to the opportunities it afforded for altering perception. The full moon had for all of human history been the setting for wild and weird human behavior because lunacy was a physiological fact. The same magnetism that drew high tides higher, propelled potatoes and peas to grow taller, and launched geese and warblers on migration worked upon the subtle inner oceans of human beings. Witches and wizards—and esoteric orders of the nineteenth century—knew that as well as moving the physical waters upon the planet, whether held in oceanic reservoirs or the aqueous cells of plants and animals, the moon moved man's subtle organism. At the full moon, the human subtle body was more active, and Thoreau's moonlit rambles always reflected this invisible activity. Diana, charging the atmosphere with "dewy fragrance," gave him "Endymion sleep," an ambrosial sense of having his "dreams awake." The ecstasies he described from his nighttime walks frequently continued into the daylight hours at the period of the full moon, a consequence of his subtle organism being "lifted" slightly out of his physical body, opening him more fully to spiritual currents.

Thoreau was reading this fall the memoirs of Benvenuto Cellini and was struck by the story he told of a prophetic dream that he had one night while confined in the Castel Sant'Angelo in Rome. After this dream, he found that a "resplendent light" appeared over the shadow of his head both morning and evening, wherever he went. Cellini found that it was particularly conspicuous when the grass was moist with dew, something that Thoreau had observed about his own shadow on certain mornings, and also by moonlight. On one occasion, Thoreau's nimbus had merged with a rainbow's arch, "dazzling" him—"If it had lasted longer it might have tinged my employments and life." Another time, catching a glimpse of his halo while walking along the railroad causeway, he "fancied [himself] one of the elect." Though he seemed at one level to accept physical science's explanation of the halo around the head's shadow as a simple diffraction phenomenon, he also suggested slyly that there was something more to it. He noted that a friend had reported that Irishmen had no halos, that they were confined to natives (though this could have been merely a slur against the Irish). Cellini had shown his halo or "glory" to only a chosen few, and Thoreau pointed out how rarely it was noticed by anyone. "Are they not indeed distinguished," he asked, "who are conscious that they are regarded at all?" The suggestion of divine favor hinted at by the halo was in some of these instances just that, for Cellini's constant aureole and Thoreau's moonlit nimbus occurred when their subtle bodies had been stirred by the moon's forces. The head and hands have always and everywhere been the places where the invisible etheric shroud could most readily be detected; along with discovering his halo this year, Thoreau one full-moon day noticed the "web" running between his fingers: "When I hold mine up to the light & bring them near together—such are the laws of light that just before they touch—a web appears to grow on them & unite them." Unaware that he was viewing his own etheric body—what today is known as the "aura"—he drew from this apparition the lesson that "each thing is attracted to each—& running to coalesce. Like drops of water." In a sense, Thoreau was seeing the medium of magnetism, the vital current that bound bodies—both earthly and celestial—together.[239]

Fate and Friction

The other stimulus for stirring his etheric body this fall was much closer at hand than the moon. The telegraph wire had, by four weeks after its erection, become for Thoreau the "telegraph harp," playing at intervals along the railroad right-of-way, particularly in the Deep Cut, the excavation through the drumlin sands flanking the west side of Walden Pond. Placing his ear up against the posts to hear more clearly, he felt the wood "rearranged according to a new and more harmonious law."

> To have a harp on so great a scale, girdling the very earth, and played on by the winds of every latitude and longitude, and that harp were, as it were, the manifest blessing of heaven on a work of man's! Shall we not add a tenth Muse to the immortal Nine? . . .
>
> To read that the ancients stretched a wire round the earth, attaching it to the trees of the forest, by which they sent messages by one named Electricity, father of Lightning and Magnetism, swifter than Mercury, the stern commands of war and news of peace, and that the winds caused this wire to vibrate so that it emitted harp-like and æolian music in all the lands through which it passed, as if to express the satisfaction of the gods in this invention. Yet this is fact, and we have attributed the invention to no God.

There were many others who heard the music emanating from the telegraph wires crisscrossing America. A correspondent to *Scientific American* wrote to describe his experience of the musical sounds, and asked for an explanation: "I trust that the subject will attract the attention of some more accurate and philosophical observer." Thoreau was that observer, in that he transcended the merely physical explanation of the sound emitted from the vibrating string of wire. The telegraph harp seemed to give Thoreau a way to hear the music of the spheres directly.[240]

Thoreau found that certain Americans put the telegraph to a more mundane use. In early October, he helped Henry Williams, a fugitive slave, get aboard a train at Concord Depot. (As he approached the ticket office, Thoreau spied what he suspected to be a Boston policeman, and they had to duck from sight until he left.) Williams told him that along with finding his way north by the stars, escaping slaves frequently followed the telegraph lines in areas where there were no railroads. Thoreau also discovered that runaway slaves sometimes carried a piece of turf in their hats as a good luck charm. For his part, Thoreau continued to carry his charm inside himself. Finding how sweet white acorns tasted, he declared them "a greater addition to one's stock of life than would be imagined." The same day he found two prehistoric stone gouges; "Is it not enough for one afternoon?" he asked gratefully. Coming upon witch hazel in blossom while all around the trees were dropping their leaves convinced him that "all the year is a spring." His perennial optimism was in sharp contrast to the outlook of some contemporaries described by Ralph Emerson, who was at the moment writing "Fate" for a series of lectures in Boston titled "The Conduct of Life." Emerson reviewed the kind of superstitious fatalism embraced by runaway African slaves, along with Turks, Arabs, Persians, Hindus, and even Calvinists of his father's generation. Though he rejected their provincial fatalisms, he admitted that Providence was "a little rude":

> The diseases, the elements, fortune, gravity, lightning, respect no persons.... The planet is liable to shocks from comets, perturbations from planets, rendings from earthquake and volcano, alterations of climate, precessions of equinoxes. Rivers dry up by opening of the forest. The sea changes its bed. Towns and counties fall into it. At Lisbon, an earthquake killed men like flies. At Naples, three years ago, ten thousand persons were crushed in a few minutes. The scurvy at sea; the

sword of the climate in the west of Africa, at Cayenne, at Panama, at New Orleans, cut off men like a massacre. Our western prairie shakes with fever and ague.

These cataclysms Emerson found less destructive than the tyrannical confines of inherited circumstance, whether race, gender, temperament, or status. Claiming "The book of Nature is the book of Fate," Emerson accepted his era's racialist notions, seemingly undisturbed by the fact that the fate of race proved grim and sometimes deadly to those born to the "fate" of slavery. Ultimately, Emerson believed, "whatever limits us, we call Fate." Set forcefully against Fate always was Intellect, striving for freedom against Necessity. Emerson saw all history as the action of Nature and Thought—"two boys pushing each other on the curb-stone of the pavement." [241]

Fate this fall was pushing Emerson and Thoreau apart. In his journal, where Emerson was always "my friend," Thoreau agonized over their increasingly distant relationship. "Ah I yearn toward thee my friend, but I have not confidence in thee. We do not believe in the same God. I am not thou—Thou art not I. . . . Here I have been on what the world would call friendly terms with one fourteen years, have pleased my imagination sometimes with loving him—and yet our hate is stronger than our love. . . . Ah I am afraid because thy relations are not my relations. . . . In the first place my friend is prouder than I am—& I am very proud perchance." Emerson, who had been so proud of Thoreau in the early years of their friendship, now found his esteem waning: "Thoreau wants a little ambition in his mixture. Fault of this, instead of being the head of American Engineers, he is captain of a huckleberry party." Elsewhere in his journal Emerson likened Thoreau to a malevolent nature spirit: "Henry Thoreau is like the woodgod who solicits the wandering poet & draws him into antres [caves] vast & desarts idle, & bereaves him of his memory, & leaves him naked, plaiting vines & twigs in his hand. Very seductive are the first steps from the town to the woods, but the End is want & madness." [242]

Emerson's imperial manner—which grew as his fame did, and by 1852 he was one of the most celebrated men in America—contrasted sharply with Thoreau's private agonies over the rift between them. "He finds fault with me that I walk alone, when I pine for want of a companion—that I commit my thoughts to a diary even on my walks instead of seeking to share them generously with a friend—curses my practice even—Awful as it is to contemplate I pray that if I am the cold intellectual skeptic whom he rebukes his curse may take effect—& wither & dry up those sources of my life—and my journal no longer yield me pleasure nor life." Anna Parsons had in her somnambulic state clairvoyantly diagnosed Emerson's fatal flaw—his inability to "sympathize" with others; Thoreau's nature by contrast was all sympathetic, and his open acceptance of Emerson's curse suggests how strongly he rejected his friend's mistaken characterization of him as an emotional miser. One December evening in front of a fire at home, Thoreau had been thinking about a disagreement he had had with Emerson over his conviction that Margaret Fuller's superstitions were the key to her character, and he decided to employ one of them—a *sortes Virgilianae*, which was the divinatory practice of opening a copy of Virgil's works or some other revered book at random and reading a passage to give guidance on some question. He took up one of Emerson's books, opened it, and let his eye fall randomly on the page. He read: "If, with a high trust, he can thus submit himself, he will find that ample returns are poured into his bosom out of what seemed hours of obstruction and loss. . . . In a society of perfect sympathy, no word, no act, no record, would be. He will learn that it is not much matter what he reads, what he does. Be a scholar, and he shall have the scholar's part of everything." The oracle spoke truly; Emerson's failure to live out his own words was clear enough to Thoreau.[243]

The quarrel between them echoed in some way the quarrel America was having with itself over its own fate. Thoreau put his faith in himself as a "common man" in a manner to which Emerson, for all his fine words about democracy, often paid only lip service. While Emerson still sought intellectual and spiritual treasure abroad, Thoreau dug deeper and deeper into his native land, convinced that the lode held there was as rich as anywhere upon earth. Thoreau's capacity for self-aware introspection—a capacity in short supply as a collective national trait—always exceeded Emerson's. America, like Emerson, was a bit glib, liked to hear itself talk, and as a consequence frequently failed as a listener. The contrariness that so disturbed Emerson was Thoreau's first line of defense against succumbing to smug confidence in wan and wayward truths. If America as a nation practiced Thoreau's adage "a man must see, before he can say," it might more readily act with wisdom.

The latest fateful event for Americans—the discovery of gold in California—nearly universally hailed as a sign of divine favor upon the nation, called out the Puritan preacher in Thoreau. He was appalled by the "philosophy—or poetry or religion of a world that will rush to the lottery of California gold digging on receipt of the first news—to live by luck to get the means of commanding the labor of others less lucky—i.e. of slaveholding—without contributing any value to society—and that is called enterprise and the devil is only a little more enterprising." From the accounts of early explorers of the North American continent, who unanimously reported to Europe how much larger and more bountiful the New World was in all its productions, Thoreau drew ammunition as he leveled his aim at American ambitions:

> Sir Francis Head says that in America "the moon looks larger" than in Europe. Here then more moonshine is to be expected.... At length perchance the immaterial heaven will appear as much higher to the American mind—and the intimations that star it will appear as much brighter. For I believe that climate does thus react on man—and that there is something in the *Mt*. Air that feeds the spirit—& inspires. We shall be more imaginative—We shall be clearer as our sky—bluer, fresher, broader & more comprehensive in our understanding—like our plains—Our intellect on a grander scale—like our thunder & lightning—our rivers & our lakes—& *mts*. & forests ... Will not man

grow to greater perfection, intellectually as well as physically, under these influences? Or is it unimportant how many foggy days there are in his life?

For Thoreau, national destiny could only be the fruit that ripened on the tree of individual self-perfection. Slavery, imperialism, philistinism— these rotten fruits would come season after season unless each American "faithfully practiced the yoga," as Thoreau had in his Walden Pond experiment and continued to do. His ascetic and martial temperament gave him to believe that Americans needed a storm or swamp to battle, in order to fashion its character. "There is something worth living for when we are resisted—threatened," he advised. "As at the last day we might be thrilled with the prospect of the grandeur of our destiny—so in these *first* days our destiny appears grander. What would the days— what would our life be worth if some nights were not as dark as pitch? . . . How else would the light in the mind shine!"[244]

Americans were much more likely to feel the brightness of their destiny reflected by American technical prowess than by the size and sublimity of their mountains and forests. As the pace of invention accelerated in antebellum America, it took on something of its own millennial momentum, entirely separate from national aspirations about territorial empire. This civic religion of technophilia was as fervently embraced by ministers as mechanics and was especially pronounced in the Spiritualist movement. In early 1853, Andrew Jackson Davis wrote a series of spirit-inspired letters claiming that soon America would have the ability to control the rain. "Now, Mr. Editor," Davis wrote to the *Hartford Courant*, "it seems to me that the equal welfare and proper development of humanity require a little closer approach to a kind of republicanism or 'democracy' among the elements and electro-magnetic circulations of the upper air! How seems it to you?" As always, Davis professed that his proposal was "in perfect harmony with the immutable laws of nature." He hinted that a future chemistry would discover the "intimate relation" between water and electricity, whose character he admitted had been assailed of late because it had been invoked as the cause of "every new 'manifestation' regarded as inexplicable." In order to produce and control rain within a hundred-mile radius of Hartford, Davis proposed to build on the city's Prospect Hill a tower that would have two large machines at the top—an electric device to accumulate the earth's negative charge, and a galvanic battery for the purpose of introducing magnetic currents and for decomposing water. The machine ("no more mysterious or impossible than the Magnetic Telegraph or the Ericsson Caloric Engine!"), operating on the same principle as the aurora borealis, would produce a beautiful exhibition of light as well. Noting that the city of New Haven some forty miles to the south was sorely in need of precipitation, Davis argued, "Let us love our neighbor as ourself, and set the machinery in operation."[245]

A few months after the unveiling of Davis's rainmaking scheme, medium John Murray Spear (a former Unitarian minister who in 1849 was one of the founding members, along with Emerson, Thoreau, and other transcendentalists, of the "Town and Country Club") received a set of two hundred communications from a spirit purporting to be Benjamin Franklin, giving plans for a machine to be driven by a "new motive power." "The New Motor"—mockingly dubbed "The Electrical Infant" by critics—was to collect atmospheric energy, concentrate it, and then transmit it for use in powering a wide variety of other machines. Via automatic writing, the spirit Franklin informed Spear that he was the earthly representative of "The Band of Electrizers," a fraternity of philanthropic spirits dedicated to advancing the human race through superior technology. Spear mobilized support from a wide group of Spiritualists—including the popular singing ensemble the Hutchinsons, who donated the land behind their estate at High Rock in Lynn, Massachusetts, for the erection of the promised perpetual motion machine. The Hutchinsons' High Rock Cottage had in 1852 become nearly as famous among Spiritualists as the Fox home in Hydesville, when Davis had a vision there of the "Spiritual Congress," a cloud-borne host of spirit representatives from twenty-four nations. The American representatives were an interesting mix: Patrick Henry, John Howard, George Washington, Samuel Fulton, Benjamin Franklin, Thomas Jefferson, James Fenimore Cooper, Thomas Paine, Alexander Jackson Downing, Jonathan Edwards, and John Wesley. Margaret Fuller Ossoli appeared with the Italian delegation.

Nine months after beginning construction, the New Motor stood atop the 170-foot-high hill overlooking the busy manufacturing town of Lynn. It looked like nothing that had ever powered the machinery in the shoe factories and machine shops below: a pair of large steel spheres hung over zinc and copper plates covering an oval platform made of magnets and metal. After it was set in motion by a small electric motor, a carefully selected man and woman were brought close to the machine to "raise its vibrations." Spear meanwhile entered a gemstone-studded box made of metal plates and entered a deep trance. After a climactic episode wherein one of Spear's followers declared that she had given birth to the new machine, Spear dismantled it and moved it to western New York, where it was smashed to pieces by a group of local people scandalized by Spear's claims that the machine was "the Physical Savior, Heaven's Last Gift to Man, New Creation, Great Spiritual Revelation of the Age, Philosopher's Stone, Art of All Arts, Science of All Sciences, the New Messiah." [246]

Along with the New Motor, Spear's spirits inspired him with designs for a telepathic stock ticker; mediums wearing specially wired hats would mentally telegraph commodity and stock prices instantly to all Americans, not just wealthy capitalists. They also sent him plans for a "self-powered" sewing machine. Spear's inventions shared with Davis's rainmaker a faith that the human will was the true "New Motive Power" at the center of the universe. Millions of Americans, having seen heavy Victorian furniture levitated by invisible spirits in the presence of Spiritualist mediums, imagined that the human mind might also move turbines and crankshafts. J. A. Etzler's dreams of a mechanized paradise on earth had a decade before evoked from Thoreau a critique centering on his reminding his audience that divine love was the only force capable of generating free energy or perpetual motion. The Promethean schemes of Spear and Davis, in putting the human will in the engine room, denied the efficacy of any higher will within the working of the physical universe.

While America busied itself seeking new motive powers without, Thoreau was still turning the "crank within," his daily routine bringing forth new transcendental energies. In March 1852, on his way to the Great Fields across from Sleepy Hollow, upon hearing a bluebird's note, he found a different sort of electricity pervading the ether:

> My life partakes of infinity. The air is as deep as our natures.... The air is a velvet cushion against which I press my ear—I go forth to make new demands on life. I wish to begin this summer well—to do something in it worthy of it & of me ... to have my immortality now—that it be in the *quality* of my daily life. To pay the greatest price—the greatest tax of any man in Concord—& enjoy the most! I will give all I am for *my* nobility. I will pay all my days for *my* success. I pray that the life of this spring & summer may ever lie fair in my memory. May I dare as I have never done.—may I persevere as I have never done. May I purify myself anew as with fire & water—soul & body—... May I gird myself to be a hunter of the beautiful that naught escape me—May I attain to a youth never attained I am eager to report the glory of the universe.— may I be worthy to do it—to have got through with regarding human values so as not to be distracted from regarding divine values. It is reasonable that a man should be something worthier at the end of the year than he was at the beginning.

A skilled mechanic himself, Thoreau loved elegantly crafted machines as well as his neighbors and was not averse to applying mechanical metaphors even to his own consciousness; meditating on the acumen of his mind in the moments just after waking either night or day, he thought his mind worked "like a machine without friction." This nineteenth-century dream—hundreds of patent applications were filed each decade for such machines—surely had its closest realization in the vault of the human mind, powered by a faithful heart.[247]

My Year of Observation

Spring burst upon Thoreau this year with greater immediacy than ever, and in his rambles to Concord's innumerable birthing places, Thoreau paused to ask "why just this circle of creatures completes the world." It was an impossible question, but one he now felt increasingly equipped to answer. After years of being stymied and surprised by the unpredictability of the cycles of birth, growth, senescence, and death of the local biota, he mused, "It takes us many years to find out that Nature repeats herself annually. But how perfectly regular and calculable all her phenomena must appear to a mind that has observed her for a thousand years!" The question would not go away. "Why should just these sights & sounds accompany our life? Why should I hear the chattering of blackbirds—why smell the skunk each year?" In April he dedicated himself to the pursuit of an answer, conscious of his own centripetal role as he prepared to launch himself centrifugally into the surrounding landscape for an answer: "I would fain explore the mysterious relation between myself & these things. I would at least know what these things unavoidably are—make a chart of our life—know how its shores trend—the butterflies reappear & when—know why just this circle of creatures completes the world. Can I not by expectation affect the revolutions of nature—make a day to bring forth something new?" The draftsman Thoreau suddenly saw the possibility of a plan view of nature's cycles; time could, with his help, become space. "For the first time I perceive this spring that the year is a circle—I see distinctly the spring arc thus far. It is drawn with a firm line."[248]

His ears were fully at work this spring, and he cataloged the calls of all the local birds. In the age before field guides, birdcalls were heard in as many dialects as there were listeners; no standard renderings existed.

The towhee called *to-wee, to-wee* and *whip-your ch-r-r-r-r*; the nuthatch, *wicher wicher wicher wich*; the white-throated sparrow (mistaken by Thoreau for the chickadee), *ha, ha, tull-a-lull tull-a-lull*. He thought *pewit pewit chowy chow* was the call of either the pewee or the vireo, and he heard the brown thrasher's *cherruwit, cherruwit* as *go ahead, go ahead, give it to him, give it to him*. (Emerson, by contrast, always heard the thrasher's call as *Indian! Indian! Go white man. White man give corn, beer, beer, beer, beer!*) The "seringo's" (savannah sparrow) name reminded him of its note, "as if it were produced by some fine metallic spring." He noticed that a bird in the meadow sounded like a cricket, "an earth song." He was just as enchanted by frog calls, christening frogs "birds of the night." The sound of a striking clock on a full moon walk was equally musical to him: "There is a grand, rich, musical echo trembling on the air long after the clock has ceased to strike, like a vast organ, filling the air with a trembling music like a flower of sound. Nature adopts it. Beautiful is sound. . . ."²⁴⁹

Thoreau had no binoculars at this point in his career as field naturalist, so identification by call was even more critical than it is for birders today. He spent the entire breeding season year after year puzzling over particularly cryptic birds; with no other authorities to assist him, he made his own way purely on observation. After a month of deep listening to an unidentified "dream frog," he concludes that it is actually a toad, and then laments his discovery: "I fear that the dream of the toads will not sound so musical now that I know whence it proceeds. But I will not fear to *know*. They will awaken new and more glorious music for me as I advance, still farther in the horizon, not to be traced to toads and frogs in slimy pools." This comment gives away a characteristic quality of Thoreau's manner of observation—his tendency to put phenomena at a little distance, or slightly out of focus, in order to grasp them fully. In the middle of May, watching cattle driven up-country from Concord village barns, he thinks he smells autumn, and says that autumn's aroma is remembered best in spring. He even discovered a rule of thumb about the ideal distance between perception and conception. "I succeed best when I *recur* to my experience not too late, but within a day or two; when there is some distance, but enough of freshness." This rule of thumb is actually a universal law, a function of the rhythm of the etheric body. It takes three days for experiences—observations, images, ideas—to become imprinted into our body of etheric formative forces, and thus permanently into our memory, and more important, even when we have lost our own individual memories of them, into the cosmos, where they are stored even after our death. After three days, the more intensively and faithfully an individual attends to some thought, the more deeply it becomes inscribed into the universe.[250]

A key to natural historical observation, and to all thinking, is the accumulation of enough experiences to form associations among phenomena, and this spring saw Thoreau forming a rich web of such associations. Watching Venus emerge as the evening star, he asked himself if the moment when the first star was seen did not mark the beginning of the whip-poor-will's dusk song. He noticed that birds that built nests in small branches of trees waited for the leaves to expand before they began construction. The triangulations of microclimate, faunal and floral phenology, and weather past and present allowed him to coin new phrases for characterizing individual days. "These are the warm-west-wind, dream-frog, leafing out, willowy, haze days," he declared on May 9. Five days later he made his first list of the appearance times of trees, shrubs, and herbs, the date of birds seen and heard, and a host of other phenomena—snow in hollows, frog spawn, toads dreaming, flies buzzing outdoors, sitting without a fire, spearing, first cricket on cliff, shad-fly, toad in garden, willows suddenly green, cows going up-country, anthills, humblebee, sweet scent of birch leaves with the ground still frozen in some places, barn swallows' twitter, and a green snake. His own body and habits became a kind of second hand on his new clock; he noted on June 9 that he had reduced the amount of cloth around his neck. All this chronicling seemed to intensify his vernal joy, so that the most plebeian phenomena elicited heavenly thoughts. Coming upon a pile of freshwater clamshells left by a muskrat, he wondered, "How did these beautiful tints get into the shell of the fresh-water clam buried in the mud at the bottom of our dark river? Even the sea-bottom tells of upper skies." [251]

As he approached his thirty-fifth birthday, Thoreau was as given to nature-induced ecstasy as ever. Taken with the many hues of green in the landscape unfolding out before him, he felt as if he were watching the growth of his own body: "Those great fields of green affect me as did those early green blades by the Corner Spring—like a fire flaming up from the earth. The earth proves itself well alive even in the skin." Exclamation points regularly punctuate his journal entries: "What a sweetness fills the air now in low grounds or meadows, reminding me of times when I went a-strawberrying years ago. It is as if all meadows were filled with some sweet mint!" "How rapidly new flowers unfold!" "How much of a tortoise is shell!" "How rare among men so fit a thing as the sound of a flute at evening!" Sounds provoke ecstasies: Crickets seem to him "like the dreaming of the earth still continued into the daylight." The cock's crowing makes him exclaim, "What a tough fellow! How native to the earth!" Hearing a man playing clarinet far off, he likens it to Apollo tending the flocks of King Admetus—"How cultivated, how sweet and glorious is music!" When he notes that a child loves to strike a tin pan or other ringing object with a stick, because, his "ears being fresh, sound, attentive and percipient, [he] detects the finest music in the sound, at which all nature assists," he is noting his own response to sound. Even the sounds of human inventions are made poetic: "The steam whistle at a distance sounds even like the hum of a bee in a flower. So man's works fall into nature." Familiar and unfamiliar scents shoot through him like arrows: "Ah those fugacious universal fragrances of the meadows and woods! Odors rightly mingled!" His surging sensuousness led him to desire constantly to "get wet and saturated with water." Watching boys bathing at Hubbard's Bend in the Concord River, he is delighted by the color of their bodies: "What a singular fact for an angel visitant to this earth to carry back in his note-book that men were forbidden to expose their bodies under the severest penalties! A pale pink, which the sun would soon tan. White men!" The ecstatic condition predisposed him to see always the hidden relations between phenomena: "Have not the fireflies in the meadow a relation to the stars above, *étincelant* [sparkling]? When the darkness comes, we see beneath also.... Do not the stars, too, show their light for love, like the fireflies?"[252]

The peak of Thoreau's perceptual powers was coincident with his ability to love, indeed, with his understanding of love, which was the force that knit together all these sensations. In July, he sent Blake an essay he had just written on the subject. He takes up first the nature of love between man and woman but addresses himself to love in its broadest scope, particularly its role in friendship. Thoreau's propensity for discretion, his respect for silence, for the sacredness of keeping counsel with oneself, led him to an exacting standard: "Love is the profoundest of secrets. Divulged, even to the beloved, it is no longer Love." Though he uses the pronoun *she*, Thoreau surely thinks particularly of Emerson when he says, "We should have no reserve; we should give the whole of ourselves to that society; we should have no duty aside from that." For all the intensity of his sympathy with the natural world, still Thoreau craved human companionship: "What a difference, whether in all your walks, you meet only strangers, or in one house is one who knows you, and whom you know. To have a brother or a sister! To have a gold mine on your farm! ... How rare these things are!" Ultimately, Thoreau celebrated as most ennobling the love standing behind all loves: "Whether to have a god or a goddess for companion in your walks, or to walk alone with hinds and villains. Would not a friend enhance the beauty of the landscape as much as a deer or hare? Everything would acknowledge and serve such a relation; the corn in the field and the cranberries in the meadow. The flowers would bloom, and the birds sing, with a new impulse. There would be more fair days in the year."[253]

Fittingly, on the heels of this season of fecundity, Thoreau wrote a companion essay, "Chastity & Sensuality." Such was the power of this lifelong bachelor's (and almost certainly virgin) imagination that he could write, "The intercourse of the sexes, I have dreamed, is incredibly beautiful, too fair to be remembered." He practiced the chastity he preached, saying, "I have had thoughts about it, but they are among the most fleeting and irrecoverable in my experience. It is strange that men will talk of miracles, revelation, inspiration, and the like, as things past, while love remains." Chastity and sensuousness Thoreau saw as preservers and augmenters of authentic love, through their transformation of sex into a sacred act. Thoreau thought the subject of sex "a remarkable one," as "one of the most interesting of all human facts[,] . . . veiled more completely than any mystery." Thoreau's penchant for paradox and punning made this most forbidding of subjects mirthfully approachable. "What presence," he asked in earnest, "can be more awful to the lover than that of his beloved?" Convinced that "whoever loves flowers, loves virgins and chastity," he cited Linnaeus's designation of the flower's calyx as the *thalamus*—bridal chamber—and the corolla the *aulaeum*, or tapestry of it. While in the animal kingdom the organs of generation were universally hidden from view, implying shame, flowers showed no shame, exposing their reproductive parts to the eye—and nose—of the beholder. In the throes of his season of solitary ecstasies, Thoreau unsurprisingly ascribed to the true marriage the delight attendant upon all perception of truth—"divine ecstasy, an inexpressible delirium of joy, as when a youth embraces his betrothed virgin." Finding it fitting that out of such a union, "the undying race of man" should come, he put off the proto-eugenicists calling for men to be bred like cattle, for physical improvement: "Let Love be purified, and all the rest will follow." Thoreau's advice for bettering the breed was but a variation on his measure for all human action: "The offspring of noble men and women will be superior to themselves, as their aspirations are. By their fruits ye shall know them." [254]

Everywhere he looked this spring and summer of 1852, Thoreau saw that Nature was shot through and through with morality. Watching a rainbow appear at sunset, he shouts: "How moral the world is made! This bow is not utilitarian. Methinks men are great in proportion as they are moral." Coming upon the carrion-flower, which he thought smelled like a dead dog, Thoreau asked himself at first why nature would have made such an atrocious thing, then answered himself: "Just so much beauty and virtue as there is in the world, and just so much ugliness and vice, you see expressed in flowers." A large white ash tree scorched and exploded by a lightning strike led him to counter the inclination to see lightning as "a brutish force or vengeance" with the suggestion that the evil was imparted rather than innate. A righteous man would see the lightning's Titanic force as "merely sublime." The philosophy expressed in his essay on Love was worked out in his daily encounters with roses, swamp-pinks, morning glories, arethusas, pogonias, epilobiums, and mountain laurel: "Nature must be viewed humanly to be viewed at all; that is, her scenes must be associated with human affections, such as are associated with one's native place, for instance. She is most significant to a lover. A lover of Nature is preeminently a lover of man. If I have no friend, what is Nature to me? She ceases to be morally significant." [255]

Such sentiments, for long ages the attitude of all human beings toward nature, was just then being eclipsed, as American natural scientists sought relentlessly to expunge from their ways of knowing the *appearance* at least of a moral dimension in nature. Thoreau was already alert to modern science's hubris about its explanatory ability. "Science affirms too much," he complained. "Science assumes to show *why* the lightning strikes a tree, but it does not show us the moral *why* any better than our instincts did. It is full of presumption. Why should trees be struck? It is not enough to say because they are in the way. Science answers, *Non scio*, I am ignorant." Thoreau's science demanded that all phenomena be seen from the point of view of "wonder and awe, like lightning." The righteous man—identical with the most perspicacious scientist—would see the lightning itself with "serenity, as the most familiar and innocent phenomena are." Such a man would easily act as a lightning rod, conducting "safely away into the earth the flashing wrath of Nemesis, so that it merely clarifies the air." Electrified by the lightning metaphor, he pushed it to its limit in asserting that "men are probably nearer to the essential truth in their superstitions than in their science. Some places are thought to be particularly exposed to lightning, some oaks on hilltops, for instance." This last little bit of folk science, presented as mere hearsay unverified and unbelieved by Thoreau, deflated science's authority because it was a bare fact within almost everyone's own experience. Coming on the heels of his validation of nature's moral dimension, the folk wisdom seemed to say that these thunderstruck oaks had brought Jove's bolts down upon themselves.[256]

Stripped of morality, science's approach to Nature inevitably dehumanized and demeaned man. Thoreau was reading Samuel George Morton's *Crania Americana*, in which he supported racist theories of human variation by filling skulls with lead shot, then emptying them into a calibrated beaker to quantify the intelligence of the indigenous peoples of North and South America. Thoreau took a dim view of Morton's "science": "By and by some Dr. Morton may be filling your cranium with white mustard seed to learn its internal capacity. Of all ways invented to come at a knowledge of a living man, this seems to me the worst, as it is the most belated. You would learn more by once paring the toenails of the living subject. There is nothing out of which the spirit has more completely departed, and in which it has left fewer significant traces." When Thoreau complained to his sister Sophia that he had become "sadly scientific," he meant that he was not sufficiently incubating his observations to hatch moral insight.[257]

No emblem of Nature's Janus-faced morality surpassed for Thoreau the white lilies that covered the surface of the Musketaquid as summer entered into its own. Out of the dank and sulfurous muds and stagnant dark waters rose this token of purity. "Nature never appears more serene and innocent and fragrant," he thought, than when "a hundred white lilies, open to the sun, rest on the surface smooth as oil amid their pads, while devil's-needles are glancing over them." As a boy Thoreau had enjoyed smoking the dried lily stems ("I have never smoked anything more noxious," he crowed) and the trick of making the yellow stamens rise and fall by blowing through the stem. Now as a man he was consumed with the desire to extract the moral essence of the white water lily. On the first of July he rowed out to a colony near Sherman's Bridge and found their twenty-nine petals—the number he counted on two individuals—fully open. Wishing "to breathe the atmosphere of lilies, and get the full impression which lilies are fitted to make," he came back after lunch to examine them again, and found that every one of the hundreds he had seen before noon wide open, were now shut, even though it was still sunny. That night he lay awake thinking about the lilies, saying that he was like them, having absorbed vigor from his encounter with them, just as the lilies absorbed nutrition from the muddy bottom of the river. He had brought an unopened bud back home, and after two days without it opening, he turned back its sepals and touched the apex of the folded petals, whereupon it sprang open "into a perfect blossom." Thoreau put the blossom in a wide dish of water and blew it from side to side, the "breeze of his half-suppressed admiration . . . [filling] its sail." He found it incredible that "men will travel to the Nile to see the lotus flower, who have never seen in their glory the lotuses of their native streams." [258]

Saturn—and Sol—Returns

The white water lily of his native stream was for Thoreau the catalyst for his realization of a watershed in his biography. The day after his lily exploration he proclaimed, "This is my year of observation." Nature, thought Thoreau, rushed "to make her report" only to the "full heart," in "the fullness of life." This was surely his condition as he turned thirty-five this July, while the water lily petals began to turn rosaceous and fade before the ripening fruit. All of his poetic powers now seemed to transform themselves into powers of pure observation. Over the next ten years of his life, he would write just ten more poems but fill volume after volume of journal and notebook with an avalanche of empirical detail, the raw material of poetry. It was as if the facts themselves had become the poetry.[259]

Despite feeling so acutely the consonance of nature's rhythms with his own mood, Thoreau was completely oblivious to the annual and septennial returns playing out in his own life. Age thirty-five was for Thoreau's generation the traditional midpoint of life and was generally invested with certain expectations about maturity, professional and social accomplishment, and physical health. The body's vitality was expected to decline some while a person's intellectual vigor and personal power continued unabated. The power of Mammon in antebellum America was potent enough that in bourgeois Concord the main measures of successful midlife were taxable acres owned or the number of domestics employed in the home. By 1852, though 80 percent of Americans still lived in rural areas and more people worked on farms or in cottage workshops than in factories, traditional agrarian rhythms were increasingly broken, replaced by the accelerated rhythms of the steam engine and telegraph signal. Americans were losing their attunement to the longer, basso ostinato rhythms of life and the cosmos.

Though it had been eclipsed by the discovery in 1846 of Neptune as the more distant, and thus "slower," planet in the solar system, Saturn still ruled as "chronocrator," Ptolemy's term for the planetary ruler of time. The seven-year rhythm of human biography had always been understood to be an expression of Saturn's progression through the signs of the Zodiac; each quarter turn through the circle brought Saturn into a "square," or ninety-degree aspect to its position at the prior seven-year point. Saturn's opening square around age seven marked the boundary of childhood, where the physical body finished its full incarnation. At age fourteen, when Saturn was opposite its natal position, the etheric body stabilized, and each adolescent then began to challenge and expand his horizons. The twenty-one-year-old who looked to take up new responsibilities in family or in work reflected Saturn's final square before returning, between age twenty-eight and twenty-nine and a half, to its position at birth. This "Saturn return" was something that Thoreau would have come upon in reading Chaucer and Shakespeare, but it simply did not live as a concept in nineteenth-century America, save among a handful of esotericists and astrologers. They understood that at age thirty-five, a man's soul "looked back" to the time of his Saturn return, either continuing his trajectory if it had proved fulfilling or abandoning it if it seemed unsuitable. This was not a conscious process but took the form of life seemingly haphazardly throwing up a series of personal crises for an individual. The seven final years of each person's "sun period" in life, from age thirty-five to forty-two, presented a chance to purify one's thinking, feeling, and willing, leading to an individualized, autonomous self.

The day after his thirty-fifth birthday, Thoreau headed his journal entry with a single fragmentary sentence: "A journal, a book that shall contain a record of all your joy, your ecstasy." A reaffirmation of his November 1850 declaration that the journal should be "the record of my love," this seemed to express a sort of midstream checking in rather than an explicit statement of a goal, as it had been two years before. There was no sign that he had wandered from his intended path. That afternoon he walked out to Emerson's woodlot near Walden Pond to check on the progress of huckleberries and blueberries; he admitted that even though he expected on his daily walks to be able to "see the first berry that turns," he was always foiled, finding that they had ripened sometime before his arrival. A similar principle operated in human biography—one might look for the certain signs of a ripening of talent or faculties in an individual, only to discover that the fruit was already red and ready for harvest, but unseen. Emerson certainly experienced this in relation to Thoreau; perhaps Thoreau was equally fooled by Emerson's entelechy. The landscape was full of temporal mysteries of this sort that frequently echoed in human biography. Commenting on the pair of annual growth spurts—fall as well as spring—of most trees, Thoreau recognized the symmetry with men, most of whom had "a spring growth only, and never get over this first check to their youthful hopes." Surely he considered himself a plant "of hardier constitution, or perchance planted in a more genial soil," like those trees displaying a "vigorous fall growth which is equivalent to a new spring." Bearing knots of disappointment, but the prospect of new growth, such individuals could be unaware of their own renewed vitality, masked as it was by a lapsed lifetime of youth. On this day after his thirty-fifth solar return, Thoreau wistfully hinted that perhaps he was prey to such a declensional view: "The youth gets together his materials to build a bridge to the moon, or perchance a palace or temple on the earth, and at length the middle-aged man concludes to build a wood-shed with them." Having impeccably built his temple at age twenty-eight, it seems hard to believe that Thoreau now looked back on it and declared his Walden cabin a woodshed.[260]

Astrologers for centuries had warned their clients of a planetary configuration called the black moon, at age thirty-five and four months, when a person might experience a period of emotional distress, the heightening of egoistic desires, or a turn away from one's inner quest. Thoreau's black moon fell in November 1852, a month that even normally was one where, according to Thoreau, "a man will eat his heart, if in any month." The month opened with a "warm, mizzling kind of rain" that lasted for days, with no impact whatsoever on Thoreau's elevated mood. "It is remarkable how native man proves himself to the earth," he wrote, "after all, and the completeness of his life in all its appurtenances. His alliances, how wide!" The next day, still overcast and raining, the leaves mostly fallen, he rowed out on Walden Pond, and seeing a place seemingly stirred by a faint breeze, or perhaps where a spring welled up from below or the last few water skaters were astir, he rowed toward it and was surprised to find a school of small perch sporting there. They darted to the surface, dimpled it, then dove, and when Thoreau struck the side of the boat with his oar, they would all together make a sudden splash. When a wind came up, they all leaped out of the water, while "the pond, dark before, was now a glorious and indescribable hue, mixed with dark . . . more cerulean if possible than the sky itself." He still heard and thrilled at the sound of the telegraph harp, delighted to see while sailing the red undersides of drowned white lily leaves, enjoyed finding the water in the pitcher plant turned to ice. When the season's first snow fell on November 23, he found it "genial," ameliorating November's harshness. Reflecting on his habit for many years of eschewing meat, tea, and coffee, he said this month that though he adopted these habits because "it appeared more beautiful to live low and fare hard," he now relented a little, carrying "less religion to the table." The black moon obviously had no purchase on America's most ardent lover of the white moon.[261]

The outset of Henry Thoreau's sixth septennial was marked everywhere by sunny, sanguine, solar forces, most spectacularly reflected by his observations of the sun itself. The summer of 1852 saw him record with painterly detail and timekeeper's precision a series of sunrises and sunsets. While in the past his journal entries would have been full of conscious poetic associations, now there was pure delicious description.

> Twenty minutes after seven . . . a roseate redness, clear as amber, suffuses the low western sky about the sun, in which the small clouds are mostly melted, only their golden edges still revealed. The atmosphere there is like some kinds of wine, perchance, or molten cinnabar . . . half past seven. The roseate glow deepens to purple. . . . The general redness fades into a pale reddish tinge in the horizon, with a clear white line above it. . . . Now, about twenty minutes after the first glow left the clouds above the sun's place, there is a second faint fuscous or warm brown glow on the edges of the dark clouds there. . . . About three quarters of an hour after sunset the evening red is deepest, i.e., a general atmospheric redness close to the west horizon. . . .

A couple of days later, up at four in the morning on the east-facing Conantum Cliffs to greet the sun, he imagined it being greeted by every cock in North America: "The salutation was traveling round the world; some six hours since had resounded through England, France, and Spain; then the sun passed over a belt of silence where the Atlantic flows, except a clarion here and there from some cooped up cock upon the waves..." At thirty-five, even in the throes of his black moon, Thoreau was still a chanticleer in the morning, bragging lustily. His thinking, feeling, and willing over these next seven years would be an intensification and deepening of the impulses he had carried into life up to age twenty-eight. All his joy, all his ecstasy *are* contained in the journal, which documents that his Saturn return was an upward spiral toward that heaven he had always kept in view. Recent generations of critics have almost universally understood Thoreau as having in 1852 abandoned transcendentalism for scientific materialism, but Thoreau's nearly daily record of his joy nowhere supports this interpretation. The heart of Henry Thoreau's quest had always been to know God by sympathizing with his surroundings. Charting the life histories of the plants and animals that he had spent half a lifetime loving was a way to move even more fully into sympathetic relation with the fair ground upon which he had been born[262]—"To prolong the time and make the most of his secret."

Manifesting his goal of life in no way spared Thoreau from life's pain—petty or grand. The winter of 1852–53 saw him working constantly at surveying to pay off his debt for the publication of *A Week*; at the end of February, he had amassed only a dollar a day for the previous seventy-six days' labor, however. He complained to Blake, "I have not only cheap hours, but cheap weeks and months... weeks of pasturing and browsing... which give me animal health, it may be, but create a tough skin over the soul and intellectual part." In January he got into a row with editors at *Putnam's Monthly Magazine* when they made changes to his "Yankee in Canada" piece without his approval. When, in March, the American Association for the Advancement of Science sent him a questionnaire after zoologist Spencer Baird proposed Thoreau for membership, he returned it perfunctorily, declining, he told Baird, because he would not be able to attend the meetings. To his journal he told the true reason: He could never explain to the AAAS the branch of science that occupied him, since they "do not believe in a science which deals with a higher law." "The fact is," he admitted, "I am a mystic, a transcendentalist, and a natural philosopher to boot." On second thought, he decided that the best way to inform the august scientific body that they would not understand him was to tell them "at once that I was a transcendentalist." [263]

As he embarked on the most "scientific" phase of his life, he was unwaveringly critical of contemporary science. "One studies books of science merely to learn the language of naturalists, to be able to communicate with them," he confessed, and said that "to look at [Nature] turns the man of science to stone." The modern science of the heavens was perhaps the most contemptible:

> A few good anecdotes is our science, with a few imposing statements respecting distance and size, and little or nothing about the stars as they concern man; teaching how he may survey a country or sail a ship, and not how he may steer his life. Astrology contained a higher truth than this.

Though astronomy was now taught at the district school and observatories had multiplied, "Nobody sees the stars now," Thoreau lamented. Sticking to his belief that the naked eye always saw farther than the telescope, he boasted "the poet's eye in fine frenzy rolling ranges from earth to heaven, but this the astronomer's does not often do." [264]

The other institution of which he had always been critical but which disappointed his hopes more than ever was the American government, because of its support of slavery. But Americans themselves came in for criticism. While in his essay "Walking" he could enthusiastically champion the spirit of westward movement when it was expressive of individual impulses toward wildness and freedom, that same migration Thoreau felt to be an indictment of American expansionism.

> The whole enterprise of this nation which is not an upward, but a westward one, toward Oregon, California, Japan, etc., is totally devoid of interest to me, whether performed on foot or by a Pacific railroad. It

is not illustrated by a single thought it is not warmed by a sentiment, there is nothing in it one should lay down his life for, even his gloves. . . . It is perfectly heathenish—a filibustering *toward* heaven by the great western route. No, they may go their way to their manifest destiny which I trust is not mine.

The destiny manifested by Americans who stayed behind was equally troubling to Thoreau, who saw most of his neighbors' cornucopia of enterprise and practicality as depauperate as Jenny Dugan's Desert. "Haven't we our everlasting life to get? And isn't that the only excuse at last for eating drinking sleeping or even carrying an umbrella when it rains? A man might as well devote himself to raising pork, as to fattening the bodies or temporal part merely of the whole human family." The richer America grew, the more endangered Thoreau felt its soul to be.[265]

One source of truth these days for Thoreau was the English language, whose nuances no one better enjoyed exploiting. Richard Trench's *On the Study of Words* (1851) contributed to Thoreau's appreciation of the word *wild*, as Trench demonstrated its relation etymologically to *will*. This was a revelation for Thoreau, who sought always to live wildly and willfully. He took off on a characteristic flight of philosophical fancy with this one linguistic liaison:

Trench says a wild man is a *willed* man. Well, then, a man of will does what he wills or wishes, a man of hope and of the future tense, for not only the obstinate is willed, but far more the constant and persevering. The obstinate man, properly speaking, is one who will not. The perseverance of saints is positive willedness, not a mere passive willingness. The fates are wild, for they *will*; and the Almighty is wild above all, as fate is.

Able to read Greek, Latin, French, German, Italian, and Spanish, Thoreau kept seventeen dictionaries in his study. "A word is wiser than any man," Thoreau believed, ". . . in its inner sense by descent and analogy it approves itself. Language is the most perfect work of art in the world. The chisel of a thousand years retouches it." Trench had a Thoreauvian sense of language, including among his select list of "true words" "transport, rapture, ravishment, ecstasy." "These are the words I want," crowed Thoreau. "These are truly poetical words. I am inspired, elevated, expanded. I am on the mount." Along with such poetic expression for his inner world, as he sharpened his skills as a field naturalist, he felt the need increasingly for a complementarily bounteous vocabulary for the outer world. He was keenly aware that his ability to experience nature was limited by his capacity to name it. After learning that the green dust on stone walls was a decaying state of a lichen, *Lepraria chlorina*, Thoreau remarked: "I have long known this dust, but as I did not know the name of it, i.e., what others called [it], and therefore could not conveniently speak of it, it has suggested less to me and I have made less use of it. I now first feel as if I have got hold of it." The relationship between signifier and signified ran in two directions, words being enriched by things as well as things being brought to life by words. "He is richest who has most use for nature as raw material of tropes and symbols with which to describe his life.... The man of science, who is not seeking for expression but for a fact to be expressed merely, studies nature as a dead language. I pray for such inward experience as will make nature significant." [266]

The spring of 1853 began for Thoreau not in late March with returning robins, blossoming crocuses, or leafing red maples, but the first week of March, when, with snow still on the ground, he cut alder, willow, and aspen twigs and brought them indoors, forcing their tightly closed catkins to relax and spill their pollen prematurely. Scrutinizing willow catkins outdoors, he found one whose reddish "silk" (stamens) projected more than the length of the protective scales, and thus "felt the influence of the year." He checked shrubs and ferreted about in last year's dead leaves for green shoots, discovering emergent leaves of goldenrod, mulberry, hawkweed, and gerardia. "What is the earliest sign of spring?" he asked in dead earnest. "The motion of worms and insects?

The flow of sap in trees and the swelling of buds?" George Minott, Thoreau's most trusted authority on all manner of outdoor lore, told him that the first sure sign of spring was the bark of the "striped squirrel" (chipmunk). On March 10 he decided that the first obvious evidence of spring was the erupting of the swamp willow catkins, followed by the withering of the alder catkins, and then the emergence of skunk cabbage spathes, but when all was said and done, the telltale of the real first spring day was that he did not think it necessary to button up his coat. Having solved the question of the date of spring's advent, he turned to dozens of others: "What is that dark pickle-green alga at the bottom of this ditch?" When was this spotted turtle hatched and where? "What is the theory of these sudden pitches . . . in the sandy bottom of the brook?" "What was that sound that came on the softened air?" "Was that a mink we saw at the Boiling Spring?" "Why are the early birds found most along the water?" "Why is the pollen of flowers commonly yellow?" Questions of identification he usually answered by the end of the season (though the "*tull-lull*" of the bird he sometimes called a chickadee, sometimes "myrtle-bird," he would not positively identify as a white-throated sparrow until January 1858); ecological questions might take two or three seasons or many more; some questions he never answered (for seven years he tried but failed to find the source of an "ineffable" fragrance smelled each spring), and some of these have even stopped being asked by naturalists.[267]

The intensity of Thoreau's observations this spring borders on compulsion, as he constantly predicts, based on the temperature of the day, whether such and such a plant will have leafed or blossomed, then makes a beeline to that plant to check its progress. On May 15, he listed sixty species in the order in which they had leafed out. The steady search after the minute-by-minute unfolding of Concord's common flora was punctuated occasionally with a manic hunt for a rare plant. At the end of May, Sophia brought home a single blossom of the *Azalea nudiflora*, or pinxter flower, from Mrs. Brooks's. Finding from Mrs. Brooks that George Melvin had given it to her son, he found him at work, only to discover that he didn't know where Melvin had got it. Hearing that someone had seen the shrub at Captain Jarvis's, Thoreau went there and found some in the house, but they had gotten theirs from Melvin and didn't know from where he had gotten it. At Stedman Buttrick's he found a young man who said that there was only one bush in town and its location was a secret. Thoreau went on to Melvin's house, expecting not to find him in, but when he arrived, there sat Melvin, bareheaded in the shade by the back door, a large pailful of the elusive azalea beside him.

Melvin, a hunter and trapper greatly respected by Thoreau for his woods knowledge—"dilly-dallied" a bit, calling to his neighbor to ask if he knew where that "red honeysuckle" grew. "This was to prolong the time and make the most of his secret," Thoreau said. Then he recalled running into Melvin up the Assabet River a few weeks previously when he had gone to collect a mustard in flower. Melvin had appeared out of the woods, and seeing Thoreau's flower had commented that it was "not so handsome as the honeysuckle." Now he realized that Melvin's "honeysuckle" was the pinxter flower, and Thoreau told Melvin that

> he had better tell me where it was; I was a botanist and ought to know. . . . I told him he'd better tell me and have the glory of it, for I should surely find it if he didn't. I'd got a clue to it, and shouldn't give it up. I should go over the river for it . . . I could smell it a good way, you know. He thought I could smell it half a mile, and he wondered that I hadn't stumbled on it. . . .

Getting into his boat with his dog, Melvin took Thoreau to the coveted bush and showed him how close Ellery Channing had once passed by it while it was in flower. Melvin had found it ten years before and went to it every year, thinking it "the handsomest flower that grows." This episode of the pinxter flower suggests the degree to which Concord's motherwit about the local landscape was dispersed throughout the entire community. Although Thoreau possessed special knowledge, he never ceased appealing to others to share what they knew with him. Thoreau complained frequently about the indifference with which most of his neighbors regarded the natural world, but there were among both the educated villagers and the humble farmers many amateur naturalists. Clearly George Melvin had the sort of intimate, affective relationship with this one rare shrub that Thoreau cultivated with many plants in many places.[268]

Once he finally arrived at the prize shrub, Thoreau approached it with the same exactness as he did any other phenomenon and gave in his journal a thorough description, commenting particularly on a characteristic—its clamminess—not noted in his botanical manuals. But the careful taxonomic examination did not obscure for Thoreau the fact that the quest for *Azalea nudiflora* was mythic as much as scientific:

> Some incidents in my life have seemed far more allegorical than actual; they were so significant that they plainly served no other use. That is, I have been more impressed by their allegorical significance and fitness; they have been like myths or passages in a myth, rather than mere incidents or history which have to wait to become significant. Quite in harmony with my subjective philosophy. This, for instance: that when I thought I knew the flowers so well, the beautiful azalea or pinxter-flower should be shown me by the hunter who found it. Such facts are lifted quite above the level of the actual. They are all just such events as my imagination prepares me for, no matter how incredible. Perfectly in keeping with my life and characteristic. Ever and anon something will occur which my philosophy has not dreamed of. The limits of the actual are set some thoughts further off. That which had seemed a rigid wall of vast thickness unexpectedly proves a thin and undulating drapery. The boundaries of the actual are more fixed and rigid than the elasticity of our imaginations. The fact that a rare and beautiful flower which we never saw, perhaps never heard [of], for which therefore there was no place in our thoughts, may at length be found in our immediate neighborhood, is very suggestive.[269]

The pinxter flower afforded Thoreau a glimpse of the mythic condition of his own life. The fact so striking to him—that such a rare plant should be found so close at hand—would have been exceptional in someone else's experience but was unexceptional in his own. It was, rather, "perfectly in keeping with my life and characteristic." Yet another level of allegory escaped Thoreau's notice, for "pinxter" was the Dutch term for Whitsuntide, or Pentecost, when the newly baptized wore white robes signifying their exalted state. Named to commemorate its blossoming time about seven weeks after Easter Sunday, it was a fit plant to elicit such passion from Thoreau, given his obsession this season with the vernal phenology of local plants. Beyond this, though, the pinxter flower was emblematic of a kind of personal Pentecost for Thoreau; he could now, after his year of observation, speak in nature's own tongue, baptizing others not yet anointed with such grace.

Gossamer

On the first of June Thoreau walked out to Walden, all the signs—leaves expanded to provide shade from the summer weather, trees and shrubs forming fruit, young birds hatching—now saying that summer had begun. George Melvin showed Thoreau a pile of blackened timber he had fished from the river after the gunpowder mills in Acton had exploded in early January. Thoreau had been at home when the explosion occurred, and he had run out of the house to see a vast column of smoke rising from the direction of the powder mills four miles away. Before jumping into a passing wagon to ride to the accident, he took notes on the color and shape of the progressively changing cloud. His report of what he found at the mill reads like a safety inspector's report, as he details the destruction of the buildings and the sight of human carnage—"Some of the clothes of the men were in the tops of the trees, where undoubtedly their bodies had been and left them. The bodies were naked and black, some limbs and bowels here and there, and a head at a distance from its trunk. The feet were bare; the hair singed to a crisp." His terse recommendation against future accidents: "Put the different buildings thirty rods apart, and then but one will blow up at a time."²⁷⁰

Melvin's display of the disaster's artifacts called forth from Thoreau the memory of the eastward-drifting smoke cloud, which he imagined carrying the news to the far-off mill proprietor. The charred timbers traveled in his imagination down the Concord to the Merrimack and out to the ocean to be carried by the Gulf Stream to the coast of Norway, where they would be cast upon the shore covered with barnacles: "Shouldered by whales. Alighted on at first by the muskrat and the peetweet, and finally perhaps the stormy petrel and the beach-birds. It is long before Nature forgets it. How slowly the ruins are being dispersed!" This reverie was as much a plea to humanize the industrial accident as it was sheer geographic fantasy. The front pages of American newspapers were constantly trumpeting headlines of such accidents, which were far too common in the rapidly industrializing nation. The men and women were frequently no more than cannon fodder, for the typical factory worker was an anonymous immigrant. But the real impact of this tragedy upon Thoreau was as an example of an event unfolding in time, with its own idiosyncratic rhythms. "Nobody takes the trouble to record all the consequences of such an event," he complained, convinced that if one attended carefully—in the manner of tracking the growth of a plant—there would be important revelations worth garnering.²⁷¹

Hearing this same afternoon a farmer's horn calling his hands in from the fields "to an early tea" (the evening meal), Thoreau noted how this sound often told him the time of day. About this same time, five P.M., he found a patch of snapdragon catchfly with blossoms wide open, and he wondered about their rhythm of opening and closing, for these also opened at night. These phenomena with their quotidian rhythms were sometimes interrupted by erratic, anomalous phenomena. On All Hallow's Eve, rowing with Sophia to Fair Haven Bay to gather grapes, they found "everywhere and on everything" fine white gossamer threads "produced in the atmosphere by some chemistry, spun out of air, I know not for what purpose." After going ashore, Thoreau inspected the bridge, which was covered with the mysterious threads. He had to keep changing his point of view, keeping the sun behind the gossamer, in order to be able to see it. Gossamer covered the grape vines he had collected in a basket in the boat, and he wondered that they did not get it in their mouths and nostrils, or cover their clothing with it, as they continually broke through the tiny strands. "It might well be an electric phenomenon," he declared, but he assumed, with his entomological authorities Kirby and Spence, that the gossamer was the product of ballooning spiders, sailing forth from aerial perches with silk parachutes. "What," Thoreau asked, "can possess these spiders thus to run all at once to every the least elevation, and let off this wonderful stream?" He put the question to Harvard entomologist Thaddeus Harris, to no avail. Henry and Sophia mused that perhaps the spiders were frolicking for one last time before the killing frost.[272]

The next day he was back out at Hubbard's Bridge to investigate further, but he found fewer strands and poorer light conditions for seeing the gossamer still present. As always, he drew some moral lesson from the phenomenon: "It was a woof, without warp, of the finest conceivable texture, as it were made to strain the air and light, catch all the grossness of the declining year and leave us the clear, strained, November air. . . . Thus Nature gathers up her trail, and finely concludes. . . . No industry is vain, and this must have a reason." Having satisfied himself with an ultimate cause, still he wondered about the proximal stimulus: "Now that the air is so cool and clear and free of insects, what possesses these little creatures to toil and spin so?" From his reading, he found that European folklore held the silken webs to be composed of dew burned by the sun, and that in Germany, where they were so characteristic of autumn, they were called *der fliegender Sommer*—the flying or departing summer. Gilbert White in his *Natural History of Selbourne* described a September 1741 fall of "angel hair" that extended about eight miles, over the villages of Bradley and Alresford as well as Selbourne;

White said that the "cobweb" was so thick that he had to scrape it from his dogs' eyes and that it had fallen all day, not in single filmy threads, but in "perfect flakes or rags" five or six inches long. Kirby and Spence said that even the poet Henry Moore concurred that gossamer was the product of field spiders.[273]

In 1856 Thoreau was still relating the gossamer to the activity of frolicking spiders. Then in 1858 he noticed that amid all the skeins of gossamer—"which every few inches are stretched from root to root or clod to clod, gleaming and waving in the sun, the light flashing along them as they wave in the wind"—there was not a single spider. He would see the gossamer display three more times in 1858, once in 1859, and thrice again in 1860, but never again comment upon the presence or absence of spiders. Look in any standard reference work on insects today, and you will find that "ballooning spiders" is the universal explanation. Neither these authorities nor Thoreau nor Gilbert White nor Charles Darwin—who in 1832, sixty miles from land, observed gossamer fall on the deck of the *Beagle*—has taken up the question as to why more often than not these gossamer events are absent the spiders. No scientific authority then or now has explained the geographic restriction—or extension, in the case of White's 1741 episode—of the gossamer falls. The Selbourne fall of gossamer lasted for nine hours in daylight and nine hours at night, all within the same triangular region of landscape. A whole series of logical leaps were made by generations of naturalists: Spiders make silken webs in grassy meadows and upon trees and sometimes even parachute forth upon their little webs, dogs nosed the stuff in the grass and got blindfolded by it, and people caught the stuff on their shirts, just like spiderwebs, so gossamer must therefore be spiderweb.[274]

"Some circumstantial evidence," Thoreau once declared, "is very strong, as when you find a trout in the milk." There was a trout in the milk of these gossamer falls, but no one, not even the consummate facer of facts Henry David Thoreau, seemed too concerned about it. Thoreau *had* noticed the circumstantial evidence that one day in 1858, though, and correspondents to American newspapers, who would write to report a spectacular fall of gossamer only to mention that they had seen no spiders, joined him occasionally. In July 1858, Thoreau had clipped that little newspaper notice of a shower of flies on the Illinois River and stuck it into his fact book in the section where he had taken notes on Kirby and Spence's pronouncements about ballooning spiders. If he had been a more regular reader of newspapers, he might have filled his fact book with reports of odd stuff falling out of the sky. In 1841 and 1846, at Memel in Asia Minor, a substance variously described as gelatinous or like cereal or paper fell from the skies; a German naturalist declared it to be the freshwater algae *Nostoc*. There fell in the fields of Kourianof (Kuryanovo), Russia, in March 1832, a combustible yellowish substance two inches thick, covering an area of six or seven hundred square feet. Naturalists pronounced it to be pollen from pine trees, but it was resinous, and when torn, it had the tenacity of cotton. A month later, a substance that was wine-yellow, transparent, soft, and smelling like rancid oil fell in the same place; a chemist who examined it called it "sky oil." An "unctuous" substance also fell near Rotterdam in 1832. An oily, reddish stuff fell at Genoa in February 1841. In November 1849, *Scientific American* reported a "fall of manna," four months after a fall of lichens. Edward Hitchcock's 1833 account of the "species of gelatinous fungus" found in Amherst in the wake of a falling star comes to mind. Thoreau's comment in *Walden* that "Sometimes it has rained flesh and blood" was not unsupported by data: In 1841 the *American Journal of Science* reviewed a number of cases. Falls of frogs and fishes and other fauna were not infrequently reported.[275]

Such filler items on anomalous phenomena of natural history crammed every corner of the popular press, and even in the early years of the nineteenth century made their way into the scientific journals, but by the late nineteenth century, they ceased to serve as facts worthy of investigation. Instead, they became a curious form of light entertainment for the scientifically uncredentialed, an irksome reminder of the lay public's gullibility—like UFOs and crop circles—to the scientific establishment. Gossamer—the word itself something of a linguistic mystery, thought perhaps to be from "goose-summer" (since it was seen most frequently in late autumn, the season of migrating geese)—became and remains a mystery not because what science "commonly see[s] is but half," but because in this instance and so many others, what it sees is "but twice," i.e., more than what is actually there. Science saw spider silk where there were no spiders, and continues to do so. A kind of quiet excommunication was performed on the phenomenon, along with the other strange stuff that fell from the sky throughout the century. Charles Fort, the indefatigable student of such anomalies, would say that "the datum has been buried alive," damned, "not by denial, and not by explaining away, but by simple disregard." As nineteenth-century natural science in America increasingly made "nature"—but in reality, its own institutional image of nature—the arbiter of truth, an invisible hand vanished certain phenomena from view, thereby preserving its hegemony.[276]

Thoreau stumbled upon other oddities. In January 1854, in a hollow east of Walden Pond, he heard a buzzing sound coming out of the ground, "like that of a large fly or bee in a spider's web." Crawling on the frozen ground on his knees, he traced the noise to a bare spot about the size of his hand, and poked at the ground with a stick, lest he be stung. Saying that the incessant sound made his ears ache, he finally traced it to a few stems of dead grass sticking up out of a pool of melted snow. He imagined for a minute that it was the "infantile cry of an earthquake," and then more reasonably conjectured that it was caused by air trapped under the frozen ground. There were no air bubbles, however. A week later, Thoreau was in Cambridge to testify in a land dispute, and went to see Thaddeus Harris about the identity of a Cecropia moth cocoon he had found. Though no mention is made of his having queried Harris about the odd noise, during their visit, Harris confessed to Thoreau that he had never seen snow fleas before! The most elementary phenomena familiar to country people were frequently mysterious to the taxonomists and other scientific experts entrusted to decode them.[277]

Others in Concord might have heard the enigmatic buzzing sound, but Thoreau never knew of it. Many had heard the strange noises from Nashoba and Nagog, and throughout America, there were other aural phenomena—such as the "Seneca Guns" and the "Moodus Noises"—which had been heard by thousands of people, generation after generation. As damned as gossamer was to the dustbin of scientific disregard, they remain mysteries. They also remain important indications of epistemological error, showing quite clearly the boundaries of scientific inquiry. Mystic, transcendentalist, and natural philosopher Thoreau constantly brought before the eyes of his contemporaries that which was *unseen*, and *unheard*, and yet there were certainly plenty of east-quarter places and phenomena in the cosmos that remained closed to him.

Transcendentalism and Turtles

The lawlessness of gossamer and kindred falls or booming and buzzing portions of the earth was arresting because it stood in such contrast to nature's lawfulness. Thoreau had begun his journal in 1837 in a state of great excitement over Goethe's *Italian Journey*, which comes to a head in Goethe's discovery of the "law of the leaf"—that all the organs of plants are but variations on the leaf. Thoreau had with his own eyes that next winter discovered the law uniting vegetative leaves and the hoarfrost foliage of ice that grew on his windowpane, and he had remained fascinated by any such organic demonstrations of the primal leaf. In February 1854 the midwinter sun was strong enough to set the sandbank in the Deep Cut melting into its characteristic leafy forms, which Thoreau had watched develop each spring since 1844 after the Fitchburg Railroad line was cut through the glacial sands flanking Walden Pond. In spring, the twenty- to forty-foot-high south-facing bank would rapidly produce this sand foliage over its entire quarter-mile length, while the north-facing bank remained inert. Overcome by the vitality of such a display, Thoreau saw more than the archetypal pattern for the leaf springing out of the thawing sand and clay; he saw blood vessels, river systems, the human skeleton spreading out to congeal in the toes and fingers. In his journal, he wrote, "That sand foliage! It convinces me that Nature is still in her youth—that florid fact about which mythology merely mutters—that the very soil can fabulate as well as you or I. It stretches forth its baby fingers on every side." Though he had long felt it, he now stated explicitly the supreme law that his observations taught him: "There is nothing inorganic. This earth is not, then, a mere fragment of a dead history, strata upon strata, like the leaves of a book, an object for a museum or an antiquarian, but living poetry, like the leaves of a tree—not a fossil earth, but a living specimen." [278]

This springlike thaw melted Thoreau too, and set his prose flowing as copiously as the clay and sand. He was working on the seventh and final draft of *Walden*, and he added now a fluid prose poem on the sandbank foliage, which became the centerpiece of the book's penultimate chapter, "Spring." This February saw Thoreau revise the newly written conclusion to *Walden* as well, and it seethed with the sandbank's vitality. All of the lawfulness that *Walden*'s seasonal structure imparted was, in the conclusion, construed as but one more bounds to walk extravagantly across. "If one advances confidently in the direction of his dreams," Thoreau counseled, "and endeavors to live the life he has imagined, he will meet with a success unexpected in common hours . . . new, universal, and more liberal laws will begin to establish themselves around and within him; or the old laws will be expanded." Thoreau's call for all individuals to reach beyond Nature's rhythmic repetition, to her capacity for fresh creation, is the heart of transcendentalism's promise, the freedom granted only after one has studied and understood Nature's immutable laws. [279]

As spring and summer came on, Thoreau peeked into creation this year by studying turtles. Having caught a thirty-pound snapping turtle in the river, he managed to get him home, then measured him in every conceivable direction. He collected stories of snapping turtles' incredible tenacity: Someone told him about a turtle's head snapping at a dog the day after it had been cut off, and he heard another tale about a snapping turtle's heart beating a day after a naturalist had dissected the animal. The animal struck Thoreau as "purely material and mechanical." After finding a nest of stinkpot (musk turtle) eggs, he brought them home and buried them in his garden. Three weeks later he dug one up and opened it to examine the embryo. In the midst of the formless yellow yolk, the turtle's eyes (two full-size dark circles) and heart (simply "a very distinct pulsation where the heart should be") were visible. In short, staccato sentences he condemned himself for killing a Blanding's turtle "for the sake of science": "No reasoning whatever reconciles me to this act. It affects my day injuriously. I have lost some self-respect." He began to have turtles on the brain, in August seized by the thought that under the ground all summer long were slowly hatching turtles. Hatching baby snappers—"this monster . . . steadily advancing toward maturity"—convinced him that there "must be an irresistible necessity for mud turtles." He wakes up one August morning thinking of snapping turtles and cannot tell whether he is awake or dreaming, then looks up from his bed to see his captive snapper lying beneath his writing table. "That the first object you should see on awakening should be an empty mud turtle's shell!!! Will it not make me of the earth earthy? . . . This too was once an infant in its egg. When I see this, I am sure that I am not dreaming, but am awake to this world." The monstrous, mechanical creature was still a consolation to him, a "terrene fact" hovering on the borderline of the Earth's widest taxonomic divisions. Just as the sandbank leaves wavered between mineral and vegetable, the snapping turtle waddled between vegetable and animal.[280]

As the season advanced, Thoreau developed a nearly maternal sympathy with turtles. In September he dug up and opened a snapping turtle egg to examine the embryo, and afterward, thinking it nearly dead, left it out in the rain. The next day he found it crawling around a few feet away from the broken shell, with the yolk still attached.

Astounded, he exclaimed, "They thus not only continue to live after they are dead, but begin to live before they are alive!" Thoreau dotes on the little yolk-trailing snapper, providing him with a tub of mud and water. The turtle begins to teach Thoreau something about the human being: "The insensibility and toughness of his infancy make our life, with its disease and low spirits, ridiculous. He impresses me as the rudiment of a man worthy to inhabit the earth." A little reminiscent of himself, he allegorizes: "He is born with a shell. That is symbolical of his toughness. His shell being so rounded and sharp on the back at his age, he can turn over without trouble." When the first of the transplanted musk turtles hatch out, Thoreau imagines the earth itself as their mother:

> I am affected by the thought that the earth nurses these eggs. They are planted in the earth, and the earth takes care of them; she is genial to them and does not kill them. It suggests a certain vitality and intelligence in the earth, which I had not realized. This mother is not merely inanimate and inorganic. Though the immediate mother turtle abandons her offspring, the earth and sun are kind to them. The old turtle on which the earth rests takes care of them while the other waddles off. Earth was not made poisonous and deadly to them. The earth has some virtue in it; when seeds are put into it, they germinate; when turtles' eggs, they hatch in due time. Though the mother turtle remained and brooded them, it would still nevertheless be the universal world turtle which, through her, cared for them as now. Thus the earth is the mother of all creatures.

This was no Darwinian natural history, telling of nature red in tooth and claw, but a sympathetic biology founded on the recognition of the "universal world turtle," that same great mother spoken of in Native American mythology, who not only supported the globe with her stout back, but also with her nurturing warmth could penetrate the cool sands to quicken the life-giving yolks below.[281]

While snappers and stinkpots were being stirred into life this summer, another long-incubated creation hatched on August 9. His journal for the day reads simply: "Wednesday. To Boston. *Walden* published. Elderberries. Waxwork yellowing." That evening he had dinner with Alcott and gave him a copy of his new book. After reading and rereading it, and then going back to reread also *A Week*, Alcott said they were "books to find readers and fame as years pass by, and publish the author's surpassing merits." Though some of the early reviews were positive, an equal number were dismissive or downright disparaging. The *Boston Puritan Recorder* begins with a common cynical remark about Thoreau "play[ing] hermit," and ends by pointing to the top of page 118 to alert prospective readers to a remark of Thoreau's "inconsistent with . . . Christianity." The *National Era* of Washington, D.C., psychologized Thoreau, accusing him of being unconscious of his own share of "the infirmities of human nature": "To go out and squat, all alone, by a pretty pond in the woods, dig, lay the foundation of a little cabin, and put it up, with borrowed tools, furnish it, raise corn, beans, and potatoes, and do one's own cooking, hermit like, so that the total cost of the whole building, furnishing, purchasing necessaries, and living for eight months, shall not exceed forty or fifty dollars, may do for an experiment by a highly civilized man, with Yankee versatility, who had had the full benefit of the best civilization of the age." The *Boston Atlas* was appalled that Thoreau's constant communion with Nature "was not able to kindle one spark of warmth in this would-be savage. . . . There is not a page, a paragraph giving one sign of liberality, charitableness, kind feeling, generosity, in a word—heart." [282]

Sometime after the publication of his masterwork, Thoreau wrote on the inside cover of his sixth journal volume: "My faults are: Paradoxes, saying just the opposite, a style which may be imitated. Ingenious. Playing with words, getting the laugh, not always simple, strong, and broad. Using current phrases and maxims, when I should speak for myself. Not always earnest. 'In short,' 'in fact,' 'alas!' etc. Want of conciseness. *Walden* published Aug 9th, 54. Sent Fields 12 copies of the *Week*,

Oct. 18th, '54." This offhand self-assessment certainly contradicted his last criticism, and these were faults that escaped the notice of his reviewers, who were more liable to fault his heretical views on religion, society, and culture. Whatever literary shortcomings he found in himself, the transcendentalism that Thoreau offered in *Walden* had the same qualities as the turtles he came to admire this summer. The heroic life called for in *Walden* was above all a life of courage, not for its author's having walked off a mile from the village to live in a cabin of his own construction for two years, but for its unshakable confidence in the human imagination. "If I were confined to a corner of a garret all my days, like a spider," he declared in the conclusion, perhaps thinking of his old hero Sir Walter Raleigh, "the world would be just as large to me while I had my thoughts about me." The fledgling snapping turtle dragging his embryonic sac behind him was nothing if not courageous; even the nearly mechanical tenacity for life of the decapitated adult displayed an undeniable form of bravery. Observing the forming of perfect organs out of the turtle egg's yolky chaos reinforced Thoreau's sense of nature's supreme lawfulness, a leitmotif running through all of *Walden*. The ultimate quality celebrated in *Walden*, however, is one possessed by no turtle or any other creature besides the human being. If men were to escape from leading "lives of quiet desperation," they had to make those lives perpetually meaningful. The men and women born generation after generation upon the back of the universal world turtle had but one transcendent task—to seek out and make sense of Nature's order, however inscrutable it might appear. Human beings—both their individual biographies and the "second nature," i.e., culture they created—were not exempt from this task but an integral part of it. The book that Henry Thoreau gave to America and to the world was a true book, prophetic not because its author was clairvoyant but because he lived eternal verities, ones that the world might have lost sight of during his lifetime and ours, but which it must regain if the universal world turtle is to go on crawling toward the stars.[283]

A Constant Mirage

The publication of *Walden* brought new invitations to Thoreau to lecture: In October he went to Plymouth to give his "Moonlight" lecture; in November a Philadelphia audience heard "Moosehunting," a reflection on his Maine trips; in early December, Thoreau—advertised as "Author of 'Life in the Woods'")—gave the fourth lecture in a series at Railroad Hall in Providence. Lecturing hardly fulfilled the aspirations for courage and integrity he had called for in *Walden*, and the experience left him feeling "cheapened":

> I am disappointed to find that most that I am and value for myself is lost, or worst than lost, on my audience. I fail to get even the attention of the mass. I should suit them better if I suited myself less. I feel that the public demand an average man,—average thoughts and manners,—not originality, nor even absolute excellence. You cannot interest them except as you are like them and sympathize with them.... To read to a promiscuous audience who are at your mercy the fine thoughts you solaced yourself with far away is as violent as to fatten geese by cramming, and in this case they do not get fatter.

At least a few listeners shared Thoreau's evaluation; a Philadelphia friend of Emerson's who missed the lecture wrote to Emerson that he had heard from others that "the audience was stupid and did not appreciate him." [284]

At the invitation of his new friend Daniel Ricketson, a New Bedford admirer of *Walden*, on the day after Christmas in New Bedford, Thoreau gave his lecture "Getting a Living." This was the draft of an essay finally published in the *Atlantic Monthly* in 1862 as "Life Without Principle"; he gave this lecture a number of times over the next six years, variously calling it "The Connection Between Man's Employment and His Higher Life," "What Shall It Profit?" "Life Misspent," and "The Higher

Law." The lecture was Thoreau's rebuke of capitalism, a naysaying expansion of his *Walden* argument that getting a living was but a *means*, not the *end*, of the very serious business of living authentically. The written version of the lecture opened with his disappointment that lyceum audiences rarely asked for and even more rarely received the "meat" rather than the "shell" of a lecturer. For his part, once engaged for a lecture, Thoreau intended to give the audience a "strong dose" of himself, determined that "they shall have me, though I bore them beyond all precedent." He even complained openly of lyceum audiences' preference for flattery over frank criticism, saying, "I have walked into such an arena and done my best to make a clean breast of what religion I have experienced, and the audience never suspected what I was about." "Life Without Principle" could not have been clearer as to what he was about: "I think there is nothing, not even crime, more opposed to poetry, to philosophy, ay, to life itself, than this incessant business." Pointing to pursuits of Mammon both small (the cheating of customers in selling cordwood) and large (the rush after California gold) Thoreau admonished that "a grain of gold will gild a great surface, but not so much as a grain of wisdom." The "news" daily seduced men into misspending their thoughts. "Read not the Times. Read the Eternities," Thoreau advised. "Getting a Living" was peculiarly an *American* problem, for despite granting of political freedom (to some, not all), Americans remained bound by an economic and moral tyrant, Mammon.[285]

America's continued myopia about the real meaning of independence—and his distaste for "Cattle Show" mobs—kept Thoreau from ever celebrating Independence Day. On July 4, 1855, Thoreau and Ellery Channing arrived at the Boston wharf at eight A.M. to take the schooner *Melrose* to Provincetown for a two-week Cape Cod excursion, only to discover that the trip was canceled because of the holiday. They made the best of it by visiting the Athenaeum gallery, where they saw Frederick Church's gigantic "Andes of Ecuador." The Cape Cod expedition as rendered by Thoreau's pen was just as dramatic and exotic a feast for the eye as Church's painting. The journal entries are a straightforward recording of impressions of people, places, and events, filled with facts and figures—the price of fresh lobsters, the dimensions of "blackfish" (pilot whales), the height of the sandbank below Provincetown lighthouse, the number of clams dug in East Harbor, the amount of money appropriated to dredge Provincetown Harbor. But in his written sketch of Cape Cod, the facts from this and his other travels there become little patches of poverty grass to hold the shifting sands of the Cape's sublime scenery in place. "Scenery" is the ostensible object of Thoreau's excursions to the Cape. "Wishing to get a better view than I had yet of the ocean," the first installment of the essay series, published in *Putnam's*, begins, "I made a visit to Cape Cod. . . ." Revisiting the first trip of October 1849, Thoreau tells how his plans to see the ocean from the outer Cape went awry when he ended up in Cohasset instead, witness to the carnage of the recent shipwreck. On his second voyage, he presents himself as a stagecoach-transported sightseer, armed with his own copy of the eighth volume of the *Collections of the Massachusetts Historical Society* as his guidebook. Thoreau enters the Cape in a fog, and at Dennis, when he puts his head out the window, he finds it difficult to believe that he is not already at the beach. "Through the mist, singular barren hills, all stricken with poverty grass, loom[ed] up as if they were in the horizon, though they were close to us, and we seemed to have got to the end of land on that side, notwithstanding that the horses were still headed that way." *As if* becomes a key construction in *Cape Cod*, which is also littered with *seemed*, *appeared*, and *but . . .* , phrases expressive of the "constant mirage" Thoreau found the Cape to be.[286]

He had long been fascinated by tricks of visual perception. Walking on Staten Island in 1846, some seven or eight miles from shore, he had caught a glimpse through a gap in some hills of a ship at full sail, twenty miles out to sea, but looking as if it were borne upon the waving tassels of the cornfield in front of him; the image stayed with him for years. Earlier in 1855, skating on the Sudbury River, he was shocked when the knotty stubs of a dead limb in front of him lifted up into the air, turning out to be partridges. Once he saw what appeared to be sequentially the yellowed skeleton of a bird, a turtle shell, and then a pile of dry oak leaves metamorphose into a woodcock. A November shadbush in full bloom on another occasion was really the feathery seed ball of the virgin's bower. "It is singular how one thing thus puts on the semblance of another," he mused. "I thought at first I had made a discovery more interesting than the blossoming of apple trees in the fall." On other occasions, he mistook a forest fire for a red flag, a young woodchuck for a piece of rusty iron, a real man for a scarecrow. Just this same illusion happened again at Wellfleet on Thoreau's second trip to Cape Cod. Paying a visit to a cheerful old oysterman with whom he had stayed the previous year, Thoreau saw the man's simpleminded son in a cornfield and mistook him for a scarecrow.[287]

Thoreau was unabashed about reporting these errors, for they were just the sort of spontaneous inversions of perception that he courted consciously in his engagement with the world. "Our minds anywhere, when left to themselves," Thoreau wrote after mistaking the sound of a waterfall for a railroad engine, "are always thus busily drawing conclusions from false premises." On Cape Cod, the curving spit of sand held out like a boxer's arm to spar with the sea, the landscape presented countless opportunities for obfuscation. The wide-open expanses of sand, absent trees or houses, tricked the eyes into mistakes of scale. Seeing a family out blueberrying a mile away, the dwarfed vegetation below their ankles, they appeared to him a "race of giants, twenty feet high at least." He would spy a windmill or herd of cows and think them far off on the horizon, then after walking a few rods, they stood right before him. On the beach, without even rocks to provide perspective, he thought a pile of driftwood left by "wreckers" (the term for people who made a living scavenging the beach for shipwrecked cargo) was a hut or wigwam. The same illusion occurred also when looking out to sea: "We were so often disappointed in the size of such things as came ashore, the ridiculous bits of wood or weed, with which the ocean labored, that we began to doubt whether the Atlantic itself would bear a still closer inspection, and would not turn out to be a small pond, if it came ashore to us." Along with the illusions, the Cape offered "surprises" to Thoreau: seeing a thousand bank swallows swoop over crashing surf stunned someone who had seen them always over inland waters; pygmy vegetation was familiar from Thoreau's alpine rambles, but here was the same dwarfed vegetation at sea level. Thoreau learned that Wellfleet villagers practiced a method of catching seagulls for food that entailed baiting a trap with whale meat; this method gave the local dialect the expression to be "gulled," i.e., to be taken in; Thoreau was certainly "gulled" by the Cape's perceptual traps.[288]

Thoreau on Cape Cod occasionally seems to be suffering a kind of perceptual vertigo. One morning, while walking on the beach with Channing, he sees the waves cast up a large black object, and as they approach it, Thoreau sees it successively take the form of "a huge fish, a drowned man, a sail or a net" before realizing it is a piece of shipwrecked cloth as two wreckers load it into a cart. Like the Arabian desert, the desert expanse spilling away from Mount Ararat near Provincetown was full of mirages. He comes upon a chain of clear, shallow pools of water apparently inclined at a distinct angle to the horizon, "like a mirror left in a slanting position," even though the land is quite level. Walking at sundown on the edge of the dune bank at Wellfleet, he has the impression that "the inside half of the beach sloped upward toward the water to meet the other half," even though the tracks of waves clearly showed this was impossible. The old oysterman tells Thoreau that when shooting at gulls along this same bank, you must always aim under them, to correct for the illusion. Even light, the transcendental symbol of divine truth, proves untrustworthy when reflected off the sand and sea of Cape Cod. The Highland lighthouse keeper tells Thoreau of sailors led astray by mistaking a mackerel fisher's or even a shore cottage's lantern for the lighthouse light, and tells about a "looming" of the sun he once witnessed, which caused him to extinguish the lighthouse lamps fifteen minutes before the actual sun had risen.[289]

Thoreau's aptitude for making the familiar strange had long served him as a rhetorical device for highlighting the perversities of human social life, and in his *Cape Cod* essays, he took aim at an institution peculiar to isolated maritime communities—the "charity" or "humane" house. Constructed on particularly desolate stretches of beach where shipwreck survivors might land, the little shelters were built to standard dimensions and were supposed to be stocked with hay or straw bedding for the stranded mariners, and even "accommodated with a bench." Thoreau's outlandish soliloquy on the disappointment he found upon looking into one of these houses is a comic tour de force about the elusive but real rewards of introspection:

> As we wished to get the idea of a humane house, and we hoped that we should never have a better opportunity, we put our eyes, by turns, to a knot-hole in the door, and, after long looking, without seeing, into the dark—not knowing how many shipwrecked men's bones we might see at last, looking with the eye of faith, knowing that, though to him that knocketh it may not always be opened, yet to him that looketh long enough through a knot-hole the inside shall be visible,—for we had some practice at looking inward,—by steadily keeping our other ball covered from the light meanwhile, putting the outward world behind us, ocean and land, and the beach—till the pupil became enlarged and collected the rays of light that were wandering in that dark, (for the pupil shall be enlarged by looking; there never was so dark a night but a faithful and patient eye, however small, might at last prevail over it,)—after all this, I say, things began to take shape to our vision,—if we may use this expression where there was nothing but emptiness,— and we obtained the long wished for insight.

Thoreau was just such a "pupil" who had been enlarged by looking into the dark, and his pun was a linguistic version of the perceptual inversions he constantly foregrounded in his Cape Cod rambles. Thoreau's "fault" of using paradoxical expressions was also perfectly matched to the Cape's landscape of deception. Turning the empty hut—he sees no matches nor straw nor hay nor bench inside—into an

indictment of the humane "charity" of all human institutions, he exclaims, "How cold is charity! how inhumane humanity!" [290]

A day or two after Thoreau and Channing visited the Wellfleet oysterman, two men broke into the Provincetown bank and robbed the safe,
and the oysterman and other locals wondered if the Concord men might
have been the thieves. Thoreau derived secret pleasure from this mistaken identification, for it paralleled the kind of leaps in perception that
the shimmering Cape sands were always provoking. The suspicion of the
given that Thoreau cultivated on Cape Cod gave him a venue to question
the received wisdom of Atlantic America's colonial history. Instead of a
settlement narrative, he offers a story of "unsettlement," doubly so, in
both the encounter with the contemporary thinly populated lands of the
Cape, and in his debunking of the inflated claims of colonial explorers.
Thoroughly unsettling the reader with wordplay, Thoreau whimsically
(he says "I suppose" and "perhaps" to undermine his own authority)
traces the etymological origins of "Cape Cod" to Latin *caput*, "head,"
and *capere*, "to take," "that being the part by which we take hold of a
thing: Take Time by the forelock. It is also the safest part to take a
serpent by." Glossing the Saxon word *codde* as "a case in which green
peas are lodged ... perhaps [related to] coddle—to cook like green peas,"
in this fanciful bit of philological invention he hints that he is going to
cook up a fresh view of the past. He decenters the triumphalist Puritan
history by beginning with Champlain's 1605 voyage, but he also con-
siders the possibility that Cabot and Verrazano in the sixteenth century,
or even the Vikings in the eleventh century, made landfall at Cape Cod.
His "Ante-Pilgrim" account leads him to ask, "If America was found and
lost again once, as most of us believe, then why not twice?" History,
Thoreau argues, is "for the most part ... merely a story agreed upon by
posterity. ... I believe that, if I were to live the life of mankind over again
myself, (which I would not be hired to do,) with the Universal History in
my hands, I should not be able to tell what was what." [291]

The reason that the wisecracking Thoreau would not have been hired
to live through the Universal History was that he lacked the proper

respect for the past, including the venerated founders of New England. Entering Provincetown, he juxtaposes the colonial account from *Mourt's Relation* of coming into the harbor with his own navigation of Provincetown hotels: "The Pilgrims say, 'There was the greatest store of fowl that we ever saw.' *We* saw no fowl there, except gulls of various kinds." He distrusts the Pilgrims' descriptions of just about everything, believing they exaggerated the fairness of the landscape "for they were glad to get any land at all after that anxious voyage." Indeed, the closest Thoreau gets to empathizing with the Pilgrims is when he gets sick from eating a clam and reads in a history that they did as well. "It brought me nearer to the Pilgrims to be thus reminded by a similar experience that I was so like them." By traveling east to Cape Cod to discover America, Thoreau practiced his contrary politics of refusal, and in doing so issued a salvo against the ideology of manifest destiny. His storytelling about his "sightseeing" trips to Cape Cod invited the awake listener or reader to reconsider the national myth of conquering wilderness, bewildering them into the realization that the real frontier was "wherever a man *fronts* a fact." The affronting facts he recovered from the Cape's sands debunked historical discovery, while reinvigorating the act of discovery each person can make if he unsettles his own prosaic patterns of perception. Thoreau's rule of thumb for seeing true was that "it is only when we forget all our learning that we begin to know. . . . If you . . . would fain perceive something, you must approach the object totally unprejudiced." [292]

In the American mythology of conquering the wilderness, after discovery followed possession, and Thoreau had as strange an outlook on this aspect of history. The only Cape Cod inhabitant Thoreau portrays as possessing the landscape is the wrecker, who gets his living by grabbing as quickly as possible that which others own but which the sea has violently wrested from them. Amoral and nakedly opportunistic, the salvager is the shrunken spirit of New World discovery, reduced to the petty entrepreneurial capitalism of bandit beachcombing. When Thoreau tries his own hand at wrecking, he does so to mock the monuments of national possession: "From time to time we saved a wreck ourselves, a box or barrel, and set it on its end, and appropriated it with crossed sticks; and it will lie there perhaps, respected by brother wreckers, until some more violent storm shall take it, really lost to man until wrecked again." This ephemeral monument, reminiscent of the mock Revolutionary War monument of tar barrels and boards erected in 1825 over the empty cornerstone on Concord's green, cast doubt on the legitimacy of all American monuments to discovery and possession, because they marked acts of theft as much as honest finding. Some of the most common objects cast up on the Cape Cod beach were sand dollars, the spineless and smoothed skeletons of sea urchins. Walking on the beach with Channing, Thoreau picked one up and pretended it was a silver coin, and Channing ran over excited to find more of the ancient treasure, only to discover that his companion had tricked him. The sleight-of-hand was telling, a sort of archetypal American mirage meant as always to draw our eyes toward true silver and gold.[293]

"He Prays for It, and So He Gets It"

Thoreau did not have to go to the cargo-strewn beaches of Cape Cod to find treasure hunters; there were plenty in Concord. In November 1854, walking to White Pond, he was hailed by John Hosmer and Anthony Wright to come see where they had been digging for money. Looking into a hole six feet square and as many deep, the men told Thoreau that three pirates in Captain Kidd's day had stopped by a Concord house asking if they could bury some treasure. After they were refused, the pirates walked on and buried the treasure in a nearby hollow. A woman followed them and spread the word around the village, and people had been digging in the vicinity ever since. As a little boy, Hosmer had unearthed three old-fashioned bottles while plowing, and he said that someone then consulted the Lynn seeress Moll Pitcher for exact instructions on where to dig. Born Mary Dimond, Moll Pitcher was the granddaughter of another noted New England wizard, "Ol'

Dimond"—Aholiab Dimond—of Marblehead, a Wampanoag Indian wonder-worker who used his clairvoyant powers to locate thieves and lost objects or to save sailors from shipwreck during storms and was reputed never to have used his gifts for his own advantage. Moll Pitcher shared this reputation, and the mere association of her name with a prospective treasure site guaranteed that it would be dug for generations. Stories were told after the Revolution that she had passed on British military secrets to General George Washington, whom she also prophesied would become president. She had also on a number of occasions predicted future inventions and, more rarely, mentioned certain sites of buried treasure. Thoreau's greatest interest in the money-digging activities was that the unearthed sand always sported blackberry bushes for a few seasons after the pits were dug. Though he loved to see the holes where they had dug "since they remind me that some are dreaming still like children, though of impracticable things,—dreaming of finding money, and trying to put their dream into practice. It proves that men live Arabian nights and days still." Thoreau viewed treasure-hunting as one more indication of how little curiosity his contemporaries had about more important mysteries.[294]

Despite his distaste for this sort of fortune-finding, Thoreau had an uncanny aptitude for discovering treasure. He repeatedly sensed where he would find Indian artifacts, and though this was at least partly due to his experience in distinguishing likely locations of prehistoric settlements, it was equally a mysterious faculty that baffled him. "I have frequently distinguished these localities half a mile off, gone forward, and picked up arrowheads." The trick occurred most often with flowers. One July day, having recently been shown by Emerson a specimen of the bog rosemary *Andromeda polifolia* that a Concord botanist had collected in another town, Thoreau discovered the plant in Beck Stow's Swamp. Thoreau called this "a common experience. When I am shown from abroad, or hear of, or in any [way] become interested in, some plant or other thing, I am pretty sure to find it soon." In the fall of 1856, he found two plants that he had never seen before—black nightshade and Pennsylvania smartweed—in Brattleboro, and a week later he discovered them in Concord. "I detected them first abroad," he reasoned, "because there I was *looking for* the *strange*." In 1857 he found the wild calla at the south end of Gowing's Swamp, then immediately began to detect it in other places. "Many an object is not seen, though it falls within the range of our visual ray, because it does not come within the range of our intellectual ray, *i.e.*, we are not looking for it. So, in the largest sense, we find only the world we look for." On a walk in January 1858, he had the thought that he would look for a new plant and instantaneously came upon dyer's greenweed, an alien that had become naturalized farther east. After years of searching in vain for Indian hemp, one day he read about it and was alerted to the small size of its blossoms; within a day or two, he found it in three different places. Having had a "presentiment" of finding the boreal shrub Labrador tea, he did so, and called "remarkable" the fact that almost all the rare plants he found in Concord were preceded by some such anticipation. On more than a few occasions, this happened with animals as well; on the Clamshell Bank, a bend in the Sudbury River southwest of Concord village, Thoreau one night suddenly wondered whether musk turtles lay their eggs at night, and lifting his lantern to look, saw a musk turtle just returning from egg laying.[295]

Stepping out of one's habitual paths could become an opportunity for discovery if one cultivated the proper "thrilled and expectant mood." That anticipation precedes discovery became the foundation of Thoreau's theory of perception:

> All this you will see, and much more, if you are prepared to see it, if you look for it. Otherwise, regular and universal as this phenomenon is, you will think for threescore years and ten that all the wood is at this season sere and brown. Objects are concealed from our view not so much because they are out of the course of our visual ray as because there is no intention of the mind and eye toward them. . . . The greater part of the phenomena of nature are for this reason concealed to us all

our lives.... Nature does not cast pearls before swine. There is just as much beauty visible to us in the landscape as we are prepared to appreciate, not a grain more. The actual objects which one person will see from a particular hilltop are just as different from those which another will see as the persons are different. The scarlet oak must, in a sense, be in your eye when you go forth. We cannot see anything until we are possessed with the idea of it, and then we can hardly see anything else. In my botanical rambles I find that first the idea, or image, of a plant occupies my thoughts, though it may at first seem very foreign to this locality, and for some weeks or months I go thinking of it and expecting it unconsciously, and at length I surely see it, and it is henceforth an actual neighbor of mine. This is the history of my finding a score or more of rare plants which I could name.

Plant hunting was the most personal arena for finding evidence of this law, but Thoreau knew it operated universally. He asked what report one would get from a Concord selectman—or Julius Caesar, Emanuel Swedenborg, or a Fiji Islander—placed on the town's highest hill: "Sharpening his sight to the utmost, and putting on the glasses that suited him best, aye, using a spy-glass if he liked, straining his optic nerve to its utmost, and making a full report[.] Of course, he would see a Brocken spectre of himself." Once upon a time Thoreau had been a hunter, and he was on intimate terms with Concord's finest hunters, so he knew that "it takes a sharpshooter to bring down even such trivial game as snipes and woodcocks; he must take very particular aim, and know what he is aiming at." Shooting at beauty obeyed the same law. The vagabond for beauty needed to know his quarry's seasons, its "haunts and the color of its wing," and would have dreamed of it incessantly, so that he flushed it at every step. "He prays for it, and so he gets it":

After due and long preparation, schooling his eye and hand, dreaming awake and asleep, with gun and paddle and boat, he goes out after meadow-hens, which most of his townsmen never saw nor dreamed of, paddles for miles against a head wind, and therefore he gets them. He had them half-way into his bag when he started, and has only to shove them down. The fisherman, too, dreams of fish, till he can almost catch them in his sink-spout. The hen scratches, and finds her food right under where she stands.... The true sportsman can shoot you almost any of his game from his windows. It comes and perches at last on the barrel of his gun; but the rest of the world never see it, with the feathers on. He will keep himself supplied by firing up his chimney. The geese fly exactly under his zenith, and honk when they get there. Twenty musquash [muskrats] have the refusal of each one of his traps before it is empty.

Mary Brown, the daughter of Vermont publisher Addison Brown, once sent Thoreau a box of live mayflowers from Brattleboro, Vermont, where they grew profusely on bare patches of the sand terraces of old glacial Lake Hitchcock. He wrote to her that on the very day that they arrived in Concord, he was out surveying in Sudbury and found more of the flowers than he had ever seen before. Owning that "a botanist's experience is full of coincidences," in that thinking about a flower never seen nearly always meant you would find it nearby someday, he turned his botanical experience into a general law of life: "In the long run, we find what we expect. We shall be fortunate then if we expect great things." [296]

Emerson—a capable amateur botanist who shared Thoreau's appetite, but not aptitude, for finding rare plants—was always astounded by this special talent of Thoreau's. He liked to tell the story that when Thoreau was climbing Mount Washington, he had a bad fall in Tuckerman's Ravine, and sprained his foot. Getting up from the ground, Thoreau saw for the very first time the hairy arnica, a rare alpine composite that was a well-known remedy for sprained joints. Though Emerson appreciated with Thoreau the importance of the desire to apprehend facts as a necessary precursor to securing them, he had a real sense that his friend was at times providentially guided by an invisible sympathetic hand. When Emerson said, "Those pieces of luck which happen only to good players happened to him," he was suggesting the agency of the daimonic, that old individualized genius whose promptings Emerson well knew from his dreams and poetic inspiration. The heightened, expectant frame of mind that brought forth poetic inspiration could as easily manifest mayflowers, music boxes, and musk turtles.[297]

One fall, walking to Fair Haven over the Conantum Cliffs, Thoreau found a swamp full of blossoming witch hazel, the yellow confetti flowers dangling from the skyward arching branches. Treasure hunters favored witch hazel branches for their divining rods, but Thoreau saw them pointing in a different direction: "Let them alone and they never point down to earth." Though he never cut himself a witch hazel branch for dowsing water or buried treasure, Thoreau daily divined the true gold of heaven. While treasure hunters throughout Concord and America pointed their rods downward and impatiently demanded results, Thoreau pointed his thoughts upward, and patiently awaited the reply of the spiritual world. Money-diggers like Hosmer and Wright (and Joseph Smith) electrified their body consciousness as in a mesmeric trance and thus opened their subconscious minds to the illusory activity of the jinn. Through his purified heart, Thoreau opened instead toward higher beings, who were happy to reply. The Old Norse word *happ* meant chance or good luck. Happiness happened to Thoreau for the same reason that rare plants and arrowheads "happened" to him; he made the daimones happy, and they responded in kind.[298]

"The Woodcraft of the Cunningest Hunter"

Sometime just before July 1855, Ralph Emerson made a brief entry in his journal:

The new professions—

The phrenologist
The railroad man

The landscape gardener
The lecturer
The sorcerer, rapper, mesmeriser, medium
The daguerreotypist

Emerson was himself acting as a kind of phrenologist in compiling this vocational roster, for it gave a characterological reading of American culture at midcentury. The "railroad man" was the easy choice, as by 1855 rail lines had penetrated every corner of the country and had transformed the social and economic lives of many Americans. Emerson's other choices hardly composed a nested set, but they all were professions that burst quickly upon the scene and then, with the exception of the landscape gardener, went extinct. Phrenology was already by 1855 losing its former cachet, displaced by other sciences of the mind; the wet developing process, which dramatically reduced the exposure time for making photographic images, came into its own this year; the lyceum movement had peaked, and though Emerson went on lecturing until 1870, lecturing as a profession was certainly on the wane; the mesmerizer had been largely replaced by Spiritualist mediums, who saw their commercial opportunities contract as spirit rapping became a hobby for millions.

Phrenology, landscape architecture, professional public speaking, Spiritualist and mesmeric performance, and daguerreotype portraiture were united by something other than their meteoric rise to obsolescence; they were all "physiognomic" pursuits, seeking to reveal or enhance hidden inner qualities. The phrenologist was the direct descendant of Franz Josef Gall and Johann Spurzheim, who in the late eighteenth century developed a science of physiognomy. Landscape architects and the gardeners who executed their plans sought to discover the inner quality of a place and then to sculpt the soil and plants to best express that quality. Lecturers like Emerson and Thoreau read the physiognomy of their fellow citizens and then suggested through their rhetoric how their audiences might better shape their ideas and actions to the pursuit of goodness, truth, and beauty. Sorcerers of all stripes—from the stage magician to the professional or amateur mediums and mesmerizers—used theatrical technique and prescribed physical gestures to lead their subjects and audiences into another world. The daguerreotypist was antebellum America's supreme recorder of gestures, to whom everyone rushed to immortalize their countenances before their facial physiognomy began to fail and fade away. Like other midcentury vocations, all aspired to scientific objectivity; in their pre-Enlightenment forms, all of these professions would have been arts, while in 1855 each one claimed for itself the mantle of science.

Thoreau's profession in the 1850s was profoundly physiognomic as well, for in making his journal a "record of his love," he was practicing the art of reading and responding to gestures. Science by 1855 was entirely analytic, always attempting to reduce complexity and ambiguity by taking living and nonliving things apart. Art—and Thoreau's natural history practice falls into this domain—enlarges understanding by seeking wholes and then rendering them synthetically. Along with artistically observing and recording a wide world of natural phenomena, Thoreau practiced a physiognomic natural history in his indefatigable attempt to place himself inside what he saw, heard, and felt. Trying to imitate the honking of geese, he instinctively flapped his arms and twisted his head as he uttered *"mow-ack"* in his best nasal twang. His large inventory of birdcalls had been won by constantly mimicking the little songsters. Whenever possible, he felt the fox's foxness, the turtle's turtleness, the frog's frogness, by leaping or crawling or croaking just like them. His physiognomic science allowed him to see and speak across structural and functional lines; he thought that the songs of frogs in late March were not only contemporary with, but analogous to, the blossoms of the skunk cabbage and the silver maple. He belittled naturalists for not being more attentive to color, believing that in both animals and plants, "color expresses *character.*" Human gestures fascinated him as well. "Why do laborers," Thoreau asked, "so commonly turn out their feet more than the class still called gentlemen, apparently pushing themselves along by the sides of their feet?"[299]

Even his ecstasies by 1855 had taken on a profoundly physiognomic cast. On an "aggravated November" day (called such by Thoreau for the lack of snow on the ground) in December, Thoreau while threading the tangle of a spruce swamp thought about flocks of lesser redpolls and pine grosbeaks and other Northern birds coming south in winter to add color and activity to Concord's drab landscape. The thought "charmed and haunted" him:

> My body is all sentient. As I go here or there, I am tickled by this or that I come in contact with, as if I touched the wires of a battery. I can generally recall—have fresh in my mind—several scratches last received. These I continually recall to mind, reimpress, and harp upon. The age of miracles is thus returned. . . .
>
> Beauty and music are not mere traits and exceptions. They are the rule and character. It is the exception that we see and hear. Then I try to discover what it was in the vision that charmed and translated me. What if we could daguerrotype our thoughts and feelings! for I am surprised and enchanted often by some quality which I cannot detect. I have seen an attribute of another world and condition of things.

In the ecstatic condition, with his etheric body slightly lifted out of its physical casing, he feels the electric "breeze" of the earth's etheric body, and the effect is to heighten his sense of the fit physiognomy of Nature. Reaching for some device to inscribe and thus fix the sensation, he imagines himself a daguerreotypist. The analogy is particularly apt in that the daguerreotype subject had to sit for long periods of time in order for an image to develop; Thoreau had to remain attentive and still for long periods in order to receive the crystalline, finely etched impressions that were characteristic of his perception. "It is only necessary to behold the least fact or phenomenon," he concluded, "however familiar, from a point a hair's breadth aside from our habitual path or routine, to be overcome, enchanted by its beauty and significance." This was the talent of the physiognomist, to heighten meaning by tilting the head slightly, thereby catching the accentuated relief of surfaces too long seen as flat and featureless.[300]

Along with drawing and describing a wealth of animal tracks, the winter and early spring of 1856 found Thoreau reflecting more often than usual on the tracks of his own past. Having the day after Christmas exclaimed, "In a true history or biography, of how little consequence those events of which so much is commonly made!" He found that most of the important events in his life, "if recorded at all," were undated. He also was struck by how difficult it was for most people even to recall in which towns or houses they had lived, and when, so the next day he made an inventory of these facts, with the help of his mother. The three-page entry in his journal is actually the most concentrated autobiographical offering since he composed his class autobiography at Harvard eighteen years before. A few months later, he reminisced on Fast Day (April 10) of baseball games played on the snow-free fields near Sleepy Hollow. Years of intense reading of the gestures of his environment had obscured for Thoreau the contours of his own physiognomy. "I am sometimes affected," he mused, "by the consideration that a man may spend the whole of his life after boyhood in accomplishing a particular design; as if he were put to a special and petty use, without taking time to look and appreciate the phenomenon of his existence." He found it impossible to believe that the "innate" passions of a person—"interest in our country, in the spread of liberty, etc."—could end with death. "It cannot be that all those patriots who die in the midst of their career have no further connection with the career of their country." The very next morning after making this heartfelt speculation about the endurance of individual destiny across the threshold of the grave, his uncle Charles died. His mother's brother had forever been the family member whose eccentric gestures—his clownish habit of swallowing his nose, his falling asleep midsentence, his trick of tossing his hat tumbling into the air and then catching it on his head—made the strongest impression on Thoreau.[301]

Gestures are what we fall in love with, the expressions that catch our eye and delight us to the bone. The day of Uncle Charles's burial, Thoreau memorialized him with but one thought—that he had been born in February 1780, the winter of the Great Snow, and that by dying in another winter of much snow, Uncle Charles had a life "bounded by great snows." While his love for his uncle melted even the greatest snows and was only augmented by death, Thoreau's feeling for another loved one was turning cold: "Farewell, my friend, my path inclines to this side the mountain, yours to that. For a long time you have appeared further and further off to me. I see that you will at length disappear altogether." In recording the growing distance between himself and Emerson, Thoreau employed gestural language—"I come here to be reminded of the past, to read your inscriptions, the hieroglyphics, the sacred writings." "Love is a thirst that is never slaked," declared Thoreau. "Under the coarsest rind, the sweetest meat. If you would read a friend aright, you must be able to read through something thicker and opaquer than horn. If you can read a friend, all languages will be easy to you." Thoreau's facility for reading physiognomies actually freed him from the constraints and possible pitfalls of language. Ultimately, he relied on pure gesture to know the status of his friendships:

> You know about a person who deeply interests you more than you can be told. A look, a gesture, an act, which to everybody else is insignificant tells you more about that one than words can. (How language is always found to serve best the highest moods, and expression of the highest truths!) If he wished to conceal something from you it would be apparent. It is as if a bird told you. Something of moment occurs. Your friend designs that it shall be a secret to you. Vain wish! You will know it, and his design. He says consciously nothing about it, yet as he is necessarily affected by it, its effect is visible to you. From this effect you infer the cause. Have you not already anticipated a thousand

possible accidents? Can you be surprised? You unconsciously through sympathy make the right supposition. No other will account for precisely this behavior. You are disingenuous, and yet your knowledge exceeds the woodcraft of the cunningest hunter. It is as if you had a sort of trap, knowing the haunts of your game, what lures attract it, and its track, etc. You have foreseen how it will behave when it is caught, and now you only behold what you anticipated.

"A friend tells all with a look, a tone, a gesture, a presence, a friendliness," thought Thoreau. "He is present when absent."[302]

The tracks that Thoreau made through his life were unmistakable to those who walked with him. Channing remarked that Thoreau's "whole figure had an active earnestness, as if he had no moment to waste. The clenched hand betokened purpose." Channing also knew well his friend's other physical characteristics—his aquiline Roman nose, large overhanging brows, prominent lips, searching eyes, hearty laughter, his peculiar rolling pronunciation of the letter *r*. Emerson and others commented how like his writing Thoreau's speech was, and that they often heard him say in conversation phrases that would later appear in his books. Thoreau was a stunning example of the very expressiveness he found in nature. Once, commenting upon the striking relationship between animals and the plants they fed or lived on, he said that it was "as if every condition might have its expression in some form of animated being." Thoreau was like the yellow spider on the goldenrod—not so much "adapted to" his place and time but called forth from it.[303]

The Sea Serpent

Since beginning his "Kalendar" project in 1851, Thoreau constantly moved back and forth mentally to see the shape of the "time body" of plants and animals. Occasionally these shapes prompted him to poetic contemplation; at the end of March 1857, he found among a half dozen

Vanessa butterflies at Lee's Cliff a few dead ones, and these made him think back thirty years to his first memory of finding dead suckers floating belly up. He knew now that the phenomenon of dead suckers was more conspicuous than living ones. Regular annual observation had transformed a former "evil" into a good: "It is a part of the *order*, not disorder, of the universe. When I realize that the mortality of suckers in the spring is as old a phenomenon, perchance, as the race of suckers itself, I contemplate it with serenity and joy even, as one of the signs of spring." He may have had suckers on his mind from a dinner conversation the week before at Emerson's with Louis Agassiz, professor of zoology and geology at Harvard's Lawrence Scientific School and founder of Harvard's Museum of Comparative Zoology. Agassiz had told Thoreau that the suckers die of asphyxia, having very large air bladders and the habit of coming to the surface to fill them with air. He also said that painted turtles do not copulate until they are seven years old and first lay eggs at eleven years, that Blanding's turtle copulates at age eight or nine, that the Eskimo dog is the only dog indigenous to North America, and that German naturalist Peter Simon Pallas showed that fishes can be frozen and then thawed again. This last fact Thoreau took exception to, and Agassiz changed his opinion. Then Thoreau showed Agassiz that a *Lycoperdon* mushroom immersed in water appeared silvery and stayed dry and told him that he had watched pouts take care of their young. Agassiz had only read about pout parenting in Aristotle.[304]

Ten years before this dinner discussion, America's most renowned zoologist had at a distance faced similar differences in opinion with the unknown young naturalist from Concord. In the spring of 1847, less than a year after Agassiz had come to America from Switzerland, Thoreau had collected fish and reptiles for him, and his secretary, James Elliot Cabot, had encouraged Thoreau to continue collecting. Agassiz was especially keen to get more musk turtles, which he called "a very rare species," and snapping turtles, along with all the species of fish that Thoreau could supply from the surface waters of Concord. Thoreau replied to Cabot with a preliminary account of Concord's fish and promised to send specimens of these and "minks, muskrats, frogs, lizards, tortoises, snakes, caddice-worms, leeches, muscles, etc." "*Here they are*," proclaimed the keen collector, adding that he needed at least another five dollars to secure the snapping turtles. Thoreau's professional demeanor did not prevent him from some sport; noting that although both musk and snappers were as common "in our muddy river as anything," they were elusive at that season. "As no one makes a business of seeking them," he advised, "and they are valued for soups, science may be forestalled by appetite in this market, and it will be necessary to bid pretty high to induce persons to obtain or preserve them." Three weeks later, Thoreau sent Agassiz fifteen pouts, seventeen perch, thirteen shiners, a wood turtle, and five musk turtles, all collected from "the pond next to my house"—i.e., Walden, for this was Thoreau's last season living there. From the river he sent seven perch, eight breams, four dace, two musk turtles, five painted turtles, and three wood turtles. He also put in a live black snake and a mouse he had caught the night before in his cellar. Cabot wrote that it was the first white-bellied mouse Agassiz had ever seen, and that at least two of the fish were new species.[305]

That an amateur naturalist from the oldest inland village in the Massachusetts Bay Colony could at midcentury casually collect a small sampling of the local vertebrate fauna and have a few of them declared new species by America's premier zoologist suggests the paucity of scientific investigation of the American landscape in the early years of the new republic. It also suggests the ease with which Louis Jean-Rudolphe Agassiz—the man who in later years boasted "Darwin's work was contrary to modern science as he [Agassiz] had defined it"—saw new species where others might see variations of one. Given that Agassiz was natural science's greatest exponent of special creation, which theorized that every species on Earth had come into existence on the first day of creation, the great zoologist imagined an incredibly robust Genesis. The dinner at Emerson's was one of a number of events planned to celebrate the publication of the first volume of Agassiz's *Contributions to the Natural History of the United States of America*. The volume's contents were devoted to Agassiz's "Essay on Classification," in which he argued that historically earlier species—some of which were now extinct—were purposefully designed by God as prophecies of later, now living species. Agassiz published his theistic, typological tour de force just months before Charles Darwin would deliver to the Linnaean Society a lecture outlining the theory of evolution by natural selection.[306]

Thoreau read the "Essay on Classification," and though his notes do not show him arguing with Agassiz, he clearly was skeptical about all the zoologist's pronouncements, not just about evolution. Despite his early collecting spree, he abhorred Agassiz's practice of killing large numbers of animals for comparative zoological study. Emerson confided to his journal "the turtles of Cambridge, on the publication of this book of Agassiz, should hold an indignation meeting, and migrate from the Charles River, with *Chelydra serpentina* marching at the head, and 'Death to Agassiz' inscribed on their shields." Thoreau rejected Agassiz's ideas about biogeography as well; finding toad eggs in a rockbound pool of rainwater on the summit of Mount Monadnock, Thoreau quipped, "Agassiz might say they originated on the top." But Thoreau's animus against Agassiz was part of a more generic distrust of scientific hubris. In the five days following the dinner at Emerson's, Thoreau made three separate remarks in his journal that, although unattributed to any particular source incident, would seem to have been sparked by his firsthand encounter with Agassiz's arrogance:

If you are describing any occurrence, or a man, make two or more distinct reports at different times. Though you may think you have said all, you will to-morrow remember a whole new class of facts which perhaps interested most of all at the time, but did not present themselves to be reported. If we have recently met and talked with a man, and would report our experience, we commonly make a very partial report at first, failing to seize the most significant, picturesque, and dramatic points; we describe only what we have had time to digest and dispose of in our minds, without being conscious that there were other things really more novel and interesting to us, which will not fail to recur to us and impress us suitably at last. How little that occurs to us in any way are we prepared at once to appreciate! We discriminate at first only a few features, and we need to reconsider our experience from many points of view and in various moods, to preserve the whole fruit of it.

Two days later he wrote that he should make two reports of his ob-servations in his journal—one immediate, the other delayed, since "the men and things of to-day are wont to lie fairer and truer in to-morrow's memory." On the third day he extended the rule of thumb from days out to years: "Often I can give the truest and most interesting account of any adventure I have had after years have elapsed, for then I am not confused, only the most significant facts surviving in my memory. Indeed, all that continues to interest me after such a lapse of time is sure to be pertinent, and I may safely record all that I remember." [307]

It may be that the dinner conversation with Agassiz found its fairer and truer expression only seven months later, when Thoreau was writing in his journal about polypody ferns, which stood out as the surrounding vegetation turned brown and died back with the killing frosts. The fore-grounding of the ferns at this season turned them into a phenomenon as exotic as a unicorn or sea serpent:

Some forms, though common in our midst, are thus perennially foreign as the growths of other latitudes; there being a greater interval between us and their kind than usual. We all feel the ferns to be further from us, essentially and sympathetically, than the phanogamous plants, the roses and weeds, for instance. It needs no geology nor botany to assure us of that. We feel it, and told them of it first. The bare outline of the polypody thrills me strangely. It is a strange type which I cannot read. It only piques me. Simple as it is, it is as strange as an Oriental character. It is quite independent of my race, and of the Indian, and all mankind. It is a fabulous, mythological form, such as prevailed when the earth and air and water were inhabited by those extinct fossil creatures that we find. It is contemporary with them, and affects as the sight of them.

A few days later the polypody was still working on him, and he noted that it was not the polypody in the field, in a pitcher of water on his desk, in the botanies, or transplanted into his garden that interested him, but "the one I pass in my walks a little distance off, when in the right mood." Historians of science—who uniformly embrace Darwinian theory— tend to fault Agassiz for his claim of scientific objectivity, which to the modern mind is laughable given Agassiz's rejection of Darwin for the theory of special creation. It was not the false claim of objectivity but the very aspiration toward objectivity that troubled Thoreau:

> I think that the man of science makes this mistake, and the mass of mankind along with him: that you should coolly give your chief at-tention to the phenomenon which excites you as something inde-pendent on you, and not as it is related to you. The important fact is its effect on me. He thinks that I have no business to see anything else but just what he defines the rainbow to be, but I care not whether my vision of truth is a waking thought or dream remembered, whether it is seen in the light or in the dark. It is the subject of the vision, the truth alone, that concerns me. The philosopher for whom rainbows, etc., can be explained away never saw them.[308]

Perhaps the last time that Thoreau saw Agassiz was in January 1858, when he stopped in Boston on the way back from a lecturing en-gagement in Lynn. He looked up ornithologist Samuel Kneeland to ask him about his "night warbler" or "myrtle bird," the evening songster whose *ah, te-te-te te-te-te te-te-te* note had baffled Thoreau for years. Kneeland identified the bird as the white-throated sparrow. The same afternoon he took around to various Boston naturalists a specimen of the common glowworm, *Lampyris noctiluca*. Agassiz had never seen the larvae of this luminescent beetle before. At Lynn, Thoreau stayed with the lyceum program secretary Jonathan Buffum, an amateur naturalist who took Thoreau on a number of outings. Riding out to Nahant, they stopped to see the syenite cobbles atop the stone fence posts of Mr. Alonzo Lewis's cottage; Mr. Lewis had fashioned one of the stones, which he collected from a beach of a nearby cove, into a sundial, and Thoreau noted the hour in his journal as told by the sundial. They also stopped to see Samuel Jillson, a skillful taxidermist who killed his own birds with clay balls shot from seven-foot-long glass blowguns he made himself. At Nahant they saw snow buntings and black ducks and studied the fossil-filled slate and porphyry dikes at Egg Rock. The next day Buffum led Thoreau to the northwest part of Lynn near Danvers, where they continued to study the local geology, and then—after making a characteristically serendipitous discovery of dyer's greenweed—they visited a quarry on the return to Lynn. From Lynn's higher hills, Thoreau realized how the native peoples out hunting or berrying would have been able to look out to see European ships sailing along the coast. He was much obliged to Buffum for his knowledge, which extended to historical lore about seven-foot-deep pits lined with smooth stone made by Lynn's first settlers to trap wolves and to a culinary tradition regarding the local clams—not to eat the "worm," the clam's penis.[309]

During these excursions in Lynn, Buffum told Thoreau that he had in 1817 or 1819 seen at Swampscott, along with hundreds of others, a sea serpent. Buffum said the first time he'd seen the creature, there were many carriages whose owners had pulled down to the edge of the water to enjoy the surf. The serpent came right at them, as if he was going to come ashore, and they all turned their horses and fled up the beach. Buffum saw him some twenty times after this; once, while alone on the rocks at Little Nahant, the monster came within fifty or sixty feet of him. Thoreau's only comment was that, "as affecting the value of his evidence, . . . he is a firm believer in Spiritualism." (In 1853, Buffum was the president of the New England Spiritualist Convention in Boston; his sister was a Spiritualist medium of some repute.) This was not Thoreau's first encounter with witnesses of the sea serpent. The year before his visit to Lynn, at Plymouth, his friend Benjamin Marston Watson, another accomplished naturalist, told Thoreau that Daniel Webster had in 1817 seen the sea serpent while he was out fishing with Plymouth's most respected sea captain, Thomas Perkins. On Sunday, August 10, 1817, just four weeks after Henry Thoreau's birth, Gloucester fisherman Amos Story was rowing his boat near Ten Pound Island when he saw a snakelike animal nearly one hundred feet long, with a head like a turtle, which was held high out of the water as it moved "with the vertical motion of a caterpillar." For the next two weeks, the monster was seen each day by the inhabitants of Gloucester and neighboring Massachusetts coastal villages. Newspapers in Boston and Salem reported on it for the next two months. On August 18, two serpents were seen playing together; on the twenty-fifth, one was seen feasting on alewives in Kettle Cove, the source of Alonzo Lewis's syenite cobbles; on the twenty-eighth, he was seen feeding on herring; by September 4, citizens were clamoring for the navy to capture it; on the tenth, the monster was seen at Salem going after schools of baitfish and then basking near Half-Way Rock, apparently digesting his breakfast of herring; on October 1, the "Panorama of Gloucester with the Great Sea Serpent" was advertised to open at Merchant's Hall on Monday next.[310]

Two weeks after the first sighting, the Linnaean Society of New England appointed a committee—composed of a prominent lawyer, a judge, and a physician/naturalist—to collect evidence of the existence of the sea serpent. Early nineteenth-century scientific committees were modeled on legal proceedings: the members examined witnesses, were cautious not to allow fraternization among them, and obeyed certain rules regarding the conduct of questioning. Among those deposed were Amos Story, the mariner who had first sighted the animal; Solomon

Allen III, a shipmaster; William H. Foster, a merchant; Matthew Gaffney, a ship carpenter; James Mansfield, a merchant; John Johnson Jr., a boy of seventeen; and William B. Pearson, a merchant. These men were all selected because they were universally trusted as reliable Gloucester citizens. Their testimony varied about the animal's length (from "forty feet at least" to "at least a hundred feet"); circumference (from "the size of a man's body" to "large as a barrel"); manner of movement ("vertical, like a caterpillar," "turns short and quick, head and tail moving in opposite directions and almost touching," "a mile in—six, five, four, three, two—minutes"); and head shape ("like the head of a sea-turtle, carried ten to twelve inches above the water," "like the head of a rattlesnake, but nearly as large as the head of a horse"). All agreed that the animal had a long forked tongue and undulated vertically.

Captain Perkins and his friend Daniel Webster arrived on the paramount day for sea-serpent watching, for the creature was seen continuously for hours not only from their ship in Gloucester Harbor, but also by people at all points on shore. Gaffney, the ship carpenter, had come within thirty feet of the animal and fired at its head with an eighteen-to-the-pound ball. The monster dove directly under the boat, and came up a hundred rods off on the other side, like a loon or cormorant. Watson told Thoreau that the sea serpent had passed directly across the bow of Perkins's boat, only six or seven rods away, and that on the sail home, Webster told Captain Perkins, "For God's sake, never say a word about this to any one, for if it should be known that I have seen the sea serpent, I should never hear the last of it, but wherever I went should have to tell the story to every one I met." Thoreau added slyly, "So it has not leaked out till now." [311]

The Linnaean Society committee's report of fifty-two pages testified to the truthfulness and accuracy of their deposed witnesses' statements and then concluded that the "large marine animal, supposed to be a serpent" was the parent of a three-foot-long black snake killed by a farmer in a field on Cape Ann. They agreed with the farmer's reasoning that the animal had appeared along shore because it had laid its eggs there. An engraving of *Scoliophis atlanticus*, the committee's Linnaean binomial for the murdered snake, accompanied the report, along with illustrations of the animal in parts after dissection and full anatomical explanations. The report never mentioned that not a single member of the committee ever went to Gloucester. This was reminiscent of the French Royal Society's in absentia investigation of Franz Anton Mesmer and subsequent damnation of mesmerism. Though naturalist Alexandre Lesueur responded to the Linnaean Society report by showing conclusively that the *Scoliophis atlanticus* was no more than a deformed version of the common black snake, no alternative explanation for the monster came forward. But more monsters came forward. In 1819 a sea serpent was sighted by thousands of people from Cape Ann to Long Island Sound. By then, everyone knew exactly what a sea serpent looked like, for John Ritto Penniman's nineteen-by-nine-foot canvas of the sea serpent in repose upon the waters of Gloucester Harbor had toured the Northeast the year before, complete with a stop at Peale's Museum in Philadelphia.

The monster continued to be sighted occasionally right into the 1850s, and certain peak years stirred scientific interest once again. In 1835, the *American Journal of Science*, reporting on another Massachusetts sighting, concluded, "We must therefore consider this case as settling the question of the real existence of a Sea Serpent. The absence of paddles or arms forbids us from supposing that this was a swimming saurian." This equivocation suggests that at least in 1835, there was still—as with the existence of the unicorn—some scientific hesitancy to unilaterally declare the nonexistence of the sea serpent. But by 1850, a number of sophisticated hoaxes had been executed, which in this age of humbug quickly provided an easy excuse for those who wished to banish the anomalous creature from any serious consideration. The dozens of explanations provided by debunkers (almost all of whom never came anywhere near the places where the spectral animal had been seen) do not alter the fact that there were thousands of eyewitnesses, among them the most trusted men of their age—sea captains. Upon hearing of the 1817 sighting from Captain Perkins, Edward Everett, a brilliant scholar and statesman, had made a special study and concluded that Perkins and the other witnesses had indeed seen a serpent. *American Journal of Science* editor Benjamin Silliman and British Royal Society scientists Joseph Banks and Joseph Hooker were all convinced of the creature's existence, and as late as 1847, *Zoologist* editor Edward Newman devoted pages of his scientific journal to an open-minded discussion of the topic. "It has been the fashion for... many years to deride all records of this very celebrated monster," his editorial stated. He chided critics for a priori approaches that ignored "fact and observation" on the grounds that the sea serpent "ought not to be." "Fact-naturalists," he said, "take a different road to knowledge, they enquire whether such things are, and whether such things are not." The following year the most famous sea serpent report of all time took place. It occurred on the afternoon of August 6, 1848, and the witnesses were the captain and crew of the frigate *Daedalus*, on their way back to England from the Cape of Good Hope. Soon after the ship's arrival at Plymouth, England, on October 4, several newspapers reported rumors of a spectacular twenty-minute sea-serpent sighting, and the Admiralty asked the captain to supply a report either denying or detailing the incident. The captain fully verified the report, which was reprinted widely in newspapers and was even noticed in *Scientific American*.

When Thoreau stopped in Cambridge on his way home from Lynn in 1858, he checked out two volumes of the *Jesuit Relations* from the Harvard Library. He had moved on to the French sources on early North American exploration after exhausting the English sources, such as John Josselyn's *Account of Two Voyages to New England*. Thoreau thought Josselyn's generation "stood nearer to nature, nearer to the facts," than his own. In his 1672 work, *New England Rarities Discovered in Birds, Beasts, Fishes, Serpents and Plants of That Country*, Josselyn, who had sailed within eight miles of Boston, told of seeing a serpent "quoiled like a Cable upon a rock at Cape Ann." The English sailors were about to shoot at the creature when two Indians on board dissuaded them, saying that if they killed the serpent, they would all be in danger of losing their lives. Though he had read this work, Thoreau never re-marked in his fact books on Josselyn's sea serpent account. Clearly, from his dismissal of Buffum's report, he placed no credence in the creature. There was something altogether gossamerish about it, and the "fact-naturalist" Thoreau had a similar response as he did to the strange sticky stuff not spun by spiders; he "damned" it by his silence as surely as the Linnaean Society did with its lame explanation. Given that he had no personal eyewitness experience of the sea serpent, as he had with the gossamer, his silence is understandable, and yet one wishes that he had taken the monster under consideration.

If Thoreau had been able to interview the Indian eyewitnesses aboard the English boat in 1672, he might have begun to get a sense of the true nature of the sea serpent. All the Algonquian-speaking peoples of the Northeast had traditions of serpentine monsters; indeed, the serpent is perhaps the most ubiquitous animal spirit in prehistoric North America. Thoreau had read about serpent spirits in Ephraim Squier's *Serpent Symbol in America* (1851), which moved out from Squier's own field research in the Serpent Mound region of the Mississippi Valley to all corners of North America. The Pawtuckets of Concord and the Wampanoag and other native peoples of coastal New England knew Chepian, the evil nemesis of the trickster god Nanabozho; the Micmac dragon Chepitchcalm (Jibijka'm) was the same beast. The Pas-samaquoddy of eastern Maine called their serpent monster Atosis. Among the Seneca and other Iroquoian speakers to the west of Bitawbagw—"the waters between," i.e., Lake Champlain—the serpent was Gaasyendietha. Bitawbagw and other large northeastern lakes, as the lakes of Quebec, were almost universally known to have been inhab-ited by serpents like the sea-dwelling ones. But the real "home" of all these creatures was in the realm of Faery, the imaginal realm of the lesser gods. Though there were specific and characteristic geographic locations where these spirits manifested—no other stretch of the Atlantic Coast has been as demon-haunted as the Cape Ann region—they shared the timeless, spaceless home of dragons, vampires, harpies, and other creatures that have always and everywhere left the Otherworld occasionally to cause mischief in our own.

Thoreau copied out from Squier's *Serpent Symbol* an Algonquian tradition of a contest between Nanabozho and Chepian, in which after the evil serpent is wounded with Nanabozho's arrow, he deluges the earth in a great flood. This was typical of the serpent mythology of native North America. Although Chepian could appear as a benevolent friend of human beings, he usually worked against them. The Gloucester sea serpent was quite different; despite having all the physical attributes that would make him a powerful adversary of man, he never attacked anyone. He seemed more like the sylphs and salamanders and gnomes and undines, in that he was relatively shy and quite ephemeral, even if he made repeated appearances in an area.[312]

Had a spectral serpent turned up in Walden Pond or the Concord River, Thoreau no doubt would have approached it as he did all of nature's phenomena—sympathetically and chronometrically. He would have felt his way into the serpent's life world, and at the same time he would have mapped him into his Concord Kalendar, attempting to understand the timing of his appearances and disappearances. Perhaps Massachusetts's sea serpent came swimming into the nineteenth-century consciousness because it was lonely, having been gradually abandoned during the colonial period as his old neighbors—the Algonquian native peoples—were decimated by disease and warfare. Perhaps it was as simple as the two Indians on Josselyn's boat pronounced it to be: If he is killed, we will all die. The sea serpent was antebellum America's wake-up call from the Great God Pan, making his appearance to remind the children of Mammon that other Powers and

Principalities once reigned on the continent. Like the faeries over which he reigned, he was nourished by loving attention and grew petulant when ignored or assaulted. After three decades of persistent searching for some small gesture of hospitality, the daimonic snake slipped away into the ether.

CHAPTER 6

Expansion and Contraction

I sing the wild apple theme enough for me.
I love the racy fruit & I reverence the tree—
— *Journal*, October 28, 1857

"What Prayers They Make!"

The day after Benjamin Watson told Thoreau the story about Daniel Webster and the sea serpent, Watson and his wife drove Thoreau to Manomet, where he resumed his solo pilgrimage to Provincetown on this fourth and last Cape Cod excursion. Along the way, they stopped their carriage for a painted turtle who was caught in a wheel rut. "Now is the time when they are killed in the ruts all the country over," he lamented, and though by "country" he meant the sandy cart paths of Cape Cod, this must have been a common occurrence all over horse-drawn America each spring, as aquatic turtles moved overland to lay their eggs. That evening Thoreau reached a desolate tract seven or eight miles from Manomet, and stopped to inquire about lodging with a Mr. and Mrs. Samuel Ellis; though Mrs. Ellis was tired from washing day, she agreed to take Thoreau in. The Ellises assumed at first that Thoreau was a peddler and asked him what he had for sale in his bag. A real peddler arrived shortly thereafter, and Thoreau asked the teenage cutlery vendor how he liked his occupation. The boy replied that it enabled him to see the world. "I thought him an unusually good specimen of Young America," quipped Thoreau.[313]

Thoreau heard Ellis praying after he had gone to bed, and at breakfast the next morning he spoke a blessing giving thanks that "we of all the palefaces were preserved alive." Though Mrs. Ellis thought their neighboring Indians "worthy people," especially since they were churchgoers, Mr. Ellis thought that if angry with you, "they wouldn't make anything of taking your life." Dismissing Ellis's remark as the "usual suspicion," he set out to see the Indians, whom he was surprised to find had just begun to erect a new meetinghouse. Meeting in the road a man with deeply tanned skin, dark eyes, and straight black hair, Thoreau asked if he was "of the aboriginal stock." "I suppose so," the man replied, to Thoreau's chagrin.[314]

Enjoying a lifetime of imaginary relationships with ghostly Indians, Thoreau had frequently been disappointed by living ones. While Thoreau was out hunting arrowheads in Concord's fields, Tahatawan and his kin always loomed heroically before his mind's eye, but their descendants fell short of his romantic imagination. The occasional Indians who appeared in Concord during Thoreau's lifetime were itinerant peddlers of a sort themselves, "gypsying" from town to town selling handicrafts—and sometimes begging. "Me want a pie" declared an Indian woman who with her two children showed up at the Thoreaus' door one day in 1850. There was in nearly every Massachusetts town an old Indian widow who lived alone with her dog, "insulted by school-children, making baskets and picking berries her employment... [with] melancholy face, history, destiny; stepping after her race." Thoreau also recognized the odd farmer in Concord and the neighboring towns who passed as a Yankee but whose skin color or movements or accent identified him as Indian. Once, when he met a group of Indians camped on the Musketaquid, they had to ask Thoreau where the river came from. By 1850, except for the intact native communities at places like Gay Head and Old Town, New England's Indian peoples had become to non-Indians a kind of collective refugee race, generic "mixed-bloods" with vague histories of displacement and decline rather than very specific individualized tales of persistence and survival through centuries of European colonial and then American occupation. The itinerant Indians who had no knowledge of the Musketaquid could have been Passamaquoddy or Penobscot from the Maine coast, Abenakis down from Saint Francis in Quebec, or Mahican from over in the Taconic Valley. They could not have been expected to know the Grass Ground River the way Thoreau imagined Tahatawan's people to have known it. In the mid-nineteenth century, the gap between most New England Indian peoples and their Yankee neighbors had grown so wide that their individual historical identities had been collapsed into one lurid captivity narrative or genocidal swampbound last stand, like King Philip's.[315]

Thoreau may not have been as baldly racist and badly misinformed as his peers, but he too fell into a variety of misconceptions about native peoples. He had undertaken to systematically inform himself about the indigenous peoples of North America in 1847, while still living in his Walden cabin. At Walden he finished the first of his "Extracts Concerning the Indians," or "Indian Notebooks"—eleven volumes and over half a million words, which represent perhaps the greatest body of knowledge about American Indian culture assembled by any individual in the nineteenth century. His handwritten notes in English, French, Italian, Latin, and sometimes in the written versions of the indigenous spoken languages, range across the continent and beyond to Greenland and South America. By the fifth volume, Thoreau was organizing all his research under a suite of topics: Travelling, Physique, Music, Games, Dwellings, Feasting, Food, Charity, Dress, Painting, Money, Government, War, Tradition & History, Superstitions & Religions, and "Naming" drew his attention the most regularly through the years. From the *Jesuit Relations*, he learned that the Micmac, when facing starvation, would sing and be succored. From John Tanner's 1830 captivity narrative—more accurately an adoption narrative, as Tanner came to love and respect his Ottawa and Ojibwa captors—he learned of the Ojibwa Wain-je-tah We koon-de-win, a feast called for by dreams. From John Heckewelder's *History of the Indian Nations* he learned that native peoples considered the earth as their universal mother, from whose womb they had emerged, and of the fabled world turtle upon whose back rode all the Indian nations. In Adrien Van der Donck's *Description of the New Netherlands* (1655) he read Mohawk creation myths. Henry Rowe Schoolcraft's ethnological works on the Algonquian-speaking peoples of the Great Lakes region, the source for Longfellow's *Hiawatha* and so many other nineteenth-century writers' works, were a special treasure for Thoreau. He copied out the Ojibwa *keekeewin*—picture-writing—of "the highest grade of the symbolic": A six-parted circle topped by rays signified "I am rising"; a man with outstretched arms, "I take the sky"; a headless and armless hatched torso and legs meant "I walk through the sky"; a woman with a heart emblazoned on her chest, holding out in her left hand an arrow and in her right a roll of birch bark, was the symbol for the call of "The Eastern Woman," i.e., Venus, the Evening Star. Schoolcraft, who married a woman of Ojibwa descent, was the best of the Victorian ethnographers and shared Thoreau's love for native myth and mysticism. From Schoolcraft he copied out a passage that sounds like a flight of fable from his own journal:

> Their ancient history or mythology; Nations creeping out of the ground—a world growing out of a tortoises back—the globe reconstructed from the earth clutched in a muskrat's paw after a deluge. A mammoth bull jumping over the great lakes; a grape-vine carrying a whole tribe across the Mississippi; an eagle's wings producing the phenomenon of thunder, or its flashing eyes that of lightning; men stepping in viewless tracks of the blue arch of heaven; the rainbow made a baldric; a little boy catching the sun's beams in a wave; hawks rescuing shipwrecked mariners from an angry ocean, and carrying them up a steep ascent in leather bags . . .

"They see the great spirit in everything," Thoreau declared in response to Schoolcraft's inventory of native myth.[316]

As a young man, while all about him were voices sounding nostalgic but unmistakably imperial laments for the fate of the "dying Indian," Thoreau had seen a different destiny, even linking the "Saxon family" fate with that of the "American race." "I find it good to remember the eternity behind me as well as the eternity before," he wrote. "Wherever I go, I tread in the tracks of the Indian. I pick up the bolt which he has just dropped at my feet. And if I consider destiny I am on his trail." Though he felt the fate of these "strange spirits, daimons" was of "another nature," he believed that some element of the Indian had to be passed forward into those who now inhabited America: "Where is this country but in the hearts of its inhabitants? Why, there is only so much of Indian America left as there is of the American Indian in the character of this generation." He sensed the historical chasm between the two cohabiting peoples, feeling that Indians, "tanned with age," had exhausted the secrets of nature, while the "fair Saxon slip" was "but commencing its career." Like his contemporaries, he was completely comfortable declaring one day that a certain individual was "the last Indian, of pure blood," and then on the next day reporting on some "wild Indian" he had encountered. At Worcester in 1854 to give a lecture, he met an Indian from Canada who was making sugar maple baskets near his banked wigwam of dry grass that he had cut from a meadow. At home, whether of old friends or new acquaintances, the portraits Thoreau gives are deeply personal. Unless he is respectfully concealing an individual's name, Thoreau tells us the name of everyone whom he meets, even the Irish and other people of lower status who often did not receive the dignity of being addressed by their proper name. But the ever curious Thoreau rarely asks the names of the Indian men and women he meets. There are other obvious questions that come to mind that Thoreau seems never to have asked when he had the opportunity. He asks the Indian man making baskets if he has ever hunted moose but never asks him what has brought him particularly to Worcester.[317]

Antebellum Massachusetts was full of Indians with complex, variegated histories and experiences, and these occasionally shine out from Thoreau's journals. In 1855, visiting Middleboro with Daniel Ricketson, he visited an Indian cemetery among whose many unmarked headstones was one marked in memory of Jean and Benjamin Squeen and

Lydia, their mother. On the shore of Betty's Neck on Assawompsett Pond they found a large rock marked with inscriptions, including one saying "Israel Felix," whom Thoreau knew from his reading in the *Massachusetts Historical Collections* to be an "old Indian preacher." The same source told Thoreau that "Betty" was Betty Sasemore, who owned that land, where, in 1810, eight families comprising thirty or forty people lived. None of these were named by Thoreau's source, which went on at length detailing the names of the four Englishmen and three Americans who had inscribed their signatures and the date on the shell of a box turtle between the years 1747 and 1791. Watching loons diving along the shore of Betty's Neck, Thoreau and Ricketson saw a man and woman in a small boat, and Ricketson called to them. "Come nearer," said Ricketson, "Don't be afraid; I ain't a-going to hurt you." The man, who appeared black to Thoreau, told them his name was Thomas Smith and that he was one-fourth Indian. The woman, who said her name was "Sepit"—"but [she] could not spell it," remarked Thoreau—said that she was one-half Indian. These "blood quotas," which were hardly the way in which the Indians thought about themselves, were constantly the first thing on non-Indians' minds when they met anyone who looked remotely native. "Your nose looks rather Indiany," Ricketson said rudely to the woman, and it's a wonder that she didn't punch him in *his* nose. Thoreau asked Tom about the turtles in the pond, how deep it was, and sketched the odd wooden grapple on their "sharpie," or oyster fishing boat. But Ricketson pressed on with his attempt to get back to the "pure" Indian past, and told the woman that he was interested in "the old stock, now that they were so few." "Yes," she replied, "and you'd be glad if they were all gone." [318]

Visiting Ricketson in New Bedford in 1856, Thoreau sought out the hut of Martha Simons, "the only pure-blooded Indian left in New Bedford." She answered Thoreau's questions "listlessly," and though from her facial features "she might have been King Philip's own daughter," Thoreau was sorely disappointed that she spoke not a word of her native language and "knew nothing of her race." When she told him she was sixty years old, he noted that she was probably nearer seventy. (Thoreau seemed unaware that very few Indian people knew their exact age; their privileging of cyclical over linear time continued even into the twentieth century.) There was between Thoreau and Martha Simons a kind of silent sparring going on about the past: Thoreau was determined to retrieve it in a form he wanted. Though she told him things about the past that from non-native informants would have delighted him—that she had been born on that spot, where her grandfather, the last Wampanoag thereabouts who could speak Indian, had lived most of his life; that she had gone out to service with white people when she was but seven years old—he hardly heard her. But she identified a plant that he was carrying in his hat vasculum as husk root and said that it had a bitter root that was good tonic for a weak stomach.[319]

Once, on the train to and from Boston, Thoreau had seen "a solitary pure-blooded Indian, looking as wild as ever," stepping onto the cars with his gun. His inclination ever was to find and follow such an Indian home to his native woods, where Thoreau might step back in time to the mysterious, mystical life he imagined the Indian to have led before the arrival of Europeans. There, he might decipher the "arrow-headed character" of North America's native peoples. He had taken the railroad east to Bangor, Maine, for just such a purpose on two occasions: In 1846, on his trip to Mount Katahdin, the errant Penobscot guide Louis Neptune had dashed Thoreau's hopes for getting close to the Indian mind. Then in 1853, Joe Aitteon led Thoreau and his cousin George Thatcher on a moose-hunting trip to Chesuncook Lake, between Moosehead Lake and Mount Katahdin. Though on that trip Thoreau got to hear Joe call the chickadee *kecunnilessu*, the kingfisher *skuscumonsuck*, the mountain ash *upahsis* and to listen to Joe serenade moose with his birch-bark horn, the overall impression left upon Thoreau was of Joe's closeness to modern civilization (he whistled Stephen Foster's popular "Oh Susanna" while paddling, and once he exclaimed, "Yes, Sir-ee") juxtaposed with the violent savagery of the killing and butchering of a moose. The only moment approaching true communion with the native mind occurred near the end of the trip, when one night he lay in the dark listening to Joe speaking with Tahmunt Swasen, an Abenaki from Saint Francis, Quebec. As the two men "gossiped, laughed, and jested, in the language in which Eliot's Bible is written," Thoreau delighted to hear this "purely wild and primitive American sound."[320]

In July 1857, only a few weeks back from his Cape Cod trip, Thoreau returned to the Maine woods for a trip to the Allagash Lakes and East Branch of the Penobscot River with Edward Hoar, the young man with whom he had set the Concord woods on fire in 1844. Determined to have a guide "well skilled in Indian lore," he hired Joe Polis, a wellborn Penobscot with "no trace of white blood in his face." Though Thoreau was still laboring under racialist notions about "pure blood," whatever physiognomic clue recommended Polis to Thoreau served him well, for Polis was the man that Thoreau had long dreamed of leading him into the forested consciousness of the Native American. When Thoreau first saw him, he was dressing a deerskin in front of his home, which looked like any white clapboard house in Concord village. Asked if he knew of any good Indians to guide them to the Allagash country, Polis answered, "Me like to go myself; me want to get some moose." George Thatcher and Thoreau bargained Polis down from his rate of two dollars a day to a dollar and a half, plus fifty cents a week for his canoe.[321]

Escorting Polis to Thatcher's house after meeting him at the railroad station in Bangor and then, the next day on the stage, Thoreau was struck by Joe's "peculiar vagueness" in reply to questions. Thinking it better than the conventional small talk of white men, still Thoreau yearned for a fluid conversationalist who could easily impart his knowledge. At first, Joe's taciturnity kept Thoreau at a distance, until Thoreau began to appreciate its inherent dignity and wisdom. After Thoreau shouted repeatedly downstream to get Hoar's attention, Joe rebuked him by saying, "He hears you." When they would reach a difficult stretch of water demanding a short portage, Joe would put out his charges, then dart downstream in his canoe, coming ashore and calling out to let them know where he was. Thoreau thought he didn't call out often enough, "forgetting that we were not Indians," and chalked it up to another example of the Indian manner of getting along "with the least possible communication and ado." Penobscot Indians were not trained on the lyceum circuit. Farther into the trip, Thoreau asked Joe a question about preparing moose hide, and after Joe replied impatiently, "What you ask me that question for?" he realizes that a question asked more than once rarely received an answer.[322]

Thoreau put lots of questions to Polis—about place names, plant lore, hunting, and woodcraft. When Polis told him that after being turned round in the woods many times, he could still make a beeline for home, he asked how and Polis replied, "O, I can't tell *you*. Great difference between me and white man." But as the trip progressed, that difference diminished, and Polis at times even seemed a kind of Indian equivalent of Thoreau. Both were skilled paddlers; both loved to play—at one point, Joe challenged Thoreau to a footrace over a carry. The two men were acutely opinionated, and their judgments were well considered. Joe, who had on his own initiative gone to meet Daniel Webster, thought that all he said was "not worth talk about a musquash." What united them most closely was their prayerfulness. Joe began and ended each day with prayers and once remarked to Thoreau, "Poor man rememberum God more than rich." One night, Joe sang an Indian hymn that Thoreau took to mean that "there was only one God who ruled the world." Moved by its "humility and reverence," Thoreau said that it carried him "back to the period of the discovery of America, to San Salvador and the Incas."[323]

That same evening of Joe's song, while everyone was asleep, Thoreau rose to bank the campfire, saw a ring of white light glowing from the end of a log, and realized that it was bioluminescent fungus (commonly called foxfire) in the sapwood of a piece of striped maple. He cut out some chips, put them in his hand, and carried them back to the tent to show to Hoar. The next morning, Joe told him the Penobscot word for the light—*artoosoqu'*—and he and Thoreau passed on to a conversation about fairies, who frequently gave off the same sort of light when they appeared. "Nature must have made a thousand revelations to them which are still secrets to us," he surmised. Thoreau was delighted to make the acquaintance of the fairy light in the dead wood while he was with Joe Polis, for his animistic view of nature gave Thoreau the chance to "let science slide":

> I believed that the woods were not tenantless, but choke full of honest spirits as good as myself any day,—not an empty chamber, in which chemistry was left to work alone, but an inhabited house,—and for a few moments I enjoyed fellowship with them. Your so-called wise man goes trying to persuade himself that there is no entity there but himself and his traps, but it is a great deal easier to believe the truth.

This was the truth that Thoreau had known firsthand as a child and as a young man, when on occasion he encountered the "honest spirits" of the forest. Joe Polis restored for Thoreau the sense that the one God who ruled the world had peopled the earth with a multitude of beings forgotten and forsaken by science. "One revelation has been made to the Indian, another to the white man," declared the one white man in America determined to share in that native revelation of the spirits standing behind Nature.[324]

Dreams

When Thoreau arrived home from Maine, he found waiting for him a pair of glowworms sent to him from Plymouth by Benjamin Watson. The package containing them (and four others, which had escaped) had arrived on the very day that Thoreau and Edward Hoar set out for Bangor, and Thoreau, writing to Watson a letter of thanks for his "glowing communication," admitted how singular it was that he should come home to them, since his mind was "full of a phosphorescence" he had seen in the Maine woods. Thoreau had found these bioluminescent beetle larvae before on his night walks in Concord, but had never studied them closely, and he kept the two surviving glowworms in a jar with sod that he replaced each day. As he measured them, he was charmed by the warm greenish light and likened them to "rare and precious gem[s]." A few days later, he found another prodigal light—a bright yellow mass of slime mold, "strong-scented and disagreeable," oozing amid the grass. The weeks spent with Joe Polis in the Maine woods created a kind of lingering altered state in Thoreau, so that his familiar Concord world loomed "a little larger" upon his return. He wrote to Blake that the Indian

> ... begins where we leave off. It is worth the while to detect new faculties in man, he is so much the more divine; and anything that fairly excites our imagination expands us. The Indian, who can find his way so wonderfully in the woods, possesses so much intelligence which the white man does not, and it increases my own capacity, as well as faith, to observe it. I rejoice to find that intelligence flows in other channels than I knew.

The discovery in Maine of the phosphorescent light somehow lit up all the landscape for Thoreau this fall. Every hue of the senescing leaves leaped out like a light: scarlet chinquapin oaks, greenish-yellow elder, crimson andromeda, clear pale yellow beach plum, reddish purple swamp-pink, sheeny russet swamp maple. He wondered how the Puritans could possibly have worshipped outdoors amid such a spectacle and figured that this was why they built meetinghouses, to dampen the riot of color a bit.[325]

Nature's cornucopia of color contrasted with scarcity in the world of men, for the worst financial panic in a generation had just come on with the changing leaves, sending Thoreau into a playful reverie about where dwelt the real capital:

> The merchants and banks are suspending and failing all the country over, but not the sand-banks, solid and warm, and streaked with bloody

blackberry vines. You may run upon them as much as you please, even as the crickets do, and find their account in it. They are the stockholders in these banks, and I hear them creaking their content. . . . In these banks, too, and such as these, are my funds deposited, a fund of health and enjoyment. Their (the crickets) prosperity and happiness and, I trust, mine do not depend on whether the New York banks suspend or no. . . . Invest, I say, in these country banks. Let your capital be simplicity and contentment. Withered goldenrod (*Solidago nemoralis*) is no failure, like a broken bank, and yet in its most golden season nobody counterfeits it. Nature needs no counterfeit-detector. . . . Banks built of granite, after some Grecian or Roman style, with their porticoes and their safes of iron, are not so permanent, and cannot give me so good security for capital invested in them, as the heads of withered hardhack in the meadow. I do not suspect the solvency of these. I know who is their president and cashier.

For Thoreau there was sweet vindication in the financial panic; he wrote to Blake that mercantile men had always laughed at transcendentalism as so much moonshine compared to the permanence of their institutions. "Hard times," he said, "have this value, among others, that they show us what such promises are worth, where the *sure* banks are." [326]

On the Allagash, Thoreau had learned from Joe Polis the Penobscot word for echo—*pockadunkquaywayle*—and the otherworldliness of the Maine trip kept echoing into this autumn. The Littleton Giant—a man from neighboring Littleton who suffered from acromegaly, a pituitary disorder—brought a load of coal, and his long familiar face and figure suddenly seemed to Thoreau as if they stepped out of a dream. The daydreaming coincided with the recurrence—Thoreau said he had dreamed this same dream at least twenty times before—of a nighttime dream that uncannily echoed his waking life:

I thought of that mountain in the easterly part of our town (where no high hill actually is) which once or twice I had ascended, and often allowed my thoughts alone to climb. . . .

My way up used to lie through a dark and unfrequented wood at its base,—I cannot now tell exactly, it was so long ago, under what circumstances I first ascended, only that I shuddered as I went along (I have an indistinct remembrance of having been out overnight alone),—and then I steadily ascended along a rocky ridge half clad with stinted trees, where wild beasts haunted, till I lost myself quite in the upper air and clouds, seeming to pass an imaginary line which separates a hill, mere earth heaped up, from a mountain, into a superterranean grandeur and sublimity. What distinguishes that summit above the earthy line, is that it is unhandselled, awful, grand. It can never become familiar; you are lost the moment you set foot there. You know no path, but wander, thrilled, over the bare and pathless rock, as if it were solidified air and cloud. That rocky, misty summit, secreted in the clouds, was far more thrillingly awful and sublime than the crater of a volcano spouting fire.

Feeling that he had even asked "my fellow" once to climb this spectral mountain with him, Thoreau was still sure that he had never *actually* ascended it. In attempting to exactly chronicle this dream excursion, words and phrases failed him; his journal entry is punctuated with parenthetical asides and qualifications:

It chances, now I think of it, [Now *first think of it*, at this stage of my description, which makes it the more singularly symbolical.] that it rises in my mind where lies the Burying-Hill. You might go through its gate to enter that dark wood, [Perchance that was the grave.] but that hill and its graves are so concealed and obliterated by the awful mountain that I never thought of them as underlying it. Might not the graveyards of the just always be hills, ways by which we ascend and overlook the plain?[327]

Comparing his dream ascent and descent with his actual walks to the cemetery, he found them entirely different, not only in their topographic details, but in the overwhelming numinosity of the dream landscape. He kept suggesting that his dream walk was upon the features of a "god reposing." When he went to put the dream to poetry, the eastern hill became an amalgam of spiritual aspiration:

> Forever in my dream and in my morning thought,
> Eastward a mount ascends;
> But when in the sunbeam its hard outline is sought,
> It all dissolves and ends.
> The woods that way are gates; the pastures too slope up
> To an unearthly ground;
> But when I ask my mates to take the staff and cup,
> It can no more be found.
> Perhaps I have no shoes fit for the lofty soil
> Where my thoughts graze,
> No properly spun clues, nor well-strained mid-day oil,
> Or must I mend my ways?
> It is a promised land which I have not yet earned.
> I have not made beginning
> With consecrated hand, nor have I ever learned
> To lay the underpinning.
> The mountain sinks by day, as do my lofty thoughts,
> Because I'm not high-minded.
> If I could think alway above these hills and warts,
> I should see it, though blinded.
> It is a spiral path within the pilgrim's soul
> Leads to this mountain's brow;
> Commencing at his hearth he climbs up to this goal
> He knows not when nor how.[328]

Thoreau had long had his own theory of dreams, one closest perhaps to ancient Greek ideas. At night, he believed, "the soul departs out of the body, and sleeps in God, a divine slumber." The thought that dreams had always been regarded as "ambrosial or divine" affirmed the divinity of this particular recurring dream but also of all his dreams. In *A Week*, Thoreau had declared, "Dreams are the touchstones of our characters," and so it was fitting that this most salient dream should find him walking in Concord toward a topographically particular Heaven. The only other recurring dream that he ever wrote about was equally numinous, a "big dream" during which he felt the presence of the spiritual world:

> I can remember that when I was very young I used to have a dream night after night, over and over again, which might have been named Rough and Smooth. All existence, all satisfaction and dissatisfaction, all event was symbolized this way. Now I seem to be lying and tossing, perchance, on a horrible, a fatal rough surface, which must soon, indeed, put an end to my existence, though even in the dream I knew it to be the symbol merely of my misery; and then again, suddenly, I was lying on a delicious smooth surface, as of a summer sea, as of gossamer or down or softest plush, and life was such a luxury to live. My waking experience *always* has been and is such an alternate Rough and Smooth. In other words it is Insanity and Sanity.

"Our truest life is when we are in dreams awake," Thoreau had once said; in both these archetypal dreams, Thoreau was only partly asleep, his waking consciousness having stayed with him into the dream world. In modern parlance, we would say that Thoreau was dreaming lucidly. In lucid dreaming, as the astral body expands out into the cosmos, a stronger than normal link is maintained with the etheric and physical bodies, preserving a partial state of wakefulness. In his ascent of the eastern hill and in lying on the smooth surface, Thoreau was touching the astral world in a manner similar to what he experienced always during his waking ecstasies. The rough surface of his childhood dream was the embodiment of *un*consciousness, of losing touch with the divine world that sustained him. That way lay insanity. The polarities of sleeping and waking, of the expansion into consciousness and the contraction into unconsciousness, of rough and smooth, were universal realities; the truly awake dreamer was called to build a bridge between the poles, to bring down into the sleeping state of everyday reality in mid-nineteenth-century America the ambrosial alertness and aliveness of the astral realm.[329]

Words and Eggs

From his reading in Native American literature, Thoreau knew that prior to European contact, North America had been a dream continent, a place where each culture's most pregnant acts had been incubated and valorized in dream before enactment in waking life. Shamans like the Pennacook chief Passaconnaway employed their dreams to guide not only their individual choices for hunting or healing, but also to shape the futures of their villages and nations. The shaman's gift was for taking dream images and weaving them into ritual action using rhythmically repeated words and phrases. Such had been the mission and destiny of all poets and oracles in all human history. In the world of binding ritual action, the wrong word at the wrong moment meant failure, disaster, even death. To be useful at all to their fellows, mages and wizards had to be masters of words.

All his life, Thoreau had a shamanic relationship with language, hunting out the right words like rare plants. On the first day of 1858, Thoreau began his journal thinking about words: "There are many words which are genuine and indigenous and have their root in our natures, not made by scholars, and as well understood by the illiterate as others. There are also a great many words which are spurious and artificial . . . such as the church, the judiciary, to impeach. . . . It is in vain to try to preserve them by attaching other words to them as the true church, etc. It is like towing a sinking ship with a canoe." Joe Polis's canoe and his words haunted Thoreau this winter as he worked up the report of his Allagash trip. In March, reading the Jesuit priest Sébastien Rasles's Abenaki dictionary, Thoreau felt it a "very concentrated and trustworthy natural history of that people," which included the Penobscot, who spoke a dialect of the Abenaki language. "What they have a word for, they have a thing for"—this directness met the test of both the shaman and the poet. By living out-of-doors—by lying on the ground with "mouse-ear leaves, pine-needles, mosses, and lichens, which form the crust of the earth"—the Indian had names for things which escaped the tongue—and thus the mind—of the white man. He faulted scientific language for its barrenness, which left him wanting to "skin the animals alive to come at them." Even a name like "arbor vitae" was "not a tree of life," in comparison to Indian languages, which had dozens of words for trees and their constituent parts that were absent from scientific botanies. The great attraction for Thoreau of Native American languages was their intimacy with Nature. He created an appendix for *The Maine Woods* that summarized his knowledge of "Indian Words," essentially a compendium of Eastern Abenaki place, faunal, and floral names gleaned from his Penobscot guides, Rasles's and William Willis's dictionaries, and Judge C. E. Potter's history of Manchester, New Hampshire. Despite all his affection for and study of Abenaki and other Algonquian languages, however, Thoreau never seems to have grasped their holophrastic nature—that individual words were built of many words. Occasionally he would give a meaning that pointed to the compositional nature of Abenaki words—as with the Penobscot word for creeping snowberry, *cowosnebagosar*, which he said meant "grows where trees have rotted." Unbeknownst to Thoreau, there was even more particular natural history lore contained in the word, for *cowos* was the word for white pine, suggesting that these little heaths liked the acid soil beneath coniferous trees. Thoreau never knew that *pilkimizi*, the Abenaki word for box elder, literally meant "new land tree," a perfect ecological description of its preference for new soils, such as those deposited upon point bars where the annual crop of samaras quickly germinate and thickly colonize the river-deposited sands. He never discovered that *ongemakw*, white ash, told of its highest use, for the word literally meant "snowshoe tree." [330]

Thoreau never even heard the poetry contained in Joe Polis's peoples' name for themselves. "Abenaki" was the English rendering of Wôbanakiak, "the People of the Dawnland." The word *aki* was "land," *-ak* the suffix denoting "people of," as in Bastoniak, the Abenaki term for Englishmen, who during the colonial era were all designated as coming from Boston. A key word for all the Algonquian speakers of eastern North America, from Labrador to the Carolinas, was wôban, "east" or "dawn," honoring the rhythm of the rising sun and by extension connoting all things full of prospect and promise. The abbreviation *wôn* was a constituent of the Abenaki greeting for those one didn't see every day: *Pakwônonzian*, "You look brand new to me." For all of his reverence for the thought-world revealed by the ancient tongues of indigenous America, Thoreau was too "brand new" to their words to fully penetrate the lore they contained.

There were other living sources for Thoreau to use to tunnel back in time to an era when words still shimmered with their aboriginal vitality. After 1858 a characteristic phrase of Thoreau's journal is "Minott says . . ." Thoreau thought of George Minott, who lived in a little house on the south-facing slope across from Emerson, as the "most poetical farmer . . . that I know." This man—whose sister said he had never once been to Boston—was the Concord equivalent of Joe Polis, the walking university at which Thoreau studied unceasingly. His stories were peppered with pungent expressions that Thoreau treasured. He called the spoiled meadow hay that was left over to the following year "old for"; the greater yellowlegs, which used to breed on those same meadows, he called "humilities"; bitterns were "belcher-squelchers"; in the river were fish like a small pout that he called "prods"; he often used "plaguy" as an idiosyncratic superlative, as in "a plaguy good dog for squirrels." His love of hunting preserved a wealth of vocabulary; Minott loved best to use a "cocking piece" and his phrase for killing game was to "give him gavel." [331]

In its preference for physical metaphors drawn from the vigorous work life of the farm, Minott's expressiveness was characteristic of rural

American culture. When Minott wanted to criticize Daniel Shattuck's *History of Concord*, he said that it was "not right by a jugful," and didn't "come within half a mile of the truth." Such metaphors of measure were pure poetry to the compulsive measurer Thoreau. Like Joe Polis—and Thoreau—Minott had a sharp ear for nature's sounds, particularly bird-calls, and Thoreau attributed Minott's ability to hear the notes of high-flying migrating birds to the fact that he had not "spoiled his ears by attending lectures and caucuses." [332]

Children were another fount of linguistic novelty for Thoreau. In April he met two little Irish boys about nine years old, playing in a brook, and after watching one catch a minnow on a line, Thoreau asked him if he used a hook. The boy replied that he used a "dully-chunk," a small horsehair slipknot at the end of a willow rod. Boys brought him eggs as well as words; in May and June, Edward Emerson, Edward Bartlett, and Storrow Higginson kept him busy with birds' eggs and nests they found all over Concord, and Thoreau in his own walks studied eggs. On the top of Mount Monadnock, he found a purple finch's nest, and theorized that this boreal breeding bird's ancestors had found this and other "arctic isles sprinkled in our southern sky." He also found bullfrog eggs in a shallow rainwater pool on the steepest side of the bare rock summit and was mystified as to how the frogs got there, thinking it more likely that they fell from the clouds than that they hopped up. Back in Concord, he came upon wood tortoises digging nest holes in a gravel bank and watched toads copulating near pools of fresh spawn in a meadow near Walden Pond. Looking for bullfrog spawn, he came upon a pout's nest and after thrusting his hand in, removed a ge-latinous mass of dull yellowish spawn the size of buckshot. Watching a crow chased by a kingbird, he knew the former to have been guilty of nest robbing and figured that the crow chasing an osprey or eagle meant that raptor had done the same. Marsh hawks dove at him to drive him off from observing their young. He watched bream on their river-bottom nests and scouted out dozens of locations for turtles' eggs, though usually skunks had found these places before he did. Suspecting she had just laid eggs, he followed a painted turtle's tracks back and found five eggs packed in the gravelly soil. Picking up gravid turtles, he consistently got wetted by them, as they carried this extra water to soften the ground before digging their nests. Watching the females at their "earnest and pressing business," he was impressed with how methodically they carried out the egg laying, alert all the while to possible predators. He found kingbirds', yellowthroats', song sparrows', ovenbirds', veeries', hermit thrushes', and scarlet tanagers' eggs, and reported on hatched catbirds, partridges, and hawks. He went to Cambridge to study the bird egg collections of the Boston Society of Natural History. He heard that a Mrs. Weatherbee had cooked a gravid snapping turtle and counted forty-two eggs in her cloaca.[333]

Oddly, all of these encounters with Concord's fecundity failed to spark one peep of celebration from Thoreau. Perhaps the intimacy of witnessing such a festival of individual births kept him silent. He also never once mentions the birth of a single child. The miracle of new life seems a given to him, while the persistence of the old and sometimes infirm surprises and delights him. Talking with a Mr. Witherell about a snapping turtle he had caught, Thoreau is moved by the fact that he keeps passing his hand over the torn place in his pants, to hide his bare skin. "How intimate he is with mud and its inhabitants," chimes Thoreau. Hearing a voice calling to oxen one May day, he instantly recognizes its cadence as that of Elijah Wood.

It is wonderful how far the individual proclaims himself. Out of the thousand millions of human beings on this globe, I know that this sound was made by the lungs and larynx and lips of E. Wood, am as sure of it as if he nudged me with his elbow and shouted in my ear. He can impress himself on the very atmosphere, then, can launch himself a mile on the wind [dispensing with the telegraph], through trees and rustling sedge and over rippling water, associating with a myriad sounds, and yet arrive distinct at my ear; and yet this creature that is felt so far, that was so noticeable, lives but a short time, quietly dies and makes no more noise that I know of. I can tell him, too, with my eyes by the very gait and motion of him half a mile distant. Far more wonderful his purely spiritual influence, that after the lapse of thousands of years you may still detect the individual in the turn of a sentence or the tone of a thought!!

Perhaps this was the real reason for the limited celebration of this spectacular season of births. Toads, turtles, thrushes, and trout—even when they sang—couldn't call forth from Thoreau the sympathy he was ever prone to give to any single individual human being striving for self-expression. Animals were types, not individuals, and rarely acted in a manner to merit idiosyncratic exploration and description. But Elijah Wood's lungs and larynx and lips shouted his being every moment of every day, and when he eventually fell silent, the whole world would be lessened.[334]

"They Teach Us How to Die"

Each October, Thoreau's journal burst into flame as he described the "autumnal tints" of the Concord landscape, and the fall of 1858—even though the foliage was not as brilliant as usual—was a particularly colorful season as painted by Thoreau's brush. Individual trees in forest stands long familiar to him now leaped out to distinguish themselves by a particularly intense burst of color. Looking across Walden Pond to Pine Hill from the Deep Cut, the maples appeared to his eyes like fires kindled at the base of every tree. Witch hazel flowers were camouflaged by their own yellowing leaves; cranberry meadows became dull red; hickory leaves turned orange at the edges while their centers remained green. He noted the progress of the shrubs—staghorn sumac, huckleberry, fever bush, even asparagus beds—as closely as the deciduous trees. On October 6 he declared the tints at their brightest. Arriving at Pinxter Swamp on October 12, he found the azaleas almost totally bare, revealing next year's leaf buds, and remarked on the contrast with man, who did not anticipate another spring: "With man all is uncertainty." After the beeches, maples, birches, and ash were past their prime, Thoreau turned his attention to the oaks, which faded at a more leisurely pace into their muted splendor. Thoreau was grateful to the town fathers who generations before had set out sugar maple saplings in Concord. "A village is not complete unless it has these trees to mark the season in it. They are as important as a town clock. Such a village will not be found to work well. It has a screw loose; an essential part is wanting." [335]

The shifting hues of dying vegetation alerted his eye to the variegated effects of autumnal light on all sorts of surfaces—the river, houses, even his notebook. He decided that there was not a single plant—down to the dullest grasses and even the lowly sphagnum moss—that did not acquire brighter colors just before the fall. The same process could be seen in every fruit, and it was inevitable that Thoreau would see such a general law extend to humans as well: "We have dreamed that the hero should carry his color aloft, as a symbol of the ripeness of his virtue. The noblest feature, the eye, is the fairest colored, the jewel of the body. The warrior's flag is the flower which precedes his fruit. He unfurls his flag to the breeze with such confidence and brag as the flower its petals. Now we shall see what kind of fruit will succeed." At the moment there was very little heroic behavior in the neighborhood to match the forest flags. Someone told him about a local man who had just slit both his jugular veins, and as he lay bleeding to death, asked his nephew to take the razor and cut deeper. A neighbor coldly remarked that "it was about time," as the fellow who committed suicide had set fire to his woodpile once, and had probably burned a number of houses and stables. [336]

This one man's suicide might be forgiven, but Thoreau could not forgive the general soul sickness he saw all around him. "What do ye want to hear, ye puling infants?" he demanded. "A trumpet-sound that would train you up to mankind, or a nurse's lullaby?" He lashed out in his journal at the hypocrisy of church and state:

Let us have institutions framed not out of our rottenness, but out of our soundness. This factitious piety is like stale gingerbread. I would like to suggest what a pack of fools and cowards we mankind are. They want me to agree not to breathe too hard in the neighborhood of their paper castles. If I should draw a long breath in the neighborhood of these institutions, their weak and flabby sides would fall out, for my own inspiration would exhaust the air about them.

Magazine editors—"afraid to print a whole sentence, a round sentence, a free-spoken sentence"—came in for Thoreau's especial vituperation. The particular editor Thoreau was thinking of was James Russell Lowell; the free-spoken sentence was one Thoreau had penned in his "Chesuncook" piece for Lowell's *Atlantic Monthly*. At the end of a meditation on the white pine tree and the necessity of saving it as a piece not only of wilderness, but also of the wilderness of the human soul, Thoreau wrote, "It is as immortal as I am, and perchance will go to as high a heaven, there to tower above me still." Lowell cut this sentence without Thoreau's permission; the incident had occurred over four months before, and Thoreau was still livid. Lyceums and institutes were no better. His own experiences as a lecturer had taught him that "they want all of a man but his truth and independence and manhood." [337]

For all his disappointment with mankind, this November still found him cheerful. "Give me the old familiar walk, post-office and all, with this ever new self, with this infinite expectation and faith, which does not know when it is beaten. We'll go nutting once more. We'll pluck the nut of the world, and crack it in the winter evenings." He was preparing his lecture "Autumnal Tints" for the cowardly lyceum audiences. He was scheduled to give the lecture in Worcester on February 15; it was postponed after Thoreau's father died on February 3. John Thoreau had been ill with consumption for nearly two years, had been mostly silent for the previous few months, and since January 13 had been confined to bed. Sitting along with his mother and sister by his dying father, Thoreau saw in his emaciated face resemblances to many members of his family, "as if . . . there was a greater general similarity in the framework of the face than in its filling up and clothing." John Thoreau had been a scarcely perceptible presence in his son's life, despite the fact that they had lived and worked together (in the family graphite business) for most of Thoreau's forty-two years. On the day of his father's death, Thoreau reflected on his father's life, noting his coming to Concord at age twelve, around 1800; his boyhood apprenticeship in the dry goods business and subsequent early business triumphs and tragedies; and his wide acquaintance with the "local, social, and street history" of Concord. "I think that he remembered more about the worthies (and unworthies) of Concord village forty years ago, both from dealing as a trader and from familiar intercourse with them, than any one else." [338]

Daniel Ricketson's letter of condolence to his friend suggests that John Thoreau shared certain qualities with his son. "I have rarely, if ever," wrote Ricketson, "met a man who inspired me with more respect. He appeared to me to be a real embodiment of honest virtue, as well as a true gentleman of the old school." Ricketson spoke of Thoreau's father's "kindly friendship" and fondly recounted a walk they had taken while Thoreau was away from home. In his reply, Thoreau offered his only assessment of his father's life:

> I think I may say that he was wholly unpretending; and there was this peculiarity in his aim, that, though he had pecuniary difficulties to contend with the greater part of his life, he always studied merely how to make a *good* article, pencil or other, (for he practiced various arts) and was never satisfied with what he had produced,—nor was he ever in the least disposed to put off a *poor* one for the sake of pecuniary gain;—as if he had labored for a higher end.

No higher tribute could this transcendentalist son pay his village merchant father than to suggest that his labors had been for a transcendental end.[339]

Thoreau interrupted his journal reflection upon his father's life and death with a short commentary lamenting how dismissively American historians had treated the history of the Indians. "One tells you with more contempt than pity that the Indian had no religion, holding up both hands, and this to all the shallow-brained and bigoted seems to mean something important, but it is commonly a distinction without a difference. Pray, how much more religion has the historian? If Henry Ward Beecher knows so much more about God than another, if he has made some discovery of truth in this direction, I would thank him to publish it in *Silliman's Journal*, with as few flourishes as possible." Thoreau was more than ever convinced of the inherent authority of the native peoples of North America, their undeniable primogeniture upon this continent. "They paddled over these waters, they wandered in these woods, and they had their fancies and beliefs connected with the sea and the forest, which concern us quite as much as the fables of Oriental nations do."

Then he went right back to the lamentation for his father, saying that "we partially die ourselves through sympathy at the death of each of our friends or near relatives. Each such experience is an assault on our vital force." Certainly this had been true of his experience of his brother John's—and to a lesser extent, his sister Helen's—death. "After long watching around the sick-bed of a friend," he concluded, "we, too, partially give up the ghost with him, and are the less to be identified with this state of things." [340]

On February 22, the Worcester audience of Thoreau's "Autumnal Tints" lecture took offense that he faulted them for not seeing as much of the kaleidoscope of fall colors as he did. What they really failed to see was that the lecture was actually a celebration of the art of dying rather than the artistry of fall foliage. The brownish-yellow masses of elm leaves made him wonder "if there is any answering ripeness in the lives of the men who live beneath them" and seeing a market-man taking his crop beneath them to sell in the village, he imagines "a husking of thoughts": "I foresee that it will be chiefly husks and little thought, blasted pig-corn, fit only for cob-meal,—for as you sow, so shall you reap." Watching the shower of fallen leaves, he shouts, "How beautifully

they go to their graves!" and at the end of an answering shower of exclamation marks, he concludes, "They teach us how to die. One wonders if
the time will ever come when men, with their boasted faith in immortality, will lie down as gracefully and as ripe,—with such an Indian-
summer serenity will shed their bodies, as they do their hair and nails."
Thoreau advised his listeners that they needed the "innocent stimu-
lants" of fall foliage to "keep off melancholy and superstition," and took
a jab at spiritualism by asserting that in villages where no elms and
maples and oaks flew their fall flags, people would "crack their dry joints
at one another and call it a spiritual communication."[341]

During the previous autumn, Thoreau had fallen in love with the
scarlet oak, likely because they above all of Concord's trees required the
"separate intention of the eye" that Thoreau always championed. Scarlet
oaks required halcyon days to show off their tints and did so late in October, after all the other trees had peaked and faded. The "late and unexpected glory" of the scarlet oak, however, was ultimately but a metaphor
for the triumphal end of human life:

> Lifted higher and higher, and sublimated more and more, putting some
> earthiness and cultivating more intimacy with the light each year, they
> have at length the least possible amount of earthy matter, and the
> greatest spread and grasp of skyey influences. There they dance, arm in
> arm with the light,—tripping it on fantastic points, fit partners in those
> aerial halls. So intimately mingled are they with it, that, what with their
> slenderness and their glossy surfaces, you can hardly tell at last what in
> the dance is leaf and what is light.

During the lecture, Thoreau exhibited a large scarlet oak leaf he had
mounted on white herbarium paper, so that those unfamiliar with its
dance of leaf and light could see for themselves. A couple of months
before his own death, while he was preparing this lecture for publication, he asked Sophia to draw a scarlet oak leaf to supply to the publisher for an engraving to accompany the article. Its deep embayments

and pointed capes were reminiscent of his own drawing of Walden Pond included in *Walden*; one could clearly see the series of leaf-vein crucifixes held lightly by the fleshy surface left behind from the evanescent whole of which it had been a part.[342]

The "Autumnal Tints" lecture concluded with Thoreau's law that "all leaves . . . acquire brighter colors just before their fall," and the veiled hint to his audience was that each of them, no matter what their unheroic disappointments and disasters in life, would display their heraldic colors as they died, just as the scarlet oak's scalloped leaves did. At the end of May, Thoreau was one of the pallbearers at the funeral of Bulkeley Emerson, Waldo's feeble-minded brother. Born three years after Waldo, Bulkeley had as a boy been merely embarrassing in his manners, but as an adult, he grew irritable and loudmouthed, and was often institutionalized after suffering breakdowns. He needed care all his life, living with a number of farm families, as well as at McLean's Asylum. In 1853, Thoreau had gone to fetch Bulkeley from a family at Scratch Flat in Acton, for his mother's funeral, and had visited him there on a number of occasions. Coming out of Sleepy Hollow Cemetery after burying Bulkeley, he picked up a three-inch-high oak sprout with its acorn still attached, and in his journal for the day, he noted that the barn swallows were beginning to lay in Hosmer's barn.[343]

How Long?

Along with taking over the running of his father's now profitable graphite business, Thoreau this year received his most lucrative surveying contract when in response to the complaints of a group of farmers whose hay meadows were being flooded by Concord's three rivers, the township hired him to measure water depths and compile a history of bridges, dams, and other obstructions. The contract gave him ample opportunity to hone his already extensive knowledge of riparian physiography and to gather unexplored arcana of local history. The rivers that he had paddled and sailed over and bathed in all his life now took on a new depth as he sounded them along their lengths. His measurements led him to call any place above Ball's Hill—opposite the end of the Great Meadows—where the water was eleven feet deep or more at summer level a "deep hole," and he found six of these. Shallows—places up to four feet deep—he located in seven spots. He also enumerated shoals and "great bends." Along with sensitizing him to the riparian requirements of various aquatic plants, the survey allowed him to describe hydraulic history and ongoing processes hitherto unknown. He found that the Concord River, formed from the junction of the Assabet and Sudbury, was much more variable in depth below the junction of the rivers than above it. He discovered the rhythmic alternation of meander scrolls and point bars, and as always, found a law that crossed over from nature to the human realm: "The deep places in the river are not so obvious as the shallow ones and can only be found by carefully probing it. So perhaps it is with human nature." From farmers along the river, he also met characteristic resistance to empirical fact; many boasted to Thoreau of one or another deep hole as being the deepest in the river, and when Thoreau went to sound it, found that "it only need to be considerably over his head to acquire this reputation." Whenever Thoreau would tell the farmer the actual depth, he would reply that Thoreau had not found the right spot.[344]

Nathan Hosmer told Thoreau when the stone piers at Hunt's Bridge had been built. Abel Hosmer told him that the Eddy Bridge was built around the time that the Orthodox Quaker meetinghouse was built. Jacob Farmer said that at that time—thirty-five years before—a friend had almost drowned just below the Eddy Bridge, so that the island that now stood there formed *after* the building of the bridge. Harrington related that at what he called the Elm Hole he found the old bed of the river some ten rods from the present one. In the middle of all this surveying and story gathering, Thoreau turned forty-two years old on July 12, 1859. The moon being nearly full, he went for a paddle upriver to listen to the bullfrogs. There were fireworks being set off in the village, and he kept being surprised by the flare of the rockets in the sky. "Such are their aspirations," he lamented about the revelers.[345]

Dampened aspirations—not his own, but others'—hovered around him on this birthday. He reflected on "Mr. and Mrs. Such-a-one ... 'going to the beach' for six weeks," marveling that such a "failure and defeat" was seen by society as the "culminating-point of their activity." He imagined that all men began by venturing off to pitch their tent twenty or thirty miles beyond that of their fathers, dreaming that they were living adventurously and originally, only to wake up and discover that they were as tame as their fathers, sleeping in their beds. Everywhere he looked, he saw failed expectations: "How unpromising are promising men! Hardly any disgust me so much. I have no faith in them. They make gratuitous promises, and they break them gratuitously." He complained of "non-producers," "bloodsuckers," and "sniveling prayers" as characteristic of "civilized life":

> There is nothing but confusion in our New England life. The hogs are in the parlor. This man and his wife—and how many like them!—should have sucked their claws in some hole in a rock, or lurked like gypsies in the outbuildings of some diviner race. They've got into the wrong boxes; they rained down into these houses by mistake, as it is said to rain toads sometimes. . . .
>
> We do everything according to the fashion, just as the Flatheads flatten the heads of their children. We conform ourselves in a myriad ways and with infinite pains to the fashions of our time. We mourn for our lost relatives according to fashion, and as some nations hire professed mourners to howl, so we hire stone-masons to hammer and blast by the month and so express our grief.

Contemplating the adventive plants around an old cellar hole, he turned his most misanthropic, saying that "a curse seems to attach to any place which has long been inhabited by man. Vermin of various kinds abide with him."[346]

For his own part, Thoreau's backward glance found only fulfillment. On this same day, he reminisced about the success of boyhood huckleberrying excursions, and a few days later, he told a story about going to buy a pair of shoes and asking for the shoemaker to replace the wooden pegs at the toes with iron ones. When the cobbler offered zinc pegs instead, along with considerable advice on the subject of shoes, Thoreau held fast: "I have learned to respect my own opinion in this matter," he stated matter-of-factly. Year after year, Thoreau had only become more and more like himself, refusing to compromise, independent of thought and action, even in the humble matter of shoes. Once again, at the turn of his seven-year biographical pulse, his instincts and inspirations were fortified. He seemed to be preparing for some new fight, summoning his old martial vigor. His shoes wanted iron; so did his soul. In September, he confessed that he felt hurried by his affairs—the graphite business and surveying—while he knew that great works of art needed "endless leisure." The great work he was now fashioning was his life:

> It is not by a compromise, it is not by a timid and feeble repentance, that a man will save his soul and *live*, at last. He has got to *conquer* a clear field, letting Repentance & Co. go. That's a well-meaning but weak firm that has assumed the debts of an old and worthless one. You are to fight in a field where no allowances will be made, no courteous bowing to one-handed knights. You are expected to do your duty, not in spite of every thing but *one*, but in spite of *everything*.[347]

As Thoreau had come more deeply into relationship with Concord's forests, he showed himself every bit the uncompromising two-fisted knight in his battle with those who saw forests as commodities. Tramping in Botrychium Swamp among larches turning golden, he dreamed that:

> Each town should have a park, or rather a primitive forest, of five hundred or a thousand acres, where a stick should never be cut for fuel,

a common possession forever, for instruction and recreation. We hear of cow-commons and ministerial lots, but we want *men*-commons and lay lots, inalienable forever. Let us keep the New World *new,* preserve all the advantages of living in the country. There is meadow and pasture and wood-lot for the town's poor. Why not a forest and huckleberry-field for the town's rich? All Walden Wood might have been preserved for our park forever, with Walden in its midst, and the Easterbrooks Country, an unoccupied area of some four square miles, might have been our huckleberry-field. If any owners of these tracts are about to leave the world without natural heirs who need or deserve to be specially remembered, they will do wisely to abandon their possession to all, and not will them to some individual who perhaps has enough already. As some give to Harvard College or another institution, why might not another give a forest or huckleberry-field to Concord? A town is an institution which deserves to be remembered. We boast of our system of education, but why stop at schoolmasters and schoolhouses? We are all schoolmasters, and our schoolhouse is the universe. To attend chiefly to the desk or schoolhouse while we neglect the scenery in which it is placed is absurd. If we do not look out we shall find our fine schoolhouse standing in a cow-yard at last.

In this same swamp, Thoreau found the odd moonwort fern, *Botrychium lunaria,* shedding its pollen, and in his journal asked, "How long?" This question had since the summer of 1851 been a perennial one punctuating an extraordinary number of his journal entries, as he worked to fill out his phenological calendar of Concord. How long since a plant had leafed out, flowered, or fruited? More than ever, the fall of 1859 saw Thoreau asking this question about the dying stages of plants. How long since the arborvitae had shed its seeds? How long since the cedar and tupelo leaves had fallen? How long has the red cherry fruit been eaten by birds? How long had the swamp pink and waxwork (bittersweet) been bare?[348]

Thoreau's question carried an existential ache as well, a prophetic plea that rang far beyond Concord. How long before America would become naturalized, become, like the plants and animals whose life histories he tracked, symbiotically embedded within its physical surround? How long before America discovered its true destiny? His forest preserve idea was meant to help effect the naturalization that had not yet taken place. The Kalendar project was Thoreau's own primary tool toward going native, by listening to the expectations of the land. If he was still triangulating the chronology of the turning year as it played out in plants, there were other signs of greater annual constancy. Seeing new muskrat houses appear on the leafless shores, he remarked that he had seen it regularly for thirty years. "It may not be in the Greenwich almanac or ephemeris, but it has an important place in my Kalendar. So surely as the sun appears to be in Libra or Scorpio, I see the conical winter lodges of the musquash rising above the withered pontederia and flags." Thoreau's New Testament would speak of these native lodges, and while others might scoff at "Americanisms," his living, indigenous speech preferred "musketaquidding" to "meandering." He fantasized a native zodiac that would incorporate as signs a dead sucker, musquash house, and snapping turtle. Instead of bumbling about like rank strangers in their native land—as did John LaMountain and John Haddock, who tried unsuccessfully to live off the land after freezing temperatures aloft forced them to end a balloon flight in the Canadian wilderness—Thoreau thought that all Americans should have been able to live bounteously in the woods, dining on wild edibles.[349]

The expectant cry of "How long?" haunted abolitionists more than any other Americans, and one abolitionist in particular, John Brown. Frustrated by the silence that greeted his plea, on October 16 he led twenty-one men—including five blacks—in an attack on the federal arsenal at Harper's Ferry, Virginia, in hopes of inciting a slave insurrection and provoking guerrilla war against the South. Five of the band escaped; Brown and the rest were killed or captured within forty-eight hours. News of the raid reached Concord the next day, and Thoreau began to fume in his journal:

When a government puts forth its strength on the side of injustice, as ours (especially to-day) to maintain slavery and kill the liberators of the slave, what a merely brute, or worse than brute, force it is seen to be! A demoniacal force! It is more manifest than ever that tyranny rules. I see this government to be effectually allied with France and Austria in oppressing mankind.

Going about his day, Thoreau met "craven-hearted" neighbors who consistently condemned Brown's actions, and he in turn condemned their hypocrisy: "They preserve the so-called peace of their community by deeds of petty violence every day. Look at the policeman's billy and handcuffs! Look at the jail! Look at the gallows! Look at the chaplain of the regiment! We are hoping only to live safely on the outskirts of this provisional army. So they defend themselves and our hen-roosts, and maintain slavery." In his journal, one hears him turn away from the historically fateful "how long?" to the ephemeral "how long?" of juniper berries and bare branches, only to be yanked back into his jeremiad voice. Channing tells him that he saw a loon on Walden Pond on the fifteenth, but Thoreau is more concerned with the lunacy of his slavery-countenancing neighbors, who pronounced Brown insane, while themselves imitating sanity. Like Brown, whom he had heard speak in Concord just five months before, Thoreau employed the rhetoric of Christianity to express his anger at America:

A government that pretends to be Christian and crucifies a million Christs every day!

Our foes are in our midst and all about us. Hardly a house but is divided against itself. For our foe is the all but universal woodenness (both of head and heart), the want of vitality, of man,—the effect of vice,—whence are begotten fear and superstition and bigotry and persecution and slavery of all kinds. Mere figure-heads upon a hulk, with livers in the place of hearts. A church that can never have done with excommunicating Christ while it exists. Our plains were overrun the other day with a flock of adjutant-generals, as if a brood of cockerels had been let loose there, waiting to use their spurs in what sort of glorious cause, I ask. What more probable in the future, what more certain heretofore, than in grinding in the dust four hundred thousands of feeble and timid men, women, and children? The United States exclaims: "Here are four millions of human creatures which we have stolen. We have abolished among them the relations of father, mother, children, wife, and we mean to keep them in this condition. Will you, O Massachusetts, help us to do so?" And Massachusetts promptly answers, "Aye!"

If Thoreau's voice seemed stridently militant in comparison to his neighbors', it should have surprised no one, for he spoke out of the same chivalric ideals he had held since he was a boy. He and his countrymen may have in youth shared the same fabled heroes, but Thoreau had given them flesh and bones, while his compatriots let them wither: "A whole nation will for ages cling to the memory of its Arthur, or other imaginary hero, who perhaps never assailed its peculiar institution or sin, and, being imaginary, never failed, when they are themselves the very freebooters and craven knights whom he routed, while they forget their real heroes." [350]

Two days after Harper's Ferry, Thoreau dug artichokes in Alcott's garden, but could not take his mind from Brown:

I know that there have been a few heroes in the land, but no man has ever stood up in America for the dignity of human nature so devotedly, persistently, and so effectively as this man. Ye need not trouble yourselves, Republican or any other party, to wash your skirts of him. No intelligent person will ever be convinced that he was any creature of yours. He went and came, as he informs us, "under the auspices of John Brown, and nobody else."

In comparison to Brown, he thought the Revolutionary heroes Ethan Allen and John Stark "rangers in a far lower field and in a less important cause." The gossip of his neighbors continued to vex him, and his daily rants frequently took their cue in response to their remarks. "But he won't gain anything," he heard; his reply: "Well, no! I don't suppose he could get four-and-sixpence a day for being hung, take the year round. But then he stands a chance to save a considerable part of his soul,—and such a soul!—when you do not. No doubt you can get more in your market for a quart of milk than for a quart of blood, but that is not the market that heroes carry their blood to." [351]

On October 22, Thoreau walked out to Conantum Cliffs and Fair Haven Bay and found on the path below the cliffs fresh blossoming violets, bringing back the spring. The afternoon saw him indignant that "the bravest and humanest man in all the country" was about to be hanged, but he felt it ultimately necessary: "We needed to be thus assisted to see our government by the light of history. It needed to see itself." Thoreau saw the smallness of Brown's band not as proof of his "insanity" but as proof of society's spinelessness. He mocked newspaper editors who mocked Brown for his sense of being divinely appointed to his task. Never had Thoreau stepped further out of bounds rhetorically:

This event advertises me that there is such a fact as death,—the possibility of a man's dying. It seems as if no man had ever died in America; for in order to die you must first have lived. I don't believe in the hearses and palls and funerals that they have had. There was no death in the case, because there had been no life; they merely rotted or sloughed off, pretty much as they had rotted or sloughed along. No temple's veil was rent, only a hole dug somewhere. The best of them fairly ran down like a clock. I hear a good many pretend that they are going to die; or that they have died, for aught I know. Nonsense! I'll defy them to do it. They haven't got life enough in them. They'll deliquesce like fungi, and keep a hundred eulogists mopping the spot where they left off. Only half a dozen or so have died since the world began.

A week later, Thoreau gathered up his journal pages for a lecture at the Concord Town Hall on "the character of John Brown, now in the clutches of the slaveholder." The selectmen would not have the town bell rung to announce the talk, so Thoreau rang it himself. Two days later, called in at the last moment to replace scheduled speaker Frederick Douglass, he gave the address as "A Plea for John Brown" at Tremont Hall in Boston, and then again on November 3 in Worcester. The substance of his ninety-minute speech was nearly identical to the thoughts contained in his journal, except that now, speaking directly to an audience, he began with a feint of mild-mannered humility: "I trust that you will pardon me for being here. I do not wish to force my thoughts upon you, but I feel forced myself." He ended with the plea:

> I am here to plead his cause with you. I plead not for his life, but for his character—his immortal life; and so it becomes your cause wholly, and is not his in the least. Some eighteen hundred years ago Christ was crucified; this morning, perchance, Captain Brown was hung. These are two ends of a chain which is not without its links. He is not Old Brown any longer; he is an Angel of Light.

Thoreau then quoted Brown's words to his captors at the armory, prophetic words that warned the South to prepare to settle "this negro question"—"the end of that is not yet." When Thoreau said that he did not plead for John Brown's life, he spoke truly, for the heroic martyrdom for which Brown was destined demanded his death. Thoreau said as much in his lecture: "I see now that it is necessary that... [he] be hung... I *almost fear* that I may yet hear of his deliverance, doubting if a prolonged life ... can do as much good as his death." [352]

Named—along with Emerson, ex–lieutenant governor Simon Brown, and former high sheriff John Keyes—on November 30 to a committee to ask the selectmen for permission to ring the First Parish church bell at the time that Brown was to be hanged, Thoreau found the same cowardly actions that he had condemned generally in his "Plea." The selectmen at first denied responsibility for the bell, then "*in any case*" refused their consent. Leading men of Concord hoped that "no such foolish thing would be done," and someone told Thoreau that five hundred people—some of whom promised to fire guns in a counterdemonstration—damned him for proposing the action. On December 2, the day of the execution, Thoreau, Emerson, Alcott, and a crowd of Concord and neighboring townspeople gathered at the Town Hall for a memorial service arranged by Thoreau. No bell was rung, but Thoreau read poetry, and Emerson read some of Brown's words. After the service, an effigy of Brown was found tied to a tree with a will attached, that included the line: "I bequeath to H. D. Thoreau, Esq., my body and soul, he having eulogized my character and actions at Harper's Ferry above the saints in heaven." [353]

The next day, Francis Jackson Merriam, one of Brown's men who escaped to Canada from Harper's Ferry, arrived in Concord after hearing of Brown's execution. Frank Sanborn asked Thoreau to take Merriam, traveling as "Mr. Lockwood," to the South Acton station in order to get a train back to Canada. The mildly insane Merriam kept insisting that Thoreau was Emerson, and put questions to him—"of Fate, etc., etc."—as if he *were*. After Merriam's departure, Brown's fate continued to haunt Thoreau, who marveled that "no theatrical manager could have arranged things so wisely to give effect to his behavior and words." Thoreau knew that many men had been hanged in the South for attempting to rescue slaves, and yet their deaths had little stirred the North. The effect of Brown's death was different because Brown was "Transcendental"—a vehicle of higher laws: "It goes behind the human law, it goes behind the apparent failure, and recognizes eternal justice and glory." Brown's revolution was a higher one than the one begun at Concord North Bridge, for it was on "behalf of another, an oppressed, people." In Henry Thoreau's eyes, John Brown lived the heroism he had abstractly described twenty years before in "The Service" and which he himself had lived momentarily when he had spent a night in the Concord jail. When "government puts forth its strength on the side of injustice," that government must be disobeyed. Instead of anxiously asking "how long?" before slavery would end, John Brown acted to end it and, in doing so, answered the question.[354]

CHAPTER 7

Faith in a Seed

As often as a martyr dies,
This opes its petals to the skies;
And Nature by this trace alone
Informs us which way he is gone.
— "Rosa Sanguinea"

Tracks

The new year 1860 brought abundant snow to Concord, and Thoreau on his walks enjoyed deciphering the impressions left by birds and mammals in their foraging. Finding that the snow showed him wood-peckers working, a flock of goldfinches feeding, a bevy of quail walking along the roadside, all after the fact, he exclaimed, "How much the snow reveals!" The animal tracks in the snow evoked thoughts about human tracks in life:

> A man receives only what he is ready to receive, whether physically or intellectually or morally, as animals conceive at certain seasons their kind only. We hear and apprehend only what we already half know. If there is something which does not concern me, which is out of my line, which by experience or by genius my attention is not drawn to, however novel and remarkable it may be, if it is spoken, we hear it not, if it is written, we read it not, or if we read it, it does not detain us. Every man thus *tracks himself* through life, in all his hearing and reading and observation and travelling. His observations make a chain.

The phenomenon or fact that cannot in any wise be linked with the rest which he has observed, he does not observe. By and by we may be ready to receive what we cannot receive now. I find, for example, in Aristotle something about the spawning, etc., of the pout and perch, because I know something about it already and have my attention aroused; but I do not discover till very late that he has made other equally important observations on the spawning of other fishes, because I am not interested in those fishes.[355]

In the previous ten years, no one else in America had made a chain of observations as tightly linked or as conscientiously transcribed as Henry Thoreau's. Amateur naturalists and professional natural scientists had by 1860 traveled to some of the farthest reaches of the North American continent and had filed their specimens and maps and surveys and reports, and in so doing had tracked themselves as well as the flora and fauna, but none of their chains of observations were graced by the extraordinary self-awareness of Thoreau's tracking endeavor. What was true for the naturalist reading Aristotle on fishes was true for the citizen reading the local newspaper or hearing the latest telegrams at the post office. Only a few Americans—Thoreau, in his collaboration with Agassiz, was one of them—could discover new species of fish, but fewer still could hear of Harper's Ferry and discover an overlooked species of man. Thoreau's observations about Brown made a telltale chain that linked both men to their singular histories but also bound them more tightly to the story of their nascent nation.

John Brown's heroism was something that Thoreau had been preparing to recognize his whole life. The stunning bravery and spectacular violence of Brown and his compatriots' act left most Americans shocked and stuttering; the same act invited more than the usual eloquence from the man who ever marched to the beat of a different drummer. Though in his "Plea" and also in "The Last Days of John Brown"—read in Thoreau's absence at the graveside celebration of Brown's life in North Elba, New York, on July 4, 1860—Thoreau had praised the

"Captain" as a stalwart soldier, it was the aim, and not the means, of Brown's martial excellence that most excited Thoreau's admiration. The steadfastness of his will, the seriousness of his purpose, the steely calm displayed both during the armory gunfight and afterward, when he addressed his captors—these were the mark of Mars, the god who made war on injustice. For Thoreau, the ultimate human battle was the one waged eternally for individual freedom, and no institution violated freedom as murderously as chattel slavery. Bearing such potent Mars forces within his soul, Thoreau could not help but be Brown's most ardent absentee collaborator against the slave owner.

After John Brown was executed, Thoreau never spoke of him as dead, preferring to speak of his "translation." In the first few days after the execution, Thoreau had a strong sense that Brown was not dead: "Of all the men who are said to be my contemporaries, it seems to me that John Brown is the only one who *has not* died." This was not just classic Thoreauvian rhetorical reversal, but a real felt sense of the transcendence brought by transcendental thought and action. "John Brown has earned immortality," Thoreau declared, suggesting that all mortals were granted it, but only a few actually earned it. Thoreau spoke of "Immortality" throughout his life, and used the word with the exactness he brought to all words. In his very first publication, at age twenty, he spoke in Anna Jones's obituary of the "living and inextinguishable flame" that burned within her. In an 1849 journal meditation on friendship, Thoreau asked, "Why should we be related as mortals merely—as limited to one state of existence—Our lives are immortal our transmigrations are infinite—the virtue that we are lives ever—the vice dieth ever." In December 1853, the sound of the telegraph harp "remind[s] me of my immortality." On a mild January day in 1858, feeling full of life, he wrote, "You discover evidences of immortality not known to divines. You cease to die." Observing ferns that had escaped the first killing frosts of fall in 1857, he saw them as "an argument for immortality. Death is so far from being universal. The same destroyer does not destroy all." Thoreau's editorial battle with *Atlantic Monthly* editor James Russell Lowell was so acrimonious because the single sentence cut by Lowell—"It [the white pine tree] is as immortal as I am, and perchance will go to as high a heaven, there to tower above me still"—was very near the core of Thoreau's philosophy of life.[356]

Antebellum America had carried on a rather confusing argument about immortality—not so much about its existence, which was still widely held, but about its nature. Nineteenth-century Christian belief in an afterlife was conspicuously short on detail, but after 1849, Spiritualism's meticulous if grossly materialist portraits of "Summerland" brought forth from ministers and lay folk alike a host of responses. Just as that debate was heating up, Darwin's theory of evolution by natural selection opened to question the traditional Christian view of the human being as divinely created and thus divinely destined after death.

In claiming immortality for John Brown, Thoreau left another unmistakable track of his own life, which had been an enactment of higher-than-mortal principles. Thoreau recognized that no other man in all America could have done what Brown had done; the attack on Harper's Ferry was the act that magnetically drew toward it every other thought and action in Brown's life. Thoreau's public proclamations of Brown's heroism were equally fated, a ripened fruit of a tree of life whose deep moral taproot served the uppermost branches. Before Thoreau's father's death, his firm had abandoned pencil manufacture as the market opened for high-quality graphite for the recently invented process of electrotyping. While the graphite business and surveying occupied his business hours, distinguishing the signs of immortality all about him—Nature's preparation for the future in the form of fruits and seeds—had become Thoreau's principal trade. In early February, he gave his last lecture at the Concord Lyceum, "Wild Apples," drawing "long, continued applause" at its close. "It is remarkable how closely the history of the apple tree is connected with that of man," he began slyly, putting his vast chronological knowledge to good use in telling his neighbors with more detail than they themselves could muster the exact timing of the growth and development of the fruit. His rhapsody to their fragrance was a thinly disguised ode to immortality:

> There is thus about all natural products a certain volatile and ethereal quality which represents their highest value, and which cannot be vulgarized, or bought and sold. No mortal has ever enjoyed the perfect flavor of any fruit, and only the godlike among men begin to taste its ambrosial qualities. For nectar and ambrosia are only those fine flavors of every fruit which our coarse palates fail to perceive,—just as we occupy the heaven of the gods without knowing it.

After dispensing quickly with the history of the cultivated apple, Thoreau went straight to the wild apple, whose transcendent qualities he prized above the well-tended orchard fruit. Whether detailing how the wild apple is crabbed by the constant nibbling of cows or rhapsodizing about the flavor of their fruit or the beauty of their flecked and blotched skin, Thoreau thought them the finest of creations. These "apples not of Discord, but of Concord" were but understudies for Men, the real subject of Thoreau's pomological essay. "*Our* wild apple," he crowed, "is wild only like myself, perchance, who belong not to the aboriginal race here, but have strayed into the woods from the cultivated stock." Like the apple, men were "browsed on by fate; and only the most persistent and strongest genius defends itself and prevails, send[ing] its tender scion upward at last, and drop[ping] its perfect fruit on the ungrateful earth." Surely he pointed right at himself when he said, "Poets and philosophers and statesmen thus spring up in the country pastures, and outlast the hosts of unoriginal men." [357]

Thoreau concluded his lecture with a lament that the era of the Wild Apple would soon be past, since commercial orcharding and the temperance movement (its animus against alcohol adversely affecting the production of apple cider, the best of which came from wild apple trees) banished the gnarly boles to only a few remaining wild places. After warning his audience that soon they would be compelled to look for their apples in a barrel, he quoted the Lord's dark and damning words to Joel in the Old Testament (Joel 1:12): "The vine is dried up, and the fig tree languisheth; the pomegranate tree, the palm tree also, and the apple tree, even all the trees of the field, are withered: because joy is withered away from the sons of men." [358]

Thoreau had become so expert at reading tracks that February was as fertile a time of observation for him as July. Indeed, the spareness of the landscape only heightened his powers of observation. Drifting snow and bare patches revealed the wind's direction; naked trees revealed the sky more fully. Remarkably, he seems this February to have seen for the very first time a pair of sun dogs (parhelia, or mock suns), bright spots flanking the low winter sun, along with an upper tangent arc, the small inverted rainbow touching the sun's halo, or nimbus, at its apex. Sun-absorbing oak leaves melted into the surface of pond ice, then blew away, leaving behind impressions of their former presence; meltwater caught in wheel ruts made diagnostic ripple marks in the sand. Thoreau could even distinguish the tracks of moles' flippered feet in the slush at Andromeda Pond. On his way home one night after tracking otter along the banks of the Assabet, seeing someone a dozen rods off—covered but for his hands and face, which he could not see at that distance— Thoreau recognized the man immediately by his walk. "We have a very intimate knowledge of one another; we see through thick and thin; spirit meets spirit." The next day, coming upon a distinctive footprint in the snow, he guessed it was the trapper George Melvin's, because it was accompanied by a hound's track. He experimented with his gait to get it to match the form of the track, and found himself walking just like Melvin, who later confirmed that the track had been his. "It is not merely by taking time and by a conscious effort that [man] betrays himself," Thoreau concluded. "A man is revealed, and a man is concealed, in a myriad unexpected ways." [359]

Since the spring of 1851, Thoreau had, along with his nearly daily journal entries, kept a pair of large notebooks for his natural history reading and reflection. This spring he began to work through these notebooks in an attempt to systematically summarize Concord's annual unfolding of phenomena, month by month. He made lists of the dates for the appearance of wildflowers, the ripening of fruits, the first appearances of birds, the sequences of tree and shrub leafing out, and dozens of categories of observation of mammals, reptiles, fishes, and insects. These lists he then began to assemble into charts that would give a picture of change and stability through time. At the top of the chart he laid out the years, beginning usually with 1851 or 1852, and listed the days of the month down the side. In the ledger boxes he listed whatever phenomenon he was tracking. Traces of this prodigious labor occasionally show up in his journal; for June 12, he calculated that spring peepers and "purring frogs" (*Rana palustris*) ceased to peep; lightning-bugs were first seen; bullfrogs trumped *"generally"*; mosquitoes began to be troublesome; afternoon thundershowers were almost regular; turtles began to lay eggs; and one could sleep with the window open and wear a light coat. But there was a great deal of variation from year to year that made Thoreau's Kalendar difficult to manage. He tried to come up with a date for the most characteristic signs of spring:

> Fair Haven Pond may be open by the 20th of March, as this year, or not till April 13 as in '56, or twenty-three days later.
> Tried by the skunk-cabbage, this may flower March 2 ('60) or April 6 or 8 (as in '55 and '54), or some five weeks later,—say thirty-six days.
> The bluebird may be seen February 24, as in '50, '57, and '60, or not till March 24, as in '56,—say twenty-eight days.
> The yellow-spotted tortoise may be seen February 23, as in '57, or not till March 28, as in '55,—thirty-three days.
> The wood frog may be heard March 15, as this year, or not till April 13, as in '56,—twenty-nine days.
> That is, tried by the last four phenomena, there may be about a month's

fluctuation, so that March may be said to have receded half-way into February or advanced half-way into April, i.e., it borrows half of February or half of April.

All of his observations now seemed focused on a single purpose—to answer the question "how long?" He would not settle for the vague generality of folk wisdom about nature, aiming instead for an almanac's chronological sureness. On March 18, even though he had been watching the skunk cabbage spathes and spadixes swell for sixteen straight days, he came up with the idea that he could use a microscope to examine pollen on the abdomens of returning honeybees and get the exact date of the first skunk cabbage flower or any other flower visited by bees.[360]

On March 25, finding along the railroad tracks a willow shedding pollen in advance of any others, he was determined to find another even "more forward." Looking over his old journals and lists that day, he made a best guess at the emblematic phenomena not of the ides of March, but of the whole month, day by day. March began with the frost coming out of the sun-warmed sandbanks, producing sand foliage, on the same day that chandelier icicles dripped from bridges. On the second, ice suddenly softened, putting an end to skating, and on the third the milkman closed the doors of his icehouse to keep out the milder air. Melted snow filled gutters on the fourth, making for wet and dirty walking, and on the fifth, a "cold mizzling rain" made the last glaze of the year on one's coat. The sixth cleared off cold and windy, and the herd's grass stubble from last summer all leaned southeast, showing the prevailing wind before the snow fell. On the seventh, while each step slumped into moist brown earth, one found the first Indian relics of the season, spit up by the thaw. On the eighth, one woke to find the water in the jug frozen, and when going out, calculated how to put the hills and woods between oneself and the biting wind. A warm southwest wind followed on the ninth, and the first lightning could be seen at dusk on the horizon. Great white cakes of ice floated down the newly opened river channel on the tenth, and on the eleventh, the bluish haze in the air was answered by the call of the first bluebird. Their welcome azure aspect vanished the next morning, as a snowstorm as memorable as the Great Snow of 1760 arrived, only to have melted by midafternoon. On the thirteenth, gusts of wind rippled the surface of the flooded meadows, and on the fourteenth, it snowed again, more successfully this time, killing some of the early songbirds. By the fifteenth—the Roman ides—the ice was all out of the river and meadows, but the thin skin formed during the freeze overnight grated downstream in the morning. Now, as soon as he could get it painted and dried, Henry Thoreau launched his boat for his first voyage of the year, eager to feel the river beneath him again after three and a half months away. On the evening of the seventeenth the first house-shaking wind knocked a neighbor's chimney down, along with all the rotten limbs of the village's trees. The dry scent of withered leaves on warm wooded hillsides marked the eighteenth; on the nineteenth gnats hummed, early birds warbled, and one coat sufficed for going outdoors. Scarlet cranberries dotted the shore wrack on the twentieth. Two days of warm and windy weather followed. A channel was worn through Fair Haven Pond on the twenty-third. On the twenty-fourth, one needed all one's winter coats again as the wind sprayed icicles off the rivers and onto the causeways. The twenty-fifth was colder yet; the twenty-sixth, warm enough to plant peas and rye. April-like rain fell on the twenty-seventh. Some sat without a fire on the afternoon of the twenty-eighth, "pellet" frost or snow was on the ground on the twenty-ninth, smoke from burning brush or accidental fires rose from the horizon on the thirtieth, and on the thirty-first, the dust on the highway foreshadowed the dusty routine of summer settling slowly upon one's mind.[361]

From such a luxurious suite of phenomena, still one invincible sign of the season emerged for Thoreau:

When March arrives, a tolerably calm, clear, sunny, spring-like day, the snow is so far gone that sleighing ends and our compassion is excited by the sight of horses laboriously dragging wheeled vehicles through mud and water and slosh. We shall no longer hear the jingling of sleigh-bells. The sleigh is housed, or, perchance, converted into a wheeled vehicle by the travelling peddler caught far from home. The wood-sled is perhaps abandoned by the roadside, where the snow ended, with two sticks put under its runners,—there to rest, it may be, while the grass springs up green around it, till another winter comes round. . . .

The boy's sled gets put away in the barn or shed or garret, and there lies dormant all summer, like a woodchuck in the winter. It goes into its burrow just before woodchucks come out, so that you may say a woodchuck never sees a sled, nor a sled a woodchuck,—unless it were a prematurely risen woodchuck or a belated and unseasonable sled. Before the woodchuck comes out the sled goes in. They dwell at the antipodes of each other. Before sleds rise woodchucks have set. The ground squirrel too shares the privileges and misfortunes of the woodchuck. The sun now passes from the constellation of the sled into that of the woodchuck. . . .

I often meet with the wood-sled by the path, carefully set up on two sticks and with a chip under the cop [steering pivot point] to prevent its getting set, as if the woodman had waited only for another snow-storm to start it again, little thinking that he had had his allowance for the year. And there it rests, like many a human enterprise postponed, sunk further than he thought into the earth after all, its runners, by which it was to slide along so glibly, rotting and its ironwork rusting. You question if it will ever start again.

If we must stop, says the schemer, leave the enterprise so that we can start again under the best possible circumstances. But a scheme at rest begins at once to rust and rot, though there may be two sticks under the runner and a chip under the cop. The ineradicable grass will bury it, and when you hitch your forces to it a year hence it is a chance if it has not lost its cohesion. Examine such a scheme, and see if it rests on two sticks and can be started again. Examine also its joints, and see if it will cohere when it is started.

You can easily find sticks and chips, but who shall find snow to put under it? There it slumbers, sinking into the ground, willingly returning to the earth from which it came. Mortises and tenons and pins avail not to withhold it.

All things decay,

And so must our sleigh.

The sleighing, the sledding, or sliding, is gone. We now begin to wheel or roll ourselves and commodities along, which requires more tractile power. The ponderous cart and the spruce buggy appear from out their latebrae [the white yolks inside the yellow yolks of birds' eggs, referring to summer vehicles' winter shrouds] like the dusty flies that have wintered in a crevice, and we hear the buzzing of their wheels. The high-set chaise, the lumbering coach like wasps and gnats and bees come humming forth.

"All things decay, / And so must our sleigh"—the last poem that Henry Thoreau wrote, its easy resignation stood in stark contrast to the iron-willed refusal he showed in the face of John Brown's death. One might put up the sleigh for winter, and eventually the sleigh would succumb to time and rust, but who could say with certainty that sleighless sleighing did not continue on other snows?[362]

The Transcendentalist at the Cattle Show

Late spring found Thoreau tracking nearly everything that moved in Concord. With his field glasses, he spied a well-dressed man pacing methodically over a field that had been used the previous September for a military muster. From the way the man poked the straw with a stick, his head prone, Thoreau knew him to be hunting for coins fallen from soldiers' pockets. He followed muskrat tracks "as usual" but was led by them this year to a stunning theory: The muskrat always stayed in the very lowest part of the muddy hollows in river meadows, with such fidelity that after the meadow dried up completely, his dragging belly essentially traced the channel of future brooks and rivers. On May 19, Thoreau's lifetime of chronicling Concord's seasons allowed him to debunk the horologic aspect of a sacred local myth. While poetic memory of the Concord Fight in April 1775 held that "the apple trees were in bloom and the grass was waving in the fields," his own observations showed that this was more likely to occur in mid-May than mid-April.[363]

Tracking animals in their habitats was one thing; getting opportunities to see them up close was another. Thoreau had always been able to get very close to animals by remaining still for long periods and allowing creatures to come to him. These moments were always filled with an exceptional poignancy for Thoreau. Once, as a young man, he had come upon a nest of partridges, and after he laid one back down on the nest, it fell to one side and remained in that position for over ten minutes, an instinctual protective behavior. Haunted by the "innocent yet adult expression" in its eyes, he felt that "away down in that dell of the woods was the whole wide heavens reflected and re-created." Startling a wood frog one September, he stooped and stroked it a little, then slid it onto the middle of his palm and brought it right up to his eye. After clearing out the leaves in an owl's nest, he found a mouse in one corner, and brought his face within seven or eight inches. When the mouse did not retreat, he placed it in his hand, where it curled up in a ball. Wanting to see its tail, he pulled on it, and the mouse ran up over his arm and shoulder, then leaped off, eighteen feet to the ground. On other occasions, he came face-to-face with garter and black snakes, foxes, and turtles. One day he played cat-and-mouse with a woodchuck: "We sat looking at one another about half an hour—till we began to feel mesmeric influences. I talked to him quasi forest lingo—baby-talk—at any rate in a conciliatory tone and thought that I had some influence on him—He gritted his teeth less. I chewed checquer berry leaves & presented them to his nose at last without a grit. . . . I spoke kindly to him—I reached checquer berry leaves to his mouth I stretched my hands over him—though he turned up his head & still gritted a little. I laid my hand on him, but immediately took it off again—instinct not being wholly overcome." [364]

In June, admiring interrupted fern in a meadow, Thoreau noticed what he took to be a large cocoon, but found it was a red bat hanging upside down on the fern stem. He broke off the top of the plant and let the bat lie on the back of his hand. For fifteen minutes he tried to waken it, but all it would do was open its mouth and eyes a bit, then drop back to sleep. He finally wakened the bat by whistling, and it fluttered off into the woods. This spring he repeatedly marveled at animals' accommodation to humans. He watched a pickerel under the railroad bridge over the Assabet; when a locomotive screamed past, it barely stirred. Finding a song sparrow nest in the bank of a drainage ditch, he wondered what the birds did before the English settlers began to dig ditches and build stone walls.[365]

Men, too, still caught his eye. Writing to Blake in his typical fatherly philosophical fashion, Thoreau continued to believe that the proper habitat of the human being was the highest ground of his own character:

> Men & boys are learning all kinds of trades but how to make *men* of themselves. They learn to make houses, but they are not so well housed, they are not so contented in their houses, as the woodchucks in their holes. What is the use of a house if you haven't got a tolerable planet to put it on? . . . Grade the ground first. If a man believes and expects great things of himself, it makes no odds where you put him, or what you show him, . . . he will be surrounded by grandeur. . . .
>
> Whether he sleeps or wakes, whether he runs or walks, whether he uses a microscope or a telescope, or his naked eye, a man never discovers anything, never overtakes anything or leaves anything behind, but himself. Whatever he says or does he merely reports himself. If he is in love, he *loves*; if he is in heaven he *enjoys*; if he is in hell he *suffers*. It is his condition that determines his locality.
>
> The principal, the only thing a man makes is his condition, his fate. . . . He works 24 hours a day at it and gets it done. Whatever else he neglects or botches, no man was ever known to neglect this work. . . .

In Thoreau's estimation, the only "unexplored land" was in "our own untried enterprises," and therefore, "You must make tracks into the Unknown." To Blake he wrote, "Let us sing."[366]

In September, Thoreau was invited to address the Middlesex Agricultural Society at the annual Concord Cattle-Show. "Cattle-Show" had long been shorthand for Thoreau for petty amusements of the mob, and yet he had a local's fondness for the variegated display of men at the annual agricultural fair. In *A Week on the Concord and Merrimack Rivers*, he had painted a warm, unsentimental portrait of the farm folk at the fair, "come to see the sport, and have a hand in what is going,—to know 'what's the row,' if there is any; to be where some men are drunk, some horses race, some cockerels fight; anxious to be shaking props under a table, and above all to see the 'striped pig.'" Thoreau thought these men were the raw material of a fruitful future:

> Though there are many crooked and crabbed specimens of humanity among them, run all to thorn and rind, and crowded out of shape by adverse circumstances, like the third chestnut in the burr, so that you wonder to see some heads wear a whole hat, yet fear not that the race will fail or waver in them; like the crabs which grow in hedges, they furnish the stocks of sweet and thrifty fruits still. Thus is nature recruited from age to age, while the fair and palatable varieties die out, and have their period. This is that mankind.

Thoreau's address began with the same sense of fondness for "those old familiar faces, whose names I do not know, which for me represent the Middlesex country, and come as near being indigenous to the soil as any white man can." Every man was welcome to the Cattle-Show, "even a transcendentalist," Thoreau asserted, but to put his audience on alert to how queer a specimen of humanity they had invited to address them, he gave a little picture of a "weak-minded and whimsical fellow" who showed up each year at the fair with his crooked walking stick, then warned the progressive farmers listening to him that they might find him as odd as this fellow.[367]

Then Thoreau went straight for the jugular, saying that in his capacity as surveyor and naturalist, he had gone across their farms regularly without detection, and yet when occasionally he met them on their properties, they asked him if he were lost, because they had never seen him in that part of the country before. "If the truth were known," he admitted, "and it had not been for betraying my secret, I might with more propriety have inquired if *you* were not lost, since I had never seen *you* before." The particular secret business he had been conducting in the last few years was the study of their woodlots, to answer for himself the question that had been asked by every generation of Concord farmers since the Puritans moved inland from the coast: Why, after any dense pine wood was cut down, did oaks and other hardwood species immediately take its place? The first step toward the answer had come to Thoreau on September 24, 1857, when he was paddling down the Assabet and noticed a red squirrel running along the bank with something in its mouth, which it buried near the foot of a hemlock tree. He paddled over to see what it was, and the squirrel watched anxiously, making a couple of abortive attempts to go dig it up. When Thoreau dug the spot, he found two green pignuts with the thick husks still on, buried about an inch and a half below the hemlock duff. Laying up a store of winter food, the squirrel was also planting a hickory wood "for all creation." Examining a number of pine woods, which when observed from outside appeared to contain not a single hardwood tree, Thoreau found they all had little oaks spaced about five feet apart growing up from their floors.[368]

Before Thoreau made his observations, the prevailing theory of forest creation among his audience was spontaneous generation. Thoreau showed these proprietors out of *that* woodlot:

Though I do not believe that a plant will spring up where no seed has been, I have great faith in a seed,—a, to me, equally mysterious origin for it. Convince me that you have a seed there, and I am prepared to expect wonders. I shall even believe that the millennium is at hand, and that the reign of justice is about to commence, when the Patent Office, or Government, begins to distribute, and the people to plant, the seeds of these things.

No doubt aware of the appearance of some sleight-of-hand behind his theory of forest succession, Thoreau playfully concluded his remarks with a series of magical allusions. He told of growing five yellow squashes weighing together 310 pounds, having for his *"abracadabra presto-change"* only performed "a little mysterious hoeing and manuring." He mused about the "perfect alchemists" who could transmute substances so, and ended in a prestidigital flurry calculated to summon his hearers away from theatrical illusion to transcendental truth:

> Here you can dig, not gold, but the value which gold merely represents; and there is no Signor Blitz [a famous magician and ventriloquist] about it. Yet farmers' sons will stare by the hour to see a juggler draw ribbons from his throat, though he tells them it is all deception. Surely men love darkness rather than light.

Two weeks later, poking about the artificial pond at Sleepy Hollow, for which he had surveyed in 1855, he found small patches of water lilies established in the otherwise vegetationless water. The lily-full river was nearly a half mile distant, presenting a new seed mystery, which was answered for him by the presence of a few pouts and pickerel in the pond—they had transported the seed to the new environment. "Thus in the midst of death we are in life," he declared.[369]

In previous Octobers, Thoreau could not take his eye off the spectacle of autumn foliage; this October he looked *inside* the tree for new revelations. Surprised to find many white oak acorns still clinging to their branches, he cut them open and found them all decayed or decaying, and wondered "what great purpose is served by this seeming waste." No Malthusian solution offered itself as it had to Charles Darwin, thinking about predation. Under the leaf litter of oak forests, he found squirrel-planted chestnuts sending forth tender sprouts, and decried the rampant shooting of squirrels. In newly settled lands out west he knew that settlers conducted squirrel hunts in which thousands were killed in a few hours. New England's chestnut forests had in the last decade been decimated for railroad sleepers, and Thoreau noted that squirrels go "a-chestnutting perhaps as far as the boys do" and imagined that by letting them alone, the chestnut woods might be recovered within a century. He continued to consider his discoveries in light of Darwin's theory:

> We find ourselves in a world that is already planted, but is also still being planted as at first. . . . Unless you can show me the pool where the lily was created, I shall believe that the oldest fossil lilies which the geologist has detected (if this is found fossil) originated in that locality in a similar manner to these of Beck Stow's. We see thus how the fossil lilies which the geologist has detected are dispersed, as well as these which we carry in our hands to church.
>
> The development theory implies a greater vital force in nature, because it is more flexible and accommodating, and equivalent to a sort of constant *new* creation.[370]

His other window into forest history this fall was the counting of tree rings. He came upon a white pine stump with 130 rings, and reasoned that this was one of the town's second-growth trees, the last remnants of which had been cut off within living memory. Counting rings of oaks and pines in Rice's woodlot, he determined four distinct periods of growth. Knocking moss off the tops of pitch pine stumps in Farrar's lot east of the Deep Cut, he found them to be about seventy-five years old. In Ebby Hubbard's wood, he found from stumps that both oak and pine were a century old. He worked out a new calculus for aging pines where there were no stumps to examine: Cut off the lowest branch still growing, count its rings, estimate or count the rings of another pine growing in a nearby opening that reaches to the height of that branch, and then add the two sums together.[371]

Roots held hidden histories as well. He went out to count rings on the oaks and pines on Emerson's Walden Pond lot and discovered an oak seedling only an eighth of an inch thick and ten inches high that emerged from an inch-thick root he figured to be some sixteen years old. In just the last week of October alone, his journal was filled with a dozen other minute revelations of Concord's forest history, afforded as much by Thoreau's own store of personal memory of the tree-planting and logging activity of neighbors as by his present observations. "I have an advantage over the geologist," he boasted, "for I can not only detect the order of events but the time during which they elapsed, by counting the rings on the stumps. Thus you can unroll the rotten papyrus on which the history of the Concord forest is written." All of this systematic, analytic investigation only served to heighten Thoreau's fidelity to a holistic, transcendentalist method of observation and reportage:

> All science is only a makeshift, a means to an end which is never attained. After all, the truest description, and that by which another living man can most readily recognize a flower, is the unmeasured and eloquent one which the sight of it inspires. No scientific description will supply the want of this, though you should count and measure and analyze every atom that seems to compose it.
>
> Surely poetry and eloquence are a more universal language than that Latin which is confessedly dead. In science, I should say, all description is postponed till we know the whole, but then science itself will be cast aside. But unconsidered expressions of our delight which any natural object draws from us are something complete and final in themselves, since all nature is to be regarded as it concerns man; and who knows how near to absolute truth such unconscious affirmations may come? Which are the truest, the sublime conceptions of Hebrew

poets and *seers*, or the guarded statements of modern geologists, which we must modify or unlearn so fast?

The true gold in the American landscape had been discovered and amalgamated by the earliest naturalists, just as those who had been present at Sutter's Mill and then observed the sudden fall in the value of the gold had described things most truly. Most Americans approached nature like a cattle show, willing to be dazzled by its sparkling treasures and odd sports but unwilling to go behind the stages and tents to uncover the foundations of what they saw. The woodcraft of the cunningest hunter was still all sympathy: "In the true natural order the order or system is not insisted on. Each is first, and each last. That which presents itself to us this moment occupies the whole of the present and rests on the very topmost point of the sphere, under the zenith. The species and individuals of all the natural kingdoms ask our attention and admiration in a round robin." From out of the treasury of memory contained within himself and the landscape, Thoreau with more regularity than ever brought forth the new.[372]

Minott's Clock

On the penultimate day of February 1861—a pleasant, warm day, with the ground half bare—Thoreau was walking the Boston Road out from Concord Common and heard the twitter of a bluebird. He stopped to listen for it again but couldn't tell whether it was singing from high up in a buttonwood along the road or from the lower trees on the hill flanking the Boston Road on the north. Hearing it again, it seemed to come from the open window of Pratt's house, and he wondered if perhaps it was merely a caged bird. Then he thought he saw it at the top of a huge elm on the common. He saw a man shingling Brooks Clark's barn and walked over to ask him if he had heard a bluebird singing that day. Yes, he had. As he climbed the hill to George Minott's little gray hip-roofed cottage across from Emerson's, he heard distinctly the full warble of a bluebird. Its notes were bittersweet to Thoreau's ears, for within the past fortnight, two of Minott's sisters—one of whom, Mary, lived with him—and an elderly friend, Miss Potter, had died, all of "lung fever," i.e., tuberculosis. After George and Mary's sister passed on the thirteenth, Mary Minott couldn't attend the funeral, for she had caught cold in visiting her. Before Mary died, she had willed her property back to her brother George, but he had also been sick and expected to die any day and so had made out his will to leave everything to her. When Thoreau entered the open door at Minott's, he found his old friend so far away in his own thoughts that he had not heard the bluebird singing.[373]

Thoreau had over the past five years often marked the time at Minott's, where he usually found his friend sitting by the stove in the corner behind the door, his cat by his side or in his lap. His failing health had confined him to the house since 1857, and his greatest recreation was to tell stories; Thoreau had heard some of these stories five or six times before. Minott was slowly excarnating, and as he did so, the memories stored deep and long forgotten in his subtle body rose to the surface and asked to be told. Minott told Thoreau of how he used to hear wildcats yell in the Fair Haven woods and of the huge flocks of passenger pigeons that used to descend each year. He said that in his youth he and all his fellow farmers had much more energy than the farmers of today, for they made liberal use of strong drink; this was why all the alders, birches, and willows were now springing up in the river meadow, as today's men, lacking the old cider-stimulated vigor, were too weak to cut them down with their scythes. Minott told Thoreau he had been born in the house where Casey, a Guinea Negro, had formerly lived and that Casey had been a slave to a man named Whitney, who lived in the house that Nathaniel Hawthorne then owned, until one Sunday sometime before the Revolution Casey had run off across the Great Meadows, was pursued by the neighbors, but hid himself in the river up to his neck until nightfall. Minott said that Casey had then run through Gowing's

Swamp and got something to eat from Mrs. Cogswell, then cleared far away, enlisted in the Continental Army, and was freed after the war. Whitney's son had thrown snowballs at Casey the day before, while he was chopping wood, and Casey had thrown his axe at the boy. Whitney called Casey an "ugly nigger" and threatened to have him put in jail, and that is when he had run away. Minott recalled that Casey had been just twenty years old when he was stolen from his wife and child in Guinea, and that he used to say that each night when he went to sleep, he went home to Africa but returned each morning.[374]

Minott said his house—to whose dooryard from decades of visits Thoreau knew spring came earlier, and from which summer left later, than any other—had been moved sixty years before to this sunny site and that it had been built by Captain Isaac Hoar. Still a boy when the house was being framed, Minott used to climb up on the post-and-beam frame and, with a teaspoon, take the eggs of the house wren out of its nest in the mortise holes. Minott's grandfather had moved the house to where it now stood and died in it in 1805 at age eighty-eight. Minott told Thoreau that his grandfather had died exactly where Thoreau sat, at such and such paces from the clock. The clock had belonged to old John Beatton, who died before Minott was born. Thoreau had found Beatton's tombstone; he had died in 1776 at age seventy-four. Despite all of his ranging through the centuries in his study of tree rings, Native American myth, and reading of history, Thoreau was particularly moved by the time travel he did whenever he visited Minott: "To sit under the face of an old clock that has been ticking one hundred and fifty years,—there is something mortal, not to say immortal, about it! A clock that began to tick when Massachusetts was a province. Meanwhile John Beatton's heavy tombstone is cracked quite across and widely opened."[375]

Only a few days after Thoreau's visit, Minott died. He learned from Minott's niece that Minott had called out to her on his last day, asking her if she didn't feel lonely. "Yes, I do," she said, and he answered, "So do I," saying he felt like an old shattered and decaying oak. Thoreau told this in a letter he began to Daniel Ricketson on March 19; when he went back to the letter a few days later, he substituted for this story an account of his own illness. Back in November, Bronson Alcott—suffering at the time from a bad cold—had stopped to talk to Thoreau about the upcoming commemoration of the anniversary of John Brown's death. While out counting tree rings on December 3, Thoreau came down with "influenza," and after it deepened into bronchitis, he had spent most of the winter housebound. He made only ten journal entries in February, nine in March. His spirits had not flagged at all; at the end of March he wrote to his cousin George Thatcher:

> I may say that I have been unexpectedly well, considering how confined and sedentary my life has been. I have had a good time in the house, and it is really as if nothing had happened; or only I have lost the phenomena of winter. I have been quite as busy as usual, reading and writing, and I trust that, as the warm weather advances, & I get out of doors more & more, my cough will gradually cease....

He did get out in April, measuring the height of the river and hearing his first hylas (tree frogs, or peepers) of spring, but on both April 12, the day that Fort Sumter was attacked, and April 19—the eighty-sixth anniversary of the Concord Fight—when forty-five volunteers left Concord to go to war, Thoreau's journal was left blank. It was all but blank the first ten days of May as well, and then on May 12, in block letters, he made the entry "SET OUT FOR MINNESOTA, *via* WORCESTER."[376]

The supposed therapeutic value of Minnesota's dry climate was being widely touted at the moment, and Thoreau also had recently read about the 1850s exploring expedition to the Canadian plains north and west of Minnesota, so he had decided to go there instead of the West Indies, which his doctor had recommended. He asked Channing and then Blake to go with him, but Channing couldn't make up his mind and Blake couldn't go, so finally he was accompanied by Horace Mann Jr., seventeen-year-old son of the recently deceased educator. Young Mann, an amateur naturalist, had within the last month brought to

Thoreau the contents of a crow's stomach, a screech owl, a hermit thrush, a bufflehead, and a pigeon hawk, so Thoreau felt he would be an able companion for the journey to the Western frontier. Emerson wrote out a list of acquaintances along the route that Thoreau was to travel, telling him, "If you come into the neighborhood of any of them, I pray you hand this note to them, by way of introduction, praying them, from me, not to let you pass by, without salutation, and any aid and comfort they can administer to an invalid traveler, one so dear and valued by me and all good Americans." [377]

On June 25, from Redwing, Minnesota, he wrote to Frank Sanborn in Concord. He described a steamer excursion he and Mann had made from Saint Paul up the Minnesota River to the Lower Sioux Agency, where the annual government payment was to be made to the Indians. Telling Sanborn of the "remarkably winding stream," he got caught up in one of his comic extravaganzas:

> It was a very novel kind of navigation to me. . . . In making a short turn, we repeatedly and designedly ran square into the steep and soft bank, taking in a cart-load of earth, this being more effectual than the rudder to fetch us about again; or the deeper water was so narrow and close to the shore, that we were obliged to run into & break down at least 50 trees which overhung the water, when we did not cut them off, repeatedly losing a part of our outworks, though the most exposed had been taken in. I could pluck almost any plant on the bank from the boat. We very frequently got aground and then drew ourselves along with a windlass & cable fastened to a tree, or we swung round in the current, and completely blocked up & blockaded the river, one end of the boat resting on each shore. . . . It was one consolation to know that in such a case we were all the while damming the river & so raising it.

At Redwood—"a mere locality, scarcely an Indian village"—they observed the council meeting, conducted through interpreters. Thoreau thought the Indians "as usual," had "the advantage in point of truth and earnestness, and therefore, of eloquence. . . . They were quite dissatisfied with the white man's treatment of them & probably have reason to be so." The entire substance of his ethnographic report was: "In the afternoon the half naked Indians performed a dance, at the request of the Governor, for our amusement & their own benefit & then we took leave of them." While at Redwing, Horace Mann wrote to his mother that "Mr. Thoreau is getting along pretty well," and told how they had been out gathering wild strawberries, and took a swim in the river.[378]

Back home in Concord in August, responding to an invitation from Ricketson to come visit him in New Bedford, Thoreau said that he had been sick so long that he had almost forgotten what it was to be well, "and yet I feel that it all respects only my envelope." A week later, he was at Emerson's for dinner, to celebrate Edward's departure for Harvard. Seeing that the boy was sad about going away, Thoreau took him aside after dinner and assured him that while in Cambridge he would never be far from home. In October Thoreau's neighbor lent him his horses and wagon, and he took a ride every other day; "I think that, on the whole, my health is better than when you were here," he wrote to Ricketson. On November 3, he played with his beloved cat Min's four three-week-old kittens. He thought their disproportionately large feet and head and legs made them look like lions, and he was astounded that despite the fact that they could barely walk, they scratched their ear with their hind leg "as effectually as an old cat does. . . . You may say that, when a kitten's ear first itches, Providence comes to the rescue and lifts its hind leg for it." His journal entry for the day reflected on Min's search for a "dark and secret place" to give birth, how the kittens could mew from the first and spit at a fortnight, and how they instinctively sought out their mother's teat. He then turned to describing the storm of the previous evening and the long striations that the winds had left in the gravel along the railroad causeway. He gave the exact dimensions of the minute tracks: From behind each pebble projected a ridge an eighth of an inch high and an inch long. The very last line in this his very last journal entry reads: "All this is perfectly distinct to an observant eye, and yet could easily pass unnoticed by most. Thus each wind is self-registering." With his last steps in life, Thoreau surely was leaving tracks that could be made by no other man.[379]

On the first day of 1862, Bronson Alcott took apples and cider to Thoreau and spent the evening with him. Finding him "failing and feeble," still Thoreau was talkative, "interested in books and men," and he talked with special delight about the Roman natural historian Pliny. In mid-January Emerson wrote in his journal, "As we live longer, it looks as if our company were picked out to die first, and we live on in a lessening minority." He made a list of local people who had died, concluding, "I am ever threatened by the decay of Henry Thoreau." In February, Alek Therien came to visit Thoreau, who saw at once that his woodsman friend had been drinking, scolded him, and told him to go home and cut his throat. When word came back to Thoreau that Therien, who didn't know what to make of Thoreau's words, was repeating them about town, Thoreau said he was glad to hear it and hoped that Therien now understood what he had meant. On the first day of spring, Sophia wrote out a letter for Henry in reply to a correspondent who had written to praise *A Week*. Thoreau said he was glad that the man liked the bits of poetry throughout the book, since they had been "least attractive" to most readers, and in reply to the man's inquiry after his health, he said, "I *suppose* that I have not many months to live; but of course, I know nothing about it. I may add that I am enjoying existence as much as ever, and regret nothing." A few days later, Thoreau's old jailer, Sam Staples, looked in on him and told Emerson that he never spent an hour with more satisfaction, never saw a man dying "with so much pleasure and peace." Staples thought that very few men in Concord really knew Thoreau. When Emerson visited his dying friend at the end of March, Thoreau spoke admiringly of the manners of "an old-established, well-behaved river," as preferable to those of a new river, which was "a torrent." "What happens in any part of the old river relates to what befalls it in every other part of it," declared the self-registering Thoreau.[380]

On May 5, Thoreau asked his friend Edmund Hosmer to spend the night with him. Hosmer had helped Thoreau raise the roof on his Walden Pond cabin and had often walked with Thoreau, who wondered why, given Hosmer's intelligence, he had never been invited to lecture at the Concord Lyceum. Hosmer whittled his own axe helves out of white oak and could manage oxen as well as any Concord farmer, and Thoreau had always admired his resourcefulness but couldn't understand why Hosmer despaired of any higher meaning to his life. In appreciation for Hosmer's kindness in coming to sit with him, Thoreau asked Sophia to give him his memorial copy of *A Week*, which had a lock of his brother John's hair taped inside it.[381]

The next morning, Sophia read to her brother the "Thursday" section of *A Week* and, anticipating the "Friday" section's description of the exhilarating return voyage home, he murmured, "Now comes good sailing." At nine o'clock on the morning of May 6, Henry Thoreau set sail.

One World at a Time

On May 9, Bronson Alcott and his daughters Anna and Louisa May, Nathaniel Hawthorne and his family, Harrison Blake, Ellery Channing, and a host of other friends of Henry Thoreau gathered at the Unitarian church to hear Ralph Waldo Emerson's eulogy. Concord schools were dismissed early for the afternoon funeral service. Emerson began by pointing out that Thoreau was the last male descendant of a French immigrant from the Isle of Guernsey, and that his character derived from the combination of this French Huguenot blood with "a very strong Saxon genius." In portraying this most affirmative of men, Emerson elaborated Thoreau's many "renunciations":

> He was bred to no profession, he never married; he lived alone; he never went to church; he never voted; he refused to pay a tax to the

State; he ate no flesh, he drank no wine, he never knew the use of to-
bacco; and, though a naturalist, he used neither trap nor gun.... He
had no temptations to fight against—no appetites, no passions, no
taste for elegant trifles.... He chose to be rich by making his wants few,
and supplying them himself.

Emerson knew perhaps better than anyone that "there was somewhat
military in his nature, not to be subdued, always manly and able, but
rarely tender, as if he did not feel himself except in opposition." But Emerson realized that Thoreau's contrariness stemmed from his impatience with the limitations of vernacular thought.[382]

Sympathy—that favorite of Thoreau's words—characterized the
stoic hermit Thoreau, and Emerson reminded the mourners of his
friend's love for children. His love of truth led Thoreau to use "an
original judgment on each emergency"—as examples Emerson gave
Thoreau's Walden Pond experiment, the night in jail, and his argument
with the president of Harvard about the rule prohibiting anyone outside
a ten-mile radius from borrowing books. "No truer American existed
than Thoreau," Emerson proclaimed, believing that his friend's fidelity
to the individual freedoms expressed in America motivated his
opposition to most reformers, who often demanded unthinking conformity.[383]

Emerson also paid tribute to the physical Thoreau:

Mr. Thoreau was equipped with a most adapted and serviceable body.
He was of short stature, firmly built, of light complexion, with strong,
serious blue eyes, and a grave aspect—his face covered in the late years
with a becoming beard. His senses were acute, his frame well-knit and
hardy, his hands strong and skillful in the use of tools. And there was a
wonderful fitness of body and mind. He could pace sixteen rods more
accurately than another man could measure them with rod and chain.
He could find his path in the woods at night, he said, better by his feet

than by his eyes. He could estimate the measure of a tree very well by his eye; he could estimate the weight of a calf or pig, like a dealer. From a box containing a bushel or more of loose pencils, he could take up with his hands fast enough just a dozen pencils at every grasp. He was a good swimmer, runner, skater, boatman, and would probably outwalk most countrymen in a day's journey.

This healthy body was married to "a strong common sense," and yet Emerson admitted that these alone could not account for the "superiority" that shone out of Thoreau's simple life. He quoted Thoreau as saying one day that "the other world is all my art; my pencils will draw no other; my jack-knife will cut nothing else; I do not use it as a means." Emerson agreed that this was "the muse and genius that ruled his opinions, conversations, studies, work and the course of his life." [384]

In speaking of Thoreau's fierce love for his native place, Emerson pointed to the recently completed survey of Concord's rivers, and described Thoreau's knowledge with a sentence of Thoreauvian exuberance:

Every fact which occurs in the bed, on the banks or in the air or over it; the fishes, and their spawning and nests, their manners, their food, the shad-flies which fill the air on a certain evening once a year, and which are snapped at by the fishes so ravenously that many of these die of repletion; the conical heaps of small stones on the river-shallows, the huge nests of small fishes, one of which will sometimes overfill a cart; the birds which frequent the stream, heron, duck, sheldrake, loon, osprey; the snake, muskrat, otter, woodchuck and fox, on the banks; the turtle, frog, hyla, and cricket, which make the banks vocal—were all known to him, and as it were, townsmen and fellow creatures; so that he felt an absurdity or violence in any narrative of one of these by itself apart, and still more of its dimensions on an inch-rule, or in the exhibition of its skeleton, or the specimen of a squirrel or bird in brandy.

Emerson honored Thoreau's powers of observation, his patience, his intimacy with animals, and the respect paid him by his townsmen, "who did at first know him only as an oddity."[385]

Emerson—one of America's most public of men—appreciated Thoreau's "reserves," his "unwillingness to exhibit to profane eyes what was still sacred in his own, and knew well how to throw a poetic veil over his experience." Though only mildly praising of Thoreau's poetry, he stated unequivocally that "his biography is in his verses." Toward the end of the eulogy, Emerson took up his old argument with Thoreau: "With his energy and practical ability he seemed born for great enterprise and for command; and I so much regret the loss of his rare powers of action, that I cannot help counting it a fault in him that he had no ambition. Wanting this, instead of engineering for all America, he was the captain of a huckleberry-party." Still, he closed with the most tender tribute, speaking of the Swiss plant congeneric with the familiar life everlasting— edelweiss, meaning "noble white," a symbol of purity in the Alps. This plant, Emerson believed, of all the species Thoreau collected, was the one that he lived to gather and that "belonged to him of right":

> The scale on which his studies proceeded was so large as to require longevity, and we were the less prepared for his sudden disappearance. The country knows not yet, or in the least part, how great a son it has lost. It seems an injury that he should leave in the midst his broken task which none else can finish, a kind of indignity to so noble a soul that he should depart out of Nature before yet he has been really shown to his peers for what he is. But he, at least, is content. His soul was made for the noblest society; he had in a short life exhausted the capabilities of this world; wherever there is knowledge, wherever there is virtue, wherever there is beauty, he will find a home.[386]

At the end of the service, the bell that Thoreau had so loved to hear peal through Concord's days and nights rang out forty-four times to mark his years on the planet. A few weeks later, Emerson rowed on

Walden Pond, and there before his mind's eye was Thoreau—"erect, calm, self-subsistent." "How near to the old monks in their ascetic religion!" he exclaimed in his journal. "Perhaps he fell—all of us do—into his way of living, without forecasting it much, but approved and confirmed it with later wisdom." Henry Thoreau's life hardly felt like one he "fell into"; it seemed instead like one of Fortunatus's magical tricks, such as that recalled by Emerson in his eulogy when he told the story of Thoreau's fall in Tuckerman's Ravine and simultaneous discovery of the *Arnica mollis*.[387]

That unmistakable mark of destiny was inscribed into Thoreau's first posthumously published piece of writing. Emerson's eulogy appeared in the August issue of the *Atlantic Monthly*; in June, the magazine had printed Thoreau's "Walking," a lecture he had given often throughout the 1850s, which he revised for publication the month before his death. When he had been preparing to speak to the Concord audience in April 1851, his thoughts had all been upon Thomas Sims's extradition from Massachusetts under the Fugitive Slave Law and the failed possibilities of the American republic. He began by quoting Wordsworth, who, while walking in Scotland one evening, was asked by a woman he passed, "What, you are stepping westward?" Struck by the originality of the query and the beauty of the place, Wordsworth had replied, "Stepping westward seemed to be a kind of heavenly destiny." These prefatory remarks were removed, but the essay was still from the outset clearly an exhortation. The inattentive listener or reader might have mistaken Thoreau's message as a patriotic ode to manifest destiny, but the alert audience member would have recognized that Thoreau was pointing to a higher calling. After beginning by saying, "I wish to speak a word for Nature, for absolute freedom and wildness," and then explicitly *not* apologizing for the "extreme statement" he was about to make, Thoreau cut capers with the word *saunterer*, playfully deriving its etymology from medieval children pointing at passing pilgrims and saying, "There goes a *Saint-Terrer*, a Saunterer, a Holy-Lander." Then he backed off, offering an alternative derivation, from *sans terre*, "without land or home," professing his own secret to the art of sauntering. The walk of life could be meaningful only if the Chevalier dismounted to become a "Walker Errant," a "fourth estate, outside of Church and State and People." One did so "only by the grace of God," for "it requires a direct dispensation from Heaven to become a walker." If it was not clear enough what sovereign territory he was speaking of, he even dismissed the pretension of his townsmen to transcendental walking by suggesting they were "elevated for a moment as by a previous existence." [388]

He quoted John Quincy Adams quoting George Berkeley—"Westward the course [Adams and Thoreau substituted *star*] of empire takes its way"—and he repeated colonial explorers' exaggerated accounts of the New World's majesty, but he also said, "You may name it America, but it is not America." Neither Americus Vespucius nor Columbus nor any other discovered it, but Thoreau had, along the Old Marlborough Road, the Concord vernacular for the spiritual path. All of Thoreau's talk about stepping southwestward toward freedom had nothing to do with Texas or New Mexico or California but everything to do with the sort of manifest destiny sought by Chaucer's Canterbury pilgrims. When he boasted that "the West is preparing to add its fables to those of the East," he was not singing a song about the American Empire but about the Empyrean road ever traveled by him toward a Holy Land fast disappearing from the view of his compatriots. Within a generation, Americans would read Thoreau's words as a visionary call for wilderness preservation, but the swamps he would have them enter "as a sacred place" were the mucky wetlands of their own minds. He speaks of an *Andromeda* swamp particularly because he wished to point toward the stars, not earth. Thoreau's prophetic confidence—"So we saunter toward the Holy Land, till one day the sun shall shine more brightly than ever he has done, shall perchance shine into our minds and hearts, and light up our whole lives with a great awakening light, as warm and serene and golden as on a bankside in autumn"—is a cosmic, eternal one but hooked to no particular star, not even the seemingly shining one called America.[389]

A few days before Thoreau's death, abolitionist Parker Pillsbury asked Thoreau how "the opposite shore" appeared to him. Thoreau had replied, "One world at a time." His answer clearly embraced the other world even as it appeared to hold to this one. About the same time that Thoreau wrote "Walking," he composed a poem, "Music," whose last stanza reads:

> Perchance the God who is proprietor
> Will pity take on his poor tenant here
> And countenance his efforts to improve
> His property and make it worthy to revert,
>   At some late day Unto himself again.

Throughout his life, Thoreau was certain that his "property"—his soul—was immortal, destined to go to God again when he died. But Thoreau hinted from time to time that he also believed that the soul was able to take up a new body and return to Earth. A couple of months after delivering the "Walking" lecture, looking into the eyes of a caged grizzly in a menagerie that was visiting Concord, Thoreau said that "it is unavoidable, the idea of transmigration; not merely a fancy of the poets, but an instinct of the race." In 1853, emphasizing in a letter to Blake his firm belief in the unchanging aspect of the eternal, he says, "As it respects these things, I have not changed an opinion one iota from the first. As the stars looked to me when I was a shepherd in Assyria, they look to me now, a New Englander." In a similar spirit, he wrote in another letter, "I lived in Judea eighteen hundred years ago, but I never knew that there was such a one as Christ among my contemporaries." From his reading of Hindu sacred literature, he was well acquainted with Eastern notions of reincarnation. In 1849, while writing out a translation of "The Transmigration of the Seven Brahmans," Thoreau remarked, "Why should we be related as mortals merely—as limited to one state of existence—Our lives are immortal our transmigrations infinite—the virtue that we are lives ever." [390]

In his journal, directly following this remark, Thoreau wrote, "I would meet my friend not in the light or shadow of our human life alone—but as *daimons*." Speaking obviously of Emerson, he said that his knowledge and intercourse of his friend "is not to be limited to a few of Nature's revolutions," but

> no! no! we are Great fellows—we shall be a long time together.... Ours is a tragedy of more than five acts—this is not the fifth act in our tragedy no, no! blow high, blow low, I will come upon my feet—& holding my friend by the hand. The undertaker will have a dusty time that undertakes to bury me—I go with the party of the gods.... A friendship which will survive despair & the grave thereafter ...

It was fitting that the champion of individualism should most emphatically insist on repeated earth lives when he came to contemplate his relation to others, especially those to whom he felt eternally bound, like Emerson. [391]

In March 1856, Thoreau wrote in his journal:

> I am sometimes affected by the consideration that a man may spend the whole of his life after boyhood in accomplishing a particular design; as if he were put to a special and petty use, without taking time to look around him and appreciate the phenomenon of his existence. If so many purposes are thus necessarily left unaccomplished, perhaps unthought of, we are reminded of the transient interest we have in *this life*. Our interest in our country, in the spread of liberty, etc., strong and, as it were, innate as it is, cannot be as transient as our present existence here. It cannot be that all those patriots who die in the midst of their career have no further connection with the career of their country.

Henry Thoreau and Ralph Waldo Emerson were surely American patriots, and patriots of the wider world, as were their fellow transcendentalists, who endeavored to keep a path open for individual spiritual freedom within a national culture that was becoming increasingly materialistic and, for all its progress in developing political freedom, frequently a nemesis of the unfettered individual creative self.[392]

If America has a particular destiny, that destiny has been and will always be inextricably linked to the actions of individual men and women. Contemporary historical explanation, which, like modern ecological science, favors contingency over certainty, allows little room for the expectancy of "destined" events. Rarely does one hear the word *destiny* these days, whether in academic circles or in popular parlance. One is more likely in America to speak of karma, though mostly in a flippant, dismissive manner that again collapses cosmic fatedness into facile accident. When Emerson wrote about Fate or Necessity and Thoreau spoke of the stars, they were not surrendering to determinism, but fighting their way toward a view of the future that let freedom ring within the admitted constraints of certain undeniable natural laws. Surrounded by a millennialist culture that saw doomsday or divine deliverance around the corner, they didn't build Fourierist enclaves or God machines or go up on their roofs to await the Rapture. They championed the sovereignty of the individual, while fully expecting the individual's progressive divinization. They believed in America as a yet-to-be-fulfilled promise to all humanity, not just an entitled few. From our twenty-first-century perspective, the dappled dreams of American destiny that in Thoreau's day gripped many of its citizens— the territorial imperialists, both slaveholding and abolitionist, the Mormon missionaries, the Freemasonic brotherhoods, the transcendentalists seeking heaven above, and the Mammon worshippers seeking heaven on earth—appear provincial rather than providential. We see all the failed aspirations and doubt that there could ever be a truly transcendental, universal vision of the possibilities for such a complex geographical, social, and political entity as the United States of America.

As a young man, Henry Thoreau dreamed chivalric dreams, inspired by his reading in chapbooks, poetry, and myth. Though in adulthood he dismounted, adopting the manner of the foot soldier, he continued to dream chivalric dreams for both himself and his country. Without ever identifying the high tableland of his dreams along any doctrinal lines, Thoreau aspired to a personal and national mythology of grand proportions. If he couldn't see to which chivalric stream he belonged, which pennant he walked under, perhaps we can, and in so doing, recover the sort of enlarged view of life that was his particular talent. Henry Thoreau, the indefatigable measurer of trees and truth, would ask that our measurement of his life hew to the facts, but that we then read those facts with an enlarged sense of meaning.

Before Henry Thoreau took his string and plumb bob out onto the Walden Pond ice, his townsmen almost to a person spoke of the pond as bottomless. With simple instruments, working from facts to law, Thoreau put his foot through illusion and hearsay to touch bottom. Let us do the same. Let us take facts—which admittedly have grown exceedingly hazy to us earthbound denizens—and strive toward law. There are great cosmic rhythms, perennial, eternal rhythms undulating around and through us, which we hear not. "How long?" this great American spirit asked. Why not now?

Notes

PRINCIPAL SOURCES: ABBREVIATIONS

A Week: A Week on the Concord and Merrimack Rivers, Carl F. Hovde, William L. Howarth, and Elizabeth Hall Witherell, eds. (Princeton, NJ: Princeton University Press, 1980)

Cape Cod: The Writings of Henry David Thoreau: Cape Cod, Joseph J. Moldenhauer, ed. (Princeton, NJ: Princeton University Press, 1984)

Correspondence: Correspondence of Henry David Thoreau, Walter Harding and Carl Bode, eds. (New York: University Press, 1958)

EJMN: William H. Gilman et al., eds. *The Journals and Miscellaneous Notebooks of Ralph Waldo Emerson,* 16 vols. (Cambridge, MA: Harvard University Press, 1960–1983)

Journal: Journal, Bradford Torrey, ed., 14 vols. (Boston: Houghton Mifflin, 1906)

P Journal: The Writings of Henry David Thoreau: Journal, John C. Broderick, Robert Sattelmeyer, Sandra Harbert Petrulionis, eds., 8 vols. (Princeton, NJ: Princeton University Press, 1981–2002)

Maine Woods: The Writings of Henry David Thoreau: The Maine Woods, Joseph J. Moldenhauer, ed. (Princeton, NJ: Princeton University Press, 1972)

Walden: Walden, J. Lyndon Shanley, ed. (Princeton, NJ: Princeton University Press, 1971)

CHAPTER 1: DECLARATIONS OF INDEPENDENCE

1. *Journal* 9:379–81.
2. *Journal* 8:93 (Jan. 7, 1856).
3. Henry David Thoreau, *Wild Fruits: Thoreau's Rediscovered Last Manuscript,* Bradley Dean, ed. (New York: Norton, 2005), 55, 57, 152.
4. Edward Emerson, *Henry Thoreau as Remembered by a Young Friend,* 14–15.
5. *Journal,* July 8, 1852; July 28, 1854.

6. "The Seasons," in Joseph J. Moldenhauer, ed., *Henry D. Thoreau: Early Essays and Miscellanies* (Princeton, NJ: Princeton University Press, 1975).

7. Kenneth Walter Cameron, "Thoreau's Three Months Out of Harvard and His First Publication," *Emerson Society Quarterly* 5 (1956): 9.

8. Walter Harding, *The Days of Henry Thoreau* (Princeton, NJ: Princeton University Press, 1982), 16–17.

9. Hubert H. Hoeltje, "Thoreau and the Concord Academy," *New England Quarterly* 31 (1948): 105–6; Cameron, *ESQ* 9 (1957): 1–21; 3, 4.

10. George W. Cooke, "The Two Thoreaus," *Independent* 58 (1896): 1671; John Weiss, "Thoreau," *Christian Examiner* 74 (1865): 98; *Early Essays*, 14–15.

11. Cameron, "Young Henry Thoreau in the Annals of the Concord Academy," *Emerson Society Quarterly* 10 (1957): 6–8.

12. On the culture of luck in antebellum America, see Jackson Lears, *Something for Nothing: Luck in America* (New York: Viking, 2003).

13. Ralph Waldo Emerson, "Ezra Ripley, D.D.," in Brooks Atkinson, ed., *The Essential Writings of Ralph Waldo Emerson* (New York: Modern Library, 2000), 744–46.

14. Kenneth Walter Cameron, *The Transcendentalists and Minerva: Cultural Backgrounds of the American Renaissance with Fresh Discoveries in the Intellectual Climate of Emerson, Alcott, and Thoreau*, 3 vols. (Hartford, CT: Transcendental Books, 1958), 17.

15. *EJMN* 4:344 (1834).

16. Denison Olmsted, "Observations on the Meteors of Nov. 13th, 1833," *American Journal of Science* 25 (1834): 363–411 and 26 (1834): 132–74; Denison Olmsted, *Letters on Astronomy, Addressed to a Lady: In Which the Elements of the Science Are Familiarly Explained in Connexion with Its Literary History*, 1840, pp. 348–49; Frederick Douglass, *Life and Times of Frederick Douglass*, 2nd ed. (1892; New York: Pathway Press, 1941), 117.

17. Ralph Waldo Emerson, "The Uses of Natural History," in Stephen E. Whicher and Robert E. Spiller, *The Early Lectures of Ralph Waldo Emerson, vol. 1, 1833–36* (Cambridge, MA: Harvard University Press, 1966), 5–26 at 6.

18. J. F. Laterrade, "On the Existence of the Unicorn" (from *Bulletin d'Histoire Naturelle de la Societé Linnéene de Bordeaux*), trans. Jacob Porter, *American Journal of Science* 26 (1834): 123–26.

19. Emerson, "Uses of Natural History," 8, 20.

20. "Anxieties and Delights of a Discoverer," 4–5.

21. "We Are Apt to Become What Others . . . Think Us to Be," in Moldenhauer, ed., *Thoreau: Early Essays*, 9–11.

22. "Introductions to the Study of the Greek Classic Poets," in Moldenhauer, ed., *Thoreau: Early Essays*, 50–58.

23. Kenneth Walker Cameron, "Thoreau's List of Phrases Gleaned from Milton, *Lycidas, Comus, Paradise Lost*, 'Christmas Hymn,' Shakespeare's *Hamlet*, Dryden,

etc.," in Cameron, *Transcendentalists and Minerva*, 1:153–62; "The Speeches of Moloch and the Rest," in Moldenhauer, ed., *Early Essays*, 79–83.

24. Cameron, *Transcendentalists and Minerva*, 1:142.

25. "The Love of Stories," in Moldenhauer, ed., *Early Essays*, 45–47.

26. Samuel Eliot Morison, *Three Centuries of Harvard, 1636–1936* (Cambridge, MA: Harvard University Press, 1946), 201, says that "curricular requirements were not exacting, so that boys like Emerson and Thoreau had ample time to browse and dream."

27. Cameron, *Transcendentalists and Minerva*, 140.

28. *JMN* 1:10–11, 26.

29. Gregg, *Letters of ETE*, 1:5 (Mar. 1851); Louisa May Alcott, *Flower Fables*, 1854. An 1847 draft manuscript (Alcott Papers, Concord Free Public Library) of the book carries this prefatory note to Ellen: "Dear Nellie ... Give my love to the Concord Fairies if you chance to see them, though I believe they spend their winters in Italy on a count [*sic*] of our climate. Still you may find them whom the gout or rheumatism keeps behind. ..." An excellent survey of the literary world of Faery in Britain during the Victorian era can be found in Carole G. Silver, *Strange and Secret Peoples: Fairies and Victorian Consciousness* (New York: Oxford University Press, 1999).

30. Cameron, "Early Records of the Concord Lyceum," *Transcendental Climate* 3: 64–73. This popular interest in the darker side of human consciousness was reflected in the contemporaneous offerings at Boston lecture halls. Just one day after Emerson finished his fourth in a lecture series on the philosophy of history at the Masonic temple in January 1837, Charles Poyen began a course of six lectures on animal magnetism. During the same week, the first of a six-lecture course in astrology was offered at Boylston Hall. [Cameron, *Thoreau's Harvard Years*, 125–30] On the relationship of Fate and Faerie, see Henry Charles Coote, "The Neo-Latin Fay," *Folk-Lore Record* 2 (1879): 1–18.

31. "Folk-Lore of Marblehead, Massachusetts," *Journal of American Folk-Lore* 7 (1894): 252–53; Emerson, "History," in *Essential Writings*, 128. The ubiquity of fairies in popular consciousness is suggested by another passage from this essay: "A lady with who I was riding in the forest said to me that the woods always seemed to her to wait, as if the genii who inhabited them suspended their deeds until the wayfarer had passed onward; a thought which poetry has celebrated in the dance of the fairies, which breaks off on the approach of human feet" (120).

32. Cameron, *Transcendentalists and Minerva*, 235–36. Thoreau's transcription of this ballad is from "Friar Rush and the Frolicsome Elves of Popular Mythology," *Foreign Quarterly Review* 18 (Oct. 1836): 180–202.

33. Marshall Tufts, *A Tour Through College*, 1832, in Cameron, *Transcendentalists and Minerva*, 297; Jean Le Clerc, *Opera philosophica*, 3rd ed., 4 vols. (Amsterdam, 1704), vol. 2: *Pneumatologia et Historia philosophiae orientalis*.

34. Ralph Waldo Emerson, *Nature*, in Brooks Atkinson, ed., *The Essential Writings of Ralph Waldo Emerson* (New York: Modern Library, 2000), 37–38.

35. William H. Gilman et al., eds., *The Journals and Miscellaneous Notebooks of Ralph Waldo Emerson* (Cambridge, MA: Harvard University Press, 1960–83), 4:199, 200, 87.

36. Emerson, *Nature*, 6, 7, 34–35.

37. *Ibid.*, 35–36.

38. Cameron, *Transcendentalists and Minerva*, 224.

39. The story of the North Bridge monument is told beautifully by Robert A. Gross in "The Celestial Village: Transcendentalism and Tourism in Concord," in Charles Capper and Conrad Edick Wright, eds., *Transient and Permanent: The Transcendentalist Movement and Its Contexts* (Boston: Massachusetts Historical Society, 1999), 251–81.

40. Louis A. Surette, *By-Laws of Corinthian Lodge of Ancient, Free, and Accepted Masons, of Concord, Mass.* (Benjamin Tolman: Concord, MA: 1859).

41. *An Investigation into Freemasonry by a Joint Committee of the Legislature of Massachusetts* (Boston, 1834), app. 31–33. The reaction against Atwell from Concord Masons was fury; he was banished from the lodge, and Louis Surette's history nearly thirty years later still was full of animus against Atwell: "We could have wished that our proverbially quiet and pleasant village—famed in history, and consecrated by the blood of the first martyrs to American liberty—had never been disgraced by the mis-deeds of a traitor to masonry.... The name of Herman Atwill [*sic*] will go down to the future as that of a Judas—a Benedict Arnold of the Masonic Institution; while those who remained steadfast and true to our Order will shine like stars in the Masonic Firmament, and be honored and remembered long after Atwill shall have turned to dust and been forgotten" (Surette, *By-Laws*, 151–52).

It is unlikely that the prominent Concord Mason noted by Atwell as having condoned the murder of William Morgan was Ezra Ripley. However, Edward Jarvis (*Traditions and Reminiscences of Concord*, 150–51) notes a "staid farmer" who had faithfully attended Ripley's sermons all of his life but had turned against the minister, calling him a "liar" after he publicly defended the Masonic lodges from accusations of complicity in the Morgan murder and other charges.

Morgan was not the only Freemason to lose his life for disclosing secrets. In February 1830, Mason Artemas Kennedy's body was discovered in the Milton River near Boston (Goodman, *Towards a Christian Republic*, 147).

42. Cameron, "Sanborn's Table Talk," p. 9. The repugnance for Freemasonry was not shared by Thoreau's ancestors; in June 1781, his maternal grandfather, Rev. Asa Dunbar of Salem and later Keene, New Hampshire, gave the founding address in old Trinity Lodge. See Franklin Benjamin Sanborn, *Life of Henry D. Thoreau* (Boston, 1882), 49.

43. John Quincy Adams, *Letters on the Masonic Institution* (Boston, 1847; Montague, MA: Acacia Press, 1996).

44. Charles Pinckney Sumner, *A Letter on Speculative Free Masonry* (Boston, 1829); Surette, *By-Laws*, 190–91; Benjamin Gleason, "Address Pronounced at the Dedication of the New Masonic Hall, in Concord" (Concord, 1820), 16–17.

45. Emerson, "The American Scholar," *Essential Writings of Ralph Waldo Emerson*, 43, 45, 59.

   Robert Richardson points out both how unoriginal was Emerson's "declaration of independence" (saying that "the general subject was so common that it had become a standard undergraduate theme topic") and how unfaithful he was at the time to his own clarion call, engaged in literary projects totally dependent on European authors. See Robert D. Richardson Jr., *Emerson: The Mind on Fire* (Berkeley: University of California Press, 1995), 262–64.

46. Cameron, *Transcendentalists and Minerva*, 234–35.

47. Harding, *Days*, 52–53.

48. Sanborn, *Life of H. D. Thoreau*, 57–58, 59.

49. *Journal*, 45; William Ellery Channing, *Thoreau: The Poet-Naturalist*, ed. F. B. Sanborn (1873; Boston, 1902), 18; *Journal*, 46.

50. "The Bluebirds," *Collected Essays & Poems*, 512–15.

51. Ibid., 514, 515; "May Morning," *Collected Essays & Poems*, 515.

52. *Journal* 1:8–9.

53. *Journal* 1:16.

CHAPTER 2: SEEING THE UNSEEN

54. "Homer, Ossian, Chaucer," *Collected Essays and Poems*, 140; *Journal* 1:31; *Walden*, 144; "Homer, Ossian, Chaucer," 139.

55. "Homer, Ossian, Chaucer," 138, 152; *Journal* 1:31.

56. "Homer, Ossian, Chaucer," 146; Cameron, *Literary Notebook*, 185; *Early Essays*, 170–71; *A Week*, 371, 373; *Journal* 2:175; *Journal* 1:31.

57. "The American Scholar," 57; "Thoreau," *Essential Writings of Ralph Waldo Emerson*, 821; *JMN* 7:229–30; *EC* 1:256.

58. "Thoreau," 820–21; *Collected Essays and Poems*, 556–59.

59. Joel Myerson, "A Calendar of Transcendental Club Meetings," *American Literature* 44 (1972): 197–207; *Correspondence of Henry David Thoreau*, 91–92.

60. *Journal*, Nov. 12, 1837; Henry David Thoreau, *The Writings of Henry David Thoreau*, *Journal*, vol. 6, *Familiar Letters*, Bradford Torrey, ed. (Boston, 1895), 13–16.

61. Cameron, *Transcendentalists and Minerva*, 172; Roger Williams's *Key into the Language of the Indians of New England*, Massachusetts Historical Society Collection for 1794, ch. 32; *Journal*, Apr. 1, 1838.

62. *Journal*, Mar. 14, 1838, and June 30, 1840; Emerson, "Thoreau," 811; *Journal* 1:49, 52; *Walden* (P. ed.), 326.

63. *P Journal* 1:87, 124.

64. "The Service," *Collected Essays and Poems*, 8, 11.

65. *P Journal* 1:38–39; *Yeoman's Gazette*, Concord, Nov. 25, 1837, p. 3, in *Early Essays*, 121, 380.

66. *Collected Essays and Poems*, 517–18.

67. "Friendship," *Collected Essays and Poems*, 510–11.

68. *Journal* 2:453, 496, 505.

69. *P Journal* 1:48; *Collected Essays and Poems*, 516–18; *Familiar Letters*, 28.

70. *P Journal* 1:51.

71. "An Address," *Essential Writings of Ralph Waldo Emerson*, 63, 68, 74, 75.

72. *P Journal* 1:53–54, 51, 57, 61, 67.

73. *P Journal* 1:50, 51; "The Peal of the Bells," *Collected Essays & Poems*, 523; *P Journal* 1:53–54, 54, 53.

74. *P Journal* 1:55, 50; *Woman in the Nineteenth Century*, 1855, pp. 358–60; Letter to a "young friend," Oct. 21, 1838.

    In Jones Very, the rhythmic revelation came slightly later, at age twenty-four, and it proved too much for him to bear. A year after graduating second in his Harvard class of 1836, Very was riding the train from Boston to Lowell when he was suddenly struck by a sense of terror at how fast he was moving through the countryside. Realizing that he was always "amid movements far more worthy of alarm yet with perfect safety," his terror was replaced by a sense of being in God's care, "borne along by a divine engine and undertaking his life-journey." But by the fall of 1838, he was in a state of religious mania, convinced that he was a vehicle for the Holy Ghost. Two months after Thoreau's ecstasy, Very arrived at Emerson's home for a five-day visit, during which he continued to declare the Second Coming to be at hand.

75. *EJMN* 7:143–44.

76. *P Journal* 1:59–60, 65, 67.

77. *Ibid.*, 1:76–77, 74. Allen Beecher Hovey, in *The Hidden Thoreau*, interprets "Sympathy" as being about Thoreau's lost youth (New York: AMS Press, 1966).

78. *P Journal* 1:79–80; Ellen Sewall to her father, Rev. Edmund Quincy Sewall, July 31, 1839, George L. Davenport Papers, Concord Free Public Library; *P Journal* 1:81.

79. *P Journal* 1:80–81.

80. *A Week*, 15–16.

81. *Ibid.*, 16–17, 21–22.

82. *Ibid.*, 62; *P Journal* 1:136.

83. *P Journal* 1:136–37; Thoreau, "Prometheus Bound," *Dial* 3, no. 3 (1843): 363–86.

84. Emerson, *Essays*, 126; *P Journal* 1:107.

85. For an exegesis of the Prometheus myth, see Rudolf Steiner, "Greek and Germanic Mythology in the Light of Esotericism," Lecture 1, unpublished transcript of Oct. 7, 1904, lecture, Rudolf Steiner Library; *EJMN* 7:383.

86. *EJMN* 7:238.

87. *P Journal* 2:17, 24, 40.

88. *Ibid.*, 2:51.

89. *Ibid.*, 2:51, 100–103.

90. *Ibid.*, 1:97; *EJMN* 203.

91. Cudworth, *True Intellectual System*, 3:514–22, 4:5–6; *Journal* 1:150.

92. *Journal* 1:140.
93. Thoreau's *Literary Notebook*, 15–20.
94. *EJMN* 7:525.
95. *P Journal* 1:121, 128, 139, 143.
96. Amos Bronson Alcott, "Orphic Sayings," *Dial* 1 (July 1840): 85–98.
97. Emerson, *Nature*, 3.
98. *Woman in the Nineteenth Century*, v. For Fuller's esotericism, see Arthur Versluis, *The Esoteric Origins of the American Renaissance* (Oxford, UK: Oxford University Press, 2001), ch. 12.
99. *Literary Notebook*, 165.
100. *EL* 2:287; *Early Essays*, 309.
101. *Letters*, 41–42.
102. *Journal* 1:122; Ellen Sewall to Prudence Ward, Nov. 18, 1840, Davenport Papers.
103. *Journal* 8:238; *Journal* 1:216; *Journal* 8:238; *Journal* 7:175.
104. *EJMN* 1:301.
105. *P Journal* 1:257; *Journal*, Feb. 4, 1841.
106. *P Journal* 1:301.
107. *P Journal* 1:296–97; *EC* 1:335; *EL* 2:402; Edward Waldo Emerson, *Henry Thoreau as Remembered by a Young Friend* (Boston: Houghton Mifflin, 1917), 104.
108. *EJMN* 7:455; *Walden*, 174.
109. Thoreau to Lucy Brown, July 21, 1841, *Letters*, 45; *Journal* 1:271–2.
110. Thoreau to Miss Lucy Brown, Sept. 8, 1841; *Collected Essays and Poems*, 566; Sanborn, *Familiar Letters*, 329n. On Thoreau's poetry from this period, see Elizabeth Hall Witherell, "Thoreau's Watershed Season as a Poet: The Hidden Fruits of the Summer and Fall of 1841," *SAR* 1990: 49–106.
111. Henry Seidel Canby's 1939 biography identified Ellen Sewall as the "maiden," and Carl Bode (*Collected Poems of Henry Thoreau* [Baltimore: Johns Hopkins University Press, 1969]) agreed; later critics and biographers have followed them. Henry W. Walls ("An Evaluation of Thoreau's Poetry," *American Literature* 16 (1944): 99–114) suspects that "The Maiden in the East" refers to the Virgin Mary, and if not, "it affords at least a remarkable coincidence."
112. *P Journal* 1:338. Both Emerson and Fuller were inspired by Sophia. While Emerson—despite ecstatic passages like the final chapter of *Nature*—remained largely unconscious of any divine feminine influence, Fuller consciously cultivated communication with the Goddess. Fuller opens *Woman in the Nineteenth Century* with the words "Frailty, thy name is Woman. / The Earth waits for her Queen." The "Queen" is either Mary or Sophia. On the Virgin Mary in America, see John Gotta, *American Madonna: Images of the Divine Woman in Literary Culture* (New York: Oxford University Press, 1997).
113. *Letters*, 56–57; *Collected Essays & Poems*, 545; *P Journal* 1:301, 343, 346, 347.
114. *Days*, 134.
115. *JMN* 8:165; *Life of LE*, 85; *JMN* 7:165.

116. Harding and Bode, *Correspondence of HDT*, 66; *EJMN*, Apr. 6–12, 1842; *JMN* 6:298; HDT to Mrs. Lucy Brown, Mar. 2, 1842, *Correspondence*, 62–63, 67.

117. *JMN* 9:387; *JMN* 8:144–45.

118. Raleigh, *Works* 2:28–33, quoted by Thoreau, in Cameron, *Transcendentalists and Minerva*, 342. Thoreau worked these thoughts into *A Week on the Concord and Merrimack Rivers* and both his "Moonlight" and "Sir Walter Raleigh" essays.

119. Cameron, *Literary Notebook*, 151.

120. *P Journal* 1:390, 380, 370.

121. Lewis Hyde, ed. *The Essays of Henry David Thoreau* (New York: Farrar, Strauss & Giroux, 2002), 22–23.

122. *Ibid.*, 13, 18–19.

123. *Ibid.*, 150; Hawthorne, *American Notebooks* 3:167–68.

124. *Familiar Letters*, 71, 82–83, 110.

125. *P Journal* 1:494, 496–97; *Journal* 2:21–25.

126. Harding and Bode, *Correspondence of HDT*, 156.

127. "Paradise (To Be) Regained," *Essays of Henry David Thoreau*, 46.

128. *Ibid.*, 60; *P Journal* 1:494.

129. Clara Sears, *Days of Delusion: A Strange Bit of History* (Boston: Houghton Mifflin, 1924), ch. 7.

130. *Collected Essays and Poems*, 591–92.

131. *P Journal* 1:460, 465.

132. *A Week*, 8–9.

133. Johnson, *Thoreau's Complex Weave*, 137.

134. *Long Book*, 116.

135. *Henry Thoreau as Remembered by a Young Friend*, 90, 131, 132, 131–32. Louisa May Alcott very likely shared in the secret fraternity of Faerie with Thoreau and the Emerson children. When she sent Ellen a copy of *Flower Fables* in 1854, she wrote: "Hoping that age has not lessened your love for the *Fairy folk* I have ventured to place your name in my little book, for your interest in their sayings & doings, first called forth these 'Flower Fables,' most of which were fancied long ago in Concord woods & fields." Speaking of her dissatisfaction with the illustrations, Alcott said, "The pictures are not what I hoped they would be & it is very evident that the designer is not as well acquainted with fairy forms & faces as you & I are, so we must each *imagine* to suit ourselves & I hope if the fairies tell me any more stories, they will let an Elfin artist *illustrate* them" (*Selected Letters*, 10–11).

136. Julian Hawthorne, *Memoirs* (New York: Macmillan, 1938), 114–15.

CHAPTER 3: PRODIGIES AND WONDERS

137. *Journal*, July 5, 1845, and July 6, 1845; *Walden*, 84; *Journal*, July 7, 1845, and July 14, 1845.

138. John L. O'Sullivan, "Manifest Destiny," *United States Magazine and Democratic Review*, July 1845.

139. Emerson, "An Address," *Essential Writings of RWE*, 78.

140. Shakespeare, *As You Like It*, II, 7. Shakespeare's awareness of the cosmic rhythms moved him to incorporate planetary-astrological motifs into his play. The first three periods described by Shakespeare (infant, schoolboy, lover) are related astrologically to the Moon, Mercury, and Venus; the soldier (42–49) to Mars; the justice (age 49–56) to Jupiter; pantaloon (56–63) to Saturn. Philo of Judea, *De opificio mundi*, 104, trans. F. H. Colson and G. H. Whitaker, *On the Creation*, 10 vols. (London: Loeb Classical Library, 1929), 1:85; Julius Pollux, *Onomasticon* 2:4, T. Hemsterhuis, ed. (Amsterdam, 1706), 153; Thomas Laycock, "Evidence and Arguments in Proof of the Existence of a General Law of Periodicity in the Phenomena of Life," *Lancet* 1 (1842–43): 124–29, 160–64; "On the Influence of the Moon on the Atmosphere of the Earth, and on the Pathological Influence of the Seasons," *Lancet* 2 (1842–43): 438–44; and "On Some of the Causes Which Determine the Minor Periods of Vital Movements." 1 (1842–43): 929–33.

141. *Collected Essays & Poems*, 610–11.

142. *P Journal* 2:165. A close examination of Thoreau's notes from his reading in English poetry this year gives direct sources for some of his images of the fairy world: In a Ben Jonson poem about Robin Good-Fellow, Thoreau had transcribed a verse where the narrator "eat[s] their cakes & sip[s] their wine," an echo of the images Thoreau gives of supping from the fairies' table (Cameron, *Transcendentalists and Minerva*, 231). In the manuscript version of *A Week* that Thoreau was composing at this time, Thoreau includes a fragment of this poem following a text section that suggests that "we live on the verge of another and purer realm," where "Echo dwell[s], and there is the abutment of the rainbow's arch." Thoreau versifies:

> A finer race and finer fed
> Feast and revel above our head,
>   And we titmen are only able
> To catch the fragments from their table.
> Theirs is the fragrance of the fruits,
> While we consume the pulp and roots,
> What are the moments that we stand
> Astonished on the Olympian land!

Saying nothing once again about the identity of this "finer race," Thoreau again hints at his own clairvoyance in the following paragraph by saying that humanity's senses are "but the rudiments of what they are destined to become," and that in the future they will realize their true purpose, to see and hear and taste and smell the gods." See Johnson, *Thoreau's Complex Weave*, 165, 167.

143. *Collected Essays and Poems*, 601–2, 606.

144. *Walden,* 49–50. This is a partial list.

145. *P Journal* 2:168–74.

146. *P Journal* 2:187.

147. D. Michael Quinn, *Early Mormonism and the Magic World View* (Salt Lake City: Signature Books, 1987), 40.

148. Nauvoo Temple Book; Catherine Lewis, *Narrative of Some of the Proceedings of the Mormons* (Lynn, MA: self-published, 1848), 9–10; see also Increase McGee Van Dusen and Maria Van Dusen, *The Mormon Endowment: A Secret Drama, or Conspiracy, in the Nauvoo-Temple, in 1846* (Syracuse, NY, 1847), 6, 9.

149. Quinn, *Early Mormonism and the Magic World View,* 158.

150. *P Journal* 2:179.

151. *P Journal* 2:233–36; HDT to Lidian Emerson, July 7, 1843; HDT to Cynthia Dunbar Thoreau, Aug. 6, 1843, and Oct. 1, 1843, *Familiar Letters,* 91, 99.

152. Charles M. Mitchill, *The Surprising Case of Rachel Baker, Who Prays and Preaches in Her Sleep: With Specimens of Her Extraordinary Performances* (New York, 1814); William L. Stone, *Letter to Dr. A. Brigham, on Animal Magnetism: Being an Account of a Remarkable Interview Between the Author and Miss Loraina Brackett While in a State of Somnambulism* (New York, 1837). On sympathy and somnambulism, see Robert S. Cox, *Body and Soul: A Sympathetic History of American Spiritualism* (Charlottesville: University of Virginia Press, 2003).

153. Emerson, *Lectures and Biographical Sketches* (Boston: Houghton Mifflin, 1886), 30. Despite his distaste for the sympathetic state of somnambulism, Emerson shared with Thoreau and the majority of his contemporaries a Romantic doctrine of sympathy. See Carl Strauch, "Emerson and the Doctrine of Sympathy," *Studies in Romanticism* 4, no. 3 (1967): 152–74.

154. Cameron, *Literary Notebook,* 357.

155. *Journal,* Oct. 5, 1840.

156. Thoreau to Lucy Brown, Jan. 24, 1843, *Familiar Letters,* 44; *P Journal* 2:45.

157. *P Journal* 2:242; *Walden,* 262.

158. *P Journal* 2:481.

159. *Journal of A. Bronson Alcott,* 184; Emerson, *Journal* 7:219.

160. "Ktaadn," *Maine Woods,* 38, 40.

161. Ibid., 63, 64, 70, 71.

162. Ibid., 78, 81.

163. John Hubbell and Robert W. Smith, "Neptune in America: Negotiating a Discovery," *Journal for the History of Astronomy* 23, no. 3 (1992): 260–91.

164. *Concord Freeman,* Feb. 20, 1846; Feb. 27, 1847; July 12, 1845; Mar. 13, 1846.

165. H. J. Moulton, *Houdini's History of Magic in Boston, 1792–1915* (1918; Glenwood, IL: Meyerbooks, 1983). See also James W. Cook, *The Arts of Deception: Playing with Fraud in the Age of Barnum* (Cambridge, MA: Harvard University Press, 2001).

166. Emerson, *Lectures and Biographical Sketches* (Boston: Riverside Press, 1883), 10; Margaret Fuller, "The New Science; or, the Philosophy of Mesmerism or Animal Magnetism," in *Life Without and Life Within*; Christopher Fahy, "Dark Mirrorings: The Influence of Fuller on Alcott's 'Pair of Eyes,'" *ESQ* 45, no. 2 (1999): 131–59; Margaret Fuller to Ralph Emerson, Jan. 28, 1844, *Letters of MF*, 3:177–79.

167. *EJMN* 6:489, 492.

168. Hawthorne to Sophia Peabody, Oct. 18, 1841, *Hawthorne: The Letters, 1813–1843*, 1984 ed., 15:588; 14:398–99. See also Chase Coale, *Mesmerism and Hawthorne: Mediums of American Romance* (Tuscaloosa: University of Alabama Press, 1998).

169. *Walden*, 95–97.

170. *P Journal* 2:334. On Morton and the eclipse of mesmeric anaesthesia by chemical methods, see Alison Winter, *Mesmerized: Powers of Mind in Victorian Britain* (Chicago: University of Chicago Press, 1998).

171. *P Journal* 2:357–58.

172. *Walden*, 289, 291.

173. *Ibid.*, 294, 296.

174. *Letters of RWE*, 3:384; *Walden*, 297–98.

175. *Journal of A. Bronson Alcott*, 190–91; *Walden*, 4.

176. *Walden*, 16.

177. *Ibid.*, 143–44, 154, 137, 182.

178. *Ibid.*, 268; *P Journal* 2:225; *Walden*, 268–70.

179. *Walden*, 165.

180. *Ibid.*, 333.

181. Richardson, *Mind on Fire*, 433–35; *Familiar Letters*, 186.

182. *Correspondence*, 216; James Russell Lowell review of *A Week on the Concord and Merrimack Rivers*, *Massachusetts Quarterly Review* 3 (Dec. 1849): 40–51.

183. *Massachusetts Quarterly Review*, 50; *Thoreau Log*, 159, 149.

184. *Thoreau Log*, 146, 145.

185. *Collected Essays and Poems*, 623; *Correspondence*, 247.

186. *P Journal* 3:18, 9–10.

187. *P Journal* 3:30, 33, 35–36.

188. *Scientific American* 5, no. 6: 42; *P Journal* 3:24, 31; Thomas Shepard, *The Clear Sun-Shine of the Gospel Breaking Forth Upon the Indians in New England* (London, 1648), in *Collections of the Massachusetts Historical Society*, 3rd series, vol. 4 (Cambridge, MA, 1834).

189. *P Journal* 3:4, 37, 25.

190. Townsend Scudder, *Concord, American Town* (Boston: Little, Brown, 1947); Austin Meredith, "A History of the Uses of Walden Pond," American Transcendentalism Web, http://transcendentalism-legacy.tamu.edu/authors/thoreau/walden/pondhistory.html.

191. Horace Hosmer, *Remembrances of Concord and the Thoreaus: Letters of Horace Hosmer to Dr. S. A. Jones,* George Hendrick, ed. (Urbana: University of Illinois Press, 1977), 101.

192. *P Journal* 3:37–38; *New York Evening Post,* Nov. 3, 1849; *Scientific American,* May 1, 1846; May 8, 1846; May 15, 1846; June 19, 1847.

193. Cameron, *Thoreau's Fact Book,* 1:129a (Thoreau had written in ink on the clipping, *Boston Journal,* July 26, 1858); *Walden,* 303, 302; *Concord Freeman,* Jan. 23, 1846; *Scientific American,* Feb. 6, 1847, and Nov. 18, 1848; *Walden,* 318.

194. *P Journal* 3:23.

195. *Ibid.,* 3:43–44.

196. Andrew Jackson Davis, *The Philosophy of Spiritual Intercourse* (Boston: Colby & Rich, 1880), 77–117.

197. Nathan Brooks Family Papers, "Spirit Papers," Box 78, Folder 3, Concord Free Public Library; Henry Thoreau to Sophia Thoreau, July 13, 1852, *Correspondence,* 1958, 283–84.

198. Emma Hardinge Britten, *Modern American Spiritualism* 1:185.

199. Frederick L. H. Willis, *Alcott Memoirs* (Boston: Richard H. Badger, 1915), 91–93.

CHAPTER 4: A TURNING POINT IN TIME

200. *Journal* 2:5; *Log,* 138.

201. *A Week,* 363; *P Journal* 3:126.

202. *Journal* 2:10.

203. *Ibid.,* 2:19, 20–21.

204. *Ibid.,* 2:21–25, 25.

205. *Ibid.,* 2:24, 25, 488–89, 39–40.

206. *Ibid.,* 2:39, 34–35. For an examination of the contingencies of the fire, see Edmund A. Schofield, "'Burnt Woods': Ecological Insights into Thoreau's Unhappy Encounter with Forest Fire," *Thoreau Research Newsletter* 2, no. 3 (1991): 1–8.

207. *Journal* 33–34.

208. Paula Blanchard, *Margaret Fuller: From Transcendentalism to Revolution* (New York: Delacorte Press, 1978), ch. 16.

209. Ibid., ch. 19.

210. Thoreau to RWE, July 25, 1850, *Familiar Letters,* 184; Blanchard, *Fuller,* 331–37.

211. Thoreau to Blake, Aug. 9, 1850, *Familiar Letters,* 185–86; *Journal* 2:80.

212. *Yankee,* 3; *Collected Essays and Poems,* 626–27, 628, 629.

213. *Journal* 2:77–78 [P ed. 125–26]; *P Journal* 3:125–26; *Journal* 2:94; *Collected Essays and Poems,* 629.

214. *Journal* 2:96–101.

215. *Ibid.,* 2:102, 103–4.

216. *Emerson Journal,* Riverside 1905 ed., 8:135–36, Oct. 26, 1850.

217. *Journal* 2:105–6, 138, 167, 118.

218. *Ibid.*, 2:106–7, 160–61.

219. *Ibid.*, 2:112–15.

220. *Collected Essays and Poems*, 632–34.

221. *Journal* 2:285, 137, 143, 138–39, 141.

222. *Ibid.*, 2:174–80.

223. *Ibid.*, 2:186, 190–91. Though the etheric realm is a staple of modern occult meta-physics, its most lucid expositor is the Austrian philosopher, educator, and eso-tericist Rudolf Steiner. Steiner, the editor of Goethe's scientific work, posited the existence of *Bildekraft*, or "etheric formative forces," universal cosmic forces streaming from Earth's periphery as opposed to the centric forces of classical physics. This nonphysical, nonspatial *Kraft*, or "working," is the key to all of nature's rhythmic phenomena, including the working down into the human being of cosmic forces. Steiner's writings take it for granted that it is also the realm in which the elemental beings of nature exist and through which per-ception of higher spiritual beings takes place. Steiner's research in and on the etheric world was carried out over a quarter of a century and can be found throughout his published work. The earliest comprehensive examination of the etheric formative forces is in his 1909 work, *Occult Science: An Outline*, recently reissued as *Outline of Esoteric Science* (Great Barrington, MA: Steiner Books, 1997); a collection of excerpts can be found in *World Ether-Elemental Beings: Kingdoms of Nature*, ed. Ernst Hageman (Spring Valley, NY: Mercury Press, 1992).

Subsequent research on the etheric formative forces can be found in Guenther Wachsmuth, *The Etheric Formative Forces in Cosmos, Earth, and Man: A Path of Investigation into the World of the Living* (New York: Anthroposophic Press, 1924); Jochen Bockemühl, *Toward a Phenomenology of the Etheric World: Investigations into the Life of Nature and Man* (Spring Valley, NY: Anthropo-sophic Press, 1985); and Otto Wolff, *The Etheric Body* (Spring Valley, NY: Mercury Press, 1990).

224. *Journal* 2:574, 194, 228–29, 237–38.

225. *Ibid.*, 2:213. Six weeks later Thoreau restated this: "The intimations of the night are divine, methinks. Men might meet in the morning and report the news of the night,—what divine suggestions have been made to them. I find that I carry with me into the day often some such hint derived from the gods,—such im-pulses to purity, to heroism, to literary effort, as are never day-born" (*Journal* 2:286–87).

226. *Journal* 2:240–48, 261–64.

227. *Ibid.*, 2:207, 214–15.

228. *Ibid.*, 2:289–91, 294.

229. *Ibid.*, 2:306–7, 316–17.

230. *Ibid.*, 2:322, 328, 330, 333.

231. *Ibid.*, 2:373–74; *Collected Essays & Poems*, 635, 636–37.

232. *Ibid.*, 2:406, 403, 472.

233. *Ibid.*, 2:403, 407, 397, 416, 423, 450, 428, 496–97.

234. Alfred Munroe, *Concord and the Telegraph* (Concord Antiquarian Society, 1902).

CHAPTER 5: "WHAT YOU COMMONLY SEE IS BUT HALF"

235. *P Journal* 3:85; Burritt, *Geography of the Heavens*, 15.

236. Burritt, *Geography of the Heavens*, 55–56, 220–21, 94, 114–15, 149–50, 96.

237. Ibid., 226; *P Journal* 3:121–22; Burritt, *Geography of the Heavens*, 130.

238. *Writings of Henry D. Thoreau, vol. 5, Excursions and Poems*, 324, 325, 326.

239. *Journal* 2:497; *Walden*, 202; *P Journal* 4:316.

240. *Journal* 3:11–13; "Music on the Telegraph Wires," *Scientific American*, Mar. 14, 1849.

241. *Journal* 3:113–14, 133–34, 136; Emerson, "Conduct of Life," *Works*, vol. 2: 194

242. *EJMN*, 11:400, 10:345.

243. *P Journal* 4:424, 134–35.

244. *P Journal* 4:317, 318–19, 407.

245. Andrew Jackson Davis, *The Harmonial Man; or, Thoughts for the Age* (New York, 1873), 40, 41, 45, 91. A Kentucky inventor named Daniel Vaughan had actually in 1852 published a circular in which he detailed the scheme proposed by Davis; he distributed it to members of the American Association for the Advancement of Science and had even given a copy to Davis. Vaughan publicly accused Davis of plagiarism.

246. Britten, *Modern American Spiritualism*, 220.

247. *P Journal* 4:390, 394.

248. *Ibid.*, 4:468.

249. *Journal* 4:4, 12, 13. Emerson's phrase for the thrasher's call is remembered by Edith Emerson in Edith E. W. Gregg, "Emerson and His Children: Their Childhood Memories," *Harvard Library Bulletin* 38, no. 4 (1986): 407–30.

250. *Journal* 4:20.

251. *Ibid.*, 4:32, 47, 63.

252. *Ibid.*, 4:64, 95, 99, 103, 108, 109, 110, 114, 85, 94, 89, 100, 92, 108.

253. "Love," *Collected Essays & Poems*, 326, 327, 328.

254. "Chastity & Sensuality," *Collected Essays & Poems*, 331, 329, 330, 331, 332.

255. *Journal* 4:128, 149–50, 157, 157–58.

256. *Ibid.*, 4:158.

257. *Ibid.*, 4:146–47; Thoreau to Sophia Thoreau, July 13, 1852, *Correspondence*, 283.

258. *Journal* 4:162–63, 149, 168, 174, 172.

259. *Ibid.*, 4:174.

260. *Ibid.*, 4:223, 224, 227–28, 227.

261. *Ibid.*, 4:405–6, 407, 414, 417.

262. *Ibid.*, 4:248, 255.

263. Thoreau to Blake, Feb. 27, 1853, *Correspondence*, 295–96; Thoreau to Baird, Dec. 19, 1853, *Correspondence*, 309; *Journal* 5:4.

264. *Journal* 5:43, 45; *Journal* 4:470, 471.

265. *Correspondence*, 296, 298.

266. *Journal* 1, July 26, 1840; 4:466–67; 5:135.

267. *Journal* 5:7, 13, 12, 13, 14, 15, 32, 58, 164.

268. *Ibid.,* 5:160, 204–8.

269. *Ibid.,* 5:203–4.

270. *Ibid.,* 4:455.

271. *Ibid.,* 5:212.

272. *Ibid.,* 5:465–67.

273. Cameron, *Thoreau's Fact Book,* 1:137–38.

274. *Journal* 9:128–29, 10, 327.

275. *Scientific American* 45:337; *Annals and Magazine of Natural History* 1–3: 185; *Annual Register* 1832:447; *American Journal of Science* 28:361; *Edinburgh New Philosophical Journal* 13:368; *Comptes Rendus*, 13:215; *Scientific American* 5, no. 9: 66; *Walden*, 318; "Shower of Red Matter like Blood and Muscle," *American Journal of Science* 1, no. 41 (1841): 403–4.

   Thoreau's "trout in milk" comment may baffle modern readers; it baffled even his contemporaries. Ellen Emerson wrote to her brother Edward after Thoreau died, saying that very few people—not even her father and mother—understood Thoreau's aphorism's meaning: The trout gave away the fact that the milk had been watered. *Letters of Ellen Tucker Emerson* 1:274.

276. Charles Fort, *Book of the Damned* (New York: Boni and Liveright, 1919), 62.

277. *Journal* 6:65–68.

278. *Ibid.,* 6:99–100.

279. *Walden*, 324.

280. *Journal* 6:276, 388, 452, 474.

281. *Ibid.,* 7:6, 10.

282. *Ibid.,* 6:429; *Journals of Bronson Alcott*, 274; *Thoreau Log*, 308, 320, 326–27.

283. *Journal* 6:7–8; *Walden*, 328.

284. *Journal* 7:79–80; Henry Horace Furness, *Records of a Lifelong Friendship* (Boston: Houghton Mifflin, 1910), 101.

285. "Life Without Principle," *Collected Essays and Poems*, 348, 358, 354, 362.

286. *Journal* 7:431–32; *Cape Cod*, 3, 19.

287. *Journal* 13:157; 10:194–95; 11:293; 10:331–32; 4:6; 5:298.

288. *Maine Woods*, 203; *Cape Cod*, 105, 48, 52, 129, 55.

289. *Cape Cod*, 84, 150, 151, 152, 135, 136.

290. *Ibid.,* 59–60.

291. *Ibid.,* 3–4, 196, 197.

292. *Ibid.,* 199, 200, 74; *A Week*, 304; *Journal* 12:371.

293. *Cape Cod*, 91–92, 127.

294. Ellen M. Griffin, *Moll Pitcher's Prophecies; or, the American Sibyl* (Boston, 1895); *Journal* 8:168–69.

295. *Journal* 5:515; 9:88, 465; 10:244, 273; 13:356.

296. *Ibid.*, 10:53–54; 1:285; *Correspondence*, 551.

297. Emerson, "Thoreau," *Essential Writings of RWE*, 815.

298. *Journal* 10:152.

299. *Ibid.*, 7:258; 9:301; 14:345; 6:128.

300. *Ibid.*, 8:41, 44–45, 44.

301. *Ibid.*, 8:64, 64–67, 270, 229, 230.

302. *Ibid.*, 8:231–32; 11:434.

303. Channing, *Thoreau: The Poet-Naturalist* (Boston, 1873), 2; George F. Hoar, *Autobiography of 70 Years* (New York: Scribner's, 1903), 72; *P Journal* 4:6.

304. *Journal* 9:309–10.

305. *Correspondence*, 178, 179–80, 182–83.

306. Lurie, *Louis Agassiz*, 338.

307. *EJMN* 14:122–23; *Journal* 10:467–68; 9:300, 306, 311.

308. *Journal* 10:153, 163.

309. *Ibid.*, 10:242, 244.

310. *Ibid.*, 10:243–55.

311. *Ibid.*, 9:415–16.

312. Richard F. Fleck, ed., *The Indians of Thoreau: Selections from the Indian Notebooks,* (Albuquerque: Hummingbird Press, 1974), 24.

CHAPTER 6: EXPANSION AND CONTRACTION

313. *Journal* 9:422–23.

314. *Ibid.*, 9:425–26.

315. *Ibid.*, 2:82, 40–41.

316. For selections from the *Indian Notebooks,* see Fleck, *The Indians of Thoreau:* 5:119, 53–54, 55.

317. *Journal* 1:445; 7:96, 100.

318. *Ibid.*, 7:472–74, 475, 476–77.

319. *Ibid.*, 8:390–92.

320. *Journal* 2:42; *Maine Woods*, 136. Despite his interest in Algonquian languages, Thoreau never seems to have figured out that many of these native acquaintances' names were glosses on their French baptismal names. Joe Aitteon's surname was from "Étienne" (Stephen), while "Swasen" was the Abenaki pronunciation of Joachim. "Tahmont" was from the Abenaki *odamôt*, "the smoker."

321. *Journal* 9:498; *Maine Woods*, 158.

322. *Maine Woods*, 162, 262, 272, 289.

323. *Ibid.*, 185, 285–86, 252–53, 197, 194, 178–79.

324. *Maine Woods*, 181.

325. *Correspondence*, 487–88; *Journal* 10:3, 6; *Correspondence*, 491; *Journal* 10:82.

326. *Journal* 10:92–93; *Correspondence*, 496.

327. *Maine Woods*, 208; *Journal* 10:103, 139–44.

328. *Journal* 10:144.

329. *Ibid.*, 10:63; *A Week*, 297; *Journal* 9:210–11; *A Week*, 297.

330. *Journal* 10:233, 290, 298; *Maine Woods*, 322.

331. *Journal* 2:41; 9:94; 11:189–90; 10:163; 11:219; 10:283–84.

332. *Ibid.*, 11:110; 10:264.

333. *Ibid.*, 10:459, 461, 480–81, 482–85, 486, 490–92, 494, 505, 502–3, 505.

334. *Ibid.*, 10:398, 389.

335. *Ibid.*, 11:192–93, 195–96, 206, 217.

336. *Ibid.*, 11:236, 244, 294–97.

337. *Ibid.*, 11:324; *Maine Woods*, 122.

338. *Journal* 11:435–37.

339. *Correspondence*, 543, 546.

340. *Journal* 11:279.

341. *Essays of HDT*, 226, 227, 230, 235.

342. *Ibid.*, 236; *Correspondence*, 636–39.

343. *Essays of HDT*, 242; *Journal* 12:194.

344. *Journal* 12:218–22.

345. *Ibid.*, 12:216, 244–45, 248, 249, 235.

346. *Ibid.*, 12:329, 339–40.

347. *Ibid.*, 12:232, 233, 296, 308, 347–48.

348. *Ibid.*, 12:384–88, 396, 399, 410, 440.

349. *Ibid.*, 12:388, 396.

350. *Ibid.*, 12:388.

351. *Ibid.*, 12:410, 411–18.

352. *Ibid.*, 12:420; *Essays of HDT*, 261, 279–80.

353. *Journal* 12:457; *Thoreau Society Bulletin* 146 (1979): 3.

354. *Journal* 12:4–5, 5–6.

CHAPTER 7: FAITH IN A SEED

355. *Ibid.*, 13:76.

356. *Ibid.*, 13:5–6; *P Journal* 3:29; *Journal* 6:39; 10:149, 263.

357. *Thoreau Log*, 554; *Essays of HDT*, 291, 294, 307, 298, 302.

358. *Essays of HDT*, 312.

359. *Ibid.*, 2, 21, 25, 5.

360. *Journal* 13:356–57, 229, 363, 199.

361. *Ibid.*, 13:222–29.

362. *Ibid.*, 13:219–21.

363. *Ibid.*, 13:271, 274, 302.

364. Cameron, *Transcendentalists and Minerva*, 2:403; *Journal* 10:31; 11:321; 10: 342, 426, 432–37; *P Journal* 4:455.

365. *Journal* 13:330, 274.

366. *Correspondence*, 578–79.

367. *A Week*, 338–39; *Essays of HDT*, 245.

368. *Essays of HDT*, 246, 250.

369. *Journal* 7:485.

370. *Ibid.*, 14:134–42, 142–48.

371. *Ibid.*, 14:155–61, 161–67.

372. *Ibid.*, 14:138, 148, 115.

373. Thoreau to Ricketson, Mar. 19, 1861, *Familiar Letters* 609–10.

374. *Journal* 11:189–90; 9:37, 94, 212; 10:276.

375. *Ibid.*, 9:282; 10:51–54.

376. *Familiar Letters*, 609–10; manuscript letter in *Concord Saunterer* 12, no. 3 (1977): 21–23; *Journal* 14:336, 339.

377. *Journal* 14:309–10, 314, 337, 338; *Correspondence*, 616.

378. *Correspondence*, 620, 621, 622; Walter Harding, ed., *Thoreau's Minnesota Journey: Two Documents*, Thoreau Society Booklet 16 (1962): 56, 58.

379. *Correspondence*, 625; Edward Emerson, *Henry Thoreau as Remembered by a Young Friend*, 147; *Correspondence*, 628; *Journal* 14:346.

380. *ABAJ* 343; *EJMN* 9:360–61, 401–2; *Correspondence*, 641; *EJMN* 9:413–14.

381. *Concord Saunterer* 11, no. 4 (1976): 16; *Thoreau Log*, 605.

382. *Essential Writings of RWE*, 810–11.

383. *Ibid.*, 812, 813.

384. *Ibid.*, 814, 815.

385. *Ibid.*, 816, 819.

386. *Ibid.*, 821, 823, 825.

387. *EJMN* 9:425.

388. "Walking," *Essays of HDT*, 149, 150.

389. *Ibid.*, 177.

390. Franklin Benjamin Sanborn, *The Personality of Thoreau* (Boston: Charles Goodspeed, 1901), 68–69; *Journal* 6:239; *Familiar Letters* 6:210; *P Journal* 3:29. After Thoreau's death, Sophia, on a walk with Daniel Ricketson to the cliffs on Fair Haven Hill, told him of her brother's "strong faith in the immortality of the soul." Daniel Ricketson Diary, Sept. 16, 1870, Parmenter Papers, Thoreau Society Archives.

391. *P Journal* 3:29.

392. *Journal* 14:229.

Index

About the Author

Historian and naturalist **Kevin Dann** received his PhD from Rutgers University in American history and environmental history. He is the author of ten books, including *Bright Colors Falsely Seen: Synaesthesia and the Search for Transcendental Knowledge, Across the Great Border Fault: The Naturalist Myth in America,* and *Lewis Creek Lost and Found.* He has taught at Rutgers University, the University of Vermont, and the State University of New York. A field agent for the New York Obscura Society, he lives in Brooklyn.